Religion and Politics in Enlightenment Europe

Erasmus Institute Books

Religion AND *Politics* IN *Enlightenment Europe*

edited by

JAMES E. BRADLEY
DALE K. VAN KLEY

UNIVERSITY OF NOTRE DAME PRESS
Notre Dame, Indiana

Notre Dame, Indiana 46556
http://www.undpress.nd.edu

Manufactured in the United States of America

Library of Congress Cataloging-in-Publication Data
Religion and politics in enlightenment Europe / edited by James E. Bradley, Dale K. Van Kley.
p. cm. — (Erasmus Institute books)
Includes bibliographical references and index.
ISBN 0-268-04051-6 (alk. paper)
ISBN 0-268-04052-4 (pbk. : alk. paper)
1. Christianity and politics—Europe—History—18th century.
2. Europe—Church history—18th century. I. Bradley, James E., 1944– II. Van Kley, Dale K., 1941– III. Series.
BR470 .R45 2001
274'.07—dc21

2001001938

∞ *This book was printed on acid-free paper.*

Contents

Acknowledgments

IN THE VERY LONGEST RUN THIS BOOK OWES ITS INCEPTION TO J. C. D. Clark and to his interest in whether it might be possible to find religious forms of political disaffection elsewhere than in eighteenth-century England and British North America where he had located and described them. As one of the general editors in a projected series of collaborative volumes tentatively entitled *History in Comparative Perspective,* Clark enlisted us on the strength of our own separate previous studies on the religious origins of the American and French revolutions, and it is a tribute to the catholicity of his approach that he did so despite the fact that both of us had published accounts that diverged significantly from the central role he attributed to religious heterodoxy in politics. The moment he chose to approach us for a comparative examination of the interrelations between religion and politics in the era of the European Enlightenment could not have been more propitious, in that by the mid-1990s a number of new studies on the importance of religion in stimulating political change had appeared, including several seminal articles by J. G. A. Pocock. Negotiated on the occasion of the American Historical Association's annual meeting of 1995, our agreement to produce the book was finally sealed and solemnized over a dinner with Clark and Pocock at the famous Chicago Chop House, during which we engaged in vigorous debate over a variety of presently contested issues, not the least of them the role of religion in political conflict across Enlightenment Europe.

But whether due to the Hegelian cunning of reason—or, more probably, to the rather more mundane influence of capitalism in the academic publishing world—this series never materialized, with the result that the present volume has finally found a yet more natural home at the head of a quite different series under the general editorship of Professor James Turner and the aegis of the Erasmus Institute, both at the University of Notre Dame. Nor would this volume in particular have come about without the generous funding awarded in 1996 by the Calvin Center for Christian Scholarship, then under the direction of Ronald Wells and now of James Bratt, both of Calvin's History Department and both ably seconded by the administrative assistance of Donna Romanowski. Not only did this grant enable us to sign on a distinguished team of contributors—Wayne te Brake, James Van Horn Melton, Charles C. Noel, Olga Tsapina, and Reginald Ward—but also served to defray most of the expenses of two conferences attended by these contributors, the first at Calvin College toward the end of November 1997, the second in the History Department of the Ohio State University in mid-March 1999. This second conference received additional crucial financial support from Ohio State's History Department and College of Humanities in the persons of Chairman Michael Hogan and Dean Marshall Swain, respectively, as well as from Fuller Theological Seminary and Dean William Dyrness. Sandy Van Kley provided unstinting logistical support for these conferences and deserves a word of thanks as well for her culinary skills and wonderful hospitality.

Characterized throughout by collegial comity and irenic give-and-take, these conferences will live on in our memory as an image and model of higher education in humane letters at its best. This is especially true of the second conference, which was devoted to the presentation and discussion of rough drafts. As this conference coincided with the end of Dale Van Kley's winter-quarter graduate seminar where these drafts had also been read and discussed, the contributors benefitted not only from the criticism of their colleagues in the project but also from that of numbers of Ohio State University graduate students in early-modern and modern European history, in particular Thomas Hendrickson, Tracy Hoskins, Jason Kuznicki, and Miles Rosenberg. The result, we dare hope, is a degree of internal coherence and integration which, while not entirely canceling the inevitable divergences of interest and emphasis among the contributors, is seldom achieved in the case of volumes of essays by diverse authors. And although the contributors will undoubtedly not wish to subscribe to every jot and tittle of the work that their essays have been made to perform in the editors' introduction, that introduction could not have been written without their advice and consent, in particular that proffered during the second conference's concluding discussion on 13 March 1999. A particular word of thanks is owed to Wayne te Brake for his close reading and helpful criticism of the introduction's first draft.

These acknowledgments would be remiss indeed without mention of the support received by the editors for their own contributions to this volume. The archival research that went into the writing of Dale Van Kley's chapter in this volume was made possible by a Summer Stipend from the National Endowment for the Humanities in 1997 and an Ohio State University Faculty Seed Grant in 1998. His work in the Utrechtsarchief and the Bibliothèques of Port-Royal and of Saint-Sulpice benefitted enormously from the expert guidance of archivists Huib Leeuwenberg, Valerie Guitienne-Mürger and Fabien Vandermarcq, and Père Noye, respectively, just as his sojourns were rendered far more pleasant—and affordable—than they would otherwise have been thanks to the friendship and hospitality of Froukje as well as Huib Leeuwenberg and Hilary Sayles in Utrecht and of Mlle Hélène Walbaum in Paris. James Bradley's chapter borrowed on research originally intended for a much larger, and now long overdue project on Religion in the English Enlightenment that was funded by a major grant from the Pew Evangelical Scholars Program. This grant provided a year-long sabbatical and supported his research for the present volume in Cambridge, Massachusetts, Cambridge, England, and in London.

In addition to the constructive criticism received by the volume's other contributors, Van Kley's essay benefitted a great deal from close readings given it by Professors Monique Cottret of the University of Paris, Nanterre, Dr. Rodney Dean of Middlesex, England and Susan Rosa of Northeast Illinois University, as did this same essay along with the editors' introduction from further critical reaction from the participants in seminars at the Ecole des Hautes Etudes en Sciences

Sociales in Paris—and in particular from Yann Fauchois and Rita Hermon-Belot—where Van Kley presented them as papers during a term as professeur invité in the winter of 2000. As this volume received its initial inspiration from J. C. D. Clark, the editors have not been unmindful of his unremitting efforts to excise the word radicalism from the vocabulary of the eighteenth century, and in particular from Bradley's essay, which sustained Clark's most rigorous scrutiny. The author's unrepentant persistence in retaining the traditional usage in no wise lessens or absolves his indebtedness, both for the constructive criticism itself and Clark's warm hospitality in Oxford in the summer of 1999. Ian McBride's tutoring on matters Irish through the exchange of numerous letters also helped place the English radical tradition in a broader, more meaningful context. And both Susan Rosa and Professor Richard Davis of Washington University in St. Louis must be thanked for their valuable criticism of the entire manuscript as readers for the University of Notre Dame Press.

Last, but certainly not least, the editors wish to thank Barbara Hanrahan, director of the University of Notre Dame Press, for her sponsorship of this volume, and with her the entire editorial board of Notre Dame Press for their decision to publish it. And to Alice Honeywell goes a word of appreciation for a superb job of copyediting the manuscript.

James E. Bradley, *Fuller Theological Seminary*

Dale K. Van Kley, *The Ohio State University*

Contributors

JAMES E. BRADLEY is the Geoffrey W. Bromiley Professor of Church History at Fuller Seminary where he has taught for the past twenty-four years. He is the author of *Popular Politics and the American Revolution in England: Petitions, the Crown, and Public Opinion* (1986) and has written on religion and quantitative history in *Religion, Revolution, and English Radicalism: Nonconformity in Eighteenth-Century England* (1990) and historical method in *Church History: An Introduction* (1995), the latter co-authored with Richard A. Muller. He serves on the editorial board of *Anglican and Episcopal History* and is currently engaged in research on the English Enlightenment for a book provisionally entitled "Religion and the Rise of Pluralism in English Society, 1662–1832: The End of the Ancien Régime."

JAMES VAN HORN MELTON is Associate Professor of History at Emory University. He is the author of *Politics, Culture, and the Public Sphere in Enlightenment Europe* (forthcoming, Cambridge University Press) and *Absolutism and the Eighteenth-Century Origins of Compulsory Schooling in Prussia and Austria* (Cambridge, 1988). His other works include *Paths of Continuity: Central European Historiography from the 1930s to the 1950s*, coedited with Hartmut Lehmann (Cambridge, 1994), and a translation (with Howard Kaminsky) of Otto Brunner, *Land and Lordship: Structures of Governance in Medieval Austria* (Philadelphia, 1992).

CHARLES C. NOEL's research has concentrated on eighteenth-century Spain. He has taught at several American and British Universities, including Princeton and Columbia and Thames Valley University in London. His articles and essays have appeared in a number of journals, among them *The American Historical Review,* and in various collections. Currently, having taken early retirement, he divides his time between writing a book on the Spanish Enlightenment and coping with teenagers as a substitute teacher in the secondary schools of south London.

Wayne te Brake is Professor of History at Purchase College, State University of New York. He is the author of *Regents and Rebels: The Revolutionary World of an Eighteenth Century Dutch City* (1989) and *Shaping History: Ordinary People in European Politics, 1500–1700* (1998) and co-editor of *Challenging Authority: The Historical Study of Contentious Politics* (1998). He is currently leading an international scholarly collaboration, funded by a grant from the Ford Foundation, on the theme "Accommodating Difference: The Politics of Cultural Pluralism in Europe."

Olga Tsapina is Curator of Manuscripts at the Huntington Library. Her publications include a complete bibliography of works on the Moscow Kremlin and articles on various aspects of the intellectual history of eighteenth-century Russia, including a study of the perception of Quakers and Old Believers, a study of church antiquities, and notions of fanaticism and enthusiasm. She is currently working on a biography of Petr Alekseev and a book about the Enlightenment and Russian Orthodoxy.

Dale K. Van Kley, as of January 1998, is Professor of History at Ohio State after having taught for twenty-eight years at Calvin College in Grand Rapids, Michigan. He also recently served as a "professeur invité" at the Ecole des Hautes Etudes en Sciences Sociales in Paris. He is the author of *The Jansenists and the Expulsion of the Jesuits from France, 1757–1765* (New Haven: Yale University Press, 1975); *The Damiens Affair and the Unraveling of the Old Regime, 1750–1770* (Princeton: Princeton University Press, 1984); and, most recently, *The Religious Origins of the French Revolution: From Calvin to the Civil Constitution, 1560–1791* (New Haven: Yale University Press, 1996). He is also the editor of *The French Idea of Freedom: The Old Regime and the Declaration of Rights of 1789* (Stanford: Stanford University Press, 1994) and co-editor, with Jeremy Popkin of the University of Kentucky, of the section on the "Prerevolutionary Debate" in Pergamon Press's microfiche French Revolution Collection.

W. R. Ward is Emeritus Professor of Modern History in the University of Durham, England, and an honorary Doctor of Theology of the University of Basel, Switzerland. His recent works include *The Protestant Evangelical Awakening and Christianity under the Ancien Régime, 1648–1789*; the seventh and final volume of his edition of the *Journals* of John Wesley, and his *Kirchengeschichte Grossbitanniens vom 17. bis zum 20. Jahrhundert* (to be published in Leipzig) are both in proof; and he is at present working on an international study of *Evangelical Identity.* He is a member of the editorial boards of *The Journal of Ecclesiastical History* and *Kirchliche Zeitgeschichte.*

Introduction

SEVENTEENTH-CENTURY EUROPE HAS BEEN VARIOUSLY CALLED a century of theological controversy and of Catholic saints, and the nineteenth century a century of Catholic revival and of Protestant missions. But the eighteenth century has eluded all religious labels. For most professionals and lay readers alike, the European eighteenth century still maintains its identity as the century of the Enlightenment, while the obscurity that this "light" supposedly dispelled is precisely that of religion. To the extent that religion has been factored into the political or social history of eighteenth-century Europe as a whole, it has been mainly as mainstay of the various Old-Regime "establishments" and hence as a force for their conservation. To the limited extent that religion has been seen as a challenge to that order, it has been in the form of heterodoxy or heresy. While heterodoxy is still religion, the temptation to see it as a religious way station to total "enlightenment" has been, and remains, very strong.

Hence the challenge of this volume. To associate, as it does, forms of Christian orthodoxy with dissent from the European Old Regime's ecclesiastical establishments is to run against that historiographical grain. And to associate such forms of orthodox dissent with the Old Regime's specifically political order, as it also sometimes does, is to go against it as well, seeing that political absolutism is commonly supposed to have been progressive only to the degree to which it became less religious and more "enlightened." In the Enlightenment Europe described in this book, established churches everywhere found themselves forced to fend off challenges from orthodox dissenters, sometimes with some help from, but sometimes also notwithstanding the hostility of, the governments that had established them. If in the short run the ecclesiastical establishments survived these challenges, they did not do so without sustaining structural changes of their own along with comparable ones in the states allied with them, regardless of the position taken by the state or the precise outcome of the conflict. In sharp contrast, therefore, to the sixteenth-century religious conflicts that tended to pit different confessions and states against each other, the eighteenth-century conflicts tended to occur within the various confessional traditions, churches, and states—within Russian Orthodoxy, for example, or Gallican Catholicism, the Anglican Establishment, or Lutheran Württemberg. These conflicts were therefore as important as any between the Enlightenment and religion, sundering the post-Reformation alliances between church and state from within and contributing a religious dimension to the late-eighteenth-century crisis of the Old Regime. However secular the issues engendered by that crisis may superficially seem, discernibly religious forces took up positions as much on the one side as on the other, and had as much to do with the emergence of "liberalism" as with "conservatism," as much to do, that is, with the advent of modern ideas of individual rights, of toleration of religious dissent, and of constitutional limitations on government, as it obviously had to do with modern notions of the imperative of political order and the need for social hierarchy. And although the Enlightenment is far from absent from the Old-Regime Europe that is the subject of this book, the perspective from which it is viewed here tends to refract it into "lights" of various hues and degress of brightness, very few of them inimical to religion as such.

Religion and the Rise of the French Revolution

The view that the European eighteenth century was above all an age of "lights" which dispelled religion and religious support for political authority was in the first instance that of the eighteenth century itself, and in particular the French eighteenth century.[1] That French philosophes and their adherents elsewhere in Europe thought that the eighteenth century was one of unprecedented light in the sense that "reason" was steadily getting the better of religious "superstition" and "fanaticism" is well known. But the celebration of "light" thus understood did not prevent the century's many would-be defenders of religion from entirely sharing this characterization of their century. Although no century since the "inundation of the barbarians" in Europe had failed to produce its share of setbacks for Christianity, none could compare with the eighteenth century, at least in the opinion of the author of some anonymous *Reflections on the Present State of the [French] Church.* For not only had the vice of self-interest been raised to the level of a virtue, but the "epidemic" of "incredulity," in the author's words, had spread from Paris "into the provinces and penetrated the remotest places, . . . enveloping even those who by their estate, simplicity, ignorance, or distance from the principal centers of contagion would seem to have been the most immune to its threat."[2] The verdict on the century was equally harsh for the anonymous denouncer of *The Secret Revealed,* who, reacting the same year to Louis XVI's Edict of Toleration for Protestants, discerned in its provisions "the revolution produced in manners and opinions by the principles consigned in the *Encyclopedia* . . . and of our modern philosophes, which all tend toward independence, revolt, and crime."[3] This concordance of judgments is all the more remarkable in that they came from opposite ends of the Catholic spectrum, Augustinian and Molinistic, and pointed to opposite ends of the social hierarchy, from the peasantry at the bottom to the king's council on top.

But it was above all the French Revolution that, by specifically designating the philosophes as its progenitors and associating the destruction of monarchy with its spectacular campaign known as "dechristianization," seemed to vindicate both the fondest hopes and direst prophecies of the preceding century and hardened them into historiographical form. On the one hand, republicans or "liberals" at pains to define and defend the legacy of the French Revolution were chary about acknowledging anything other than "enlightened" origins, lest they associate it with things too "fanatical" for comfort. Although she regretted the Revolution's association of political liberalism with atheism, Madame de Staël, one of the founders of the "liberal" interpretation, regarded the Revolution as "inevitable" and "one of the great epochs in the social order" precisely because it represented the "triumph of lights" or of "philosophical lights, that is to say, the judgment of things according to reason rather than habit."[4] And however lively his own sense of religious transcendence, her fellow founder Benjamin Constant was also convinced that this sense had long vacated the eighteenth century's institutional and confessional forms, hopelessly contaminated as these had become by subservience to the Old Regime, especially in France.[5]

On the other hand, Catholics and conservatives were equally reluctant to acknowledge the religious origins of a Revolution they loathed. Responding to de Staël, the vicomte Louis de Bonald, one of the architects of "conservatism," allowed that the Revolution was religious only in the sense that, like the Enlightenment, it directed itself primarily against religion, instinctually sensing that any effort to "demonarchialize" France would have to be accompanied by an effort to decatholicize France as well.[6] Other French "conservative" thinkers were, if anything, even more insistent on this score. The French Revolution, maintained Hughes Félicité de Lamennais in 1825, demonstrated that "no Christian monarchy could ever have degenerated into a democracy if religious principles had not previously sustained a profound alteration," one brought about by the philosophes and the principle that unaided individual "reason" was a reliable guide to the truth.[7] The only exception to this curious consensus of ideological opposites discounting the valence of religion from the making of political dissent in the eighteenth century was the occasional association of the Enlightenment with religious "heresy," in particular, with Protestantism or Jansenism.

Because the radical nature of the Revolution made it the kind of event that provoked adhesion or opposition everywhere even before it crossed French boundaries in armed form after 1792, it also exported its view of the eighteenth century to a Europe hitherto less inclined than the French to view the relation between religion and the cause of enlightenment in such mutually hostile terms. That is to say that as Europeans and even Americans defined themselves either for or against the Revolution, they ironically did so in largely French terms. And as these terms included the Revolution's bipolar historiography ascribing revolutionary change to the influence of lights and assigning the defense of the Old Regime to religion, they also tended similarly to celebrate or to deplore all eighteenth-century reform movements as harbingers of the Revolution, even ones associated with religion, and to interpret religion in either case as "heretical" way stations toward total enlightenment.

This process is clearest in Catholic Europe. Writing in Rome in 1791, but already taking his cues from French counterrevolutionary ideologists, the Sicilian pro-papal publicist Nicola Spedalieri conceptualized the whole eighteenth century as a vast conspiracy of deistic or atheistic philosophes aided and abetted by heretical Jansenists and Protestants to undermine the authority of both thrones and altars, a conspiracy he thought had culminated in the French Revolution to which he assimilated all earlier instances of even absolutist reform.[8] Minus the conspiracy and the association with Jansenists, Italian Jacobins would eventually agree with him, avowing only an enlightened ancestry while leaving it to erstwhile Italian Catholic proponents of ecclesiastical reform like Pietro Tamburini to wash their hands of association with either the Revolution or the philosophes.[9]

But the process is not foreign to Protestant Europe either, despite the possibility there of invoking the sixteenth-century Reformation as an alternative impetus for political reform. Thus in England did Edmund Burke beat even Spedalieri into print, attributing the French Revolution to atheistic French philosophes with whom he paired heretical Dissenters and political radicals in England like Richard Price and Joseph Priestley who, true to form, indeed defended the French Revolution as the triumph of the enlightened "reason" in human affairs. Idealistic counterparts of Price and Priestly in Germany like Johann Gottlieb Fichte or Immanuel Kant greeted the Revolution as a secular sort of sacramental "memorative sign" and promise of future human progress that could "never be forgotten," while Justus Möser and Adam Müller, Protestant and Catholic alike, opposed the Revolution in terms very similar to those of Burke whose *Reflections* Friedrich Gentz, a Protestant convert to Catholicism, admiringly translated into German in 1793.[10]

The shadow thus cast by the French Revolution—and European counterrevolution—over the historiography of eighteenth-century religion and its relation to politics and the Enlightenment was a very long one, stretching over the whole nineteenth and much of the twentieth century. Under its cover there occurred a curious collusion between "liberal" and "conservative" histories to see the Enlightenment as sole promoter of liberal reform and ultimately revolution, on the one hand, and eighteenth-century established religion as a defense of the Old Regime's political order, on the other. The difference between the two were largely evaluative, the one celebrating and the other deploring a "history" about whose "facts" they essentially agreed. This pattern is starkest in Catholic Europe, especially France, where the Revolution never ceased to dominate the interpretation of the eighteenth century in a nation that remained hell-bent on replaying all of the conflicts of the Revolution and experimenting at greater leisure with every constitutional or even anticonstitutional alternative that it had briefly thrown up, and where the polarization of historical interpretation into opposing schools increased rather than decreased as the nineteenth century went on.[11]

The most glaring exception to this historiographical pattern in Catholic Europe is the case of early nineteenth-century Italy where the identity of the papacy as the peninsula's only indigenous Italian state made it possible for Italians to imagine it as a possible nucleus around which national unification might coalesce and to produce the liberal Catholic historiography—that of Alessandro Manzoni, Carlo Troya, and Vincenzo Gioberti—that underscored the medieval papacy's alliance with the Lombard League of communes against the "foreign" Holy Roman Empire.[12] In the long run, however, that historiographical tradition was a casualty of the failure of the Italian revolutions of 1848 and the conspicuous refusal of the papacy to play the role assigned to it. Although it left behind an enduring legacy in the form of work on the Catholic, and specifically Jansenist, origins of the Risorgimento by Ettore Rota and Ernesto Codignola, that legacy in turn sustained collateral damage by association with the philosopher Giovanni Gentile—and Italian fascism's—quest for a "third," more Catholic way to political modernity between anticlerical liberalism and ultramontanist conservatism.[13] Despite a harvest of distinguished scholarship on Italian Jansenism since World War II, the fiasco of fascism in that war paved the way for the triumph of the

French—or, in Italian terms, Ghibelline—model of interpretation of the Italian *Settecento* and its emphasis on the enlightened origins of political modernity, especially in such influential works as Luigi Salvatorelli's history of Italian political thought and of course Franco Venturi's massive and magisterial *Settecento riformatore*.[14]

The pattern holds largely good for Protestant nations as well, once allowances are made for different emphases attendant upon variations in national development. If, in the case of England, the long regnant "Whig interpretation of history" and particularly of English history gave the Protestant Dissenting tradition a very privileged place, it was less as a religious phenomenon than as a carrier of liberal and democratic values that came to prevail in the nineteenth century. For G. M. Trevelyan and W. E. H. Lecky, for example, seventeenth-century Puritans and their Dissenting—and often Unitarian—descendants were "vigilant champions of liberty and critics of government" and the mainstay of the Whig "party," while their Tory opponents were above all defenders of an Anglican Establishment which justified its privileges and intolerance in terms similar to those used by the Church of Rome.[15]

When this history of the "progress" of "liberty" reached the eighteenth century it further demanded the subordination of the Dissenting tradition to the moderate English Enlightenment which, especially in the more philosophical renditions of Whig history like Leslie Stephen's, was seen as the logical fulfillment of the liberal promise of the sixteenth-century Reformation as well as the condemnation of the Anglican Establishment as a hopelessly rearguard action.[16] The conservative response to this metanarrative was an all too predictable evaluative inversion of the image that, without really contesting the image, featured the Anglican Establishment as fighting a heroic if ultimately unsuccessful effort to uphold law and order in the face of the American Revolution, the French menace, and its own disloyal—and heterodox—sons at home.[17] In both schools, the results were the same: a slighting of eighteenth-century religion itself as having already served its prescribed purpose and a general inability to grasp the complex interplay between religion and politics.

Across the North Sea in the Calvinist Netherlands, reaction to the French Revolution and its after-tremors in the revolutions of 1830 and 1848 produced a Calvinist counterrevolutionary conservatism in the form of the Anti-Revolutionary Party and, in historical form, Willem Groen van Prinsterer's *Unbelief and Revolution.*[18] Locating the origins of the French Revolution and even like-minded reform exclusively in the Enlightenment and defining both as the destructive progress of "unbelief," Groen's history was cut from the cloth of French Catholic conservative ideologies of the early Lamennais except in its denial of papal infallibility and refusal to accept the stock judgment that the Calvinist Reformation of the sixteenth century could have prepared the way for the Enlightenment and revolutions of the modern period. The liberal reply came in the form of P. J. Blok's *History of the Dutch People,* and, later, Peter Geyl and Johann Huizinga's classic histories of the Netherlands, which, although sympathetic to the work of the French Revolution, similarly insisted upon the Old-Regime character of Calvinism and religion more generally in the Dutch eighteenth century and their incompatibility with even the ideology of the Dutch "patriotic" reform at the end of the century.[19]

A Protestant conservatism in reaction to the French Revolution similarly set the tone in the Protestant Germanies in the first half of the nineteenth century, especially in Prussia, where Friedrich Stahl played a role in relation to the Hohenzollern dynasty not unlike that of Groen van Prinsterer vis-à-vis the House of Orange-Nassau in the Netherlands.[20] So pervasive was the negative reaction to the French Revolution and Napoleonic occupation in Germany that the only political and ideological current openly to avow the parentage of the French Enlightenment and Revolution was that of Georg Wilhelm Friedrich Hegel, for whom the Enlightenment and the Revolution represented the "last stage of history," that of the idea of freedom, as well as of course Hegel's atheistical intellectual progeny culminating in the dialectical materialism of Karl Marx and Friedrich Engels.[21] For Protestant liberal and nationalist Germans in search of a more "usable past" it was of course always possible to root the legitimacy of their aspirations in the German Reformation read—or reread—

as the first stirring of German nationhood and liberation from the Roman papal yoke rather in the manner of the patriotic celebration of the Reformation's tricentennial at the Wartburg Castle in 1817 or Felix Mendelssohn's interpretation in his Reformation Symphony in 1832.

This line of interpretation reached its apogee in the work of the "Prussian School" of German historians during and in the wake of the unification of Germany under Prussian auspices in the 1860s. In Heinrich Von Treitschke's vision of the eighteenth century, for example, the distinctively German enlightenment developed "the fundamental ideas of the Reformation into a right of absolutely free and unprejudiced investigation" and again made the country "the central region of heresy" and fit object of "national pride." As for the apparently religious Pietistic enterprise of Jakob Spener and August Hermann Franke in Prussia, Treitschke deemed it a movement that recovered the purely "moral content of Christianity" as opposed to the "tyranny of the theological belief in the letter of the written word," enabling the eighteenth-century German, alone in this respect in Europe, "to be at once pious and free," and "for his literature to be Protestant without the taint of dogma."[22] Such was the power of this Prussian Protestant metanarrative that Catholic Germans excluded by it never came up with an adequate narrative to counter it at the national level, having recourse instead to regional histories and the memory of the medieval reich. Yet it is hard to see how such a counternarrative could have taken any form other than that of the negative mirror image of the Protestant one, faulting the Reformation, Pietism, and the Enlightenment for having contributed to the combination of bureaucratic omnipotence and corrosive individualism that characterized modern Germany in the Catholic view.[23]

Not even imperial Russia has altogether escaped from the interpretational net cast by the French Revolution. To be sure, the Russian eighteenth century stood quite apart from the West's, inasmuch as Russia remained little affected by the French Revolution much less by the religious upheavals of the sixteenth-century. The Revolution of 1917, moreover, interrupted the Orthodox Church's history even more brutally than the French Revolution did that of the Gallican

Church.[24] Yet certain distinct parallels with the treatment of religion in western Europe are discernable. For just as, say, French radical historiography's image of an entirely retrograde Gallican Church in the eighteenth century is in large measure a backwards projection of the Third Republic's pitched battles with the church over education and monastic orders in the 1880s, so nineteenth-century liberal Russian historiography's image of an Orthodox Church entirely subdued by Catherine the Great's "enlightened" absolute state is a retrospective projection of the conflicts provoked by the liberal reforms of Tsar Alexander II in the 1860s. In negative yet concordant response, Orthodox clerical historians, in Olga Tsapina's words, were "prone to treat the history of the Russian Church with a certain halo of martyrology," valuing as they did the Church as the last viable defense against the new secular order.[25] The advent of Soviet historiography only reinforced this pattern, as did for that matter Marxian historiography in the West.

The main legacy of nineteenth-century liberal historiography was a cluster of classic, highly influential texts that prolonged the life of this enlightened image of the eighteenth century and the retrograde relation of religion to it. Pride of place among these works must go to Ernst Cassirer's *The Philosophy of the Enlightenment* and Paul Hazard's two-volume treatment of the transformation of European thought in the late seventeenth and eighteenth centuries, neither of which did anything to modify the prevailing teleology.[26] For while Cassirer noted in passing the essential differences between religious expressions in eighteenth-century England, France, and Germany, his persuasive treatment of the progressive unfolding of unbelief since the sixteenth-century Protestant revolt logically culminated in France and was celebrated there, while Hazard's story both begins and ends in Paris and depicts an even sharper mutation of thought and starker contrasts between the champions of reason and the devotees of religion.[27] Derived to some degree from both of these sources, the eighteenth century more recently depicted in Peter Gay's *The Enlightenment: An Interpretation* is an entirely passive tabula rasa written on by a uniquely active and unitary Enlightenment characterized as "the rise of neo-Paganism" and defined in essentially French terms.[28]

Not even the great syntheses of enlightened thought in political context by Robert Palmer and Franco Venturi entirely transcended this view. Although Palmer's operative division between "democratic" and "aristocratic" thought and political action helpfully dissected Gay's artificially unitary enlightenment into opposing political camps, it also tended to reduce any religious dimensions of "the struggle" to its purely political plane. Descendants of Calvinists though they were, he argued, radical English Dissenters spoke uniquely in "the language . . . of the European Revolution," wishing to "forget religious differences."[29] And although Franco Venturi's massive *Settecento riformatore* devoted much of its sprawling space to the European periphery where, he thought, the tensions within enlightened thought were much more visible than in the center, his enlightenment never ceased to be that of Paris, precisely because it was the French "philosophes who, above and beyond the decadence of the churches and [occasional calls for] toleration, affirmed the values of liberty."[30]

Toward the end of the nineteenth century and into the twentieth, the liberal occlusion of the role of religion in eighteenth-century Europe received powerful reinforcement from socialist historiography for which the only possible ideological expression of the ascending bourgeoisie in the eighteenth century was the secularized thought in the enlightened mold, limiting religion's politically and economically "progressive" phase to the sixteenth and seventeenth centuries and consigning its eighteenth-century manifestations to rearguard defenses of the old order. The "classics" of socialist historiography of the eighteenth century characteristically concentrated on revolutions and rumors of revolutions. Although Louis Blanc and Jean Jaurez manifested a certain interest in religious phenomena—in particular, Jansenism—their more "orthodox" Marxian successors like Albert Mathiez, Georges Lefebvre and Albert Soboul did not. In a book about the "civilization" of the Old Regime and the beginnings of the French Revolution of more than six-hundred pages, Soboul devoted precisely six pages to religion, dividing these six into the social categories of the devotional practices of the peasantry and the "apologetics" of an "aristocratic ideology" in full "feudal reaction."[31]

As for England, E. P. Thompson's estimate of Methodism as a "ritual of psychic masturbation" that thwarted class consciousness and hence French-style revolution on the part of the eighteenth-century English working class is well enough known. And the one place where he was willing to locate religious sources for "progressive" politics was, not surprisingly, precisely where the older Whig historians had seen it: in Nonconformity, in his view a leading "vector of the Enlightenment," and in Socinian or Unitarian positions, from which "liberal principles were argued."[32] Thus did such tidy, well-used categories again confirm the old paradigms. Conversely, to the considerable degree that liberal historiography engaged the Marxian challenge on its own terrain, the social history that dominated the field in the 1960s and 1970s all but excluded consideration of religion and completed its historiographic ghettoization as ecclesiastical or church history, a specialized subdiscipline that tended not to engage the wider field.[33]

Religion and the Fall of the French Revolution

What has more recently changed this—or what, in other words, has made a book such as this one feasible—is first and most simply the demise of the Marxian interpretation of the whole early-modern period in the West, culminating of course with the collapse of Eastern-European Marxian governments themselves as the twentieth century entered its final decade. The process began in the 1960s with the successful assault on the hitherto regnant Marxian or class-oriented interpretation of the English Revolution of the mid-seventeenth century by H. R. Trevor-Roper, Jack Hexter, among others, and then extended to the equally successful siege of Marxian historical interpretation's ultimate Bastille, the French Revolution itself, at the hands of William Doyle and François Furet and many others during the 1970s and '80s—the alliance of Anglo-Saxon empiricism and Left-Bank intellectualism, in Robert Darnton's exasperated estimation—beginning with Alfred Cobban's *Social Interpretation of the French Revolution* in 1964.[34] The result was that what had long been mere "superstructure"—the world of politics, intellection and ultimately religion—now found itself bereft of its socioeconomic underpinnings and free to acquire historical agency in its own right, something capable of effecting as well as reflecting historical change. Along with the "new cultural history" in general, the field of religious thought and experience hence acquired a potential valence that it had not had before, even, and most especially, in the eighteenth century.[35]

Perhaps the collapse of the Marxian interpretation of the French Revolution will have carried in its debris the beginning of the end of the French Revolution itself, in the sense of being the alpha and omega of the interpretation of the eighteenth century. If, in Furet's phrase, the French Revolution is finally "over," not only for the French but for historians, French and non-French alike, then perhaps there will also be an end to the long shadow it has cast over the preceding century as well as to the spell it has cast over its historians until now, beginning with the contemporaries of the Revolution itself.[36] We may see an end as well to the incessant antiphony of "liberal" versus "conservative" interpretations which, sharing at least as much as ever divided them, have managed to drown out all sound of religion between them. It is certain that any historiographical appreciation of religion as a political factor in eighteenth-century Europe ultimately depends on getting behind the French Revolution, of pretending that it might not have happened, or at least might not have happened in the way that it did, of seeing the eighteenth century as something more and other than a long prelude to the Revolution, and the Revolution itself as the historical contingency that, like all history, it merely was.

A second interrelated development that has opened up the eighteenth century to a new appreciation of religion is more amorphous, of longer duration, and, accordingly, harder to state: the modernist and then postmodernist collapse of confidence in enlightened "reason," its privileged access to "nature," including human nature, and the metanarrative of "progress" these categories sustained. The demise of the prospect of the "progress" promised by dialectical materialism is thus only a special, if indeed especially poignant, case of the demise of what the Enlightenment promised in its loudly touted triumph of empirical "reason" over "superstition" and habit. A long time coming before Max Horkheimer's and Theodor Adorno's landmark *Dialectic of Enlightenment* made it "official" in 1947, the West's loss of confidence in the objectivity of "reason" and the transparency of "nature" was perhaps slowest in making its impact felt in the historical profession, especially in North America.[37] (This despite Carl Becker's precocious perception in the 1930s that the creed of the Enlightenment was just that, a creed akin to the Christian one requiring faith in either case, and his personal loss of faith in this creed under the cumulative impact of the Great War and the Great Depression.)[38]

When this "failure of nerve," as Peter Gay would probably have it, finally hit the profession with full force, it did so under the combined impact of the fragmentation of national identity in the 1960s and poststructural linguistics and hermeneutics by way of literary theory associated with the names of Jacques Derrida and Michel Foucault.[39] Among the many victims of this impact, none is more illustrious than the Enlightenment and its metanarrative of triumphant reason over superstition, which suddenly looked like just a "discourse" or internal system of meaning—and a new way of rationalizing power—replacing another, or a linguistic system just as self-referential and lacking an anchor in "reality" as any other.[40] While the collapse of the Marxian interpretation may well spell the end of the French Revolution, this loss of confidence in the capacity of language to engage "reality" may well mean the end of the Enlightenment. And although the consequences of this development are unlikely to be uniquely benign, they have opened up the possibility of reconsidering eighteenth-century religious phenomena in something other than the self-validating "enlightened" categories of, say, the leftover mythological or the revenge of the emotions.

The effect of these developments on the treatment of the eighteenth century are already numerous and visible. On the one hand, the once lordly and unitary Enlightenment of Cassirer, Gay, Hazard, and Venturi with its center and sun in Paris and its philosophic rays penetrating the peripheries seems to be refracting into numerous plural lights in a spirit more in keeping with eighteenth-century parlance. J. G. A. Pocock has located a distinctively Protestant Enlightenment of which Edward Gibbon, hardly a "philosophe," is an exemplar, that was anti-"enthusiastic" but not anti-Christian, and that stretched like a crescent from England and Scotland through the Protestant Netherlands and western Germanies only to end in the Swiss cities like Geneva and Lausanne.[41] At the same time, a distinctively Catholic Enlightenment, for whose existence Bernard Plongeron and Samuel Miller have made a persuasive case, seems to have formed another and southern crescent from the Catholic Germanies in the southeast through the north-central Italies, including Rome in the center, and on through the Iberian peninsula in the West.[42] Opposed though it was to the excesses of "baroque" Catholicism and open to the newer sciences, it bears everywhere the marks of a revival of Christian humanism.

Between and within these crescents, a distinctively civic humanistic and proto-republican Enlightenment which, opposed to commerce, "luxury," and many aspects of modern "civilization," made common cause with certain forms of British Nonconformist and Jansenist dissent, has forced itself onto the scholarly agenda. Among the English bearers of this kind of enlightenment, the less than orthodox "commonwealthmen" originally brought to light by the work of Caroline Robbins have recently joined company with entirely orthodox divines like Philip Doddridge and Isaac Watts as well as the editors of the *Occasional Paper* uncovered by research during the last two decades. The discovery of a classical but not at all impious republican in the person of the abbé Gabriel Bonnet de Mably has established the existence of such an enlightenment in the seemingly inhospitable home of absolutist France as well.[43]

Much in the work of Jean-Jacques Rousseau, too, overlaps with civic humanism's secular austerity. Yet the misanthropic "citizen of Geneva" also concocted his own religion out of the elements of existing ones, and "Rousseauism" as a quasi-religious phenomenon acquired enough "mass" at least in France to lay claim to being a separate strand of enlightenment. Those who in opposition to both Rousseau and civic humanism celebrated "modern" and often monarchical progress in civility and commerce formed a school of political economy which is hard not to categorize as a fifth strand of enlightenment, and which, in the form of physiocracy, produced the most pious enlightenment in France. And although the radical free-thinking, materialist, and "encyclopedic" enlightenment denounced by the pious of both Protestant and Catholic traditions did indeed mount a frontal assault against the "infamous thing," this latter enlightenment, examples of which Margaret Jacob has called attention to in England and the Netherlands, seems to have predominated only in France.[44]

While this attenuation and refraction of a single enlightenment have made many erstwhile figures of the Enlightenment look a lot more religious—Gaspar Jovellanos in Spain, the Latitudinarians, and even the Deists in England—they have also made a lot of hitherto irreducibly religious figures into bearers of enlightenment.[45] Eighteenth-century English "enthusiasm" incarnate in the person of John Wesley has emerged from Frederick Dreyer's seminal study as a conscientious student of the empirical epistemology of John Locke, on the lookout for a sixth sense that could help account for religious experience.[46] Similarly, the Russian white (nonmonastic) clergy turn out to be the warmest friends of Catherine the Great's efforts to bring the Orthodox Church into the modern world.

Not only did such people make common cause with *Aufklärer* during the early decades of the century, in the case of England, and much later in the case of Russia, but German pietists also, in James van Horn-Melton's analysis, cleared out the "public space" later occupied by the more radical enlightenment of Lessing and Kant. A Benedictine monk and priest, Benito Gerónimo Fejyóo y Montenegro and Antonio Muratori, turn out to be central figures in the Spanish and Italian enlightenments respectively, and champions of the newer sciences there. Sincere defenders of papal and episcopal authority like Spedalieri in Italy and Lefranc de Pompignan were perfectly capable of wielding the language of natural rights and social contract to "conservative" purpose. "Patriotic" curés like Claude Fauchet and Adrien Lamourette found in Catholic Christology "reason" enough to stay with the French Revolution until its falling out with the Gironde.[47] And although the proximity of the Molinistic or humanistic theology of the Jesuits to the enlightened rehabilitation of human nature has long been recognized, those most incorrigible opponents of any hint of "natural religion," the French Jansenists, turn out in Monique Cottret's recent study to have had numerous and growing points of convergence with the philosophes, especially in matters political.[48]

But in some national settings, the reaction to social interpretations has been so severe and the recourse to "discourse" so unreserved as to have ironically ended by rehabilitating a certain enlightenment's own auto-discourse, an identity of which Marxism was only a later and more materialistic embodiment. Although, in an English context, J. C. D. Clark has done much to resurrect the role of religion in the formation of eighteenth-century Tory and radical political theory, his work nonetheless continues to insist upon heterodoxy as the main if not sole "matrix of ideological innovation"; while J. G. A. Pocock, despite arguing for the existence of a more religious or at least less "philosophic" enlightenment in England than in France, has similarly underscored "the extent to which all discourse of toleration, liberty, and enlightenment was a polemic against the orthodox theology of Christ's divinity, against the Trinity and the Incarnation . . . because it explains so much in the political, philosophical, theological, and historical controversies of the long eighteenth century."[49] Thus do certain aspects of Clark's and Pocock's work come full circle, ending in the reaffirmation of the thesis first propounded by H. R. Trevor-Roper in 1968 that traced the intellectual ancestry of the European Enlightenment exclusively through forms of seventeenth-century Protestant heterodoxy on back to pre-Reformation humanism, in large part on the grounds that these are the ancestors that the eighteenth-century philosophes acknowledged.[50] The post-Marxian effort to avoid materialistic reductionism in the study of religion has hence led by degrees to the nearly total subordination of the social experience of disaffected religious minorities to a neo-enlightened narrative of the progressive secularization of thought and the advent of a post-Christian modern world. Recent studies have therefore provided not only the occasion but the need for comparative analyses.

Orthodox Dissenters

Jansenists and philosophes as political co-belligerents? Presbyterian and Independent ministers, on the one hand, and Russian Orthodox white clergy and Catherine the Great, on the other, all advocates of reform? Such de facto alliances suggest that something like a religiously inspired political radicalism was still possible in the eighteenth century. That possibility may well still seem as much of a contradiction in terms as the possibility of, say, a religiously grounded "reason" might have seemed to contemporary enlightened readers of Immanuel Kant's *Religion within the Bounds of Reason Alone.*

In contrast, the possibility of alliance between religion and the defense of the European Old Regime seems all too obvious. Tautology though it may be, it nonetheless boasts an imposing mass of empirical evidence in its favor with which it would be well to come to terms. The French monarchy's occasional attempts at reform to equalize the fiscal burden or to grant toleration to Protestants met no greater or more effective resistance than from the French clergy which, with the leverage of its General Assembly, successfully opposed all the monarchy's efforts to tax its property or to accord a civil status to Protestants from the 1750s until the Revolution. In Anglican England, by contrast, the government's sole attempt to grant a measure of toleration to Catholics provoked in 1780 the largest urban public disturbances of the whole eighteenth century in Western Europe before the French Revolution, enabling the government to fend off the reformist Association Movement's effort to make the House of Commons more representative. The same seemingly anachronistic confessional rivalry ultimately broke the momentum of the Irish Volunteers and their attempt to reform the Irish Parliament; religious disagreements over the "Catholic question" finally frustrated efforts for Parliamentary reform in 1785.[51] Similarly, religious divisions plagued the ranks of the Dutch "patriots" in their attempt to reform the Dutch municipal councils and provincial estates in a "democratic" sense, at least in some provinces like the Overijssel studied and presented in this volume by Wayne te Brake.[52]

In Catholic Europe, Charles Noel sketches a similar picture for Bourbon Spain, where the efforts of royal reformers like Pedro

blessed the Dutch patriot movement as fervently as the Catholic ecclesiastical hierarchy and rank-and-file Protestants condemned it; James van Horn Melton's Lutheran pietists who were just as anti-absolutist in Württemberg as they may have been the allies of Hohenzollern absolutism in Prussia; the Austrian and Spanish Jansenists, as profiled by Reginald Ward and Charles Noel, and who sponsored and defended "enlightened" reforms, especially in higher education and the emerging discipline of history, or finally the many Gallican Catholics, who were able to reconcile their Catholic consciences to their commitment to a revolution which, if in the end it defined itself against Catholicism, did so despite their very best efforts. The point is that these conflicts, many of them politically defining for the eighteenth century, were not ones that uniformly pitted Catholics or Protestants against the "enlightened" proponents of political reform or revolution, but that rather also divided Catholics from other Catholics and Protestants from other Protestants, often within the same ecclesiastical structures.

Further, the dissenters from the various "establishments" who figure most prominently in this volume are more likely to be orthodox than heterodox. As employed here, the term "orthodox" means quite simply only those dissenters who had no quarrel with the givens of Christian doctrine within their various "establishments," and in particular with the doctrines of the Trinity and the full deity of Christ, as in the case of Presbyterian, Congregationalist, or Baptist Dissenters in Great Britain who continued to be "orthodox" in the sense of agreeing in substance with the Westminster Confession or the Thirty-Nine Articles. But this doctrinal orthodoxy did not prevent them from objecting to the hierarchical ecclesiastical establishments or advocating radical parliamentary reform in equal or greater numbers than their Arian or Unitarian "rational Dissenting" counterparts in test cases at the end of the century in the England, Scotland, and Ireland comparatively analyzed by James Bradley. On the opposite side of Europe, in Russia, the focus of Olga Tsapina's analysis is on the parish or "white clergy" whose commitment to Russian doctrinal "orthodoxy" was seamless and entire as opposed to the better known "Old Believers," even though Old Belief's dissent from the

Russian Orthodox Church was not doctrinal either, but rather liturgical in content. The Russian Orthodox Church faced no real challenge in the form of doctrinal heterodoxy or heresy.

Between these two geographical extremes, in what was still the Holy Roman Empire, Pietist dissent from the German Lutheran or even Reformed polities fell well short of any doctrinal quarrel with Lutheran or Reformed "orthodoxy" as defined by the Augsburg Confession or the Belgic Confession, nor did it even have any real bone to pick with the hierarchical polity, since Lutheran Pietists in particular never quarreled with the church's episcopal structure or the appointment of bishops from above. While Dutch and German Pietists typically accented the importance of praxis and deplored the preoccupation with doctrine, they did not for the most part call for a different doctrine. As for the Netherlands, neither Reformed nor Catholic participants in the political protest known as the "patriot" movement had any quarrel with doctrinal orthodoxy in their respective churches. Nor does the propensity of relatively disenfranchised Mennonites really change this picture, since they were as orthodox Trinitarians as any of the others.

Problems with this consistency arise mainly in connection with Jansenism—a mainly Flemish, French, and Dutch Catholic phenomenon, but by the end of the century also Austrian, German, Italian, and Spanish—which was condemned as a "heresy" by the papacy as early as 1641 and 1653. The second of these condemnations, the papal bull called *Cum occasione* fulminated by Innocent X, singled out five famous—or infamous—propositions for condemnation supposedly extracted from the tome entitled *Augustinus,* composed by the Bishop of Ypres, Cornelius Jansen, who posthumously gave his name to the movement. An attempt to restate the theology of Saint Augustine for post-Reformation Catholic Europe, the book was accused of teaching that God had chosen some people for salvation and others for damnation quite apart from their foreseen behavior, that a certain kind of grace called "efficacious" was irresistible, that Jesus' death on the cross was not really intended to save everyone—the sorts of doctrines, in other words, recently defined as "orthodox" by the Reformed Synod of Dordrecht in 1618–19. From the point of view of papal "orthodoxy," the Jansenist "heresy" hence consisted in covert Calvinism.

The trouble with accepting this papal judgment has always been and still is that, with few exceptions, Jansenists themselves disclaimed the name of "Jansenist," claimed only to be defending the Catholic sense of the theology of Saint Augustine against their principal foes in the Society of Jesus, professed to condemn the five propositions in any heretical sense they might be construed to have, and quarreled only about whether they were in fact contained in *Augustinus*. Except for the diocese of Utrecht in 1723–24, no Jansenist group ever separated from the Catholic Church, while Utrecht, for its part, spent the rest of the century—vainly, it is true—trying to negotiate its way back into communion with the papacy. The situation of Jansenists within the Catholic Church worsened somewhat, when in 1713 Clement XI's bull *Unigenitus* condemned many more "Jansenist" propositions which were incontestably extracted from another book, Pasquier Quesnel's *Réflexions morales sur le Nouveau testament*. Still, the form of even this bull left enough wiggle room for Jansenists to deny that the bull had condemned anything at all as clearly "heretical," enabling them to persist in regarding themselves as orthodox Catholics. Nor did they quarrel with any other aspect of Catholic doctrine, certainly not with the doctrine of the seven sacraments, much less with that of the Trinity. In the last analysis, the only reason for regarding Jansenists as "heterodox" is the series of papal judgments to this effect, and since the doctrine of papal infallibility was anything but universally accepted by Catholics at the time—all of Gallican France rejected it—to accept its validity here would seem anachronistic at the least.

In fact, Jansenists and Jesuit and "Molinistic" antagonists were among the few opposing groups in eighteenth-century Christendom to engage in very much theological quarreling, and between these two, Jansenists did the lion's share of the theologizing. Nor did their theologizing match the originality and brilliance of the generation of Pascal and Antoine Arnauld, unless, as has been recently done, much ado be made of the hermeneutics and eschatological theology called "figurism."[53] Truth to tell, with the exception of Jonathan Edwards in far off Massachusetts and John Wesley's rather original attempt to reconcile the Pauline doctrine of justification by faith alone with the freedom of the human will, eighteenth-century Europe was not a century of very distinguished or original theological reflection. Even English Arians and Socinians traced any innovations in their views back to their founders in the fourth and sixteenth centuries, respectively. But lest this judgment be taken as an admission of the unimportance of religion as a political—or even religious—factor in the eighteenth century, it should be added that theological activity and originality is only one among many possible indices of religious vitality, and probably not the most important one.

The century that ended with the publication of Kant's *Critique of Pure Reason* was not as a whole very kind to the enterprise of speculative or dogmatic theology. It was rather in the more practical domains of pastoral and penitential theology, liturgical and devotional experimentation, and ecclesiological and political action and reflection where eighteenth-century European Christianity most left its mark. To be sure, the century produced no small number of defenses of Christianity against the Enlightenment's more obvious epistemological challenges to the validity of faith and revelation—Bishop Butler's *Analogy of Religion* and the abbé Nicolas-Sylvestre Bergier's *The Certainty of the Proofs of Christianity* are two noteworthy examples—in part by trying to wield the Enlightenment's own criteria of "reason" and sensate "experience" on religion's behalf. But it was a century far more fecund in the development of domestic missions and revival, the composition of hymnody, the invention of new forms of religious association, in new translations of Scripture, the writing of ecclesiastical history, the production of canon law, and in rethinking the relation between *civitas terrena* and *civitas Dei*. But these were also all matters that divided Christians from other Christians and in which "dissent" most manifested itself, as all branches of European Christendom assimilated and creatively deployed the eighteenth century's twin criteria of "reason" and empirical "experience," sometimes collaboratively, but very often against each other.

This contest, such as it was, took place *within* the major confessions far more than between them. Gone were the days of the great post-Reformation set-to's between Protestants and Catholics, or even between Calvinists and Lutherans—and that despite Louis XIV's brutal suppression of the revolt of Huguenot peasants in the Cévennes in the early eighteenth century, the spectacular ouster of Protestants from the Archbishopric of Salzburg in 1731, and similar but increasingly anachronistic episodes as the century went on.[54] In England, the defining episodes of ecclesiastical conflict for the eighteenth century were between branches of the same confession, for example, in the ejection of some 2,000 English "Nonconformist" ministers and schoolmasters in the wake of the forcible restoration of the Anglican Church in 1662. In Scotland, the United Provinces, the Germanies, and Russia, the story is the same. This intra-confessional nature of religious contested ground must be reckoned as one of the major ways that the eighteenth century was distinguished from the previous two, although it would be well to remember that the Seven Years' War, which aligned Europe's major Catholic states against the major Protestant ones, was not without a confessional dimension, even for some of the royal actors like Louis XV. The disappearance of the international religious civil war from the eighteenth-century scene did not, however, prevent the eighteenth century's intraconfessional conflicts from assuming international dimensions of their own, as demonstrated by pan-Germanic conflict between Pietism and Lutheran or Reformed Orthodoxy or the trans-Catholic face-off between the Jansenist and ex-Jesuit "internationals" on the eve of the French Revolution, both described in the pages below.

The conflicts described in the following essays are therefore not, at least with rare exceptions, ones between Catholics and Eastern Orthodoxy, Catholics and Protestants, or between Calvinists and Lutherans, but rather between equally Reformed clergy and some of their parishioners on political issues in the Netherlands, between equally Lutheran Pietists and defenders of "orthodoxy" in the Germanies, between equally "Orthodox" parish or "white" clergy and monastic clergy in Russia, between equally Catholic Jansenists and Jesuits in France, Spain, Austria, the Netherlands, and Italies; and finally, between equally Presbyterian antisubscriptionists and subscriptionists in Northern Ireland doubled by equally Presbyterian

Secessionists and defenders of the Established Kirk in Scotland. While all of these intraconfessional conflicts, like the English one, had deep roots in the seventeenth and even sixteenth centuries, none of them had come to occupy the ecclesiastical foreground until the second half of the seventeenth century and the eighteenth century. Although one or another of the parties in conflict usually laid claim to the title of "orthodox," all were orthodox enough by the standards within each polity. The sources of conflict in most of these cases arose from unsettled issues of authority centering around the interplay between ecclesiastical and civil polities and the related questions of the status of established religions, religious minority rights, and toleration.

Nothing more eloquently attests to the intraconfessional nature of religious debate in the eighteenth century than the apparent evidence of its opposite: namely the persistence of anti-Catholic rhetoric among Protestants and anti-Protestant rhetoric among Catholics.[55] Not that such rhetoric did not play on real fears and traumatic memories of past centuries' religious civil wars on either side of the Catholic-Protestant divide, as the Gordon riots in London, Edinburgh, and Glasgow in 1780, the Catholic scare in the Netherlands in 1734, or the fears of a Huguenot uprising in Catholic France during the Seven Years' War more than amply attest.[56] These fears had to be real in order for the rhetoric to work. And yet the real function of the rhetoric was far more intraconfessional than interconfessional in either case. That is to say that if, in the absence of very much conflict with real Catholics, disaffected Protestant Dissenters in England, Scotland, and Ireland continued to denounce "popery" and "Romish tyranny" throughout the length and breadth of the eighteenth century, it was the better to tar their Protestant foes in the established churches with a clericalism reminiscent in their view of the Roman Catholic hierarchy. And so relentlessly, on the Catholic side, was the charge of creeping Calvinism or "Presbyterianism" leveled against Jansenist critics of episcopal and papal authoritarianism not only in France but in all of Catholic Europe by the end of the century, that if real Jansenists did not in fact become more Protestant as time went on, they might just as well have, seeing that they were bound to be damned as such whether they did or did not.

Pieties and Politics in Comparative Perspective

Indeed, the conflicts in question were so uniformly intraconfessional that the significant lines of convergence are often interconfessional. That is to say that, where the content of the issues of contestation are concerned, the parties across confessional lines often had much more in common than they did with their adversaries in the same church. At the most general level, such areas of interconfessional convergence united Congregational and Presbyterian Dissenters, continental Catholic Jansenists, Lutheran and Reformed Pietists, and even Russian Orthodox "white" clergy in favor of the parish clergy against the episcopal hierarchy as well as against the whole monastic establishment and things "monkish." The same dissenting coalition tended also to espouse the interests of the laity against an exclusive clericalism, plainer and more intelligible forms of worship against baroque "excess" and Latinate liturgies, a more interior and "enlightened" faith against "superstitious" or merely exterior motions of devotion, and, last but not least—and although not without some severe limits—the rights of the individual conscience against "blind obedience" to sheer authority. From the British Isles to Russia and from the northern Germanies to the Mediterranean, "dissent," in other words, took the form of a call for more personally assimilated faith, more intelligible forms of worship, and less hierarchical ecclesiastical structures. Almost without exception, in the context of the eighteenth century, such concerns were as much political as they were religious.

Within these broad limits, the strongest convergence emerges between the situation of French Jansenist Catholics and British dissenters on the one hand, and between the Gallican, Anglican, and presbyterian church-state "establishments" and its defenders on the other. Although Jansenists still argued with their adversaries on behalf of an Augustinian conception of divine grace and predestination while dissenters in Britain had for the most part put this issue behind them, both stood for a "spiritual" and purified devotion and an austere liturgy, both defended the laity against their pastors and these in turn against their superiors, both denounced the prevailing system of ecclesiastical preferment and what they called ecclesiastical "despotism," both invoked the unmediated authority of Christ and the example of the early church, and in both cases their ecclesiastical radicalism eventually spilled over into political radicalism and opposition to royal "despotism." Although Catholics, French Jansenists were almost as strident in their denunciations of "popery"—the "despotism" of the curia, at least, as opposed to what they called the Holy See—as their Protestant counterparts across the Channel, and although latecomers to this cause, French Jansenists had by the end of the century also joined British dissenters in advocating greater civil toleration of religious minorities, if not outright disestablishment.

If the issue of political or antiabsolutist radicalism be excepted—and this is a big exception—this same series of congruencies between British dissenters and Jansenists came to hold as well for European Jansenism generally—in Austria, Italy, Spain, the Catholic Germanies, and the Netherlands—in the course of the second half of the century. If among these convergences the issue of an explicit and antihierarchical ecclesiology be singled out and the devotional aspect played down, then it can be stretched to include the cause of the Russian "white" or parish clergy, assuming that Petr Alexeev, archpriest of the Kremlin Cathedral of Saint Michael, spoke for more than himself on the subject of the basic equality of bishops and priests. For all these forms of dissent developed explicit ecclesiologies based on the authority of Christ or the example of the early church that diminished the distance between orders and ranks within the clergy and called for a less hierarchical church.

But if, on the other hand, the ecclesiological issue be set aside and such matters as lay participation in worship and the translation of Scripture and the Mass into the vernacular be privileged, then the Lutheran Pietists join Jansenists and British dissenters in a common cause that seems to have excluded the Russian white clergy, even though—it is well to remember—they were obliged to be married and were often elected by their congregations. All of these groups insisted

guild membership and public offices here and there by largely local governments at the behest of the Reformed Church, but otherwise able to worship as Catholics in a bewilderingly decentralized republic where the "public" church did not have the power of a real state church to coerce confessional conformity. With a "constitution" more closely approximating a separation of church from state than anywhere in Europe, the Dutch Republic was the only state in eighteenth-century Europe where religious dissent and controversy could take place without much perturbing the public sphere, and where it did not translate into anything very "radical" in the domains of either church or state. For Dutch Catholics in the city of Deventer, a decisive moment came during the "patriot" agitation for constitutional reform in the 1780s when lay Catholics broke ranks with their own clergy to press their case for full citizens' rights in partial alliance with Reformed clergymen, among others. This limited kind of public political participation signaled the Catholic community's definitive abandonment of any residual hegemonic claims and the acceptance of their place in the Netherlands as one minority among many others.

This brief attempt at a typology of structural variation among ecclesiastical establishments in eighteenth-century Europe falls well short of exhausting all the possibilities presented even in these essays, if only because combinations of elements from among them were also possible. Perhaps the most peculiar such combination was, not England, but rather the Greater Britain after the Union of Anglican England and Presbyterian Scotland in 1707, which combined the weak Empire's constitutional capacity to preside over more than one ecclesiastical establishment with the existence of two strong establishments more typical of confessional territorial monarchies. Aside from the Holy Roman Empire itself, perhaps the closest precedent for this monstrosity was France after the Edict of Nantes, especially between 1598 and 1629, when an officially Catholic dynasty ruled over two rather independent and mutually hostile ecclesiastical establishments, one Catholic and of course episcopal and the other Calvinist and consistorial.

Whether, in the case of England, this anomalous situation was of a sort to strengthen or discourage dissent from either or both establishments is a matter of dispute. On the one hand, the existence of two established churches under the same civil polity would seem in principle to have relativized both establishments and thereby legitimized resistance by dissenters in both.[58] But on the other hand, especially after the law of 1712 reestablished patronage in Scotland, these two privileged "corporations" operated as though they were identical, parallel, and self-enclosed worlds, the main difference being that the Presbyterian General Assembly did not send any clerical representatives to the English House of Lords. In England, the Union may have simultaneously reinforced the Anglican establishment even as it provoked nonconformist resistance, because one of the main causes of Anglican suspicion of the English Dissenters' appeal for a full toleration, and thus one of the main arguments for staving off that appeal, was the existence of the Presbyterian establishment in Scotland.

Religion and the Crisis of the Old Regime

Viewed from afar, the picture of this largely intraconfessional dissent in eighteenth-century European Christendom would seem to be one of the final failures of European states to prop up a semblance of Christendom after the reformations had shattered the unity of the medieval church in the sixteenth century. *Cujus regio, ejus religio* (whosoever reign, his the religion) was the famous formula originally enshrined by the Religious Peace of Augsburg only to be reaffirmed by the Peace of Westphalia in 1648 after the failure of the Habsburgs to transform the Holy Roman Empire into a Catholic empire during the last and most devastating of Europe's international-civil religious wars. That formula held not just for the constituent parts of the Holy Roman Empire, but for all of the fragmented and composite states of Europe, as each state and dynasty sought to give itself legitimacy by replacing the medieval church with an established confessional church which, even if Catholic, acted as a state or dynastic church as well. Each of these religious establishments was also expected to provide the confessional unity and motives for obedience which were widely thought to be indispensable to political unity and stability, even as late as the French Revolution and after. Everywhere, too, confessional conformity to these establishments stood in lieu of citizenship, even after the word "citizen" began to replace "subject" in the vocabulary of lettered Europeans and to acquire some of the secular connotations that the word possesses today. The refusal to conform to these religious establishments was in consequence visited with civil penalties and physical punishments of varying degrees of severity, ranging from the violent persecution of Huguenots in post-Louis Quatorzian France *toute catholique* to the comparatively benign civil disabilities of Catholics in the Protestant Dutch Republic. As Wayne te Brake observes, the sovereign right to coerce the conscience and enforce religious conformity was one of the defining attributes of post-Reformation absolutism in particular.[59]

But to perceptive observers, the refusal of religious dissenters to dutifully oblige these states sounded the death knell of post-Reformation state church establishments and their theories of unified sovereignty and good order—and with them, an essential feature of what the Revolution would soon call the Old Regime—however distant formal death still was in many cases. In fact, from the point of view of that Old Regime, the situation was worse than the refusal of religious dissenters to conform, since, on the contrary, religious controversy increased in many of these states as the eighteenth century neared its end, especially in England and in Catholic states.[60] For in England, contemporaries perceived a resurgent Toryism touting the Hanoverian dynasty's divine and indefeasible right and the necessary union of Throne and High Anglican Altar facing off against a body of Nonconformists newly radicalized by the episodes surrounding John Wilkes, the American War of Independence, and the early attempts at Parliamentary reform. And in the Catholic Germanies, Spain, and especially Italy, a militantly Molinistic papal monarchicalism and heightened episcopal hierarchicalism confronted Augustinian proponents of secular authority and a radically spiritual and democratized conception of the church newly derived in part from Gallican and Jansenist sources in France.[61] And if in Catholic France itself that final confrontation took the form of a militantly anti-Catholic Enlightenment and a religiously empowered counterrevolutionary ideology before the fact, that was only because a century of religious conflict unique in its duration and intensity had already done its worst.

In fact as well, all of the persistent issues of dissent and contested authority represented still unfinished business from the reformations of the sixteenth century—divine grace versus human free will, papal hierarchicalism versus conciliarism, spiritual authority versus temporal power—issues that perversely reappeared within both Protestantism and Catholicism in the course of the seventeenth and eighteenth centuries. In that sense, the issue of religion and religious dissent and contestation constitute the core of the confrontations that Robert Palmer and Franco Venturi have taught us to think of as the "crisis of the Old Regime," an Old Regime, which came apart as much from the inside as it was stormed by any "enlightenment" from without.[62] Although not without some conceptually disconcerting exceptions—both the Protestant republican and Catholic Austrian Netherlands being the most notable—it was forms of religious dissent in the Augustinian mold that tended to be most conspicuous as constituents in the "patriot" movements of constitutional defense and reform in the 1770s and 1780s that signaled the beginning of the end of the Old Regime in England, the Anglo-American colonies, and France.[63] Which is to say that religion was as conspicuous on the proto-"liberal" side of these barricades as on the other.

At the heart of this involvement there undoubtedly occurred a redirection of human energy from the vertical or transcendent to the horizontal along with the creation of new space for fallible and contingent, and in this sense "secular," human agency. But "secularization" simultaneously took the form of partial transfer of the sacred from the vertical to the political and social, or "ideological" horizon. But to acknowledge the occurrence of "secularization" in either or both of these forms is not, of course, to concede the premature disappearance of religion from the Western European scene, nor is it to admit a uniquely one-sided "influence" of a secular enlightenment on religion. On the contrary, it is to contend in the spirit of Carl Becker that for both better and worse religion and religious controversy acted as the chrysalis as well as a casualty of the modern political world, and that if ideology and ideological conflicts gradually preempted religion's place in a politicized "public sphere" largely of religion's own making, they did not cease in one way or another to bear the marks of various Christian origins.[64] Evidence of religion's own catalytic role in the eighteenth century's transmutation of religion into ideology is accumulating in recent and ongoing research, which seldom fails to display the political valence of virtually all eighteenth-century expressions of religion, whether in perception or in practice, and conversely the essentially religious grounding of virtually every political theory, and even of the majority of constitutional and bureaucratic structures.

This transformation was for both better and for worse because the receding sense of transcendence raised the stakes of temporal ideological conflicts, making them fraught with the infinite implications that religious conflicts had borne before. Thus were the perennial tensions in Christian theology and ecclesiology—between grace and the law, faith and good works, orthodox truth and toleration of error—often played out in secular ideological form and in modern political space, not always with happy effect, as parties did battle with each other over the influence of religion by means of ideologies constructed on the model of religion. The irony, as Alexis de Tocqueville saw in the middle of the nineteenth century, is that it was where religion parted paths with the state the soonest that its influence persisted the longest, and that it was where it persisted the longest that it was best able to cushion the shock of ideological conflict and confrontation.[65]

James E. Bradley, *Fuller Theological Seminary*

Dale K. Van Kley, *Ohio State University*

Notes

1. On this subject, see Darrin M. McMahon, "Enemies of the Enlightenment: Anti-*Philosophes* and the Birth of the French Far Right, 1778–1830" (Ph.D. dissertation: Yale University, 1997).

2. [Bernard de La Plaigne Lambert], *Réflexions sur l'état actuel de l'église* (n.p., 1787), 2–3.

3. *Le secret dévoilé: dialogue entre l'évêque Y et l'abbé Z* (n.p., 1789), 72–73, in Newberry Library, Case FRC (French Revolution Collection) 8205.

4. Madame Germaine de Staël-Necker, *Considérations sur la Révolution française* (originally, *Considérations sur les principaux événements de la Révolution française*), ed. Jacques Godechot (Paris: Tallandier, 1983), 63, 138, 604.

5. Benjamin Constant, *De la religion considérée dans sa source, ses formes et ses développements,* in *Oeuvres,* ed. Alfred Roulin (Paris: Gallimard, 1964), 1365–95.

6. Louis de Bonald, *La vraie Révolution, ou Observations sur l'ouvrage de Madame la baronne de Staël ayant pour titre: Considérations sur les principaux événements de la Révolution française, par Monsieur de Bonald,* ed. Michel Toda (Etampes: Clovis, 1997), 142–46.

7. Hughes Félicité de Lamennais, *De la religion considéréé dans ses rapports avec l'ordre politique et civil* in *Oeuvres complètes,* 12 vols (Paris: P. Daubrée and Cailleux, 1836–37), 7:19.

8. Niccola Spedalieri Siciliano, *De' diritti dell' uomo libri VI, ne' quali si dimonstra, che il più sicura custode de' medisimi nella società civile è la religione christiana; e che pero l'unico progetto utile alle presenti circonstanze è de far riforire essa religione* (Assisi, 1791).

9. Pietro Tamburini, *Lettere teologico-politiche sulla presente situzione delle cose ecclesiastiche* (Pavia, Baldassare Comini, 1794).

10. Immanuel Kant, *Der Streit der Facultäten in drey Abschnitten,* in *Werke in sechs Bänden,* 6 vols. (Frankfurt am Main: Insel-Verlag, 1960–64), 6:357, 361.

11. Marginalized by this process was the social Catholic Pierre-Joseph Buchez, who saw the policies of the government of the Committee of Public Safety as representing the social fulfillment of Catholicism, and the neo-Protestant interpretation of Edgar Quinet, who blamed the Terror on the failure of the French Reformation. See Edgar Quinet, *La Révolution* (Paris: Belin, 1865); and Paul Buchez and Pierre Roux, *Histoire parlementaire de la Révolution française, ou Journal des assemblées nationales depuis 1789 jusqu'en 1815,* 40 vols. (Paris: Paulin, 1834–38).

12. Benedetto Croce, *Storia della storiographia italiano nel secolo decimonono,* 2 vols, 3d ed. (Bari: Laterza, 1947), 1:96–207; 2:1–34. If, in the very long run, a tendency existed for the Italian debate to conform to French lines, it is, as Michael Broers has argued, because there "was one point of agreement between the Napoleonic state and its opponents, which the nineteenth-century apostles of each inherited, and that was the identification of the institutions of the state with the reforming impulses of the Enlightenment." See Michael Broers,

"Italy and the Modern State: The Experience of Napoleonic Rule," in *The Transformation of Political Culture, 1789–1848,* eds. François Furet and Mona Ozouf, vol. 3 of *The French Revolution and the Creation of Modern Political Culture* (Oxford: Pergamon Press, 1989), 500. We wish also to thank Professor Claudio Fogu of Ohio State University for his help on this paragraph.

13. For a perceptive overview of this literature, see Carlo Fantappie's first chapter, "Scipione de' Ricci tra mito e storia" in his *Riforme ecclesiastiche e resistenze sociali: la sperimentazione instituziale nella diocesi di Prato all fine dell' antico regime* (Bologna: Il Molino, 1986), 1–42.

14. Luigi Salvatorelli, *Il pensiero politico italiano dal 1700 al 1870* (Turin: G. Einaudi, 1949); Franco Venturi, *Settecento riformatore,* 5 vols.: I, *Da Muratori a Beccaria;* II, *La chiesa e la republica dentro lori limiti;* III, *La prima crisi dell' Antico regime, 1768–1776;* IV, *La caduta dell' Antico regime, 1776–1789;* V, *L'Italia dei lumi, 1764–1790* (Turin: G. Einaudi, 1969–87).

15. G. M. Trevelyan, *History of England* (London: Longmans, Green and Co., 1926), 474, 615; W. E. H. Lecky, *A History of England in the 18th Century* 2nd ed., 8 vols. (London: Longmans, Green and Co., 1879–1890), 1:177–81; 187–93; W. E. H. Lecky, *Democracy and Liberty* 2d ed. 2 vols. (London: Longmans, Green, and Co., 1896), 1:434–46, 438, 442.

16. Sir Leslie Stephen, *History of English Thought in the Eighteenth Century* 3d ed., 2 vols. (London: John Murray, 1902; New York and Burlingame: Harcourt, Brace and World, 1962), 1: 76–77. The interpretation reaches the pinnacle of refinement in Unitarian historiography: H. McLachlan, *The Unitarian Movement in the Religious Life of England: Its Contribution to Thought and Learning, 1700–1900* (London: Allen and Unwin, 1934); and Raymond V. Holt, *The Unitarian Contribution to Social Progress in England* (London: Allen and Unwin, 1938). Both works place Unitarians in the "vanguard of the age."

17. C. J. Abbey and J. H. Overton, *The English Church in the Eighteenth Century* 2 vols. (London: Longmans, Green and Co., 1878), 2:222–25; see especially pp. 404–8 comparing the treatments of Hannah More and Edmund Burke to Joseph Priestley.

18. Willem Groen van Prinsterer, *Ongeloof en revolutie: een reeks van historische voorlezingen* (Leiden: S. and J. Luchtmans, 1847).

19. P. J. Blok, *Geschiedenis van het Nederlandsche Volk,* 4 vols., 1st ed. (Gronigen: J. B. Wolters, 1892–1908); and Pieter Geyl, *Geschiedenis van de Nederlands Stam,* 1st ed. (Amsterdam: N. v. Maatschappij tot verspreiding van goede en goedkoope lectuur, 1930–1937).

20. The information in this paragraph is dependent in various ways on Thomas Nipperdey, *Germany from Napoleon to Bismarck, 1800–1866,* trans. Daniel Nolan (Princeton: Princeton University Press, 1996), 333–98; and James

Sheehan, *German History, 1770–1866,* Oxford History of Germany (Oxford and New York: Oxford University Press, 1989).

21. For the quotation from Hegel, see Georg Wilhelm Friedrich Hegel, *Vorlesungen über die Philosophie der Geschichte* in *Werke,* eds. Eva Moldenhauer and Karl Markus Michel, 20 vols. (Frankfurt am Main: Suhrkamp Verlag, 1970), 12:524.

22. Quotations from Heinrich von Treitschke, *Deutsche Geschichte im neunzehnten Jahrhundert. Erster Theil. Bis zum zweiten Pariser Frieden,* Sechste Auflage (Leipzig: Verlag von S. Hirzel, 1897), 51, 90, 93.

23. On the role of Catholicism and Protestantism in competitive visions of Germany as a nation, see Helmut Walser Smith, *German Nationalism and Religious Conflict: Culture, Ideology, and Politics, 1870–1914* (Princeton: Princeton University Press, 1995). We are indebted to Professor Deborah Fleetham of Calvin College for this reference as well as for very helpful advice on the paragraphs on German historiography.

24. Paul Bushkovitch, *Religion and Society in Russia: The Sixteenth and Seventeenth Centuries* (Oxford and New York: Oxford University Press, 1992), 4–6.

25. See Olga A. Tsapina's chapter in this volume.

26. In the same category of classics belongs Guido de Ruggiero's *Storia del liberalismo europeo* which, just as the publication in 1934 of Ernst Cassirer's *Philosophie der Aufklärung* was an implicit indictment of the Nazi seizure of power in Germany, read like a rebuke to the fascist seizure of power in Italy when it first appeared in 1925. Although rather far in spirit from the celebratory anticlericalism of Hazard, the book nonetheless locates the origins of "liberalism" almost exclusively in the Enlightenment, according agency to religion only in the case of English Dissenters and to the (largely unintended) effects of shattering of the medieval church in Protestant Europe and the conflict between the Catholic Church and national states in Catholic Europe. See the Laterza edition (Rome, 1984), 121–210, 424–32.

27. Ernest Cassirer, *Die Philosophie der Aufklärung* (Tubingen: J. C. B. Mohr, 1932); and *The Philosophy of the Enlightenment* (Princeton: Princeton University Press, 1951), 134–96; and Paul Hazard, *La crise de la conscience européene,* trans. J. Lewis May (Paris: Boivin, 1935); and *The European Mind, 1680–1715* (Cleveland and New York: Meridian, 1963), 7.

28. Peter Gay, *The Enlightenment: An Interpretation,* 2 vols. (New York: Alfred A. Knopf, 1967–69), I, *The Rise of Modern Paganism,* 3, 10. See Roy Porter, "The Enlightenment in England," pp. 4–5 in Roy Porter and Mikuláš Teich, eds., *The Enlightenment in National Context* (Cambridge: Cambridge University Press, 1981).

29. Robert R. Palmer, *The Age of the Democratic Revolution,* 2 vols. (Princeton: Princeton University Press, 1959–64), 1:192–94, 317–20; and 2:20, 23, 466, 492, 573. In *Catholics and Unbelievers in Eighteenth Century France* (Princeton: Princeton University Press, 1939), Palmer began to challenge some religious stereotypes by demonstrating that Catholic intolerance was greatly overdrawn.

30. Franco Venturi, "Les lumières dans l'Europe du 18e siècle" in *Europe des lumières: Recherches sur le 18e siècle,* trans. Françoise Braudel (Paris and The Hague: Mouton & Ecole Pratique des Hautes Etudes, 1971), 25–26.

31. Albert Soboul, *La civilisation et la Révolution française,* 3 vols (Paris: Arthaud, 1970), "pratique religieuse et dévotion paysanne" under "mentalité et culture paysanne," 1:167–71; and "l'apologétique nouvelle" under "idéologie aristocratique," 1:239–41.

32. E. P. Thompson, *The Making of the English Working Class* (Harmondsworth: Penguin, 1968), 402–11, 429, and "The Peculiarities of the English," in *The Poverty of Theory and Other Essays* (London: Merlin Press, 1978), 58.

33. The impact of Norman Sykes's important works on eighteenth-century English church history made little impact on the broader historiography of the period. See J. C. D. Clark, *Revolution and Rebellion: State and Society in England in the Seventeenth and Eighteenth Centuries* (Cambridge: Cambridge University Press, 1986), 108.

34. Alfred Cobban, *The Social Interpretation of the French Revolution* (Cambridge and London: Cambridge University Press, 1964). For a readable overview of the unraveling of the Marxian paradigm for understanding the origins of the French Revolution, see William Doyle, *The Origins of the French Revolution* (Oxford and New York: Oxford University Press, 1999), 1–40.

35. As applied to eighteenth-century France, the chief pioneer of the "new cultural history" was Lynn Hunt in *Politics, Culture, and Class in the French Revolution* (Berkeley, University of California Press, 1984).

36. François Furet, "La Révolution est terminée," in *Penser la Révolution française* (Paris: Gallimard, 1978), 14–109; or "The Revolution is Over," *Interpreting the French Revolution,* trans. Elborg Forster (Cambridge and London: Cambridge University Press; Paris: Editions de la Maison des Sciences de l'Homme, 1981), 1–79.

37. Max Horkheimer and Theodor W. Adorno, *Dialektik der Aufklärung. Philosophische Fragmente,* trans. John Cumming (Amsterdam: Querido, 1947); *Dialectic of Enlightenment* (New York: Continuum, 1972, 1999).

38. Carl Becker, *The Heavenly City of the Eighteenth-Century Philosophers* (New Haven: Yale University Press, 1932).

39. See Peter Novick, *That Noble Dream: The "Objectivity Question" and the American Historical Profession* (Cambridge and New York: Cambridge University Press, 1988), 415–629; and "AHR Forum: Intellectual History and the Return of Literature," *American Historical Review,* 94 (June 1989): 581–698. On the "failure of nerve," a phrase borrowed by Gay from Gilbert Murray, see *The Enlightenment: An Interpretation,* II, *The Science of Freedom,* 5–6.

40. See, for example, Dorinda Outram, *The Enlightenment* (Cambridge and New York: Cambridge University Press, 1995).

41. J. G. A. Pocock, *Barbarism and Religion: Volume One: The Enlightenments of Edward Gibbon, 1737–1764;* and *Barbarism and Religion: Volume Two: Narratives of Civil Government* (Cambridge and New York: Cambridge University Press, 1999).

42. Bernard Plongeron, "Recherches sur l' 'Aufklärung' catholique en Europe occidental, 1770–1830," *Revue d'histoire moderne et contemporaine* 16 (1969): 555–605; and Samuel J. Miller, *Portugal and Rome, c.1748–1830: An Aspect of the Catholic Enlightenment* (Rome: Università Gregoriana, 1978).

43. Henry May first drew attention to the importance of Philip Doddridge of Northampton for furthering a Christian Dissenting Enlightenment, and Donald Davie argued that Isaac Watts popularized Locke's logic more effectively than anyone else. Henry F. May, *The Enlightenment in America* (Oxford and New York: Oxford University Press, 1976), 18–19, 38; Donald Davie, *Dissentient Voice: Enlightenment and Christian Dissent* (Notre Dame: University of Notre Dame Press, 1982), 107. R. K. Webb examines Doddridge at length in "The Emergence of Rational Dissent," 29–36 in Knud Haakonssen, ed. *Enlightenment and Religion: Rational Dissent in Eighteenth-Century Britain* (Cambridge and New York: Cambridge University Press, 1996). On the authorship of the *Occasional Paper,* see Joshua Toulmin, "Notice on the authorship of the Occasional Paper," *Monthly Repository* 8 (1813): 442–43. And on Mably, see Johnson Kent Wright, *A Classical Republican in Eighteenth-Century France: The Political Thought of Mably* (Stanford: Stanford University Press, 1997).

44. Among recent studies on this variant of enlightenment in France, see Dena Goodman, *The Republic of Letters: A Cultural History of the French Enlightenment* (Ithaca: Cornell University Press, 1994); and Daniel Gordon, *Citizens Without Sovereignty: Equality and Sociability in French Thought, 1670–1789* (Princeton: Princeton University Press, 1994). For evidence for a radical enlightenment in the Netherlands, see Margaret Jacob, "Radicalism in the Dutch Enlightenment," in *The Dutch Republic in the Eighteenth Century: Decline, Enlightenment, Revolution,* eds. Margaret C. Jacob and Wijnand W. Mijnhardt (Ithaca: Cornell University Press, 1992), 224–40.

45. W. M. Spellman, *The Latitudinarians and the Church of England, 1660–1700* (Athens, Ga.: University of Georgia Press, 1993); and J. A. I. Champion, *The Pillars of Priestcraft Shaken: The Church of England and its Enemies, 1660–1730* (Cambridge and New York: Cambridge University Press, 1992). These developments were examined by James E. Bradley in "The Role of Religion in the Question of an English Enlightenment," The American Society for Eighteenth-Century Studies, Brown University, Providence, 1993. See also B. W. Young, *Religion and Enlightenment in Eighteenth-Century England: Theological Debate from Locke to Burke* (Oxford: Clarendon Press, 1998).

46. Frederick Dreyer, "Faith and Experience in the Thought of John Wesley." *The American Historical Review* 88 (1983): 25–26; see also Richard E. Brantley, *Locke, Wesley, and the Method of English Romanticism* (Gainesville, Fla.: University of Florida Press, 1984).

47. The best treatment of this political theology is in Rita Hermon-Belot, "La politique et la vérité: l'abbé Grégoire et la Révolution française," 2 vols. (doctoral thesis, E.H.E.S., Paris, 1999), 1:54–190; published in a much shortened version as *L'abbé Grégoire: la politique et la verité* (Paris: Editions du Seuil, 2000), 63–129, 183–226 .

48. Robert R. Palmer, *Catholics and Unbelievers in Eighteenth-Century France*, 1–76; and Monique Cottret, *Jansénismes et lumières: pour un autre dix-huitième siècle* (Paris: Albin Michel, 1998), esp. 112–305.

49. J. C. D. Clark, *English Society 1660–1832: Religion, Ideology and Politics during the Ancien Regime* 2d ed. (Cambridge and New York: Cambridge University Press, 2000), 319, 368. See also J. C. D. Clark, *The Language of Liberty, 1660–1832: Political Discourse and Social Dynamics in the Anglo-American World* (Cambridge and New York: Cambridge University Press, 1994), 41; and J. G. A. Pocock, "The Definitions of Orthodoxy," in Roger D. Lund, ed., *The Margins of Orthodoxy: Heterodox Writing and Cultural Response, 1660–1750* (Cambridge and New York: Cambridge University Press, 1995), 36, 50. These views are reinforced by A. M. C. Waterman, "The Nexus between Theology and Political Doctrine" pp. 193–218 in Knud Haakonssen, ed., *Enlightenment and Religion: Rational Dissent in Eighteenth-Century Britain.*

50. H. R. Trevor-Roper, "The Religious Origins of the Enlightenment," in *The Crisis of the Seventeenth Century: Religion, the Reformation and Social Change* (New York: Harper and Row, 1968), 206–7, 214, 223; and Pocock, *Barbarism and Religion*, 1:8–9, 53–55, 60, 62–63, 73, 295, and especially 297–98 where he characterizes the Enlightenment as "the anti-Nicene consequences of a subordination of spiritual to civil authority."

51. Colin Haydon, *Anti-Catholicism in Eighteenth-Century England: A Political and Social Study* (Manchester: University of Manchester Press, 1993),

204–44; I. R. McBride, *Scripture Politics: Ulster Presbyterians and Irish Radicalism in the Late Eighteenth Century* (Oxford: Clarendon Press, 1998), 152–61.

52. See Wayne te Brake, *Regents and Rebels: The Revolutionary World of an Eighteenth-Century Dutch City* (Cambridge, Mass. and Oxford: Basil Blackwell, 1989), 100–9.

53. Catherine Maire, *De la cause de Dieu à la cause de la nation: le jansénisme au XVIIIe siècle* (Paris: Gallimard, 1998).

54. For example, in neighboring Hungary. W. R. Ward, "An Awakened Christianity: The Austrian Protestants and Their Neighbours in the Eighteenth Century," *Journal of Ecclesiastical History* 40 (1989): 72. The situation in Salzburg, ironically, gave rise to a significant, if short lived, movement of reform in the University, described in this volume by Ward.

55. James E. Bradley, "Anti-Catholicism as Anglican Anticlericalism: Nonconformity and the Ideological Origins of Radical Disaffection," in Nigel Aston and Matthew Cragoe, eds., *Anticlericalism in Britain c. 1500–1914* (Stroud Gloucestershire: Sutton Publishing, 2000), 67–92.

56. On the French case, see John Woodbridge, *Revolt in Prerevolutionary France: The Prince de Conti's Conspiracy against Louis XV, 1755–1757* (Baltimore: Johns Hopkins University Press, 1994).

57. This interpretation of Augustinian Christianity is partially dependent on Marcel Gauchet's *Le désenchantement du monde: Une histoire politique de la religion* (Paris: Gallimard, 1985).

58. This is in effect the argument of W. A. Speck in "Some Consequences of the Glorious Revolution" in Dale Hoak and Mordechai Feingold, eds., *The World of William and Mary: Anglo-Dutch Perspectives on the Revolution of 1688–98* (Stanford: Stanford University Press, 1996), 38–41.

59. Wayne te Brake, *Shaping History: Ordinary People in European Politics, 1500–1700* (Berkeley: University of California Press, 1998), 182–83.

60. James J. Sack, *From Jacobite to Conservative: Reaction and orthodoxy in Britain, c. 1760–1832* (Cambridge and New York: Cambridge University Press, 1993).

61. For England, see James E. Bradley, "The Anglican Pulpit, the Social Order, and the Resurgence of Toryism during the American Revolution," *Albion* 21 (1989), 361B88; G. M. Ditchfield, "Ecclesiastical Policy under Lord North," 228–46 in John Walsh, Colin Haydon, and Stephen Taylor, eds., *The Church of England c. 1689–c.1833 From Toleration to Tractarianism* (Cambridge and New York: Cambridge University Press, 1993). For the confrontation in Catholic Europe, see the essays by Noel, Van Kley, and Ward in this book.

62. Palmer, *The Age of the Democratic Revolution*, vol. 1, *The Challenge;* and Franco Venturi, *Settecento riformatore,* vol. 3: *La prima crisi dell' Antico Regime, 1776–1789* (Turin: G. Einaudi, 1969).

63. See, for example, Dale Van Kley, "The Religious Origins of the Patriot and Ministerial Parties in Pre-Revolutionary France: Controversy over the Chancellor's Constitutional Coup, 1771–1775," in *The Maupeou Revolution: The Transformation of French Politics at the End of the Old Regime,* ed. Keith M. Baker, a special issue of *Historical Reflections/Réflexions historiques* 18 (Summer, 1992): 17–63.

64. In addition to James Van Horn Melton's chapter in this volume, see also Pasi Ihalainen, *The Discourse of Political Pluralism in Early Eighteenth-Century England: A Conceptual Study with Special Reference to Terminology of Religious Origin,* Bibliotheca Historica, vol. 36 (Helsinki: Suomen Historiallinen Seura, 1999).

65. Alexis de Tocqueville, *De la démocratie en Amérique,* in *Oeuves complètes,* ed J. P. Mayer (Paris: Gallimard, 1951–), vol. 1, pt. 1, 301–15.

ONE

Catholic Conciliar Reform in an Age of Anti-Catholic Revolution

France, Italy, and the Netherlands, 1758–1801

DALE K. VAN KLEY

IN 1795, ON THE MORROW OF THE TERROR AND THE CAMPAIGN to "dechristianize" France, the ragged ranks of the "constitutional" Catholic clergy that had accepted the French Revolution and initially served it as salaried priests tried to make the best of its situation of enforced independence by reconstituting itself as a new national Catholic Church. This enforced independence was of two kinds: from the revolutionary state which officially cut its ties with the constitutional clergy in 1795 after closing just about all Catholic churches during the Terror of 1793–94, but also from the papacy and Rome, which had all but excommunicated this clergy for its loyalty to this same state and its new constitution as early as 1791.

Defiantly regarding itself as both Catholic despite papal anathematization and "patriotic" despite continuing hostility by the national state, the leadership of this clergy—the abbé Grégoire and the so-called "United Bishops"—convened something which the Catholic world had not seen since the late Middle Ages: two national church councils, which actually met in Paris in 1797 and again in 1801. These councils in turn called for and enacted an ambitious array of forward-looking reforms, among them the election of the clergy by their parishioners, the establishment of deliberative structures from local synods to the national council, a purged devotional style that stressed reasoned belief over ritual conformity, and the accommodation of national differences in liturgical styles, including the use of vernacular languages in the administration of the sacraments. The councils went so far as to call for renewed efforts to resolve the Protestant schism as well as the Catholic Church's earlier break with the Eastern Orthodox Church. Failing, however, to obtain any sign either of recognition from the papacy or of reconciliation with the "refractory" French clergy that had originally joined Rome in condemning the French Revolution, both councils appealed—perhaps their most signature act—to a general or ecumenical council of all Catholic churches as the only legitimate judge of the French constitutional church's differences with Rome.

To be sure, this extraordinary conciliar moment was a uniquely French by-product of the French Revolution's unsuccessful attempt at integrating the French Catholic or Gallican Church into the new constitutional order it set up in 1789. For far from formally separating the new state from any "ecclesiastical establishment" on the American model, the French Revolution's first instinct was to try to transform the French Catholic Church from a branch of an international institution deriving its authority from On High into a national church almost entirely subordinate to a state deriving its legitimacy from the will of its citizens below.[1] Without altering the substance of Catholic doctrine—its sole concession to the principle of an independent spiritual authority—the revolutionary National Assembly unilaterally abolished the tithe, nationalized the church's property, loosened its ties with Rome, redrew its diocesan and parochial boundaries, dissolved most of its monastic clergy, and reformed the secular clergy into salaried civil servants elected by the "citizens" in their secular capacity as citizens alone. Known as the Civil Constitution of the Clergy—that is, that part of the constitution that pertained to the clergy—this legislation gave the Gallican Church all the disadvantages of a state church without any of its advantages. For while the Revolution restricted its salaries to members of the Catholic "constitutional" clergy alone, it refused to accord Catholicism the status of a state religion and with it exclusive rights to public worship which that clergy had hence to share with Protestants, Jews, to say nothing of those numerous dissident Catholics and their "refractory" clergy who refused to accept the Civil Constitution at all.[2]

Numerous enough as a result of the revolutionary requirement of an oath of loyalty by all would-be beneficed clergy imposed in late 1790, the dissident or refractory clergy enrolled many more recruits after the papacy's condemnation of the Civil Constitution became known in the spring of 1791, a condemnation that provoked a full-scale schism between those French Catholics who accepted the papacy's condemnation of the French Revolution and those still shepherded by the constitutional clergy who persisted in trying to have their Catholicism and their revolution too. That schism in turn set in motion a polarizing cycle of action and reaction that radicalized the Revolution against religious "fanaticism" and "charlatanism," enlisted French Catholicism in the cause of the ideology of the counterrevolution, and exposed the constitutional clergy ever more directly to the crossfire between these contending forces. By the time that what little remained of this church sustained formal disinheritance by the revolutionary state in the wake of the Terror in 1795, the relative freedom of movement by means of which it organized its national councils was the only compensation for its isolated and shriveled estate.

That independence, the conciliar reforms, and the hopes that these engendered proved ephemeral enough and fragile even while they lasted, casualties that they were of the Concordat negotiated by Napoleon Bonaparte with the papacy in 1801. Although that Concordat restored the French Catholic Church to the position of subsidized appanage of the state for the duration of the nineteenth century, this restoration was unable to arrest—and on the contrary did much to accelerate—the putatively "progressive" parting of the paths between French Catholicism and political as well as other aspects of "modernity" inaugurated by the revolutionary experience. By the time all the revolutionary dust had settled, French Catholicism had been purged of most of its reformist elements and redefined in militantly traditionalist fashion while revolutionary republicanism had developed a tradition of its own that voluntarily relinquished any fulcrum in the nineteenth-century Catholic conscience. And although the French Revolution was in the last analysis a uniquely French affair, its armed exportation to most of the rest of Europe ensured that the conflict between republicanism and Catholicism would become a European experience as well.

The story of Catholicism's falling out with the French Revolution and all that followed from it is usually explained as the institutional consequence of the secularization of thought in the form of the Enlightenment and the resistance of "retrograde" religious forms of thought as embodied in the Catholic Church. Although this familiar version of events is not without elements of truth, it has about it an aura of inevitability belied by the possibilities of radical liturgical, ecclesiastical, and theological reform from within eighteenth-century Catholicism—possibilities of a kind briefly realized by the two national councils of Paris which, had they found more durable institutional expression, might have given this story a significantly different outcome. For while these two national councils undoubtedly drew inspiration from the French or Gallican Church's peculiar tradition of independence from Rome, they were also hardly unique to France, and represented the culmination of reformist impulses and conciliar precedents that had found earlier institutional expression in the Provincial Council of Utrecht in 1763 and the Synod of Pistoia in Tuscany on the eve of the French Revolution in 1786. The full story culminating in the two national councils of Paris cannot therefore be told without reference to these earlier precedents.

Since, moreover, the prospect for liturgical or theological reform ultimately depended on the possibility of some institutional means or agency other than the papal curia or the state's authority as well as on some margin for maneuver between these two, it is on the efforts directed toward ecclesiastical reform—in particular, on giving the Catholic Church a less autocratic and hierarchical, more deliberative and conciliar structure—that is the primary focus of this analysis. And although the cause of church councils is in principle separable from any particular theology or religious sensibility, this cause was in fact locked in a fatal embrace with Jansenism during most of the century, making it impossible to tell the story without recounting elements of the other.

The Diocese of Utrecht and the Provincial Council of 1763

Among the precedents available for the Civil Constitution, the most obvious was the ecclesiastical legislation of the Habsburg Emperor Joseph II, who during the 1780s had similarly abolished contemplative monastic orders, redrawn diocesan boundaries, secularized much church property, and tried to sever communications between Austrian bishops and the papacy, and all this on his secular authority alone. It was in part because he had managed to do all this without incurring formal papal condemnation that the National Assembly thought that it could do as much. One important difference between the two situations, however—for the papacy it was undoubtedly the decisive one—was that while Joseph II acted as a divine-right sovereign without a conciliar much less a democratic bone in his body, the France that the National Assembly was remaking in 1790 was already a republic with only a monarchical facade and so provided that the "constitutional" clergy be elected by lay "citizens," just as its legislators were to be.

A perhaps more pertinent if less obvious precedent for the National Assembly might have been the situation of the Dutch Protestant Republic where two Catholic churches, a larger one obedient to Rome and a smaller one without formal relations with the papacy, had uneasily coexisted while enjoying toleration by a non-Catholic republic since 1723. This situation has at least some resemblance to that of the French Republic between 1795 and 1801 after it formally ceased to pay salaries to the constitutional Church which, still condemned by the papacy, then tried to reconstitute itself as a Gallican Catholic church in competition with a pro-papal missionary church under a government that was not Catholic at all. The similarity of these situations thus poses the question of why the Revolution could not simply have begun at that point—why, as Edgar Quinet asked, did the Revolution not immediately declare the separation of church and state? Or, once having arrived at that point, why did it not stay there much longer?[3] The question is all the more pertinent in that the smaller of the two churches, the one centered in

Utrecht, had long taken its theological and canonical cues from French Catholics, many of whom had left France to live there. It was also a French Catholic bishop, Dominique Varlet, who had consecrated the first four archbishops of Utrecht, thereby enabling the diocese to maintain Catholic episcopal succession despite papal condemnation and furnishing the model whereby, sixty-six years later, the clergy loyal to the Revolution and its Civil Constitution similarly maintained themselves as Catholic in the face of papal condemnation.

The origins of an independent Catholic archdiocese in Utrecht lie in the conflicts between the indigenous Dutch secular clergy and regular orders, especially the Jesuits, in the wake of the Calvinist conquest of the northern Netherlandish provinces and the creation of an independent Protestant Republic in the sixteenth century. While what remained of a native Catholic clergy tried to preserve itself as an ordinary hierarchy despite the loss of its property and the secularization of its chapters, the papacy tended to see the northern Dutch provinces as mission territories, subjecting them to its direct spiritual governance by means of Jesuits and other counterreformational orders who undermined the authority of ordinary priests and bishops. From the very outset, the "apostolic vicars" of Utrecht, as they were officially called, found themselves in conflict with the papal curia not only over the number and behavior of the Jesuits but also over the nature of their own authority, whether they administered the diocese as bishops in their own right or only as papal delegates, as the title of "apostolic vicar" seemed to imply. For if the real episcopal authority they exercised was not as archbishops of Utrecht but rather as bishops of some other territory formerly Christian—bishop *in partibus infidelium*, as the phrase went—this was not uniquely at the insistence of Rome but was also the doing of the States General of the Netherlands, which then forbade the use of the title of Archbishop of Utrecht. Usually more latent than overt, this conflict between Utrecht and Rome came to the fore especially on the occasion of episcopal succession when the local "vicariate" with which the first apostolic vicar had replaced the defunct cathedral chapter tried to assert its rights to elect a successor against Rome's insistence on naming him.[4]

But by the end of the century this conflict had become further complicated by the Jansenist controversy which, originating in the Spanish Netherlands where the Louvain theologian Cornelius Jansen had given his name to the movement, had spread both south to France and north to the archdiocese of Utrecht. From the beginning this controversy was most explosive in France where Jansen's attempt to restate Saint Augustine's theology of predestination and unmerited grace in his *Augustinus* was translated in terms of a rigorous penitential discipline for the convent of Port-Royal by his friend Duvergier de Hauranne, abbé de Saint-Cyran. Here, however, it also provoked the hostility of the Jesuits and their partisans seconded by the absolute monarchy, whose renewed persecution of the movement in the 1680s added a rivulet of Jansenists to the stream of Huguenots fleeing Louis XIV's France *toute catholique* for the more tolerant Netherlands. French Jansenists were well received there by Utrecht's apostolic vicar Jan van Neercassel, who for his part found himself attracted to a Catholic Augustinianism potentially more intelligible to a surrounding Calvinist population that his church was trying to reclaim. And so it was only natural that Jesuit missionaries who were already in jurisdictional conflict with the secular clergy in Utrecht should have tried further to undermine the authority of this clergy by means of the accusation of the heresy of "Jansenism." These accusations were the more plausible in that Neercassel had befriended such well-known Jansenists as Sorbonne theologian Antoine Arnauld and his associate, Pasquier Quesnel, and had earlier overtly associated himself with the convent of Port-Royal des Champs, visiting it several times. Neercassel's principal book, *Amor poenitens*, seemed sufficiently inspired by Arnauld's *La fréquente communion* to warrant charges of Jansenist sacramental rigorism as early as in the 1680s, while his successor, Pieter Codde, although Rome's own choice as apostolic vicar, undertook a trip to Rome in 1700 to answer similar accusations against his pastoral theology and choice of liturgical books and catechisms.[5]

As it happened, Codde was about the last apostolic vicar to enjoy immediate communion with the papacy. Although he was retained in Rome for three years, it was only from the vicariate in

Utrecht that he learned of his deposition as apostolic vicar and it was only at the insistence of the States General of the Republic that he was finally able to regain his homeland. Meanwhile, in Utrecht, the vicariate refused to acknowledge the authority of Rome's replacement for Codde while Rome for its part persisted in trying to govern the diocese directly through the nuncios in Cologne and Brussels in defiance of both the vicariate and the States General, which sided with the more "national" of the rival Catholic clergies. The result was a twenty-year interregnum during which the local clergy, unable to replace itself without a bishop who could celebrate ordinations, found itself reduced to inactivity as numerous priests defected from its ranks or as "missionary priests" obedient to Rome seized control of local churches as their incumbent curés died. The only factors preventing the total attrition of Utrecht's clergy were occasional ordinations of clergy by sympathetic bishops from Ireland and Gallican France supplemented by fresh influxes of French Jansenist clerics dislodged by a new round of persecution in the wake of the French monarchy's determination to enforce the last of the papal condemnations, the bull *Unigenitus*, as a law of church and state. Dependent as Utrecht was on these sources of survival, it was only natural that its clergy should have prevailed upon Varlet, in Amsterdam on his way to Persia as missionary bishop *in partibus infidelium* of Babylon, to ordain six hundred priests in 1719; or that the Utrecht vicariate should have decided the same year to adhere to the appeal of the bull *Unigenitus* to a general council interjected by four French Jansenist bishops in 1717.

As it happened, however, these developments spelled Utrecht's definitive union with the Jansenist cause, its perennial entanglement in the affairs of France—and its eventual break with Rome. For it represented only a canonical upping of the ante of surreptitious ordinations of priests by bishops outside their own dioceses when, back in Holland after having been interdicted by Rome, the same Varlet consecrated Cornelis Steenhoven as Archbishop of Utrecht—a title unused since 1572—in 1724. And it was only an extension of its previous condemnation of the appeal of *Unigenitus* when Rome responded to this consecration with anathemas and a formal sentence of excommunication of the whole Utrecht clergy. The result in what was in principle a Protestant republic was a Catholic Church containing only a minority of a Catholic minority—the losses incurred during the interregnum were never made good—which, opposed to episcopal as well as papal "despotism" and committed to conciliar forms, found itself vulnerable to Protestant-like discussion and chronic dissension within its own diminished ranks. By way of compensation this church boasted its own ecclesiastical hierarchy which, later reinforced by the erection of bishoprics in Deventer and Haarlem, was able to administer the sacraments of confirmation and ordination without waiting for these from itinerant bishops to come from the outside. The church of Utrecht also enjoyed the Dutch Republican government's de facto favor, which, while still denying basic civic rights or *burgherrechten* like guild membership to old Catholics, allowed this church a publicity in a polity that came closer than any other in eighteenth-century Europe to realizing a separation of church from state.

The public presence enjoyed by this conciliar Catholic Church in a non-Catholic state is hence unique in old-regime Europe, and never more so than on the occasion of the meeting of a provincial council in Utrecht during the week of 13–21 September 1763—perhaps the high point of its existence after decades of internal dissension and dwindling numbers. The purpose of this council, which was called for, planned, and dominated throughout by the French, was in the first instance to demonstrate the diocese of Utrecht's catholicity by condemning the "errors" of a certain Pierre Le Clerc, a French Jansenist living in exile in the Netherlands since the mid-1750s who had progressively taken his opposition to Rome's anti-Jansenist pronouncements to the Protestant point of denying the primacy of the papal see, the divine basis of the episcopacy, and finally the validity of anything not clearly spelled out in Scripture.[6] Against Le Clerc the council loudly touted its adherence to the doctrine of papal primacy, the divine institution of bishops, and the validity of tradition, and solemnly reaffirmed its Catholic faith as expressed in the profession of Pius IV.[7] Situating itself in the orthodox middle, the council took the occasion to condemn the equally "pernicious" but opposite "errors" of the French Jesuits Jean Hardouin and Isaac Berruyer who, in an attempt to magnify reliance on the papal magisterium, had similarly undermined the scriptural and patristic basis of central dogmas like the trinity as well as, more predictably, the Augustinian doctrines of grace and predestination. Along with Jean Pichon, whose "lax" defense of the practice of frequent communion the council also condemned, these Jesuits had long functioned as *bêtes noires* in the Jansenist bestiary.[8] But for this council to condemn them in 1763 was politically opportune, inasmuch as the Society of Jesus had been expelled from Portugal in 1759 and had just been condemned to dissolution by the Parlement of Paris in France. Indeed, by adding a tenth and eleventh report condemning sundry "errors" by "new casuists," who were in fact all Jesuits, the Council of Utrecht furnished a badly needed ecclesiastical sanction for the Parlement of Paris's condemnation of the same "assertions" earlier the same year. And by including in this condemnation Jesuits who defended the papacy's "indirect authority" to sanction resistance to "tyrannical"—that is, heretical, princes—the council also found a convenient occasion to affirm the principle of obedience to secular authorities—including the Protestant Republic that had allowed it to convene.[9]

But the holding of a council was also its own justification, an occasion to vindicate Utrecht's conciliar conception of the ecclesiastical hierarchy: for that hierarchy "to practice," in the words of Archbishop Meindaerts's opening discourse, "the form of governance established by Jesus Christ himself, and since then constantly observed in all Catholic churches."[10] But however loudly the Council of Utrecht may have trumpeted its catholicity and resultant commitment to the doctrine of papal "primacy," the holding of such a council to judge doctrine apart from Rome—and along the way, to defend the contested Augustinian doctrines of efficacious grace and divine predestination—was a rebuke to papal claims to infallibility or the rights of "a universal and ecumenical bishop" who might "despotically order other bishops about," neither of which qualities the council had very clearly distinguished from the pope's legitimate identity as "visible and ministerial head (*chef*) by divine right."[11]

In addition to so dramatically witnessing to its orthodoxy, wrote the abbé Augustin Clément, one of the council's French architects, in a letter to the Archbishop of Utrecht in the following year, "we cannot doubt that the *éclat* of the [conciliar] canonical forms, equally applauded by the whole church, will bear its own fruit, and that sooner or later it will contribute to the reestablishment of so salutary and holy a practice."[12] These canonical forms were moreover given a peculiar twist by the council's inclusion of ten priests as voting members and designation of two of them as reporters for congregations, a practice that spoke louder than the council's condemnation of Pierre Le Clerc's conflation of bishop and priest and constituted an implicit challenge even to "orthodox" notions of councils, which reserved the right to judge doctrine for bishops alone. Lest any of this ecclesiological meaning remain merely implicit, the Jansenist weekly *Nouvelles ecclésiastiques* further radicalized it in an account of the council, pointedly noting how the Dutch bishops subscribed to the judgments of the council "along with the pastors of the second order who," stressed the weekly, "had exercised a deliberative voice in the synod following the usage commonly observed since the Council of Jerusalem (the model for all others) where priests judged with the apostles."[13] Glossing over the extent of the real disagreements in the council regarding the subscription to the profession of Pius IV and judging Le Clerc without hearing him, the *Nouvelles ecclésiastiques* similarly underscored the "unanimity" of the council followed by the similarly unanimous acceptance of its decrees by "the entire clergy of Holland."[14] And where the Dutch feared to tread the French rushed in with the publication of the council's acts, commissioning the comte Dupac de Bellegarde's French translation and soliciting "testimonies" of communion and adhesion from as many Catholic quarters as possible.[15]

Failing the reunion of the church with the papacy—and negotiations undertaken with this view invariably failed—Utrecht's long-run tactic of soliciting adhesions to these acts or other testimonies of communion was to establish a state of direct communion with enough other Catholic churches supported by their sovereigns to surround the Holy See. The intent was to lead the papacy to the conclusion that it was she and not Utrecht who was isolated, forcing her to conform to a fait accompli and thereby also to alter the structure of the Catholic Church. The model for this sort of action was thought to be the tactic whereby the overwhelming majority of the French *parlements* had taken the initiative against the Society of Jesus, eventually forcing the monarchy either to acknowledge that they could undertake so important a measure without royal authority or to give their action its belated imprimatur.[16] Failing any such happy ending, the publication and selective sending of the council's *Actes* at least produced not only a thousand or more signatures of adhesion on individual and collective letters to the Archbishop of Utrecht, especially in France in the years immediately following the council, but it also lent contemporary substance to the half mythical image—as well as hope for the miraculous revival—of a pre-curial apostolic church in which everything had been decided on collegially and in council. In an entirely typical letter of adhesion to the acts of the council, one Honoré Audibert, chaplain in the cathedral church of Aix-en-Provence, assured Archbishop Meindaerts and his colleagues in 1764 that their council had "had the effect of reviving apostolic times in our days and of renewing in these unhappy times those venerable assemblies of bishops of antiquity who are the subject of our respect . . . by virtue of their zeal in the combat against error and their attachment to evangelical doctrine which by their channel has come down all the way to us."[17]

That these acts never saw publication in Dutch is perhaps evidence of the limits of the Protestant Republic's policy of de facto toleration, as was the States General's refusal to grant passports to delegates from the archdiocese of Utrecht to the Rome of Pope Clement XIV later in the same decade on the occasion of the century's most serious negotiations toward reunion with the papacy.[18] But for the most part the presence of a Jansenist Catholic hierarchy, even one both backed and bedeviled by a cadre of querulous French exiles, did not constitute a major affair of state for the Dutch Republic which, on the contrary, domesticated it within the filaments of its bewildering constitutional particularism and blended it into its muted and waterlogged landscape.

Jansenism, the Gallican Church, and the Monarchy in Old-Regime France

The contrast could not be more total than with Catholic and monarchical France where from the very outset the Jansenist movement carried a political charge peculiar to that time and place. That was perhaps the crucial difference between a state like the Dutch Republic where, since the Reformation, the victorious Reformed Church became not a state church but just the only public church, and a state like France where, the Reformation having been defeated, religion remained inseparable from royalty.[19] A religious movement whose profoundest tendency was to regard "fallen" creation as totally "concupiscent" and utterly incommensurate with the order of "charity" could not but sit uneasily with a traditionally sacral monarchy that had long justified its domination of the Gallican Church by virtue of its mediating place in the cosmic hierarchy. The French monarchy had just survived the desacralizing challenge of Calvinism in the sixteenth-century wars of religion, and while Jansenism's elimination of "faith" as a means of assurance deprived it of Calvinism's activism—it is hard to imagine a Jansenist iconoclastic riot—it was easy to misread the movement as Calvinism in Catholic clothing. At the same time Jansenism's origins in the ultra-Catholic "devout party" or *parti dévot,* and initial interest in the reform of the church clashed with the monarchy's need to maintain control over the Gallican Church and, in particular, with Louis XIV's project of using the bishops as partners in the construction of absolutism. The monarchy had only recently survived a threat of that sort too, this one in the form of the ultra-Catholic and pro-papal Holy Union or League that had seized and held onto Paris against two French kings at the end of the wars of religion.[20]

It was effective control over the Gallican Church by an absolute but also sacral monarchy, and not that church's liberty, that was most at stake for the monarchy in the so-called liberties of the Gallican Church which that church's General Assembly solemnly proclaimed at Louis XIV's behest in an extraordinary assembly in 1682. In an era of growing absolutism, a lessening of papal power necessarily translated into an increase in royal control. That was the main meaning of this declaration's first article which, crucial to royal "absolutism" and new to the seventeenth century, proclaimed the King of France to be independent of the papacy in temporal affairs and answerable for them to God alone. For this article disallowed any disobedience to the king as temporal sovereign by virtue of any connection to spiritual affairs, even in cases of excommunication. Although the same assembly also reasserted the Gallican Church's right to judge doctrine concurrently with Rome as well as reiterating its adhesion to the Council of Constance's proclamation of the ultimate authority of general councils over the papacy in the church, the monarchy of Louis XIV had a declining stake in these traditional tenets.[21] For one thing, as Louis XIV was soon to realize, they stood in the way of the monarchy's need for the papacy's help in his effort to suppress Jansenism in France. In contrast to the Protestant Netherlands, there were no Catholic councils in the one Catholic realm where the supremacy of the council was formal law.

Whether or not the papacy would have on its own initiative so single mindedly condemned the Jansenist "heresy" is an open question, seeing that the initiative was taken by the French monarchy from the start. Both the bull *Cum occasione,* which condemned the five "heretical" propositions supposedly extracted from Jansen's *Augustinus* in 1653, and Alexander VII's *Ad sacram,* which specifically attributed these propositions to Jansen in 1665, came at the behest of France as represented by Cardinal Mazarin acting for the minor king in the first instance and by Louis XIV in person in the second. And after the reprieve of the so-called Peace of Clement IX in 1668–79 during which Louis XIV fought his Dutch wars—and for a brief time restored Catholicism to a position of dominance in the province of Utrecht—it was again the Sun King who demanded and got Clement XI's bull *Vineam domini,* which disallowed any distinction between Jansen's text or intentions and the condemned propositions, followed by the same pope's bull *Unigenitus* in 1713. Each of these pronouncements facilitated new acts of persecution in France—*Cum occasione* Arnauld's expulsion from the Sorbonne, *Ad sacram* the dispersion of the sisters of Port-Royal, *Vineam domini* the physical destruction of Port-Royal, and *Unigenitus* the lion's share of the persecution in the eighteenth century. When one adds the condemnation of LeMothe Fénelon's "quietism" in 1699, also at Louis XIV's initiative, the impression is hard to avoid of a papacy doctrinally dominated by French religious and political divisions from the onset of the Jansenist controversy to the condemnation of Lamennais's liberal Catholicism in 1834.[22]

The most divisive of the papal pronouncements solicited by France was incontestably the bull *Unigenitus,* and while the papacy itself along with most of Catholic Europe remained relatively unaffected by its fallout until the 1760s or so, in France it dominated the scene until that decade. This is so very much the case that, in the reputed capital of the Enlightenment, the eighteenth century may be as plausibly christened the century of *Unigenitus* as of *lumières.* The result there was little short of a full-scale religious conflict played out on political and social as well as theological and ecclesiastical registers, a conflict that in fact replayed the religious civil wars of the sixteenth century, if not in physical violence at least in sheer litigation. The conflict also relived the sixteenth-century religious civil wars in memory, as defenders of papal and royal authority as symbolized by the bull *Unigenitus* never ceased to regard Jansenists as rewarmed Calvinists while Jansenists were no less certain of descrying a reborn Catholic League in the rhetoric and comportment of their Jesuitical and episcopal persecutors.[23] Forty or fifty thousand *lettres de cachet* and several major political crises later, the French clergy and the religious orders found themselves largely purged of Jansenists who had replaced Protestants as the single most numerous category of residents of the Bastille while Jansenists in revenge had exploited just about every possible form of resistance to absolutism short of armed rebellion, recalling and recirculating much of the literature of both the Huguenot and Leaguer revolts.[24] No other religious conflict in eighteenth-century Europe, whether Protestant or Catholic, presents anything comparable to the French case in point of duration or intensity.

So ardently did the French protagonists in these conflicts nurse the memories of the wars of religion that, to a degree, they transformed eighteenth-century "reality" in their image. On the one side, Jansenists obliged those who persistently accused them of covert Calvinism by actually becoming a little more Protestant. Thus, while continuing and updating Port-Royal's project of translating Scripture into the vernacular, Quesnel and his successors enjoined the regular reading of Scripture on all the laypeople, including women, and extended the effort toward vernacular translation and explanation to the Catholic liturgy and Mass in an effort to involve laypeople in public worship.[25] The negative side of the importance attached by Jansenism to knowing the sources of Catholicism and understanding its doctrines was a steady hardening of its attitude against the sensual side of baroque Catholicism symbolized for Jansenists by the Jesuit-sponsored devotion to the Sacred Heart as well as the ritualistic aspects of baroque devotion like novenas, rosaries, and the veneration of saints, all of them regarded as "ignorant," "superstitious," and "mechanical."[26] Giving a certain significance to these developments was a Jansenist campaign on behalf of civil toleration of Protestants that, beginning in mid-century, culminated with significant Jansenist support for Louis XVI's Edict of Toleration in 1788.[27] On the other side, meanwhile, a few French Jesuits like Berruyer, Hardouin, and Jean Pichon exaggerated the doctrinally latitudinarian and penitentially lax tendencies associated with their "Molinist" theology—the Jesuits specifically condemned by Council of Utrecht—while others connived at the League-like vilification of the person of Louis XV after royal religious policy began to deviate from their desires during the tempestuous 1750s.[28]

But when all had been said and done, the French eighteenth century was not the sixteenth century, nor was it any less the century of "lights" for being that of *Unigenitus*. That is to say that the religious conflict apropos of the condemnation of Jansenism in France took place during a period of rising literacy, rapidly expanding print culture, and in the wake of geographical discoveries and scientific revolutions that had created conceptual possibilities unavailable to the sixteenth century. And while elsewhere in Europe the cause of "lights" took shape in reaction against the memory of the Reformation's religious slug-outs, for French philosophes this conflict was an ongoing and oppressively present reality, as the many Jansenists and Jesuits who people Voltaire's philosophical stories attest. When Voltaire quipped, as he often did, that there were "no sects among geometricians," he made a point polemically that would have lacked the same punch outside of France.[29] Although the Jansenist controversy is not the only factor in the making of the anticlerical character of the French Enlightenment, it is far from the least of such factors. The result was an enlightenment that Jean Le Rond d'Alembert, author of the *Encyclopédie*'s famous "preliminary discourse," self-consciously defined as a "third party" of "philosophy" on the occasion of the dissolution of the Society of Jesus in France, a "party" productive of a militantly anti-Christian form of incredulity that, whether atheistic or deistic, surfaced as the Voltairian campaign against the "infamous thing" in the declining Old Regime. And of course it rose even more spectacularly as "dechristianization" during the French Revolution.[30] The role of the monarchy in the making of the controversy also gave rise to calls for a state so adamantly secular as to be as intolerant in this sense as sacral absolutism had ever been in a confessional sense, a potential that similarly surfaced as the French Revolution's quest for ideological "orthodoxy" with all of its attendant secular "schisms" to say nothing of its sponsorship of the cult of theophilanthropy.[31]

This brand of enlightenment was also peculiar to France, for not even in the England of John Toland and David Hume did Edmund Burke, reacting to the French Revolution in 1790, have any trouble distinguishing local lights from the French variant.[32] By the time of the demise of the Jesuits in the 1760s or by 1770 at the latest, militant unbelief had attracted enough alarmed attention in France itself as to produce occasional calls for a common Catholic front against "unbelief" from Jansenists if not from their adversaries, and from institutions as hitherto at loggerheads in the Jansenist controversy as the General Assembly of France in 1775 and the Parlement of Paris in 1776.[33] Although such a common Catholic front never really became a reality—and the Jansenist-devout standoff never entirely went away—the decades after the demise of the Jesuits did indeed witness the formation of a Catholic "counter-Enlightenment" in France which, exemplified by ex-Jesuits such as the abbé Lenfant or, in a more secularized vein, journalists like Elie-Catherine Fréron, subordinated Jansenism along with Protestantism to auxiliary roles in what it saw as a multi-pronged "philosophic" plot to destroy papal altars the better to undermine absolute thrones and to replace both with "anarchy" and "unbelief."[34] A counterrevolutionary religious "right" before the letter, it tended to displace the Jansenist-devout division with a Catholic-philosophic one as the dominant bipolar polemical motif in France, and that just at the moment, as we shall see, when the international campaign against the Jesuits was bringing the hitherto mainly French Jansenist-*zelanti* standoff to the rest of Catholic Europe.

What remained unique to the Jansenist controversy in France, at least until the end of the French Revolution, was that there it subjected Jansenism to a process of precocious politicization that ultimately did not stop short of absolute monarchy itself, arguably giving the movement a more pronounced anti-absolutist political point than in the case of the philosophes as late as on the eve of the Revolution. Whether such a radically pessimistic religious sensibility as Jansenism's would ever have developed in the direction of active opposition had French absolutism known how to leave well enough alone is also an open question, since the persecution of the movement based on the assumption of its subversive potential made that assumption self-fulfilling in the longer run. But that long run was long indeed. To be sure, the two elements of Gallicanism and parlementary constitutionalism that were later to coalesce with Jansenism and bring out its political potential while attenuating its other-worldliness—these were already at hand in the seventeenth century, even during the mid-century uprising known as the Fronde. But the Fronde did not yet cause them to coalesce while in the short run it worsened Jansenism's image in the eyes of the monarchy by associating it with the memory of French Huguenot resistance and both of these in turn with the Puritanism that was simultaneously playing so rambunctious a role in the English Civil War.[35]

It really took another half century of condemnation and persecution culminating in the papal bull *Unigenitus* in 1713 to effect a synthesis of the elements in question. Although the book anathematized by this bull, namely Pasquier Quesnel's *Réflexions morales,* already contained a radically Gallican conception of the Catholic Church as the "assembly of all the faithful," the condemnation of such Gallican propositions along with classically Jansenist ones linked the cause of Jansenism with conciliar—in other words, late medieval or "old Sorbonne"—Gallicanism from which the Louis Quatorzian absolutism had been retreating since 1682. The adoption of conciliar Gallicanism by Jansenists culminated in the formal appeal of *Unigenitus* to a general council by four bishops in the Sorbonne in 1717, an appeal initially supported by three quarters of the Parisian clergy with whom the diocese of Utrecht associated itself two years later.[36] And by forcing a reluctant Parlement of Paris to register this anti-Gallican bull as a law of state—one of the Gallican liberties was that no papal pronouncement was binding in France unless accepted by state as well as church—the bull also firmed up an alliance between Jansenists and the Parlement of Paris, the realm's principal royal court, which in the absence of the Estates General had intermittently claimed to "represent" the nation by means of its rights to register and remonstrate against new royal legislation, most notably during the Fronde. These Frondish claims acquired new life when, soon after the Sun King's death in 1715, the Parlement regained the right to remonstrate against royal edicts and declarations prior to registering them as law, a right withdrawn after the Fronde by Louis XIV in 1672.

As the century progressed and persecution continued, the conciliar Gallican element in this synthesis underwent a process of radicalization and democratization in the hands of Jansenist canonists, especially after Louis XV's first minister Cardinal de Fleury used conciliar forms against the Jansenist cause by staging a provincial council composed of the Archbishop of Embrun and his suffragan bishops to depose the appellant Jean Soanen as bishop of Senez in 1727.[37] With conceptual help from the Gallican tradition of conciliar thought going back to the works of John Major, Jean Gerson, and Edmond Richer, syndic of the Sorbonne in the early seventeenth century, Jansenist canonists developed a radical ecclesiology that vested supreme spiritual authority in the whole church, or "assembly of the faithful," including the parish priests so loudly touted by the Jansenist press on the occasion of their participation in the

Provincial Council of Utrecht. This brand of Gallicanism or "Richerism" hence defined itself against the Gallican bishops themselves, the majority of whom accepted *Unigenitus*, holding that parish priests derived their sacerdotal mission directly or "radically" from Christ rather than indirectly through bishops and that, though jurisdictionally subordinate to bishops, they had a right to attend both synodical and general councils as "judges of the faith."[38]

Further democratizing this ecclesiology was the influence of the eschatological theology and biblical hermeneutic called figurism which, developed by Jansenist theologians at the Oratorian seminary of Saint-Magloire in the wake of *Unigenitus*, offered an active role even to the laity as "witnesses" if not judges of the faith, competent to raise a "cry of conscience" amidst the prophesied "obscurity" caused by a largely apostate hierarchy.[39] In the most radical statement of this ecclesiology—radical in the literal sense of appealing to the root of spiritual power in Christ's gift of it to the whole believing community—even general councils were infallible only to the extent that they were free, observed canonical forms, and genuinely represented and spoke for the entire church.[40] As secularized and applied to the state by the abbé Claude Mey and Gabriel-Nicolas Maultrot in their *Maxims of French Public Law* published in defense of the French "constitution" against Chancellor René-Nicolas de Maupeou's suppression and "reform" of the French parlements in 1775, this line of argument produced a sort of conciliar constitutionalism that, bypassing while respecting the parlements, located legislative sovereignty in the whole nation as represented in the Estates General which "has the right to change the form of its government, when it has good reasons for doing so."[41] The culmination of this line of argument was in a sense the Parlement of Paris's appeal to the Estates General in 1787, an appeal which of course actually resulted in the meeting of the Estates two years later.

As applied to relations between state and the church, this combination of figurism and conciliarism might have conceivably produced a relatively free conciliar church in a constitutional monarchy or republic not unlike the state of affairs that obtained for the diocese of Utrecht in the Dutch Republic after 1724 or, at moments, for the constitutional or self-styled "Gallican" Church in the revolutionary French Republic after 1795.

But in the absence of any Estates General the only laymen whose "witness" or "cry of conscience" was of any consequence for Jansenism were the magistrates and barristers in the parlements of France, especially the Parlement of Paris, which, aside from occasional sympathetic bishops, afforded the only institutional protection that Jansenists ever enjoyed from public refusals of sacraments or interdiction from sacerdotal functions. Hence the second element of symbiosis, that between Jansenism and constitutionalism in terms of which the Parlement claimed the right to oppose the religious policies of both monarchy and church. Conciliar constitutionalism as articulated by a Mey or Maultrot thus ran tightly entwined through most of the century with another, which, similarly extending elements of figuristic theology to Frondish constitutionalism, substituted the Parlement of Paris for the defunct Estates General as the secular counterpart, not to the general council, but rather to the faithful lay remnant in the church. In what in contrast to the conciliar variety might be called "judicial constitutionalism," the proper role of the Parlement and its remonstrances were passively to "testify" or "witness" to antique constitutional "truth" amidst the defection of royal despotism, much as a faithful lay remnant might also "witness" to patristic "truth" amidst the "obscurity" of episcopal and papal apostasy. Most influentially articulated by the Jansenist barrister Louis-Adrien Le Paige, this constitutionalism rooted the Parlement's rights of registration and remonstrance in the mythical memory of Merovingian national assemblies to which the Parlement stood as legitimate successor and thus bound, in that capacity, to suffer passively in defense of the "repository" of fundamental law against all comers including the episcopacy and royal ministers.[42] And although eclipsed after Chancellor Maupeou brutally revealed the fragility of the parlements as a constitutional bulwark in 1771, this kind of judicial constitutionalism remained enough of a going concern to have produced a still distinct strain in the proparlementary pamphlet literature on the eve of the Revolution in 1787–89.[43]

But although judicial constitutionalism surely embraced the conciliar tenets of the Gallican tradition, it also committed Jansenism to the defense of royal Gallicanism, or at least of the parlementary version of it. For, as the realm's chief royal lawcourt claiming also to be the Court of Peers, the Parlement of Paris arrogated to itself the right to speak in the name of the king to the nation as well as in the name of the nation to the king, and, routinely confounding the two, to vindicate regalian rights even against the king and his ministers should they compromise such a "national" heritage. Since these regalian rights included the king's prerogative both as quasi-sacral "exterior bishop" and secular "political magistrate" to a certain purview and control over the Gallican Church, the Parlement naturally defended these rights as well. Indeed, it was in the name of these rights that the Parlement intervened against the bishops—and against the king so long as he supported them—to protect Jansenists in such apparently "spiritual" affairs as the refusal of sacraments to appellants in the 1750s or, again, to prosecute their enemies, as in dissolution of the Society of Jesus in the 1760s.

In the hands of Jansenist canonists in the heat of battle against the "independence" of ultramontanist bishops, the justification for thus extending the jurisdiction of the *regnum* at the expense of the *sacerdotum* went very far. Beginning with a conception of the church as "purely spiritual," and prepared to give the state coactive power over everything external, they could think of few if any things so ethereally spiritual as not to discern some admixture of the external that would justify some form of state intervention. The same Maultrot who so radicalized and laicized the conciliar legacy also maintained that the "prince," by which in practice he meant the Parlement, had the right to prevent unjust public refusals of sacrament to appellants because he was duty bound to protect any citizen's public reputation and therefore external "possession" of the sacraments because the "legal possession of even spiritual things is a purely profane matter."[44] This jurisprudence could not but impinge on the autonomy of even general councils, seeing that whether they were ecumenical or not depended on the observance of all the canonical forms of which, external as these were, the "prince" was a valid judge.[45] So far was this line of argument taken that by the end of the 1760s it had produced an intellectual and spiritual twilight zone where typically judicial Jansenist appeals to canon law and early church precedents jostle for position with Rousseauian states of nature and social contracts in the very same texts, and where moderate conclusions justifying parlementary intervention to prevent abuses in ecclesiastical justice rub up against much more radical ones calling for the nationalization of church property. This polemical literary genre makes it hard to say exactly where judicial Jansenist "discourse" fades away and enlightened discourse dawns.[46] Just as conciliar constitutionalism led logically to the Parlement's appeal to the Estates General in 1787, so judicial constitutionalism pointed the way toward the Civil Constitution of 1790.

It goes without saying that judicial constitutionalism and the Erastian tendencies that went with it existed in no little tension with the commitment to councils and conciliar procedures as well as with the ecclesiastical independence that these presupposed. Yet eighteenth-century French Jansenists were only imperfectly aware of these tensions, as the chief architects of conciliar constitutionalism like Mey and Maultrot often lent their weighty authority to justifications for judicial intervention in "spiritual" affairs, while the high priest of judicial constitutionalism, Adrien Le Paige, also wielded the language of conciliarism when it suited his purposes.[47] So long as it was a question of the Parlement of Paris manipulated by Jansenist magistrates and barristers in defense of the "good cause" of efficacious grace, the synthesis of royal Gallicanism and judicial constitutionalism did not get in the way of a conciliarism that would have remained without any practical import in the best of Old-Regime circumstances. With no prospect of holding councils in their own country, French Jansenists showed their good faith by staging them elsewhere, as in Utrecht in 1763, or by applauding them elsewhere, as in Pistoia in 1786. Moreover, the same reasoning used to justify judicial intervention at the expense of ecclesiastical jurisdiction—that the state might enforce Gallican canon law against bishops acting in contempt of it—could also be used on behalf of the rights of bishops, as when the Dutch States General permitted the election and consecration of an archbishop of Utrecht in defiance of papal disapproval. It was not until the revolutionary National Assembly, assuming all of the old monarchy's crown rights in its turn, used the same lines of argument in arranging for episcopal succession to legitimate a "constitutional" Church that it had almost entirely subjected to a "national" state, that the latent tension between judicial and conciliar constitutionalism broke into open conflict.

Italy and the Jansenist International

To be sure, the refusal of sacraments controversy did indeed produce some pro-Jansenist and anti-clerical popular disturbances, particularly in Paris. And there, as in other northern French cities like Troyes and Orléans, a socially judicial public opinion most surely took shape and sided with Jansenists against sacrament-refusing priests and the Jesuits.[48] But it is hard to assign causal weight to crowd action or public opinion as factors in the two most signal Jansenist successes in France: the de facto fall of the bull *Unigenitus* from its status as a law of state in 1757 followed by the trial and dissolution of the Society of Jesus by the parlements led by that of Paris in 1762 and confirmed by royal declaration in 1764. For by the early 1760s, when the Council of Utrecht also added its voice to the anti-Jesuit chorus, the campaign against "the court of Rome" and the Jesuits as its chief symbols was not the work of French Jansenists alone or even, as it turned out, limited to France alone. For by that time Jansenism had become an international cause.

The decisive event in the internationalization of Jansenism and the successful offensive against the Jesuits was the sojourn in Rome in 1758–59 by the abbé Augustin-Charles-Jean Clément de Bizon, a French Jansenist canon in Auxerre and brother of several influential magistrates. His purposes were first to help negotiate a doctrinal statement from Benedict XIV favorable to French appellants, and then, after Benedict's improvident death in 1758, to observe and if possible influence the outcome of the papal conclave.[49] By themselves, the election of Carlo Rezzonico as Clement XIII followed by the death of the well-disposed secretary of state Cardinal Alberico

Archinto and his replacement by Torrigiani may not have been the pro-Jesuitical catastrophes calling for a counteroffensive that Clément and his Italian friends deemed them to be. But so deem them they did, with self-confirming effects for Catholic Europe as a whole.

One all but invisible but important result was the institutionalization of what had been an occasional correspondence between Clément and some Italian Augustinians—Giovanni Gaetano Bottari, for example, first guardian of the Vatican Library and confidant of Cardinal Neri Corsini; or again the indefatigable Neopolitan correspondent Carlo Armano, comte di Gros, one of Italian Jansenism's rare lay adepts. Italian Augustinians and anti-Jesuits, they now entered a kind of Jansenist International. This International remained primarily a correspondence concerned with the publication and dissemination of "good books" on behalf of "solid doctrine" as well as the circulation of news and ecclesiastical news sheets like the *Nouvelles ecclésiastiques* throughout Catholic Europe. In part it existed for its own sake as an historical record of dedication to the "good cause" that was precious enough to Clément that he thought of sending it to Utrecht for safekeeping on the eve of the Terror in January 1793.[50] But its purpose was also to establish and nourish contacts near the centers of power in the papal curia and in the various princely courts of Catholic Europe with a view toward influencing the course of events in favor of the status of the diocese of Utrecht and the situation of appellants in France. And in this domain of activity the International might have laid claim to one concrete accomplishment, namely the suppression of the Jesuits in France and elsewhere, culminating in their abolition by the papacy in 1773.

The first of the Jesuit dominoes to fall, it is true, was in peripheral Portugal, where Sebastian Carvalho e Melho, the marquis de Pombal and chief minister to José I, alleged the complicity of the Jesuits in an attempt on the king's life in order to expel them from both the metropolis and the American colonies. Besides causing a crisis in relations between Lisbon and the papacy, this literal expulsion revealed that the deed could be done, no doubt encouraging the French to try to do as well.[51] Yet even more crucial for France was the advice that Clément, Le Paige, and their cohorts received in late 1758 and 1759 from their Italian friends, notably Bottari, that because the papacy would never disavow *Unigenitus*, the French "friends of the truth" should "attack the Jesuits from whatever angle that does not concern the bull or that unites their cause with the court of Rome."[52] Once rid of the Society—so Clément summed up this advice—"and all the rest will be easy."[53] To be sure, neither the Italian nor French Jansenists could have created the right circumstances—the bankruptcy of the French Jesuits' mission in Martinique in 1759, the favorable disposition of the duc de Choiseul—but their close connections to the Parlement of Paris through Le Paige and Clément's brother Clément de Feillet are by themselves enough to account for the parlementary *parti janséniste*'s determination to profit from such circumstances as arose, providentially or otherwise. By 1764 the Society of Jesus was no more in France.[54]

The fall of the Jesuits in France was also much more decisive than in Portugal—as decisive, indeed, as the Italian Jansenists had hoped and predicted it would be. Being an international state within many states, the Jesuits suffered the adverse consequences of the dynastic alliance or "family pact" negotiated by Choiseul between the Bourbon rulers of France, Spain, Naples, and Parma in 1761, just as the Parlement of Paris was striking the first decisive blow against the Jesuits in France. Even if less directly, the Jesuits were also the victims of the "diplomatic revolution" of 1756 which, by realigning Habsburg Austria with her erstwhile enemy Bourbon France until the French Revolution, deprived the Jesuits of any support from Austria where Jansenists had become sufficiently influential in the ministry by the late 1760s to interest Empress Maria Theresa in Utrecht's case against Rome.[55] Thus, when the government of Carlos III of Spain alleged Jesuit complicity in a popular riot in Madrid a year earlier in order to motivate an edict expelling Spanish Jesuits and confiscating their property on 2 April 1767, the Bourbon rulers of Naples and Parma felt free to follow suit without fear of local Habsburg disapproval whether in Lombardy or Tuscany.[56] Moreover, in each if not in all of these states, philo-Jansenist councillors were on hand to encourage these Bourbon rulers, and Jansenist theologians or court preachers to reassure royal consciences. To a very real if limited extent, the expulsions and final dissolution of the Society of Jesus was the work of the Jansenist International.

But when the duke of tiny Parma in the shadow of the papal states tried to emulate France and Spain by asserting control over ecclesiastical appointments and banning all papal briefs and bulls that did not carry the duke's permission, a humiliated Clement XIII struck back, issuing a brief annulling Ferdinand's edict as well as fulminating a bull of excommunication—events recalling the specter of *Unam Sanctam* and medieval papal claims to temporal power. Whereupon it was the turn of the Bourbons and their sympathizers in Italy to be outraged, as Naples seized the papal enclaves of Benevento and Portecorvo while French troops occupied Avignon—events raising the specter of Philip the Fair if not the hated Hohenstaufens.[57] This sequence of actions and reactions was repeated with even more polarizing effect from 1769 to 1774 when Ganganelli emerged from the papal conclave as Clement XIV with both Bourbon and Habsburg support on the implicit condition, most insisted upon by Spain, that he dissolve the Society of Jesus. Again, as in 1759, Italian and especially Roman "friends" advised their French and Dutch co-belligerents that if, in the words of Pier Francesco Foggini, all other causes "do not wait until after the suppression of the Jesuits, nothing fundamental can . . . be hoped for"; while once again, as in 1759, an apparently amenable pope died an untimely death, not long after fulminating the bull dissolving the Jesuits but only a day before Dupac de Bellegarde was to see him on behalf of Utrecht. Thus were Jansenists once again left empty-handed as an even deeper curial reaction than under Clement XIII set in under Pius VI.[58]

But it should not have taken until 1775 for the "friends of Rome" to have realized that as soon as the offensive against the Jesuits reached Italy itself it was no longer possible, assuming it ever had been so, to effect a clean separation between the cause of the Jesuits on the one hand and that of the papacy and the Catholic Church's spiritual authority on the other. The papacy was after all among the few genuinely indigenous institutions in an Italy which, except for old aristocratic republics of Genoa and Venice, had become a patchwork of Bourbon and Habsburg dynastic satrapies. Italians of diverse stripes were thus bound to feel a sense of humiliation to see these hitherto rival Catholic dynasties of Europe all but broker their differences at the expense of the papacy to which, in the person of Clement XIV, they virtually dictated the brief dissolving the Jesuits in 1773. And so while in the mid-1770s—to single out one among many telltale examples—the Archbishop of Siena had been almost persuaded to make a public profession of communion with the appellant diocese of Utrecht, "he has changed so much since the time of the expulsion of the Jesuits," to believe the Jansenist professor Paolo Marcello Del Mare, "that no one can now remove from his head the idea that the Jansenists are out to destroy religion."[59] The 1770s also witnessed the final dispersion of the Jansenist group called the Archetto in Rome concentrated around Bottari in Cardinal Corsini's palace and Foggini in the Chiesa Nuova.[60]

The dissolution of the Society of Jesus did nothing if not also create a host of angry ex-Jesuits, many of them concentrated in the papal states where Gianvincenzo Bolgeni and Francescantonio Zaccaria emerged as the most prolific polemicists. When under Pius VI they became objects not only of pity but of favor, they came to constitute a kind of ex-Jesuit International corresponding and opposed to the Jansenist one with representatives and journals scattered throughout Catholic Europe. For every Jansenist periodical modeled on the *Nouvelles ecclésiastiques*—Follini's *Annali ecclesiastici* in Florence, Scheidel's *Mainzer Monatschriften von geistlichen Sachen* in Mainz, Wittola's *Wienerische Kirchenzeitung* in Vienna, Grégoire's *Annales de la religion* in post-Thermidorian Paris—there came to correspond an ex-Jesuit one at the opposite end of the ecclesiastical spectrum: Feller's *Journal politique et littéraire* in Luxembourg, Goldhagen and his *Religionsjournal* in Mainz, and of course Barruel's *Journal ecclésiastique* in France. But it is altogether characteristic of the eighteenth century's closing decades that these ex-Jesuits enjoyed the support of all manner of Catholic—and some even not so Catholic—allies and hangers-on whom they would have been hard pressed to enlist in their cause before the dissolution of their order. When Rome itself came to have a journal comparable to many ex-Jesuit ones, the *Giornale ecclesiastico di Roma* founded in 1785, the ex-Jesuit Zaccaria was joined by the Dominican Maria Tomasso Mamachi and even an Augustinian, Luigi Cuccagni, as editors.[61]

Italian Jansenists

While this militant ex-Jesuit International took shape in defense of papal authority on the ecclesiastical "right," Dupac de Bellegarde's abortive journey to Rome followed by the reactionary pontificate of Pius VI prompted a fresh contingent of Italian Augustinians and moral rigorists to become regular correspondents with the church of Utrecht, which increasingly took the place of Paris as the capitol of the Jansenist International. And even more than for the previous generation, this affiliation tended to remake them into Jansenists in the full French sense of the term. What this means exactly is that, in addition to a commitment to theological Augustinianism and moral rigorism, Italian philo-Jansenists began to adopt the polemical party tone and anti-papal Gallican ecclesiology as radicalized by French Jansenists in alliance with the parlements in the course of the earlier *Unigenitus*-related controversies. It was this development that transformed some Italians, in the language of Mario Rosa, from would-be Catholic "reformers" into anti-curial "rebels."[62] The tone in question was one of single-minded commitment to the "good cause" of "solid" or "sane doctrine" and "the truth" against "fanaticism" and "ignorance," omnipresent ex-Jesuits, "Hildebrandists," and last but not least the "court of Rome." As to the ecclesiology—hard as it may be to separate from the rhetoric—not all may have gone so far as Scipione de' Ricci, Bishop of Pistoia and Prato in Tuscany, who held the Gallican articles of 1682 to be "articles of faith" and who, writing in French, excoriated the curia for its "ultramontane pretensions," visibly forgetting on which side of the Alps he himself resided.[63] At the very least this generation of Jansenists were episcopal Gallicans, regarding the spiritual authority of bishops as no different in kind from that of the pope, while at the most they were also parochialists or Richerists, standing for the independent if subordinate authority of the parish priest in the ecclesiastical hierarchy.

What slipped out of the Gallican baggage in its journey over the Alps was the conciliar tenets. While eighteenth-century Frenchmen at least witnessed a formal appeal to a general council, Italians no more contemplated such an eventuality than they did the rebirth of an Ostrogothic Kingdom in Rome. A general council was without doubt the best remedy for the ills of the church, conceded the Paduan professor Giuseppe Pujati to the abbé Clement in 1786, "but this just and pious desire is not at all understood by our princes and is little understood by our bishops, while in the center of Catholic unity it is condemned as an attempt to break it."[64] Given papal hostility, and in the absence of anything like French parlements—and hence in a trajectory quite different from France's or Utrecht's—Italian Jansenists' only recourse was to Italy's sundry secular sovereigns whose "divine" right to undertake ecclesiastical reform without the concurrent authority of either papacy or councils they tended accordingly to magnify. By the eve of the French Revolution, Jansenists in Italy as everywhere else in Catholic Europe had come to stand for the right of secular authority not only to defend local episcopal authority against "the court of Rome" in such matters as the right to grant dispensations from the canonical laws prohibiting marriage within degrees of familial relatedness—the so-called "diriment impediments" to marriage—but also to change those laws, revise seminary curricula, dictate the content of theological education, and to reform or suppress monastic orders, not to mention the right to limit and tax ecclesiastical property. Only in the language of French Jansenists did the "secular authority" thus aggrandized potentially mean anything other than royal or ducal authority.

Precisely when and why in the 1760s Italian Augustinians began to "give up" on the papacy is less germane than to see that, even if radical Jansenist or Gallican ecclesiology was supposed to be subordinate to theology, it was the ecclesiology that made the difference. Writing from the University of Siena, the theologian Fabio de Vecchi came to think that it was "from the false notions of the church that the great [doctrinal] errors have been born," rather than the other way around.[65] The conviction gained ground that if the unredeemed human will had come to play a prominent role in Catholic theology, the root cause was the play of despotic will in the structure of the church. Augustinian orthodoxy would arise naturally from the practice of correct or conciliar canonical forms, even if these could be implemented only at the synodical level.

If the priority of Gallican ecclesiology in the transformation of Italian Augustinians into Jansenists be insisted upon, it is because in the absence of that ecclesiology the purely doctrinal issues had not been terribly divisive in eighteenth-century Italy or for that matter anywhere else outside of France where, alone in Catholic Europe, a sacral monarchy's allergic reaction to even a Catholic Augustinianism had helped metamorphose it into a challenge to its own authority. Unlike French appellants, Italian Augustinians long refused to accept the notion that *Unigenitus* had necessarily condemned Saint Augustine's doctrines of grace and predestination, and had therefore carved out for themselves an Augustinianism within, or at least not belligerently outside of, the bounds of *Unigenitus* alone. Hence in part the mixed chagrin and incomprehension with which, earlier in the century, they had observed the tyranny exercised by *Unigenitus*-related quarrels over French domestic politics, and their conviction—and consequent advice—that it must not be *Unigenitus* itself but rather the abuse of its authority by French Jesuits that best explained the French *malaise*. As late as 1772 Pujati, then a Dominican monk in Bergamo in the Venetian Republic, was still trying to convince friends there that their veneration for the doctrine of Saint Augustine was incompatible with their acceptance of papal infallibility or *Unigenitus*, "which I call the sepulture of this supposed infallibility and the worst scandal of the church."[66]

Indeed, it was precisely the presence of consensus and the absence of *Unigenitus* as an issue that had made possible the so-called Catholic Enlightenment in Italy, as well as the place of Augustinianism in it. A movement displaying much more continuity with the Christian humanism of Erasmus or Lorenzo Valla than the French Enlightenment, Catholic "lights" had flourished just about everywhere in Catholic Europe before the 1760s outside France although the Catholic character of this enlightenment was perhaps most salient in Italy where it enjoyed the patronage of a pope, Benedict XIV, and personification by a priest, Antonio Ludovico Muratori. Described by Bernard Plongeron as a new "religious anthropology" open to the rights of "reason" within a more christological faith as well as to the prospect of secular amelioration with some help from a less hierarchical church, the Catholic Enlightenment endorsed textual and historical criticism of the Scriptures and the dissemination of the Bible in the vernacular, called for more honest, less partisan church histories and what Muratori called a "moderate devotion" purged of baroque excesses and "superstitious" accretions, and opposed both Aristotle and scholasticism, in the one case in favor of newer sciences and in the other in favor of older or "purer" patristic sources. [67]But it is obvious from even this thumbnail description that the existence of such a movement presupposed a modicum of consensus between moderates from both Augustinian and Molinistic camps, a consensus made possible in turn by the non-existence of *Unigenitus* and papal authority as issues. While the interest in secular amelioration presupposed a more benign view of human nature than a rigid Augustinianism could readily accommodate, and the openness to scriptural criticism sat more easily with those for whom the papacy in principle spoke the very last word, Augustinians could make common cause with the movement's opposition to scholasticism, the project of translating the Scriptures into the vernacular, and the campaign in favor of a more austere and introspective style of devotion. The place of Augustinians in the movement was such that, in contrast to the sharply triangular relation of Jansenism to "lights" and Jesuits in France, what was called "Jansenism" only imperceptibly shaded off into "*lumi,*" or "*luces*" in Italy, Spain, and elsewhere in Catholic Europe.

But the "gallicization" of Italian Augustinianism undermined the doctrinal consensus on which the Catholic Enlightenment rested because, far from diminishing the doctrinal issues, Gallican ecclesiology exacerbated them, relating them as it did to so much else. With the once powerful Society of Jesus extinct but the pro-Jesuitical Pius VI as new pope, Dominicans and Augustinians allowed themselves the luxury of a great falling out, Dominicans making common cause with the fallen ex-Jesuits and the papal curia against the Augustinians who responded not only with a neo-Gallican ecclesiology but with a hardening of their theology of grace. The result of this fratricide was what Emile Appolis has called "the fragmentation of the third party" or theological center which gave way to the extremes on either side.[68] While theological reflection on the Molinist side of the debate was perhaps only a little more prolific than in France—it was less necessary to be loquacious with authority on its side—it attracted some of the best talent including the ex-Jesuit Giovan Vincenzo Bolgeni who quite simply eliminated "contrition" or disinterested love for God from his confessional theology, arguing that "attrition" or expanded self-love was the only and therefore legitimate means of relating to God.[69] And while in the second half of the century French Jansenists all but abandoned theology in favor of canon and public law, the end of the century in Italy was one of prolific Jansenist theological production. Natali, Georgi, De Vecchi, Palmieri, Tamburini, Zola—this "who's who" of Augustinian or Jansenist theological eminences at the end of the *Settecento* is also a list of those who produced multi-volume works on grace, predestination, and confession, among other characteristically Jansenist subjects, all the while holding or even hardening the Augustinian position on such edifying subjects as the damnation of infants who died without baptism.[70] While the French Jansenist theologian Etienne Gourlin's treatise on grace fell on stony ground in France when posthumously published there in 1781, it was avidly read and much appreciated by all Italian Jansenists except perhaps for Carlo di Gros who, *mirabile dictu*, thought it too Thomist.[71]

This fin-de-siècle's widening of the theological faultlines entailed the collapse of Italy's Catholic Enlightenment, which, a fragile combination of incompatibles held together by a common faith and certain "enlightened" assumptions, fell prey to polarization reminiscent of how the Italian Renaissance gave way to rival reformations followed by foreign intervention two centuries earlier. Eloquently illustrative of this disintegration is the literary itinerary of Giovanni Lami, Florentine editor of the *Novelle Letterarie* and in some sense the successor to Muratori, who used his position as international spokesman for the Italian republic of letters to mount ever harsher attacks against the Jesuits, show ever less patience with the papacy, and fulminate ever more dogmatic condemnations of the theater.[72] The result was that the Jansenists and *zelanti* divided up the Catholic Enlightenment's harvest between them, appropriating those parts of it that seemed most compatible with very partial confessional agendas. To the *zelanti* went the Enlightenment's sensate epistemology, rehabilitation of will and self interest, optimistic estimate of human nature, and openness to the prospect of at least limited progress—in short, all the real compatibilities between ethical and theological Molinism and the Enlightenment that Jansenists in Italy as well as in France never tired of denouncing. And to Jansenists went an anti-scholastic rationalism, the Renaissance quest for pristine origins, the reformational rehabilitation of secular government, an anti-clerical campaign against the regular clergy and the papal curia, and the Muratorian project for a more enlightened or better "regulated devotion."[73] In Jansenist hands, this project took the form of a catechetical campaign to stamp out popular ignorance and "superstition" with "solid doctrine" and reasoned conviction that had its basis in the doctrine that, ignorance being one of the chief consequences of the "fall," it was itself a sin and hence excused no other sins.[74]

For Italy and Roman Jansenists in particular the result, in sum, was ironic indeed. On the one hand, the stated purpose and expected result of the advice to French Jansenists to put the campaign against the Jesuits ahead of that against *Unigenitus* was to take the sharp edges off the religious and political divisions in France. And by both discrediting religious disputes and depriving French Jansenists of their preferred scapegoats—that is, for reasons that these Jansenists would not have liked—their victory over the Jesuits seems to a degree to have had that effect, creating the possibility of something like an autumnal Catholic Enlightenment there. But the effect of the same campaign in Italy, on the other hand, was the reverse, bringing the French political, ecclesiastical and even religious divisions there in its train. The grand offensive against the Jesuits thus returned to Italy like a boomerang, dividing Italian Catholics into latter-day

Guelfs and Ghibellines. And without anyone's seeming to have noticed it, the French thereby contrived to foist their polarized ecclesiastical situation onto Italy, ironically by Italian invitation, as the abbé Clément and Dupac de Bellegarde replied to requests for "good books" and "solid doctrine" by engineering an avalanche of French Jansenist publications from over the Alps onto the Italies where they found local publication, imitation, or Italian translation.[75] About the same time, and perhaps not incidentally, complaints began to be heard from both sides of the Italian religious divide about the influx of deistic and atheistic books from France.[76]

The Era and End of Jansenist Absolutism

One of the chief differences between France and the Italies, however, is that whereas the supposed capitol of the Enlightenment produced no very enlightened much less Jansenist despots, the Habsburg principalities of late eighteenth-century Italy produced at least one of each in the persons of Joseph II, who directly ruled Lombardia as province of the Empire, and his brother Peter Leopold, Grand Duke of Tuscany. That remarkable contrast reflects an anterior difference between the French and Italian situations: that whereas the French monarchy had long vindicated its Gallican liberties vis-à-vis the papacy, Italian princes and potentates had yet to gain them, and could only do so and still remain Catholic with the aid of Catholics and a theology that, although Catholic, were also anti-papal. Hence the late-eighteenth-century alliance or at least marriage of convenience between absolutists in need of clerical help in aggrandizing the secular jurisdiction's control over people as subjects at the expense of the church's as "faithful," and Jansenists, who, having given up on the papacy, looked to secular rulers to help them undertake the reform of the church. Indeed, so typical is this alliance in prerevolutionary Catholic Europe outside of France—Jovellanos or Rhoda and Carlos III of Spain, Simioli or Sarao and Don Carlos of Naples, Blarer or De Haën and both Maria Theresa and Joseph II in Austria, Nény and Le Plat and the same set of sovereigns in the Austrian Netherlands—that the whole period might as plausibly be dubbed that of Jansenist despotism as of enlightened despotism. It was with much nostalgia and only a little exaggeration that, writing after the French Revolution had scared Catholic kings into abandoning ecclesiastical reform, Professor Pietro Tamburini in Pavia recalled the "support that by divine mercy [the truth] had found among princes" thanks to which it had been possible "to promote in a short space of a few years the most felicitous revolution in the memory of man."[77]

Nowhere, however, did the concept of Jansenist absolutism come nearer to being a reality than in the Tuscany of Grand Duke Peter Leopold whose favorite reading included Jacques Duguet's *L'institution d'un prince*. Thus the grand duke's "fifty-seven points," his blueprint for ecclesiastical reform sent to Tuscan bishops and others, were largely oriented toward producing the *buon paroco* or good pastor as the model for all clergy at the expense of the regular clergy and priests holding benefices without cure of souls, as well as toward making the parish church the center of worship at the expense of confraternal chapels, public oratories, and other loci of devotion. But Leopold's chief theological inspiration came not from books but from a resident Tuscan Jansenist theologian and churchman, Scipione de' Ricci, whom Leopold had promoted from being grand vicar in Florence to the bishopric of Pistoia and Prato in 1780.

The most spectacular result of this Tuscan edition of the Jansenist-absolutist entente was the Synod of Pistoia in 1786. Convened by Ricci but presided over by the synod's "promoter" and chief theologian Pietro Tamburini of the University of Pavia, the synod included just about every curé and curate in the diocese, which was of course canonical enough for a diocesan synod in contrast to a provincial council.[78] What gave conciliar point to the presence of these priests was the synod's place in Leopold's plan as the first in a series leading to a national council along with Ricci's assurances to them that they were to be voting with their bishop as "judges of the faith."[79] The agenda entrusted to these judges was also universal—that is to say conciliar—in scope, as Ricci and Tamburini persuaded them to subscribe to a series of decrees that articulated an unmistakably Jansenist theology of grace, predestination, and penitence, enjoined the reading of Quesnel's *Réflexions morales* among other Jansenist works, and proclaimed the four Gallican articles of 1682 to contain the true doctrine of the church and the pope to be only its "ministerial head."[80] Four references to "times of obscurity" suggested that Pistoia's Gallicanism had not failed to keep up with French figurism, and that the visible magistracy, even if it were a majority of bishops and not the papacy alone, was not always to be trusted.[81] Nor of course did Ricci and the synod fail to go on record, as had the council of Utrecht, in favor of councils and conciliar forms, opposed as these were to the "spirit of domination" or any hint of "monarchy and despotism" in the church.[82] Indeed, the church of Utrecht was never far from Pistoia's agenda, as numbers of priests wanted the synod to avow its communion with that church which for its part adhered to the *Acts* of the Synod of Pistoia in 1789.[83]

In sharp contrast to Utrecht's provincial council of 1763, however, which had downplayed its differences with Rome in an effort to give public proof of its "orthodoxy," the Synod of Pistoia bore a frankly reformist and anti-curial stamp. For not only did it stake out controversial doctrinal and ecclesiastical positions but also—a third category of decrees—deduced from these positions a program of liturgical and pastoral reform that at once ratified and radicalized the assault on "baroque piety" that Ricci with Leopold's support had been visiting on unreceptive parishioners ever since his episcopate began in 1780. Thus, on the grounds that the clergy's only purpose was "the sanctification of the faithful," the synod hailed the grand duke's attempts to reallocate church resources to the service of the parish and its clergy at the expense of the monastic clergy which it all but urged him to destroy.[84] From the premise that the Eucharistic sacrifice was "spiritual" and not "material," the synod concurred with Ricci's campaign against visual and auditory "distractions" like loud organ music and the display of relics in favor of instructional books and vernacular translations whereby the laity might "even participate in the sacrifice."[85] And on the principle that Christ and not "created things" was the only cause of true prayer, the synod endorsed Ricci's crusade against repeated novenas and numbered recitations, and called upon the grand duke to restrict the number of religious feast days and required oaths. It was this bookish offensive against devotional practices it considered "exterior," "material," or smacking of "superstition" that so deepened the gulf between Jansenist and indigenous popular religious sensibility and proved to be the synod's undoing.[86] For unlike the original thing in the more typographically attuned north, Italian Jansenism was fated to remain a mainly clerical and professorial phenomenon, never acquiring much of a popular urban much less rural lay constituency.

Another contrast to the church in Utrecht is of course that the Tuscan Jansenists had an absolute Catholic sovereign to account to. Yet a remarkable feature of Peter Leopold's rule in Tuscany is that, until the going got rough and in the sharpest contrast to the more autocratic style of his brother in Vienna, he was willing to experiment with conciliar forms instead of promulgating reforms without the church's concurrence. And even though the Synod of Pistoia was the only one of Peter Leopold's planned synods to meet, it was the example of the conciliar form as well as the synod's doctrinal pronouncements that resonated and ricocheted so widely in Catholic Europe, as for that matter it was intended to do. Like the "unanimity" of Utrecht earlier touted by the Jansenist press, it was as much the "uniformity" of more than two hundred priests despite their nearness to "the court of Rome" and its "lackeys" as it was the synod's "plan of doctrine and ecclesiastical discipline" that gave its promoter Pietro Tamburini "reason to hope for a felicitous revolution in the church of Italy."[87] But the hope thus inspired extended well beyond the Italies, especially after the belated publication of the council's *Acts* in 1789. As far away as Mainz, Professor Scheidel of the archepiscopal university there tried to arrange for a German translation of "such a celebrated assembly," hoping that it would help unite the German suffragans behind their archbishops in a statement against "Roman pretensions" that the congress of the four Rhenish prince-archbishops in Ems, also in 1786, had failed to fulfill.[88] Reacting to the Synod's *Acts* in Paris in 1789, the abbé Clément had never dared hope to see anything so good, especially the parts on history and penitence, and called for a speedy French translation in the hopes that the synod might serve as a model for ecclesiastical reform in the upcoming meeting of the Estates General.[89] Back in Utrecht, Dupac de Bellegarde altogether shared Clément's enthusiasm and promptly produced the desired translation—his last major activity before his death.

It was, alas, also all too good to be true, because the "revolution" that overtook Tuscany was neither the "felicitous revolution" that Tamburini hoped for nor the one that soon transformed the awaited Estates General into the National Assembly in France. For "revolution" in Tuscany took a conservative, even pointedly anti-Jansenist direction, as those segments of the clergy alienated by Ricci's reforms allied themselves with elements of the lay population that perceived these reforms to be an attack on religion as such. This coalition of anti-Riccian forces first reared its revolutionary head in May of 1787 when popular riots erupted in Pistoia and Prato at the very moment that Ricci and his allies in the Tuscan episcopacy sustained decisive defeat at the hands of a majority of Tuscan bishops in an assembly convened by Leopold in Florence in an effort to take a shortcut to the convocation of the desired national council. Never to meet, the council was the main casualty of these events. Even more disastrous for Ricci and the Synod of Pistoia was the riot in Florence itself three years later on 9 June 1790. In the absence of Peter Leopold who had left Florence for Vienna to take the place of his deceased brother, a regency council reacted to the riot by abandoning just about all of the reforms that the grand duke had sponsored, including the liturgical and ecclesiastical ones.

It is of course true that the economic conjuncture of rising grain prices along with a crisis in the textile industry—silk production in the Tuscan case—was no more foreign as a factor in these popular uprisings than it was in the disturbances surrounding the outbreak of revolution in France. But while in prerevolutionary France popular hostility already often made scapegoats of Catholic clergymen without discernible distinctions among them, the Tuscan riots, preceded and accompanied by clerical pamphlets against Ricci and the Synod of Pistoia, pointedly sought to undo the ecclesiastical and liturgical reforms promoted by these two in defense of other priests and or even the regular clergy and a more traditional Catholicism. The immediate occasion of the uprisings of May 1787 was the rumor of the impending removal of the altar dedicated to the relic of the Virgin's garter—a typical target of Riccian reform—while the riots of June 1790 demanded and to a degree obtained the restoration of sundry altars, oratories, images, and even of abolished monasteries to their monks—all objects of the synod's decrees. They also drove Ricci himself out of Pistoia and Prato and his friend and ecclesiastical provost Antonio Baldovinetti out of Leghorn, and both to submit their resignations within the year.[90] Indeed, from the perspective of these Jansenist victims the riots were directed principally against them and clearly orchestrated by Rome.[91] Viewing the same events from Rome, Joseph II's Jansenist imperial postal agent there, Girolamo Astorri, went so far as to advance a complex conspiracy theory to show how "emissaries of the court of Rome," aware of time spent by Tuscan peasants as seasonal farmhands in the papal states each winter, "took advantage of this time to instruct them, to turn them against the reforms, and to embolden them for the explosion which has just gone off."[92]

Astorri's conspiracy theory is symptomatic of how, by raising the stakes in the debate, the coming of the era of revolutions and the end of the European Old Order would further exacerbate relations between Italian Jansenists and their *zelanti* opponents. And in the competition between rival conspiracy theories the *zelanti* were bound to prevail to the precise degree that the French Revolution came to overshadow the Catholic and conservative "revolutions" in Tuscany and the Austrian Netherlands that preceded and initially accompanied them. For while it seemed not at all implausible to traumatized Jansenists that the papacy and its agents would have fomented the popular revolts directed against Jansenist-like ecclesiastical, liturgical and devotional reforms, it seemed no less implausible to defenders of "orthodoxy" and papal primacy that Jansenists might have been in league with philosophes in the making of a revolution that promulgated anything like the Civil Constitution of the Clergy. Among the "authors" of the French Revolution the Jansenists were the most dangerous, in the opinion of one pro-papal pamphleteer, in that, unlike philosophes or Protestants, they passed as Catholics.

Taken in by Jansenism's "appearance of moral severity, cultic purity, disciplinary reform, and dogmatic antiquity," adepts of this sect came to challenge first sacerdotal, then royal authority, thereby planting a "mine under the throne of France."[93] While the further evolution of the debate subordinated Jansenists to philosophes in the French counterrevolutionary rendition of this plot, the Jansenist in the role of chief plotter remained much more pronounced in the counterrevolutionary imagination in Italy than in France.[94]

It goes without saying that Italian Jansenists did not readily recognize themselves in the role of proto-Jacobins. Had it not been they, and not their enemies, who had been the mainstays of secular authority and absolutism in late Settecento Italy? Reading the *Nouvelles ecclésiastiques* with mixed chagrin and disbelief in Rome in 1791, Astorri could not "understand how the admirers of Arnauld, Nicole, etc. can accept the principles being erected about obedience and the nature and power of the authority of princes," thus lending credence to the thesis that Jansenists were just as subversive in the eighteenth century as Protestants had been in the sixteenth.[95] The most memorable Jansenist utterance to emerge from this Italian situation was Pietro Tamburini's *Lettere theologico-politiche sullo presente situazione della cosa ecclesiastica*, which, coming to the defense of secular authority—and Jansenism—against Spedalieri's *De' diritti dell' uomo*, perforce also distanced itself from Gabriel-Nicolas Maultrot and the *Nouvelles ecclésiastiques* who had indeed put the absolutism of their seventeenth-century predecessors behind them. The situation was very particular, as Tamburini's colleague Zola apologetically explained in 1795 to the abbé Jean-Baptiste Mouton who had become one of the *Nouvelles ecclésiastiques*'s editors.[96] But it was also general enough inasmuch as just about all Italian Jansenists reacted negatively to the Revolution, seeing it as did Carlo di Gros as a divine "punishment" on a country which, "instead of profiting from the great lights that God had spread there for over a century . . . had visited persecution on those who had disseminated them."[97] Whether in the longer run their conciliar conception of Catholic polity and the language of anti-despotism would have forever remained confined to the church or whether they would have followed the French pattern and come to accept a version of national sovereignty once the alliance with absolutism had run its course—these are questions that history did not allow Italians the luxury of answering at their own pace.

As it happened, occupation by French revolutionary armies forcefully imposed republics on Italy in which Jansenists, to the extent that they were visible as a group, delineated a collective profile as defenders of a moderate constitutional and officially Catholic republicanism where religious dissent was accorded "civil" toleration but not rights to a public presence. That is to say that, minus the formally republican component—as unexpected in prerevolutionary France as it was imposed on Triennio Italy—Italian Jansenists had found their way to positions not very far from their prerevolutionary French counterparts who had similarly come to stand for a kind of consultative constitutionalism in both church and state and a tie between the two that at least allowed for the rights of citizenship for religious dissenters.

If there was one aspect of the early French Revolution to which Italian Jansenists tended to react favorably—more favorably, as a whole, than their confessional counterparts in France itself—it was the Civil Constitution of the Clergy. Although promulgated by the French "people" as represented by the National Assembly over the obvious reservations of their king, the Civil Constitution bore a close enough resemblance to the Erastian and anti-papal legislation that Italian Jansenists had been celebrating in the form of "Josephism" for them to have withheld an at least initial and cautious approval. While worried about the French Revolution's reactionary effect on the project of absolutist ecclesiastical reform, Astorri as late as September 1791 called the papal examination of the Civil Constitution a "farce," hoping that the French National Assembly would go as far as to secure the abolition of the Formulary. "If this moment escapes us it is not likely that another so propitious will come around again."[98] As in the offensive against the Jesuits by the parlements thirty years earlier, Italian Jansenists lifted their eyes beyond the Alps whence came perhaps their salvation, hoping that the National Assembly's ecclesiastical legislation would score the decisive blow against the "court of Rome" that the suppression of the Jesuits had not.

From the Civil Constitution to the Concordat

Meanwhile, however, the abbé Clement had also been turning his eyes toward the Alps, but from the French side of them, hoping that Dupac's French translation of the Acts of the Synod of Pistoia would inspire the National Assembly to sponsor similar reforms for the French Catholic Church, long convinced as he had been that the torch of Truth had passed from France into the more enlightened monarchies of Italy and Spain.[99] That the National Assembly did no such thing is perhaps the understatement of the French Revolution. Jansenists of one stripe or another were nonetheless conspicuous in the debates that led to what was called the Civil Constitution of the Clergy, which to their delight restored diocesan synods and subjected bishops to the advice of a council; instituted the consecration of bishops by their metropolitans and all but bypassed the "court of Rome"; gave curés independence from bishops and subjected both to election by the people; and although without naming the Formula of Alexander VII or *Unigenitus,* forbade the sorts of oaths and formulas that had tormented Jansenist consciences for more than a century.

The trouble in part was that, unlike the Synod of Pistoia, the National Assembly was not a church council despite some efforts to feature it as such by virtue of the presence of nearly three hundred clergymen in its midst. The National Assembly therefore imposed its "reform" on the Gallican Church in its purely secular capacity as a constituent power, without recourse to the "spiritual" power of the Catholic Church whether in conciliar or papal form. Hence the care taken by the National Assembly to make it clear that its "reform" was purely secular or "civil," affecting only what was external about the church while leaving the substance of Catholic belief alone. While that line of argument bothered many French Jansenists more than it initially did Italian ones, the National Assembly and its apologists derived it from a largely Jansenist body of jurisprudence previously used to justify the intervention of the Parlement of Paris in the controversy over the refusal of sacraments and in the suppression of the Jesuits: to wit, that these secular initiatives either only implemented or enforced Gallican canon law or that they concerned, not the faith, but only the external aspects of church organization or discipline over which secular courts exercised a legitimate purview. And as no one could make these arguments better than Jansenist jurists themselves, Jansenists again figured among the Civil Constitution's most outspoken apologists, led by canon lawyer and Third-Estate deputy Armand-Gaston Camus.

If the National Assembly's reform of the Gallican Church had not gone beyond measures that bore the imprimatur of Christian antiquity or the Gallican past, these arguments would no doubt have been more persuasive than they were and the issue of the National Assembly's authority in "spiritual" matters would never have provoked the crisis of conscience that it did. But a National Assembly that prided itself on breaking new ground was no more likely to content itself with hoary precedents in this than in any other domain, and in fact burdened its legislation with several provisions quite alien to any ecclesiastical past. For Catholic consciences, two such measures stood out like the planks of a cross: first, the unilateral reduction in dioceses from about 135 to 82, thus severing the tie of more than 50 bishops from their former dioceses; and, second, the replacement of royal or other forms of nomination of clergy with popular election by "active citizens" in their purely secular capacity as citizens alone, depriving the clergy of any corporate role in its own recruitment. When combined with the National Assembly's abolition of the tithe, nationalization of church property, and refusal to allow the church any corporate identity beyond the diocesan level—none of these, strictly speaking, part of the Civil Constitution—these provisions had the effect of stripping the Gallican Church of all autonomy in relation to the state, as though in compensation for its almost complete independence from the papacy, and thereby seeming to vindicate Pius VI's harsh judgment of the Gallican "liberties" as the slavery of the French clergy to the state in lieu of the only real liberty available to it in obedience to the papacy.[100]

Not surprisingly, the National Assembly's ecclesiastical legislation confirmed the devout opinion's most apocalyptic prophecies of a coming godless "revolution," and helped transform this Catholic counter-enlightenment into a counterrevolution. And in the Civil Constitution in particular the devout imagination also saw the nightmare of Jansenist ecclesiology come true.[101] Nor is it surprising that this opposition to the Revolution came to include most bishops, stripped as they were by the Civil Constitution of much of their own jurisdiction. Initially finding its voice in the works of an abbé Augustin Barruel, a Jean-Baptiste Duvoisin, or a Capmartin de Chaupy, this "religious right" gave the coming counterrevolution a cause more exalted than the interested defense of aristocratic privilege or even the royal prerogative could possibly have been. It also gave the cause of counterrevolution a full-blown ideology derived from the premise of the ultimate sovereignty of God.[102]

More surprising is that the Civil Constitution of the Clergy also split what remained of the French Jansenist community. In other words it split the core of the Catholic constituency most eager for ecclesiastical reform. While most Jansenists were able to swallow their qualms about the reduction of dioceses and mode of clerical election and defend the Ecclesiastical Committee's whole proposal as more beneficial than harmful, a hard core of critics led by the veterans Mey, Maultrot, and the abbé Henri Jabineau took the field against these measures, pointing to their clear lack of canonical precedents and announcing them as unacceptable so long as they remained unsanctioned by the "spiritual power" deliberating as a Gallican National Council. In taking this position, they laid bare and widened the issue of lay versus ecclesiastical authority, or of judicial versus conciliar constitutionalism, that had run like a fault line through Jansenist political and ecclesiological thought throughout the whole eighteenth century.[103] They also made it clear that part of the issue was the "absolutist" quality of the National Assembly's ecclesiastical legislation—indeed, of its constitutional legislation as a whole.

For what was objectionable to the majority of the National Assembly about the prospect of a church council deliberating on the merits of its ecclesiastical legislation was not necessarily that such a council represented the church, but that it represented anything other than the nation, thus dividing the sovereignty that Jean Bodin had long taught them was indivisible. Presiding over the National

Assembly's abolition of the church's corporate property, separate organization, and general assemblies was the same bias against all partial associations that caused it to abolish separate orders, privileged provinces, municipal guilds, and to disallow workers' associations, a bias arguably inherited from the ideology of absolutism whether in monarchical or—even more ironically—ultramontanist form. Although judicial Jansenists like Camus proved willing enough to extend the logic of Old-Regime argumentation to defend this aspect of the Civil Constitution, it is most improbable that they would ever have eliminated the "independence" of the church so totally had they been left to their own devices. And although there is nothing specifically anti-clerical much less anti-Catholic about this bias, it was in fact those deputies most marked by the century's "philosophic" spirit who, at crucial points in the debate, most surgically brought this absolutist logic to bear. Arguing for example against giving the clergy any separate voice in the election of its own ranks, Robespierre held that to do so was "to reconstitute a solitary corps."[104]

And so it is perhaps not accidental that the Jansenists most adamant in opposing this absolutist aspect of the National Assembly's ecclesiastical legislation had also been among those first in the field with a thesis of national sovereignty in opposition to royal absolutism before the onset of the Revolution. Published as early as 1775 as an addition to his and Mey's monumental *Maxims of French Public Law*, Maultrot's *Dissertation on the Right to Convoke the Estates General* circulated separately as one of the more politically radical pamphlets in 1787, while his three volume *Origins and Rightful Limits of Temporal Authority,* published in 1789, was one of the targets of Tamburini's apology for enlightened absolutism in an Italian context in 1794.[105]

It was this absolutist aspect of revolutionary ideology that prevented the National Assembly from playing the conciliar card: of allowing, that is, the Gallican Clergy to be Gallican enough to convene in a national council to deliberate on the Civil Constitution of the Clergy. The prevention is tragic not only because it split the most obvious core constituency in favor of radical ecclesiastical reform, but because it also split Gallican sentiment as a whole, dividing it as it were into its political and ecclesiastical halves. This painful choice was imposed upon the Gallican episcopacy at a time when, with the Jansenist controversy largely behind it, the Gallican cause had begun to lose its association with "heresy," arguably making the episcopacy more Gallican than at any point in the eighteenth century since the advent of *Unigenitus*. Speaking for his fellow bishops, Boisgelin de Cucé, Archbishop of Aix, virtually offered clergy's acceptance of the Civil Constitution to the National Assembly on 29 May, new dioceses, lay elections, and all, if only the Gallican Clergy were allowed to convene itself as a national church council in order to formalize its acceptance.[106]

By splitting the Gallican community, it also split whatever France had by way of a Catholic Enlightenment. For in sharp contrast to what happened in Italy where the suppression of the Jesuits had ended the Catholic Enlightenment, in France it had made one possible. And while in Italy the importation of Gallican ecclesiology had envenomed the doctrinal debate, in Gallican France it was the diminution of the theological controversy that "tamed" Gallicanism and made it available for other causes. Wedded to Jansenism ever since the appeal of *Unigenitus* to a general council, Gallicanism had to put that exclusive association behind it before being able to associate itself with some of the century's more optimistic estimates of humanity's secular prospect and become an essential element in the creation of a uniquely French Catholic Enlightenment between the extremes of Holbachian "reason" on the one side and an ever more strident Catholic counter-enlightenment on the other. It was during the Old Regime's last several decades that future patriotic priests like Claude Fauchet, Adrien Lamourette, and Henri Grégoire were able to put together the political theologies representing just such a synthesis and that enabled them to travel so many miles with the Revolution.[107]

The result of the refusal to exercise the conciliar option was ironically to make the approval or disapproval of these concentric communities dependent on the decision of the international Catholic Church in the only form that, in the absence of a general council, it then existed, namely the papal curia. As it happened, papal disapproval threw many of them into the curial camp whether they wanted to be there or not, thereby disrupting the formation of a clear Gallican-ultramontanist or reformist-traditionalist division that might have reinforced the identity of the constitutional church as a national church and an ally of the Revolution. And since the crisis of conscience posed by papal disapproval in the absence of conciliar approval was far from unique to the episcopacy or monastic clergy, including as it did about half of the secular second order as well, the resultant schism also prevented a clear hierarchical split between "privileged" and "unprivileged" clergy that might have diluted the Revolution's anti-clericalism in the larger pool of hostility to "privilege" and "aristocracy." Whether considered vertically or horizontally, clerical opposition to the Revolution was hence representative enough of the clergy as a whole as to make the whole clergy into targets of revolutionary anti-clericalism. These targets soon came to include the "constitutional" clergy as well—that is, that portion of the clergy that had sworn fidelity to the constitution—which, being more vulnerable precisely because more visible, bore the brunt of the revolutionary hostility to the clergy provoked by the "refractory" clergy's contribution to the counterrevolution and its ideology.[108]

Whether without these circumstances the French Enlightenment's peculiar distillation of militant anti-Catholicism would have come to play the spectacular role in the Revolution that it did is open to question. Suggesting that it would not have is the evidence of the *cahiers de doléances*, which called for the reform but certainly not the destruction of the Gallican Church as a corps, or even the much more radical prerevolutionary literature where pamphlets written in the vulgar Voltairian mode surface as no more than trace elements in the whole.[109] What was quite predictable from either source is that the monastic clergy might very well bite the dust, that the parish clergy would improve their status in relation to the regular clergy and their bishops, even that the clergy as a whole might lose its status as a privileged *constitutional* order and a good deal of its wealth, but not that Catholicism itself would come under attack. But pointing in the opposite direction is the growing polarization between the cause or "religion" championed by a proto-"right" and the cause of an anti-Catholic "philosophy" on the "left" visible in the literature at large, as well as evidence of popular hostility to the clergy as a whole in the cities, particularly Paris.[110] Paris even witnessed a full-scale anti-clerical riot on 29–30 September in the wake of a curé's reluctance to bury the body of a deceased journeyman carpenter for less than twenty-three livres. Since the parishes where the riot took place had been ones repeatedly purged of its clergy and traumatized by public refusals of sacraments in the course of the Jansenist controversy, this evidence is suggestive of the impact of this controversy in the making of popular anti-clericalism in cities where Jansenism had put down popular roots.[111] It also highlights how different the French situation was from elsewhere in Catholic Europe like Tuscany or Brabant where, even in urban settings, popular violence tended to break out with the support of priests in defense of a traditional Catholicism against Jansenist-inspired or enlightened legislation toward ecclesiastical reform.

But whatever the potential for something like revolutionary "dechristianization" in 1789, it was certainly if inadvertently increased by the Civil Constitution of the Clergy which, by alienating and "ultramontanizing" half the clergy, placed the remaining clergy in the crossfire between counterrevolutionary right and revolutionary left. And once the Catholic clergy as a whole had become a symbol of counterrevolution, revolutionaries were bound to have recourse to the heaviest anti-clerical artillery available by virtue of the polarizing logic of alliance with the enemies of one's worst enemy.[112] In France, that meant the Voltairian enlightenment against the "infamous thing" and the Holbachian one against "charlatanism," themselves in part the product of the confessional polarization of an earlier eighteenth century. Hence the Revolution's campaign against Catholicism stretching from the beginnings of "dechristianization" in the fall of 1793 to the directorial Terror following the coup of 18–19 Fructidor 1797, a campaign that put a permanent rift between the republican principle and Catholicism well into the twentieth century. Nor were the consequences confined to France alone, seeing that French revolutionary armies and the Convention's "representatives on mission" crossed French borders into the Austrian Netherlands, the Catholic Germanies, and of course Northern Italy, bringing parts of the Revolution's ecclesiastical legislation with them. Thus did France impose its divisions on the rest of Europe a second time, replacing the rift between Jansenism and Jesuitism with that of Catholic conservatism and militant unbelief, as the Revolution spawned imitators on the one hand while reform Catholic and Jansenists found themselves labeled as "Jacobins" by conservative *zelanti* on the other.

A last chance for a more complicated and Catholic outcome to a century of lights came in the form of the remnants of the constitutional church that had survived the Terror and regrouped itself under the de facto leadership of the abbé Henri Grégoire, constitutional bishop of Blois and deputy to the Convention and then to the Council of 500 until Bonaparte dismissed it in 1799.[113] Formally cut off from all state support by the Convention on 18 September 1794—a measure that only legalized a de facto situation that had existed since 1793—this church at least regained a small margin for maneuver after Grégoire, exploiting his access to the national podium and invoking the principle of religious toleration, called for the liberty of worship in a speech drowned out by the cries of still hostile colleagues on 21 December 1794.[114] But the Convention did not remain indefinitely insensitive to the current of opinion released by the printed distribution of Grégoire's speech, and responded with decrees which, tantamount to the formal separation of church and state, declared that the freedom to worship might "not be disturbed" and even allowed for the limited use of nationalized church buildings.[115] Using this opening to good advantage, a small group of "united bishops"—Grégoire and four other formerly constitutional bishops resident in Paris—took it upon themselves to address an encyclical letter to the remaining bishops and vacant churches, a letter that began the task of reconstituting what remained of the constitutional church and giving it a new reason for existence.[116]

The task was staggering. As it emerged from the trial of the Terror, this church counted at most twenty active bishops of its original contingent of eighty-two, the others having died natural deaths, perished during the Terror, or in one way another renounced their episcopate whether from fatigue or under pressure from the Terror. The percentage of survivors from the priesthood was no better and possibly worse, and for the same reasons. Whole dioceses, even areas, found themselves with virtually no constitutional clergy.[117] This vacuum was easily occupied by the refractory "missionary" and itinerant clergy which, in circumstances not entirely dissimilar to those obtaining in the Netherlands in the first quarter of the century, was better able to take advantage of the regime of semi-liberty after 1795 than was the constitutional clergy and may have won a majority of Catholics to its side by the time of the Napoleonic Concordat of 1801. And while the refractory clergy may have also been the preferred target of state-sponsored persecution because of its continued reluctance to swear loyalty to a republican government, the constitutional clergy hardly benefited from the protection of a regime that remained hostile to Catholicism. And as a consciously Catholic clergy, this clergy remained bedeviled by Pius VI's condemnation of the constitution of 1791 and their oaths of loyalty to it. If the issue of this oath be substituted for the refusal to accept *Unigenitus* or the Formulary of Alexander VII, then the position of this clergy bears a real structural resemblance to that of the clergy of Utrecht.

It should hence come as no surprise that the general posture of this church was not unlike that of Utrecht either.[118] That posture was in the first instance one of obedience to temporal authority extended in either case to a non-Catholic republic. So just as the Provincial Council of Utrecht had proclaimed the duty of obedience to temporal authorities including the Protestant republic that allowed it to convene, so too did this "Gallican Church"—thus had the constitutional church re-christened itself in 1795—declare its "entire submission to the laws of the [Directorial French] republic" as soon as it convened in a national council with that government's permission on 14 August 1797, a gesture reiterated by swearing the oath of "hatred for royalty and anarchy" imposed on all Catholic clerics in the wake of the Directory's anti-royal and anti-clerical coup d'état of 18–19 Fructidor just a few weeks later.[119] This declaration represented the Gallican Church's dogged commitment to the principle of obedience to secular authority: that is, to the first or "royal" of the four Gallican articles of 1682 which, like the Synod of Pistoia, it regarded as "founded on the holy canons and the tradition of the [church] fathers."[120] Obedience to secular authority in all matters within its temporal competence was of course this clergy's foundational act in the form of its constitutional oath of 1791, a stance that also continued to distinguish that clergy from the refractory priests who challenged the legitimacy of the republic and much that it had done.

In contrast to its stand of 1791, however, but like the Church of Utrecht, this church's self-proclaimed Gallicanism finally included a real commitment to the conciliar tenets of the Gallican tradition, convening two national councils in the space of its short six-year life. The first of these councils in 1797 took advantage of the de facto abrogation of the Civil Constitution of the Clergy to root deliberative and electoral procedures and structures at every level of the clerical hierarchy by means of a nexus of metropolitan councils, diocesan presbyteries, diocesan and rural synods and ecclesiastical conferences that made collegial consultation a constant, bound bishops to the counsel of their parish clergy, and both to election by a combination of clergy and laity.[121] And with the precedent of Utrecht's still pending appeal to a general council in mind, the same council formally submitted its case to the "legal and canonical judgment of the universal church" in the form of an "ecumenical council" if the pope consented to convene it or by other national churches and Catholic universities if he refused.[122] As in the case of Utrecht, but more explicitly so, this conciliar stance and structure also enabled the Gallican Church's first National Council of 1797 to be Catholic in spite its rupture with the papacy because, while confessing with the same formula as the Provincial Council of Utrecht's that the pope was "by divine right the ministerial and visible head of the universal church" enjoying a "primacy of honor and jurisdiction," the United Bishops' *Second Encyclical Letter* convoking this council also specified that "he would exceed the powers given to the first of the Apostles of whom he is the successor were he to arrogate to himself an authority superior or even equal to the Church's, and were he to govern without the concourse of other bishops." That much was enough to enable this church to reject Pius VI's condemnations of the Civil Constitution as a "usurpation violating the rights and majesty of the universal church," seeing that "it was in the power of no church, not even that of Rome, either to separate another church from universal communion or to declare it schismatic short of a declaration of separation by that church itself or unless it were summoned, heard, and judged following canonical forms."[123] Placing, as had the clergy of Utrecht, the onus of schism on their enemies, the delegates of the National Council of 1801 challenged the ultramontanist "dissidents" to show them "a single error proscribed by that same church to which we do not say anathema."[124]

Still, lack of legitimacy as a Catholic Church in the view of the papacy made it imperative for the Gallican Church to replace it, as had Utrecht, in the form of public testimonies to its Catholicity from as many other Catholic churches as possible. The subject of such relations with other churches already occupied pride of place in Grégoire's report to National Council of 1797 on the work of the "united bishops," and this council wasted no time in imitating the Provincial Council of Utrecht by addressing its decrees to as many "foreign" churches as would receive them as well as by establishing a bureau of international correspondence, which was really an extension of Grégoire's own.[125] In this domain of endeavor the relation to the clergy of Utrecht is thus less a parallel than it is a simple continuation—so much so indeed that the very first layperson to have spontaneously written a "letter of felicitation" to the National Council of 1797 was a certain Le Comte, director of postal services and former commissioner of the taille in Richelieu in Poitou, who had individually adhered to the Council of Utrecht's *Acts* in 1766.[126] Although Grégoire bore the burden of this correspondence, the aged abbé Clément—still alive if not entirely well as bishop of Versailles—remained on duty at the crossroads of the Jansenist International and most certainly rerouted its traffic to take in Grégoire, whose epistolary traces first show up in Utrecht in 1795.[127] In using this correspondence to elicit letters of communion, Grégoire like Dupac de Bellegarde before him was most successful in Italy, which sent the only genuine foreign delegates to the National Council of 1801 in the persons of Giovanni Francesco Bergancini and Eustachio Degola from Casal and Genoa.[128] To the surviving veterans of the Italian Jansenist International who stayed at home, the sight of these quasi-independent Gallican councils could not but stir all but extinguished ashes of hope for one last time. "The National Council of France now interests me for the sake of the church," wrote Pujati to Mouton in Utrecht of the first of these councils in 1798. "While the French [armies] are now taking away [territory] from Rome that their ancestors once gave her, perhaps God can yet reform the church in head and members by means of a French clergy that the supercilious Romans regard as schismatic."[129]

Reliance on the Jansenist International and relative independence from the state perforce gave the post-Thermidorian constitutional church a somewhat more Jansenist caste than was the case at the beginning of its career in 1790.[130] At ground level—to cite only one such index—the overwhelming bulk of lay donations for the support of the impoverished delegates to the National Council of 1797 meeting in Paris came from the traditionally most Jansenist parishes of Paris, with Saint-Médard in the lead followed by Saint-Etienne-du-Mont and Saint-André-des-Arts.[131] Among bishops, such Jansenists as Clément and Jean-Baptiste Saurine were more influential in the leadership of the church than before, as were Paul Baillet and Paul Brugière among priests and Pierre-Jean Agier and Charles-Jacques Saillant among lay consultants. Although he had not clearly been a Jansenist in a strictly theological sense before 1795, Grégoire himself became more of one after that date. He penned the first edition of his *Ruines de Port-Royal* in 1801, and, as one of the founders of the Gallican Church's periodical mouthpiece, the *Annales de la religion,* Grégoire availed himself of the editorial assistance of Jansenists Noël de Larrière as well as Guénin de Saint-Marc, who was also the principal editor of the *Nouvelles ecclésiastiques.*[132] If neither of the councils produced an Augustinian doctrinal statement comparable to that of Utrecht in 1763 and or the Synod of Pistoia in 1786, this was not for want of good intentions, as the abbé Clément drafted a statement of doctrine—the same one he had never succeeded in obtaining from the papacy—condemning such post-Tridentine "errors" as Molinism and ultramontanism, and had submitted his report to the Council of 1801 on 4 July, a month or so before it came to a premature conclusion at Bonaparte's command.[133]

That much said, this short-lived Gallican Church can no more be simply categorized as Jansenist than its two councils as simple replays of the provincial council of Utrecht or the Synod of Pistoia. To be sure, the Gallican church "fathers" were well aware of the precedents of 1763 and 1786, to which Grégoire made reference in his inaugural address to the second National Council of Paris in 1801.[134] But while Utrecht and Pistoia had opposed a factitious "unanimity" to papal infallibility, the two councils of Paris, with the legislative experience of the whole French Revolution behind them, shelved the desideratum of "moral unanimity" each time it was invoked, contenting themselves with simple majorities and making no effort to conceal the extent or subject of the divisions in their ranks. That of 1797 featured spirited debates on the use of vernacular languages in the liturgy, the relation of the civil contract to the sacrament in marriage, and the respective roles of the laity and clergy in the election of the clergy. And the large number of curés delegated by the presbyteries of vacant or "widowed" dioceses outnumbering the bishops in both national councils—that of 1797 by as many as fifty-seven to thirty-one—produced procedural tensions that erupted in an all-out set-to in the Council of 1801 between the bishops of Auch and Saint-Claude on the one hand, partisans of a purely episcopal Gallicanism, and on the other hand the curés François Detorcy and Augustin Frappier—the latter a veteran signer of circular letters of communion to Utrecht—who defended the rights of curés as voting members along with bishops in national and general councils. In this debate delegates heard the names of Maultrot and Mey not only reverentially cited but also taken vitriolically in vain.[135] And while Jansenism was far from unrelated to such projects as the purification of Roman ritual, the vernacular translation of the Scriptures and liturgy, the campaign against the "ignorant piety of scapulars and rosaries," and ecumenical conversation with Protestant and Orthodox churches—all initiatives undertaken by the two national councils—these were causes that also linked the Gallican Church to projects of the

Catholic Enlightenment of the earlier eighteenth century.[136] For yet another of Grégoire's creations, the Society of Christian Philosophy, expressly set out to reclaim the century's "lights" from their distortion by unbelief.

Here, in these two councils in Paris, all the conciliar possibilities of eighteenth-century European Catholicism were finally if only fleetingly realized: a conciliar Catholic church enjoying a modicum of independence from a constitutional state which, since the extension of French borders since 1794, intermittently included both Utrecht and Pistoia. Indelibly associated with Jansenism throughout the century, the conciliar cause here also had a prospect of including Jansenism without being dominated by it, and of acquiring a momentum of its own.

From the perspective of the Directorial Republic of 1795–99, it would seem to have made good sense to maintain toward this church a policy of benevolent neutrality. After all, the Gallican Church was "republican" both in its internal structure and external stance toward the state, going well beyond Utrecht's acceptance of the Dutch Republic's legitimate authority as a temporal state by proclaiming in the Council of 1797 that "republican government is that which most closely conforms to the principles of the gospel," founded as it was on principles recalling "the very order that Jesus Christ came to restore on earth."[137] Every indication is that Grégoire at least also sincerely accepted the principle of separation from the state and the freedom of religion it entailed, even if, as Bernard Plongeron reminds us, nobody in the constitutional clergy entirely broke with the notion of Christendom and Grégoire viewed separation as a means for the revival of Catholicism in France.[138] The capacity of this church to survive under a republic was assured by the existence of enough Frenchmen who wished "to be republicans while never ceasing to be Christians," in the words of a petition sent by communes in the Drôme to the Convention just as "dechristianization" was getting under way in 1793.[139] About all the Gallican Church asked of the state was to be spared the obligation of active compliance with laws calculated to torment Catholic consciences, as in the case of the *décadi*—and of course an end to persecution.

That is what it never obtained from the Directorial Republic. Indeed, the persecution that befell the Gallican clergy after the coup of 18–19 Fructidor by reason of non-compliance in the enforcement of the *décadi* was more purely governmental than that of the "dechristianization" of the year II and the Terror. That government's conceptual incapacity to come to terms with the post-constitutional church ought perhaps to be seen as one of the causes of its failure, along with its inability to put up with the results of its own elections or the formation of political parties.[140]

It was not until after Napoleon Bonaparte's coup d'état of 18–19 Brumaire and the formation of the government of the consulate that this church enjoyed a reprieve from the persecution, holding the Council of 1801 with the government's permission. "At the epoch in question, that it to say in 1800 or 1801," wrote Grégoire eight years later, "nothing was easier than to maintain this constitutional clergy in place."[141] Whether easy or not, it is not implausible to imagine this church continuing to exist and negotiating with the papacy and refractory clergy as best it could, even if the schism had never come to an end and the republic, as in the Netherlands, had had to contend with two catholic churches instead of one. To the formerly refractory clergy the two national councils in fact proposed conciliatory conferences and offered bishoprics and even mass resignations in their favor on condition of accepting the republican government and the formerly constitutional clergy as Catholic. To these overtures the refractory clergy responded with hostile pamphlets and, often, the practice of baptizing and remarrying the constitutional clergy's former parishioners—something that the Catholic Church had not even demanded of converted Protestants in the worst days of the sixteenth-century wars of religion—although in the very long run it is possible to imagine them settling down, becoming a missionary clergy under the authority of the papacy, and even accepting the republic, as Pius VI himself finally recommended that they do in the brief *Pastoralis Sollicitudo* issued in 1796.[142]

Vis-à-vis the papacy, the Gallican Church would at the minimum have held out for what it considered the canonical mode of election of the clergy by clergy and people, for the right of metropolitan bishops to confirm their newly elected suffragans, as well as for the right of both the clergy and the government to approve of or reject new papal bulls and briefs.[143] It is of course unlikely that the Gallican Church would have obtained these conditions even with the support of the government, whereupon it would have probably convened the general council that the second National Council in 1801 had included in its agenda.[144] As late as April 1802—that is, just as the provisions of the Napoleonic concordat were being revealed—one of Ricci's old allies, Bishop Pannili of Chiusi and Pienza in Tuscany, still dared to nurture the "hope . . . that this quarrel [between the Gallican Church and the papacy] would create the need for a general council in which, besides this affair, other matters would be resolved, such as the recognition of our union with Utrecht . . . as well as the annulment of the bull [*Unigenitus*] that serves as such an obstacle for the weak-minded, persuading them to condemn precious propositions from the Sacred Scriptures and Holy Fathers." But failing this council he hoped that a Bonaparte advised by Grégoire would insist on "at least a little compassion for the poor Utrechters and get the four Gallican articles recognized by all . . . as Catholic not only in France but by the whole church."[145]

But all that supposed the continued existence of the French Republic whereas Napoleon's concordat with the papacy, which put an end to the Gallican Church, was already negotiated as though by a monarchy. That Napoleon Bonaparte was more of a philosophe than a Catholic could have been known in 1801 by anyone who cared to know it, but what was perhaps not duly appreciated by most of the Gallican Clergy much less Pannili in 1801 is that he was not a very fervent republican either. Arguably, he was a better Catholic than he was a republican because he at least appreciated the force of a hierarchical and authoritarian ecclesiastical structure that commanded obedience, and which, if he could commandeer it, would enable him better to command in France as well. Years later while on visit to Holland he spoke disparagingly of the so-called Archbishop of Utrecht and the so-called Bishops of Deventer and Haarlem.[146]

Negotiated on high and above the heads of all concerned, the Concordat gave Bonaparte the power enjoyed by the Old Regime kings to nominate all of France's bishops while his unilaterally added "organic articles" gave these bishops in turn a power never enjoyed by their predecessors: that of naming their parish curés. The only Gallican feature of these provisions was the "royal" one of state control of the church: the papal acceptance of the Revolution's nationalization of church property, the inclusion of twelve formerly constitutional bishops in the new episcopacy, and of course the state's right to inspect and reject all papal bulls and briefs destined for France. Thus did the concordat make short shrift of the Gallican Church's experimentation with synods, presbyteries, metropolitan and national councils—and with them, a half century's hopes for conciliar ecclesiastical reform and the limited independence that formal separation from the state had finally promised. Such "liberties" as were to be had vis-à-vis the state could therefore only be sought by means of the total sacrifice of the Gallican liberties in relation to the papacy, whose power over the Gallican Clergy the Concordat enormously enhanced. Not only did the papacy regain the power to consecrate bishops at the expense of their immediate metropolitan superiors, but it was by virtue of papal authority that the entire episcopacy was abolished and reconstituted *de novo,* as though this church had never existed before. (The clergy of Utrecht had always resisted such a papal reconstitution in negotiations toward reunion with Rome.) In order to effect this canonical revolution the pope demanded and obtained the resignations of just about all the formerly constitutional bishops and most of the formerly refractory ones, dismissing the thirty who resisted. Those formerly constitutional bishops who were reappointed as bishops squared this unprecedented procedure with their Gallican consciences by submitting their resignations in what they deemed a canonical way, most of them to their metropolitans, and by signing a letter to the papacy that fell short of retracting their oath to the Civil Constitution. But they were joined by formerly refractory bishops who, armed with papal briefs, were soon demanding such retractions from the curés who fell under their authority.

Neither the influence of the formerly refractory clergy in the Gallican Church nor the future increase in papal power were widely foreseen in 1801, and Grégoire could legitimately congratulate himself in negotiating a discharge for the constitutional clergy far more honorable than it would have obtained from a Bonaparte left to his own authoritarian instincts.[147] Yet the long-term implications of the Concordat did not go unperceived by worldly-wise Italians or a seasoned observer of curial diplomacy like the abbé Clément, who excoriated the Concordat even before he knew its chief provisions.[148] Getting wind of the Concordat's chief provisions, Vincenzo Palmieri wrote to Degola from Genoa in August 1801 that although the plan of resignations by both clergies "did not displease" him, he would have liked to see it paired with "an authentic and solemn act acknowledging the reason and zeal of the constitutional bishops." Otherwise, he warned, the papal briefs against the constitutional clergy of 1791 and the bull *Auctorem Fidei* condemning the Synod of Pistoia of 1794 were so many means at the papacy's disposal to validate its interpretation of events in due course.[149] Degola himself, who attended the Second National Council, was even more prescient, warning the council on 15 July 1801 that any mass resignations on the part of the constitutional clergy would sooner or later mean "the most complete victory of ultramontane maxims."[150]

Thus ended a half-century's efforts to reform the Catholic Church. Whether it be called "reform" Catholicism, "enlightened" Catholicism or "Jansenism," the general drift of these efforts tended toward a more deliberative and decentralized ecclesiastical structure better able to accommodate national liturgical differences and forms of lay initiative as well as a church more open to renewed conversation with Protestants and Orthodox and some of the coming century's profounder movements, most notably the political coming to age of "the people." The greatest risk in attempting to dismantle papal centralization was of course the division of the Catholic Church into so many national churches and the subjection of each to "absolute" states. It is in the light of that risk that the Provincial Council of Utrecht, the Synod of Pistoia, and the two French national councils of 1797 and 1801 constitute such special if fragile moments. The chances of success for this reformist endeavor were slim enough, and are perhaps of interest only to devotees of lost causes. What is certain is that these efforts, having everywhere sustained a rude blow by the French Revolution from the "left," were then—and just when it seemed as though all might not be lost—dealt the *coup de grâce* by the Concordat from the "right." The Napoleonic Concordat is as good a candidate as any for marking the end of the French Revolution. For while the constitutional clergy knew very well that they could not survive the demise of the Republic, the republicans never understood that the Republic could not survive the demise of the constitutional Gallican Church.

Notes

1. In the immense literature on the Catholic Church and French Revolution, the work to begin with is André Latreille, *L'église catholique et la Révolution française,* 2 vols. (Paris: Hachette, 1946–50).

2. On the history of the Civil Constitution, Ludovic Sciout's work remains indispensable. See *Histoire de la Constitution civile du clergé et de la persécution révolutionnaire (1790–1801),* 4 vols. (Paris: Firman-Didot, 1887). And on the "constitutional" clergy that accepted it, another indispensable "classic" is Dom Henri Leclercq's *L'église constitutionnelle, juillet 1790–avril 1791* (Paris: Letouzey, 1934).

3. Edgar Quinet, *La révolution* (Alençon: Belin, 1987), 150.

4. M. G. Spiertz, *Eglise catholique des Provinces-Unies et la Saint-Siège pendant la deuxième moitié du XVIIe siècle* (Louvain: Publications Universitaires de Louvain, 1975).

5. For this and the following account, I am largely dependent on B. A. van Kleef, *Geschiedenis van de Oud-Katholieke Kerk van Nederland,* 2d ed. (Assen: Gorkum, 1953). But Dupac de Bellegarde's Jansenist and obviously partial history remains in many respects a useful source of detailed information. See Dupac de Bellegarde, *Histoire abrégée de l'église métropolitaine d'Utrecht, principalement depuis la révolution arrivée dans les 7 provinces unies des Pays-Bas, sous Philippe II, jusqu'à présent* (Utrecht: J. Schelling, 1784).

6. On this council in general, and the French domination of it in particular, see B. A. van Kleef, "Das Utrechter Provinzialkonzil vom Jahre 1763" in *Internationale kirchliche Zeitschrift;* "Die Zeit vor dem Konzil" 49, no. 4 (1959): 197–228; and "Das Konzil" 49, no. 2 (1960): 65–91, esp. 222–27.

7. Pierre Le Clerc's "errors" and "heresies" are analyzed and condemned in "reports" I–VII by François Meganck, dean of the metropolitan church of

Utrecht, in *Actes et décrets du II*[e] *Concile provincial d'Utrecht, tenu le 13 septembre MDCCLXIII dans la chapelle de l'Eglise provinciale de Sainte Gertrude, à Utrecht* (Utrecht: au dépens de la compagnie, 1764), 108–231.

8. The "errors" of Hardouin, Berruyer, and Pichon are analyzed and condemned in reports VIII–IX in *Actes et décrets du IIe Concile provincial d'Utrecht,* 236–376. For an example of the treatment of Hardouin and Berruyer in the Jansenist press, see the *Nouvelles ecclésiastiques, ou Mémoires pour servir à l'histoire de la constitution Unigenitus* (Utrecht, 1728–1803), 19 March 1760, 49–64.

9. *Actes et décrets du IIe Concile provincial d'Utrecht,* 376–94.

10. "Discours de M. l'Illustrissime et Révérendissime Archévêque d'Utrecht, président, au Concile provincial," in *Actes et décrets du IIe Concile provincial d'Utrecht,* 10.

11. "IIIe rapport. De la primauté du pape, par François Meganck," in *Actes et décrets du IIe Concile provincial d'Utrecht,* 142–43, 171–73.

12. Het Utrechts Archief (hereafter HUA), Inventaire des pièces d'archives françaises se rapportant à l'Abbaye de Port-Royal des Champs et son cercle et à la résistance contre la bulle Unigenitus et à l'appel, (henceforth 215), Ms 2767, Clément to Pierre-Jean Meindaerts, Archbishop of Utrecht, 13 September 1764.

13. The Council of Jerusalem refers to the meeting in Acts 6:1–7 where the twelve apostles and the "disciples" chose seven "deacons."

14. *Nouvelles ecclésiastiques* (28 May and 11 June 1764), 85, 93.

15. Van Kleef, "Das Utrechter Provinzialkonzil vom Jahre 1763: Das Konzil," 91.

16. This tactic is spelled out in so many words in manuscript notes from a conference of "friends" in Vienna, 27 December 1767, in HUA, 215, Ms 2630. On the example of the parlements in the case of the Jesuits, see Jean Egret, "Le procès des jésuites devant les parlements de France," *Revue historique* 204 (July-Dec.): 1–27.

17. HUA, OKN Aartsbisschoppen Utrecht (henceforth R86–1), Ms 107, 9 October 1764.

18. HUA, 215, Ms 2439, Archbishop van Nieuwenhuizen to Dupac de Bellegarde, 22 April 1770.

19. On the status of the Reformed Church in the Netherlands, see Wayne te Brake's chapter in this volume.

20. For a fuller version of this argument, see Dale K. Van Kley, *The Religions Origins of the French Revolution: From Calvin to the Civil Constitution, 1560–1791* (New Haven: Yale University Press, 1996), 15–74.

21. I am here dependent on the work of Aimé-Georges Martimort, *Le gallicanisme de Bossuet* (Paris: Editions du Cerf, 1953), 70.

22. On the condemnation of Fénelon, see Denis Richet, "Fénelon contre Bossuet: La querelle du quiétisme," *De la réforme à la Révolution: Etudes sur la France moderne* (Paris: Aubier, 1991), 119–39.

23. See Van Kley, *The Religious Origins of the French Revolution,* 100, 160–70.

24. On Jansenists in the Bastille, see Monique Cottret, *La Bastille à prendre: histoire et mythe de la forteresse royale* (Paris: P.U.F., 1986), 35–73; and on their tactics of resistance, the same author's *Jansénisme et lumières: Pour un autre dix-huitième siècle* (Paris: Albin Michel, 1998), 270–301.

25. On Quesnel's injunction to read Scripture, see *Unigenitus*'s condemnation in Augustin Gazier, *Histoire générale du mouvement janséniste depuis ses origines jusqu'à nos jours,* 2 vols. (Paris: Honoré Champion, 1924), 2: 326. On Jansenist translations after Sacy's in the course of the eighteenth century, see Bernard Chédozeau, "Les traductions de la Bible, le jansénisme, et la Révolution," in *Jansénisme et Révolution,* ed. Catherine Maire, *Chroniques de Port-Royal* 39 (Paris: S.A.P.R., 1990), 219–39. And on Jubé's innovations, see Cottret, *Jansénisme et lumières,* 250–53.

26. Michel Albaric, "Regard des jansénistes sur l'église de France de 1780 à 1789," *Jansénisme et Révolution,* 72. See also Van Kley, *The Religious Origins of the French Revolution,* 100–8, 164–66.

27. On Jansenists and toleration, see Jeffrey Merrick, *The Desacralization of the French Monarchy in the Eighteenth Century* (Baton Rouge, La.: University of Louisiana Press, 1990); and the many articles by Charles O'Brien, summed up in his "Jansénisme et tolérance civile à la veille de la Révolution," in *Jansénisme et Révolution,* 131–45.

28. Van Kley, *The Religious Origins of the French Revolution,* 180–90.

29. Voltaire, "secte," in *Dictionnaire philosophique, comprenant les 118 articles parus sous ce titre du vivant de Voltaire avec leurs suppléments parus dans les Questions sur l'Encyclopédie,* ed. Raymond Naves (Paris: Garnier Frères, 1967), 385.

30. Jean Le Rond d'Alembert, *Sur la destruction des jésuites en France, par un auteur désintéressé* (n.p., 1765), 103.

31. A homology nowhere more brilliantly suggested than in Edgar Quinet's *Le christianisme et la Révolution française* (Paris: Fayard, 1984), 229–45, esp. 240–41.

32. Edmund Burke, *Reflections on the Revolution in France* (Indianapolis and New York: Bobbs-Merrill, 1955), 95–102.

33. For an example of such a call, see the anonymous, *Lettre à M. xxx, chevalier de l'ordre de Malte, touchant en écrit 'Sur la destruction des jésuites en France'* ("en France," 1765), 26.

34. The full lineaments of this "Counter-Enlightenment" have now been ably sketched out by Darrin McMahon in "Enemies of the Enlightenment: Anti-*Philosophes* and the Birth of the French Far Right, 1778–1830" (Ph.D. dissertation: Yale University, 1997).

35. Elisabeth Labrousse, "*Une foi, une loi, un roi?": Essai sur la révocation de l'Edit de Nantes,* no. 7, Histoire et société (Geneva and Paris: Labor et Fides, 1985), 39–44.

36. Marie-José Michel, "Clergé et pastorale janséniste à Paris, 1669–1730," *Revue de l'histoire moderne et contemporaine* 27 (April–June 1979): 177–97.

37. Charles de Labriolle, "Le concile d'Embrun de 1727, révélateur de la société du 18e siècle," *Bulletin de la Société d'études des Hautes Alpes* (1966): 143–56; and Marcel Laurent, "Jean Soanen, évêque de Senez devant le 'Concile' d'Embrun (1727)," *Revue d'Auvergne* 82 (1968): 94–112.

38. On Richerism, see of course Edmond Préclin, *Les jansénistes et la Constitution civile du clergé: le développement du richérisme, sa propagation dans le bas clergé* (Paris: Libraire universitaire J. Gamber, 1929).

39. *Atti e decretti del concilio diocesano di Pistoia dell'anno 1786,* 2 vols., ed. Pietro Stella (Florence: Olschi, 1986), "Decreto della fede e della chiesa," sessione III, 1: 77. See as well Stella's "L'oscurimento delle verità nella chiesa dal sinodo di Pistoia alla bolla 'Auctorem fidei' (1786–1794)," *Salesianum rivista trimestrale di cultura ecclesiastica* 43 (1981): 731–56. On figurism in general, see Catherine L. Maire, *La cause de Dieu à la cause de la nation: le jansénisme au dix-huitième siècle* (Paris: Gallimard, 1998), 163–234.

40. [Abbé Claude Mey and Gabriel-Nicolas Maultrot], *Apologie de tous les jugemens rendus par les tribunaux séculiers en France contre le schisme,* 2 vols. ("en France," 1752).

41. [Abbé Claude Mey and Gabriel-Nicolas Maultrot] et al., *Maximes du droit public françois,* 2 vols. (Amsterdam: Marc-Michel Rey, 1775), 1: 269.

42. [Louis-Adrien Le Paige], *Lettres historiques sur les fonctions essentielles du parlement, sur le droit des pairs, et sur les loix fondamentaux du royaume,* 2 vols. (Amsterdam, 1753–54).

43. For example, *La conférence entre un ministre d'état et un conseiller au parlement* (n.p., n.d.) and *Suite de la conférence. . . ,* pamphlets in which Le Paige himself probably still had a hand judging from his handwritten corrections in his copies of them in Bibliothèque de Port-Royal (henceforth BPR), Collection Le Paige, Ms 915, no. 6.

44. [Gabriel-Nicolas Maultrot], *Les droits de la puissance temporelle, défendue contre la seconde partie des Actes de l'Assemblée du clergé de 1765 concernant la religion* (Amsterdam, 1777), 82.

45. [Mey and Maultrot], *Apologie de tous les jugemens,* 1: 348.

46. For an extended treatment of all these texts, see Dale K. Van Kley, "Church, State, and the Ideological Origins of the French Revolution," *Journal of Modern History* 51 (December 1979): 629–66.

47. For example, in Le Paige's anonymously published *Lettres adressées à mm. les commissaires nommés par le roi pour délibérer sur l'affaire présente du parlement au sujet du refus de sacrements, ou Lettres pacifiques au sujet des contestations présentes* (n.p., 1753).

48. Dale Van Kley, *The Damiens Affair and the Unraveling of the Old Regime, 1757–1770* (Princeton: Princeton University Press, 1984), 13–55, 226–65.

49. Abbé Augustin-Charles-Jean Clément du Tremblay, *Journal de correspondances et voyages d'Italie et d'Espagne pour la paix de l'église en 1758, 1768 et 1769 par M. Clément, alors trésorier de l'église d'Auxerre, et depuis évêque de Versailles,* 3 vols. (Paris: Longuet, 1802), vol. 1.

50. HUA, 215, Ms 3441, Clément to Mouton, 3 January 1793.

51. Samuel J. Miller, *Portugal and Rome, c.1748–1830: an Aspect of the Catholic Enlightenment* (Rome, Università Gregoriana, 1978).

52. For Bottari's advice, see Archives de la Bastille, Bibliothèque de l'Arsenal, Ms 12883, fols. 152, 157; and for Clément's summary, HUA, 215, Ms 2676, Clément to Rivière, 31 January 1761.

53. Ibid.

54. Dale K. Van Kley, *The Jansenists and the Expulsion of the Jesuits from France, 1757–65* (New Haven:Yale University Press, 1975), 37–136.

55. See Anton de Haen's "Résultat de la conférence tenue à Vienne le 27 décembre 1767 fête de Saint-Jean" in HUA, 215, Ms 2630. On Maria Theresa and Austrian Jansenism, see Reginald Ward's "Late Jansenism and the Habsburgs" in this volume. On De Haen, see J. Broersma, *Antonius de Haen, 1704–1776: leven en werk* (Assen: Vrije Universiteit van Amsterdam, 1963).

56. On the riot in Madrid, see Charles Noel's chapter in this volume.

57. Owen Chadwick, *The Popes and the European Revolution* (Oxford: Clarendon Press, 1981), 364–68. *Unam Sanctam* was issued by Boniface VIII in 1302 and represented the apogee of papal imperial claims. Philip the Fair of France was the king whose attempt to tax the Gallican clergy provoked the bull in question.

58. On Foggini's advice, see HUA, 215, Ms 2207–2, Foggini to Clément, 13 November 1771; and on Dupac de Bellegarde's trip to Rome, see his manuscript "Journal du voyage de Dupac d'Utrecht à Rome et de son séjour à cette ville, 1774 juin 19–Oct 2," in HUA, 215, Ms 2619. See also Pontien Polman, OFM, *Katholieke Nederland in de Achttiende Eeuw,* 3 vols. (Hilversum, 1968), 2: 157–59.

59. Ibid., 215, Ms 2557, De Vecchi to Dupac de Bellegarde, 25 January 1775; and Ms 2153, Del Mare to same, 23 March 1787.

60. Enrico Dammig, *Il movimento giansenista a Roma nella seconda meta del secolo XVIII* (Cita del Vaticano, Bibliotteca Apostolica Vaticana, 1945), 207–12.

61. Giuseppe Pignatelli, *Aspetti della propaganda cattolica a Roma da Pio VI a Leone XII* (Roma: Istituto per la Storia del Risorgimento Italiano, 1974).

62. Mario Rosa, *Riformatori e ribelli nel '700 religioso italiano* (Bari: Dedalo, 1969).

63. HUA, 215, Ms 2489, Ricci to Dupac de Bellegarde, 6 January 1782 and 2 February 1783.

64. Bibliothèque de Saint-Sulpice (henceforth BSS), Collection Clément (henceforth CC), Ms 1291, no. 761, Pujati to Clément, 24 January 1786. Pujati's correspondence with Clément has been published by Maurice Vaussard, *L'epistolario di G. M. Pujati col canonico Clément di 7 di ottobre 1776–19 di dicembre 1786* (Venice: Fondazione Giorgio Cini, 1964).

65. HUA, 215 Ms 2557, De Vecchi to Dupac, 30 June 1783.

66. BSS, CC, Ms 1291, nos. 747–49.

67. Bernard Plongeron, "Recherches sur l' 'Aufkläring' catholique en Europe occidental, 1770–1830," *Revue d'histoire moderne et contemporaine* 16 (1969): 555–605.

68. Emile Appolis, *Le "tiers parti" catholique au dix-huitième siècle* (Paris: Picard, 1960), 369–512. For first-hand evidence of this falling out, see the Augustinian General Francisco-Xavier Vasquez's letter to Dupac in HUA, 215, Ms 2556, 28 May 1775.

69. Giovan Vincenzo Bolgeni, *Della carita o Amor di Dio Dissertazione* (Roma: Stampiera Salomini, 1788).

70. Alberto Aquarone, "Giansenismo italiano e rivoluzione francese prima del Triennio giacobino" in *Rassengna storica del Risorgimento: organo della Societa nazionale per la storia del Risorgimento italiano* 39 (1962): 559–624.

71. Maire, *De la cause de Dieu à là cause de la nation*, 363; and HUA, 215, Ms 2551, no. 100, Di Gros to Dupac de Bellegarde, 28 March 1783.

72. On Lami, see Eric Cochrane, *Florence in the Forgotten Centuries, 1527–1800: A History of Florence and the Florentines in the Age of the Grand Dukes* (Chicago: University of Chicago Press, 1973), 317–96.

73. Lodovico Antonio Muratori, *Della regolata divozione de' Christiani, trattato di Lamindo Pritanio* [pseudonym] (Trent: Monauni, 1766).

74. On this point, see Acquarone, "Giansenismo italiano e rivoluzione francese prima del Triennio giacobino," 613–14. On a clear statement of the doctrinal basis of this campaign, see the "Decreto delle grazia, della predestinazione,

e dei fondamenti della morale" in *Atti e decreti del concilio diocesano di Pistoia dell' anno 1786*, ed. Pietro Stella, ristampa dell'edizione Bracali, 2 vols. (Florence: Olschki, 1986), 1:90.

75. For an idea of the extent of this exportation, see Maurice Vaussard, *Jansénisme et gallicanisme aux origines religieuses du Risorgimento* (Paris: Letouzey et Ane, 1959).

76. For example, the Roman Oratorian and professor Andrea Micheli's complaint in 1767 that to the "ignoranze" and "indolenza" all too natural to Italians now "s'aggiungo, che molti de quei, che leggono qualche cose, se perdono nella lettura e dei Rousseau, e di Voltaire, e d'altri simuli libri pieni d'irreligione, e d'impietà." BSS: CC, Ms 1291, no. 293, Micheli to Clément, 21 October 1767.

77. Pietro Tamburini, *Lettere teologico-politiche sulla presente situzione delle cose ecclesiastiche*, 2 vols. (Pavia: Stampiera di Baldassara Comini, 1794), 1:2.

78. The synod's published acts and decrees contain a detailed account of participants of which "parochi" is no. 171. See *Atti e decreti del concilio diocesano di Pistoia*, 18–27.

79. "Scipione de' Ricci per la misericordia di Dio vescovo di Pistoia e Prato, ai venerabili fratelli consacerdoti e cooperatori suoi della citta, e diocesi di Pistoia," in *Atti e decreti del concilio diocesano di Pistoia*, 1–8.

80. "Decreto della grazia, della predestinazione, e dei fondamenti della morale," 84–96; "decreto della penitenza," 141–57; and "decreto della fede e della chiesa," 75–83, but esp. 78, 81–82; and "decreto della preghiera," 209–10 in *Atti e decreti del concilio diocesano di Pistoia*.

81. References to the occasional "obscurity" of the truth are to be found in *Atti e decreti del concilio diocesano di Pistoia*, 5, 32, 77, 84, 216. On this point see Pietro Stella, "L'oscurimento della verità nella chiesa dal sinodo di Pistoia alla bolla 'Auctorem fidei' (1786–1794)," *Salesianum rivista trimestrale di cultura ecclesiastica* 43 (1981): 731–56.

82. Scipione de' Ricci's letter of convocation dated 31 July 1786 and printed as part of *Atti e decreti del concilio diocesano di Pistoia*, 1–8.

83. HUA, R86–1, Ms. 170, Scipione de' Ricci, met minute van akte, waarbij van Nieuwenhuizen, Broekman en Nobelman hun adhsesie betuigen aan het concilie van Pistoia 1789. For Dutch reaction to the Synod of Pistoia, see Peter J. van Lessel, "Il Paesi Bassi e il sinodo di Pistoia," in *Il sinodo di Pistoia del 1786: Atti de Convengo per il secondo centenario Pistoia-Prato, 25–27 settembre 1986*, ed. Claudio Lamioni (Rome: Herder, 1991), 401–9.

84. "Decreto dell' ordine" in *Atti e decreti del concilio diocesano di Pistoia*, 163–80, esp.165–66, 171–79; along with "promemoria riguardante la riforma dei regolari," 235–39.

85. "Decreto della eucharistia" in *Atti e decreti del concilio diocesano di Pistoia,* 123–33; quotations on 125, 130.

86. "Decreto della preghiera," and "della preghiera pubblica," in *Atti e decreti del concilio diocesano di Pistoia,* 196–211; as well as "promenoria circa la riforma dei giuramenti" and "sulla riforma delle feste," 225–33. For critique against "superstition" in the name of a "regulated" devotion, see 200, 202.

87. HUA, 215, Ms 3603, no. 64, Tamburini to Zola, 18 December 1786.

88. Ibid., Ms 2518, Scheidel to Dupac, 7 March 1789. On the Congress of Ems, see Timothy C. W. Blanning, *Reform and Revolution in Mainz, 1743–1803* (Cambridge, London and New York: Cambridge University Press, 1974), 177–79, 220–28. And on reaction to the Synod of Pistoia in general in the Germanic world, see Peter Hersche, "Eco del sinodo di Pistoia nel mondo germanico," *Il sinodo di Pistoia del 1786,* 393–95.

89. HUA, 215, Ms 2207–2, Clément to Dupac, 11 January 1789; Ms 3441, Clément to Mouton, 3 September 1790; and Ms 2489, Dupac de Bellegarde to Ricci, 5 January 1789.

90. On the riots in the spring of 1790, see Cochrane, *Florence in the Forgotten Centuries,* 399–418; on the riot in Pistoia and Prato of 20–21 May 1787, see Carlo Fantappiè, *Riforme ecclesiastiche e resistenze sociali* (Bologna: Mulino, 1986).

91. HUA, 215, Ms 3397, Baldovinetti to Mouton, 2 November 1790; and Ms 2489, fol. 277, Ricci to Dupac de Bellegarde, 12 August 1787.

92. Ibid., Ms 3394, Astorri to Mouton, 29 May 1790.

93. *Dal "problema se i giansenisti siano giacobini"* (Rome: Luigi Perego Salvioni, 1794), as reprinted in Vittorio E. Giuntella, *Le dolci catene, testi della contro-rivoluzione cattolica in Italia* (Rome: Istituto per la Storia del Risorgimento Italiano, 1988), 298, 300, 306.

94. For examples of Jansenism in French counterrevolutionary literature, see Emmanuel-Louis-Henri, comte d'Antraigues, *Dénonciation aux Français catholiques, des moyens employés par l'Assemblée nationale, pour détruire en France, la religion catholique* (London: Edward Pall-Mall, 1791), 5–6; and Joseph de Maistre, *De l'église gallicane dans son rapport avec le souverain pontif* (Lyon: J.-B. Pélagaud, 1862), 106–8.

95. HUA, 215, Ms 3394–2, Astorri to Mouton, 13 July and 19 August 1791.

96. Ibid., Ms 3606, fols. 30–32, Zola to Mouton, undated (but written in spring or late winter of 1794). On Tamburini's *Lettere teologico-politiche* as a defense of secular authority, see Luigi Salvatorelli, *Il pensiero politico italiano dal 1700 al 1870* (n.p.: Giulio Einaudi, 1949), 113–18.

97. HUA, 215, Ms 3441, Di Gros to Mouton, 26 May 1791.

98. Ibid., Ms 3394–1, Astorri to Mouton, 22 September 1790.

99. Ibid., Ms 3441, Clément to Mouton, 3 September 1790.

100. Words attributed to Pius VI by the Neapolitan diplomat L. A. Ferdinandi in correspondence with the Archbishop of Utrecht, to the effect that "le clergé de France ayant voulu soutenir ses libertés, s'est trop tard apperçu qu'au lieu d'être libre comme il auroit été en dépendant du pape qui l'auroit soutenu dans le grandeur où il étoit, il est devenu esclave du Parlement avec ses libertés," in HUA, R86–1, Ms 65, Ferdinadi to van Niewenhuizen, 5 December 1779.

101. [Jacques-Julien Bonnaud], *Découverte importante sur le vrai système de la Constitution du clergé, décrétée par l'Assemblée nationale* (Paris, n.d.), 9–10. This pamphlet has also been attributed to the abbé Barruel.

102. For example, Abbé Augustin Barruel, *Question nationale sur l'autorité et sur les droits du peuple dans le gouvernement, par M l'abbé Barruel* (Paris: Crapart, 1791); Bertrand Capmartin de Chaupy, *Philosophie des lettres qui auroit pu tout sauver. Misosophie Votairienne qui n'a que tout perdre. Ouvrage inutile à la présente tenue des Etats, pour laquelle il avoit été entrepris, mais qui pourra servir à celle qui pourra lui succéder,* 2 vols. (Paris: J. Beuchot, 1789–90); and Jean-Baptiste Duvoisin, *La France chrétienne et vraiment libre* (n.p., 1989). On the formation of this "Religious Right," see J. M. Roberts, "The French Origins of the 'Right'" in *Transactions from the Royal Historical Society,* 23 (1973): 27–53.

103. For recent analyses of this fissure, see Monique Cottret, "Les jansénistes juges de Jean-Jacques," in *Jansénisme et Révolution,* 81–102; and Yann Fauchois, "Les jansénistes et la Constitution civile du clergé: aux marges du débat, débats dans le débat," in *Jansénisme et Révolution,* 195–209.

104. *Archives parlementaires de 1787–1860, première partie (1787–1799),* 94 vols., eds. M. J. Madival and M. E. Laurent (Paris, 1867–), 9 June 1790, 16:154–56.

105. Gabriel-Nicolas Maultrot, *Origines et justes bornes de la puissance temporelle suivant les livres saints et la tradition sainte,* 3 vols. (Paris: Le Clère, 1789). On the *Dissertation sur le droit de convoquer les Etats-Generaux, tirée des capitulaires, des ordonnances, et les autres monumens de l'histoire de France* (n.p. 1787), see Dale Van Kley, "The Estates General as Ecumenical Council: The Constitutionalism of Corporate Consensus and the *Parlement*'s Ruling of September 25, 1788," *Journal of Modern History,* 61 (March 1989): 1–52.

106. On Le Clerc de Juigné, see *Archives parlementaires* (10 August 1789), 8:394; on Boisgelin, 29 May 1790, 15:724–31.

107. The best treatment of this political theology is in Rita Hermon-Belot, "La politique et la vérité: l'abbé Grégoire et la Révolution française," 2 vols. (doctoral thesis, E.H.E.S., Paris, 1999), 1:54–190, now published in shortened form as *L'abbé Grégoire: la politique et la vérité* (Paris: Editions du Seuil, 2000), 63–129, 183–226.

108. Michel Vovelle, *La Révolution contre l'église: de la raison à l'Etre suprême* (Paris: Editions complexes, 1988), esp. 101–54.

109. On the unanticipated novelty of the provisions of the Civil Constitution, see Timothy Tackett, *Religion, Revolution, and Regional Culture in Eighteenth-Century France: the Ecclesiastical Oath of 1791* (Princeton: Princeton University Press, 1986), 6–16; and Dale K. Van Kley, "The Debate over the Gallican Clergy on the Eve of the French Revolution: A Supplementary Introduction to Section III of the Pre-Revolutionary Debate," in Jeremy Popkin and Dale Van Kley, eds., *The Pre-Revolutionary Debate,* section #5 of *The French Revolution Research Collection,* ed. Colin Lucas (Oxford: Pergamon Press, 1989), 19–22.

110. See, again, McMahon, "Enemies of Enlightenment," esp. ch. #1.

111. Siméon-Prosper Hardy, "Mes loisirs, ou Journal d'événemens tels qu'ils parviennent à ma connoissance," 8 vols., Bibliothèque Nationale (henceforth BN), Nouvelles acquisitions (henceforth Nouv. Acq.), Manuscrits Français (henceforth Mss Fr) 6687 (29–30 September 1789), 493–94, 497. The parishes in question are Saint-Jacques de la Boucherie and Saint-Nicolas-des-Champs.

112. For a very similar emphasis on the contingency but decisiveness of this break between the Gallican Church and the Revolution, see Claude Langlois's excellent analysis, "La rupture entre l'Eglise catholique et la Révolution," *The Transformation of Political Culture, 1789–1848,* eds. François Furet and Mona Ozouf, vol. 3 of *The French Revolution and the Creation of Modern Political Culture* (Oxford: Pergamon Press, 1989), 375–90.

113. The most authoritative history of this final phase of the constitutional church's history is now Rodney Dean's "L'Eglise Constitutionnelle, Napoleon et le Concordat de 1801," which he kindly shared with me in ms. I would here like to thank Mr. Dean for his careful critique of this part of the essay, a critique that saved me from many errors.

114. Henri Grégoire, *Discours de Grégoire à la Convention sur la liberté des cultes* as reprinted in Augustin Gazier, *Etudes sur l'histoire religieuse de la Révolution française, d'après des documents originaux et inédits* (Paris: Armand Colin, 1887), "pièces justificatives," 346–47.

115. Joseph Lacouture, *La politique religieuse de la Révolution* (Paris: Picard, 1940), 106–8.

116. "Lettre encyclique de plusieurs évêques de France à leurs frères les autres évêques et aux églises vacantes" in Gazier, *Etudes sur l'histoire religieuse de la Révolution française,* 390–411.

117. John McManners, *The French Revolution and the Church* (New York and Evanston: Harper and Row, 1969), 121.

118. On this structural similarity, see René Taveneaux, "Les anciens constitutionnels et l'église d'Utrecht: à propos de quelques inédits d'Henri Grégoire

et de Joseph Monin," in *Jansénisme et réforme catholique* (Nancy: Presses Universitaires de Nancy, 1993), 177–93.

119. "Recueil des délibérations du Concile national du clergé de France en 1797," in BN, Nouv. acq., Mss Fr. 277079, sessions on 14 August and 7 September, fols. 8–12, 34–35.

120. *Decret de pacification proclamé par le Concile national de France, dans l'église métropolitaine de Notre Dame de Paris, le dimanche 24 septembre 1797*, in *Collection des pièces imprimées par ordre du Concile national de France,* no. 5 (Paris: Imprimerie-Librairie Chrétienne, 1797), 14.

121. *Decret du Concile national de France [de 1797] sur les élections* in *Collection des pièces,* no. 15; and *Seconde lettre encyclique de plusieurs évêques de France, réunis à Paris, à leurs frères les autres évêques et aux églises veuves, concernant un réglement pour servir au rétablissement de la discipline de l'église gallicane* (Paris: Imprimerie-Librairie Chrétienne, 1795), chapters III–IV, 64–120. See also Bernard Plongeron, *L'abbé Grégoire ou L'arche de la fraternité, 1750–1831* (Paris: Letouzey et Ane, 1989), 73–78.

122. *Quatrième lettre syndique du Concile national de France, aux pasteurs et aux fidèles, pour leur annoncer la fin de sa session* (Paris: Imprimerie-Librairie Chrétienne, 12 November 1797), in *Collection des pièces,* no. 12, 8; and *L'église gallicane, assemblée en concile national à Paris, à Sa Sainteté le pape Pie VI,* in *Collection des pièces,* no. 13, 10–11.

123. *Decret de pacification,* in *Collection des pièces,* no. 5, 23–13, 18; and *Seconde lettre encyclique,* 19, 24.

124. "Lettre synodique au clergé incommiquant,"in *Actes du second concile national de France, tenu l'an 1801 de J[ésus] C[hrist] (an 9 de la République française) dans l'église métropolitaine de Paris,* 3 vols. (Paris: Imprimerie Chrétienne, 1801), 1:241.

125. "Recueil des délibérations," BN, Nouv. acq., Mss Fr 277079, sessions of 17 and 19 August, 16 September, and 2 and 24 October, 1797, fols. 20–21, 40–41, 60–61, 83.

126. Ibid., session of 14 August afternoon, fols. 8–12; and HUA, R86–1, Ms 166, 13 July 1766, 3 September 1770.

127. HUA, 215, Ms 3458, Grégoire to Mouton, 23 Frimaire, IV (1795).

128. BPR, Collection Grégoire (henceforth CG), correspondance étrangère, Bishop of Noli to Grégoire, 22 Dec. 1800; and *Actes du second concile nationale de France,* 3:21–54.

129. HUA, 215, Ms 3546, Pujati to Mouton, 23 February, 1798.

130. On the Jansenism of the post-constitutional church, see Rita Hermon-Belot, "La politique et la vérité, 2:664–705; and, in shortened form, *L'abbé Grégoire,* 427–61.

131. A summary count based on the manuscript procès-verbal of the National Council of 1797, "Recueil des délibérations, BN, Mss Fr, 277079, sessions of 5, 11, 13, 18, 22, and 29 September; 3, 5, 8, 10, 20, and 23 October; 11 November.

132. Catherine Maire, *De la cause de Dieu à la cause de la nation,* 577.

133. *Recherches historiques et dogmatiques, de ce que a interessé la doctrine chrétienne depuis le Concile de Trente,* in BPR, GR, RV 108–38 (8292), no. 23, 3–21, a doctrinal statement repeated in Clément's published *Lettre de M. l'évêque de Versailles à S. S. le Pape Pie VII* (n.p., 1801) in BPR, GR, RV 108–38 (8292), no. 38, 1–11. For its place on the agenda of the Council of 1801, see the *Actes du second concile national de France, tenu en 1801,* 1:68, 463.

134. Henri Grégoire, "Discours pour l'ouverture du concile," in *Actes du second Concile national de France, tenu l'an 1801,* 1:130–31.

135. On the mode of election, see "Recueil des délibérations," BN, Mss Fr 277079, sessions of 25, 27, 28, and 29 September; and on the liturgy, see sessions 2, 6, 7, 8 and 9 November. For the debate between proponents of episcopal and parochial Gallicanism, see *Actes du second concile national de France, tenu l'an 1801,* 1:161–425.

136. See Grégoire, *Réclamation des fidèles Catholiques de France au prochain concile national, en faveur de l'usage primitif de la langue vulgaire dans l'administration des sacraments et la célébration de l'office divine* (Paris: Brajeux, 1801); *Traité de l'uniformité et de l'amélioration de la liturgie, présenté au concile nationale de 1801 par le citoyen Grégoire* (Paris: Imprimerie-Librairie, an X), pp. 67, 102–21; and *Compte rendu par le citoyen Grégoire au concile nationale, des travaux des évêques réunis à Paris* (Paris: Imprimerie-Librairie Chretienne, 1797), 65.

137. *Lettre syndique du Concile national de France, aux pasteurs et aux fidèles, sur les moyens de rétablir la paix religieuse,* in *Collection des pièces,* no. 6, 12. Or again, when a draft enjoining obedience to government came up for adoption on 28 July 1801, the Second National Council followed Grégoire's insistence that its reference to republican government be retained, fending off the Bishop of Rennes's attempt to reword the statement to designate only temporal government in general. "I believe," he said, "that in this letter we should display the principles of the government under which we live: it is republican, and so our language, it seems to me, ought to follow suit." See *Actes du second concile national de France, tenu l'an 1801,* 2:283–84.

138. Bernard Plongeron, *Théologie et politique au siècle des lumières, 1770–1820* (Geneva: Droz, 1973), 149–82.

139. BPR, RV168, fol. 25; see also Suzanne Desan, *Reclaiming the Sacred: Lay Religion and Popular Politics in Revolutionary France* (Ithaca: Cornell

University Press, 1990), 135–58. For a recent example of a hostile and very "Roman" treatment of the post-constitutionalist church as non-Catholic, see Jean de La Viguerie, *Christianisme et révolution: Cinq leçons d'histoire de la Révolution française* (Paris: Nel, 1986), 197–203.

140. Lynn Hunt, David Lansky, and Paul Hanson, "The Failure of the Liberal Republic in France, 1795–1799: The Road to Brumaire," *Journal of Modern History* 51 (December 1979): 734–59.

141. Henri Grégoire, *Mémoires de Grégoire, ancien évêque de Blois, député à l'Assemblée Constituente et à la Convention Nationale, Sénateur, membre de l'Institut, suivies de la Notice historique sur Grégoire d'Hippolyte Carnot,* ed. Jean-Michel Leniaud (Paris: Editions de Santé, 1989), 155.

142. The reference is to Pius VI's brief, *Pastoralis Sollicitudo,* on which subject see Plongeron, *Théologie et politique au siècle des lumières,* 131–32, 141–42. La Viguerie, in *Christianisme et révolution,* 200, persists in raising the question of its authenticity.

143. BPR, GR2405ms, doc. 9 "Observations au citoyen consul," 28 August 1801, by Le Coz, Bishop of Rennes; Dufraisse, Bishop of Bourges; Grégoire, Moyse, Bishop of Saint-Claude; and Perier, Bishop of Clermont.

144. *Actes du second Concile national de France, tenu l'an 1801,* session of 7 August, 2:471.

145. BPR, GR, Correspondance étrangère, Italy I, Pannili to Degola, 1 April 1802.

146. L. J. Rogier, "Henri Grégoire en de Katholieken van Nederland," in *Terugblik en Uitzicht: Verspreide Opstellen van L. J. Rogier* (Hilversum and Antwerp: Paul Bland, 1964), 1: 198–99.

147. On the negotiations culminating in the Concordat of 1801 and on Grégoire's role in obtaining more favorable provisions for the formerly constitutional clergy, I am again indebted to Dean, "L'Eglise Constitutionnelle, Napoléon et le Concordat de 1801," chapters I, VI.

148. HUA, 215, Ms 3441, letters from Clément to Mouton from 28 September 1801 to 31 January 1803.

149. BPR, GR, Correspondance étrangère, lettres rendues par Mlle Pernaud le 16 février 1950, Palmieri to Degola, 10 August 1801.

150. Actes du second concile national de France, tenu l'an 1801, 2:87.

TWO

Clerics and Crown in Bourbon Spain, 1700–1808

Jesuits, Jansenists, and Enlightened Reformers

CHARLES C. NOEL

ON THE MORNING OF 2 APRIL 1767, THE HERALDS OF CHARLES III read out a royal pragmatic to the crowds which had gathered before the new royal palace on the western edge of Madrid. The decree initiated one of the most significant events of the age in Spain, a marker for both contemporaries and historians. During the following days, as the pragmatic ordered, a clean, efficient, political and military operation expelled Spain's 2,700 Jesuits. No one, neither the Jesuits themselves, taken by surprise, nor their sympathizers resisted.[1]

Because the decree of 2 April had ordered absolute silence regarding the Jesuits, we know little of Spaniards' reactions. But we can easily imagine the jubilation the news brought the Society's numerous opponents—most of the king's ministers, many bishops, the members of rival religious orders such as the Augustinians, and Jansenist clerics and laymen and anyone jealous or afraid of Jesuit influence. For them, April 1767 was a turning point, a decisive moment in the evolution of eighteenth-century religious ideas, clerical behavior and the complex relationships among religious thinkers, clergy, laymen, and the men who dominated the Spanish monarchy. Examining the Jesuit expulsion helps us understand how complicated these relationships were and to see the anti-Jesuit attack as part of a free-for-all, with deep roots in old quarrels begun as early as the later sixteenth century. Personal rivalries, frustrated clerical and lay ambitions, irrational hatreds, intellectual clashes, competing religiosities, and reasons of state all characterized the enduring confrontation between the Society and its enemies—and among its enemies and supporters, too. In this, the expulsion is a revealing reflection of the context in which it occurred. Rather than a two-way fight—the church versus the state—eighteenth-century Spain endured a protracted series of conflicts which were partly religious, partly political, partly cultural, even partly economic and financial. A varying balance of interests made one episode different from the next, but there was never a straightforward, simple lineup of clerics against laymen. Moreover, we shall see how some of these conflicts and the political and spiritual assumptions they reflected helped generate a degree of ecclesiastical radicalism in the last years of the century.

Although relationships of clerics and laymen were troubled throughout the century, the years from 1753 to 1767 witnessed a particularly crucial series of developments. These began to transform the relationship between the government and many clerics, between the Spanish crown and the papal curia, and between the papacy and Spaniards. The language of debate began to change as well as the aims of the protagonists. During the first half of the century quarrels between the crown and the Curia usually focused on two outstanding issues: the jurisdictional authority of the pope and his nuncio in Madrid, and the patronage in papal hands of many thousands of Spanish church offices. The Hispano-Papal Concordat of 1753, which inaugurated nearly fourteen years of changes, helped to settle the jurisdictional dispute and virtually resolved the question of patronage. Thereafter, the crown and the Curia found themselves on a new and normally less rocky footing. During the 1750s other events helped change the relationship between the government and some clerics and laymen. The fall from power in 1754 of the marquess of la Ensenada, Ferdinand VI's powerful reformist and pro-Jesuit chief minister, initiated a thirteen-year period of anti-Jesuit moves. The next stage was the removal of Ensenada's ally, the Jesuit Francisco Rávago, in 1755. Rávago, confessor to Ferdinand VI, had used his office to dominate the Inquisition, to influence royal ecclesiastical policy, and to shore up the king's Jesuit sympathies. Rávago's fall was another clear victory for the anti-Jesuits.[2] But their greatest stroke of fortune was the death in 1759 of Ferdinand VI and the accession of his half-brother, Charles III. Deeply suspicious of the Society, Charles was determined to control and weaken it, and filled most key ministerial posts and ecclesiastical offices with keen anti-Jesuits. The expulsion of 1767 ended this period of transition leaving the crown, the enemies of the Jesuits, including the Jansenists, the episcopacy, most cultural reformers, and many others strengthened. To show why the fall of the Jesuits and the achievement of the Concordat of 1753 should be emphasized as both symbols and causes of changed relationships in the mid- and later-eighteenth century is the main object of this essay.

The eighteenth-century Spanish Bourbons were fortunate in being able to effectively centralize policymaking and legislation in their own and their ministers' hands. Philip V (1700–46), Ferdinand VI (1746–59), Charles III (1759–88), and Charles IV (1788–1808) or their ministers ensured that royal authority was generally respected and moderately effective, at least until the 1790s. Although they sometimes failed to achieve their goals, they imparted to government a characteristic discipline and energy. Of the four eighteenth-century monarchs, however, only Charles III was a first-rate leader.[3] Philip V and Ferdinand VI were often incapacitated by physical or mental illness and allowed themselves to be dominated by their able but unpopular queens. Charles IV, too, was dominated not only by his wife, the unfortunate María Luisa of Parma, but also by Manuel Godoy. The latter, despite some attractive personal and political qualities, was a disastrous choice as personal favorite and chief political adviser. In contrast, the dutiful and able Charles III possessed many political talents and was a dedicated and resourceful reformer who maintained a particularly outstanding team of ministers and advisers.

Bourbon ministers and councilors were the chief glory of four generations of eighteenth-century government. They were mainly experienced and energetic civil and canon lawyers, usually laymen, though some, like Manuel Ventura Figueroa, who negotiated the Concordat of 1753 and later served as governor of the Council of Castile (1773–83), were clerics. Others were army officers and a very few were grandees—rich and well-connected aristocrats like the count of Aranda, president of the Council of Castile (1766–73), overseer of the Jesuit expulsion and recipient of some avid praise from Voltaire. Whatever their background, Charles's leading administrators were almost always dedicated and imaginative reformers whose principal objectives were to strengthen monarchical authority, bolster modern science and culture, make Spain more prosperous, and enhance her power and standing in Europe and on the seas. Among their many targets for change were the church and clergy. To develop and execute their policies the reformers employed a few prominent bodies in the central administration, particularly the ministries of Finance and Justice and the ancient Council of Castile, the monarchy's highest judicial and administrative forum. Among many other tasks, the councilors of Castile in conjunction with the clerical hierarchy were the foremost watchdogs over clerical behavior and church organizations and inevitably played a key role in the story of the church in the period. Moreover, from the first years of the reign of Charles III, the Council was strongly influenced by reformers determined to impose closer controls over the church and clergy and to remold these in their own reformist image.[4] Outstanding in this regard were the Council's successive chiefs, Aranda and Ventura Figueroa, and several of its *fiscales,* its expert legal advisers. These included José Moñino, later count of Floridablanca, and the best-known and probably most influential of the Caroline reformers, Pedro Rodríguez Campomanes—historian, economist, and an outstanding canon lawyer. The latter in particular was a tough and demanding critic of the clergy, well prepared to confront the church on almost any issue. Campomanes sat on the Council for nearly thirty years, as a fiscal and then as its governor (1762–91). Nor was confrontation unknown within these organs of power. Neither the Council nor its committee for clerical appointments, the Chamber of Castile, were mere rubber stamps for the reformers. Councilors were often divided among themselves, and traditonalists sometimes resisted reformist pressures. Thus Campomanes and his supporters had to work hard to achieve whatever successes they had on the Council, the Chamber, and other commissions.[5]

Some of their opponents in their own day and conservative Catholic historians of later generations repeatedly accused the reformers of being atheists or deists. They were said to aim to destroy Christianity and the church and to undermine morality. Some, like Aranda, were believed to be either Freemasons or their dupes, while others were supposedly motivated by greed and ambition or were simply stupid or ignorant of genuine Catholicism. Nowadays, few historians would agree with any of this. There is no evidence that any of the reformers was not a believing Catholic. Campomanes, often singled out for attack, was typically a member of the Third Order of St. Francis and, like thousands of Spaniards every year, instructed that he be buried in the Franciscan habit. Manuel de Roda, minister of Justice (1765–82), a leading reform figure and bitterly hostile to the Jesuits, was a devoted reader of Thomas à Kempis's *Imitation of Christ* and one of Charles III's most influential advisers.

Roda, like his reformist colleagues, knew the church and its history well and like many thoughtful Christians was unhappy about its state. Post-Tridentine Spanish Catholicism was a richly varied conglomeration of practices and beliefs. While it was typically extravagant, sensual, and emotional, there were always quieter, more austere streams of belief which gained increasing prominence in the eighteenth century. But most Spaniards found exuberant baroque Catholicism more congenial and it was its manifestations that were heavily criticized by the reformers.

Baroque Catholicism has often been identified by historians with popular religion, the slightly degenerate offspring of the wiser and calmer patriarchs who met at Trent—an accidental and abnormal growth generated by popular mishandling of soundly conceived practices. Or, more approvingly, it has been understood as the manifestation of the people's own religiosity, the relatively unfettered spirituality of the unlettered. Recently, several historians have proposed more complex interpretations, at least in the Spanish case.[6] There was, in fact, no substantial difference between the religious practices of the educated elite on one hand and of the largely illiterate masses on the other. Baroque Catholicism was a religion for all, flourishing at all social levels: dukes, archbishops, and kings, as one of Spain's preeminent historians has suggested, "were no less emotional and miracle-seeking than nuns and artisans."[7] Indeed, it had been the spiritual and intellectual elite at Trent who knowingly encouraged "extreme, exaggerated and unmeasured," characteristically baroque piety.[8] To revitalize and extend catholic Christianity, the Tridentine reformers and their successors seized on the emotions and the senses, and encouraged clerics to utilize feeling to promote devotion, to cultivate piety with works of art, myriad images, and specialized devotions, like that of the rosary. They fomented the collection and reverence of relics, an activity spearheaded by cultivated and wealthy laypersons and prominent clerics. With the support of Roman archaeologists and rapacious dealers in antiquities, enthusiasts advanced the age-old interest in Christian relics to new heights of fervor in the seventeenth and early eighteenth centuries. The veneration of relics exemplifies the way in which material objects were employed to create or intensify faith (and loyalty to the church and its clergy). This sacralization of objects was almost unlimited as faith became more highly externalized, directed to what could be touched, adorned, and collected. Statues, paintings, and other images of Christ and the saints multiplied endlessly. Places, too, were sacralized in large numbers. Shrines along country tracks, at city street corners, and in churches and cathedrals increased. Religious processions became an even more common occurrence than earlier, and new popular devotions arose in the seventeenth and eighteenth centuries to join that associated with the rosary. In these, images were used, as in the Sacred Heart of Jesus, promoted by the Jesuits, to intensify spirituality and channel it in particular directions.[9]

The Tridentine model of Christianity was founded in the "social presence" of the church in the midst of society, especially in its parts where the church had heretofore been least present or influential. Thus, possibly more than previously, early modern Spanish religiosity intertwined with sociability. In towns and cities the foremost expression of this link were the pious associations or brotherhoods (or confraternities, *cofradías, hermandades*). They brought together laity and clerics to encourage a specific shrine, altar, image, saint, or devotion, or a certain manifestation of spirituality such as penitence.

Members cared for their altar or image, carried it proudly in street processions, or otherwise advertised and praised it. But while their ostensible objective was spiritual, one of the brotherhoods' ultimate purposes was often mutual social support against inevitable hazards and social injustices. Like British friendly societies, they provided financial and moral aid to members and their families and comforted the distressed. Such associations, while employing the language of religion and sacralized imagery, found their main work dealing with the daily needs of material life, including relaxation and "jollifications," usually at table. Thereby the brotherhoods won the hearts of the masses who cherished the touch of security and pleasure they offered. Although there is some evidence the brotherhoods attracted fewer members in the later eighteenth century, there were still some 24,100 pious associations in 1770.[10]

This confusion of the worldly and festive with the spiritual concerned some observers, as they fretted over the other excesses of baroque religion. The attempt to purify Catholicism of extravagances gave rise to the Spanish Jansenist movement of the eighteenth and early nineteenth centuries. Jansenism in Spain was only weakly tied to the better-known French Jansenist phenomenon. Spaniards shared almost none of the French Jansenists' strictly theological heritage and there is no evidence that Spanish Jansenists were formally heterodox. Rather, Spanish Jansenism was deeply rooted in Iberian humanist and Erasmian traditions of sixteenth-century scholarly and spiritual criticism. Those roots were nourished during the later seventeenth and early eighteenth centuries by French Gallicanism with its deep suspicion of papal authority; by the Maurists and modernizing Jesuit scholars with their respect for the new sciences and for intellectual rigor; and by the numerous thinkers, like Zeger van Espen and Justinius Febronius, who had contributed to widespread questioning of the Tridentine church and its apparent undermining of episcopal power.[11]

By mid-century Spanish Jansenism had become an extraordinarily varied movement, an intellectual tribe, as Joel Saugnieux, one of its leading historians, suggested, composed of different intellectual families. It evolved as its propagators and circumstances changed and became richer and increasingly multifaceted. Thus it became many things at once: political, theological, moral, administrative, undermining some authorities while bolstering others. Its diversity mirrored the wide-ranging interests of its formulators: bishops who favored episcopalism; politicians who pushed royal authority in the form of regalism; theologians who supported conciliarism; other clerics and laymen, intellectuals, who preferred to emphasize enlightened ideas; and so on. Bringing together so many tendencies, the movement was naturally prone to contradictions and inconsistencies. One, for example, was the contrast between its Erasmian heritage—humanistic, Christian, gently yet strongly critical—and the more puritanical stripe, fiercely opposed to much of the enlightened spirit of the period. Jansenism of the first kind easily accommodated itself to many enlightened reform programs; the second, as in the ideas and writings of Francisco Armañá, archbishop of Tarragona, although dedicated to numerous reforms was also deeply hostile toward most enlightened thought. For Armañá, Jansenist reform was principally a means to defeat what he denounced as the "criminal enterprises" of the philosophers.

Thus, the Jansenists were divided on some important issues. But they normally held together against their powerful traditionalist opponents. Not until the 1780s and above all in the mid- and late 1790s did they achieve the predominance they hoped for, and then for a mere few years. It is easy to list the aims most Jansenists shared. Most basic was their desire to weaken papal authority primarily by building a strong alliance between crown and altar, by enhancing episcopal power and by eliminating the Jesuits against whom they were bitterly antagonistic. Because it was so frequently used against them, at least during the first sixty years of the century, the Inquisition, too, was a target to be weakened or abolished. Regarding faith and religious practices, they wished to defeat what they believed was dangerous moral relaxation, to defend the "*camino estrecho*"—the narrow way—against the Jesuits and libertines whom they judged to be "laxist." They wished to bolster interior spirituality, at the cost of baroque extravagance with its externalization of faith. And they campaigned against superstition and ignorance.

To accomplish these tasks they planned to fortify the role of the parish priest, to improve his intellectual and spiritual training; to emphasize the clergy's pastoral and pedagogical mission; and to promote what was for Spaniards a daring experiment—a deeper and direct understanding of Scripture among both clerics and laymen. They also wanted, through charity and economic improvements, to better the material lot of the poor.[12]

Jurisdiction and authority, morality, spirituality, and education were perhaps the primary themes of Jansenism. Such concerns attracted lay supporters, both men and women, as well as clerics. Many of Spain's most influential Jansenists were laypeople. In Madrid, for example, María Francisca de Sales, countess of Montijo, presided over a well-known salon which in the 1790s nourished Jansenist ideas. Other leading lay Jansenists included Gregorio Mayans y Siscar and Gaspar Melchor de Jovellanos, both giants of intellectual reform, and political figures like Roda and Mariano Luis de Urquijo, chief minister, 1798–1800, who employed their political influence or writings to promote Jansenist programs. Jansenism found most of its outstanding supporters among the clergy, however, especially from mid-century onwards. Beginning in the 1760s a number were promoted into the church hierarchy in a deliberate ministerial attempt to shore up Jansenist reform and undermine Jesuit and ultramontane influences. Bishops José Climent of Barcelona, Antonio Tavira y Almazán of Salamanca and Felipe Bertrán, one of several enlightened Jansenist Inquisitor Generals, were among them.

The Jansenists' appreciation of the intellect and rejection of baroque excess made them natural though sometimes uneasy allies of most enlightened intellectual and cultural reformers. Moreover, the Jansenists, never satisfied only to cry out from the wilderness, very much sought power. Thus, they and the regalists, the most ambitious political reformers of the early and middle decades of the century, were also natural allies. Thus, men and women of the enlightenment, regalists, and Jansenists formed a loose but strong network of thinkers and practioners who enjoyed a wide-ranging impact in the second half of the century. Despite their talents and energies, however, the Jansenists were never to dominate Spanish religious life. For most Spaniards, religion remained in 1800 substantially what it had been a century earlier. Some historians have identified a slow process of simplification, a tendency to purify baroque extravagance and to turn faith to the inside. For example, by the end of the century fewer testators were invoking saints in their wills and a slowly increasing number of funerals were kept simple and relatively austere. Not only did many pious associations have difficulty keeping up their numbers, but many clerics joined in the government's attack against them in the 1770s. This very slight and gradual evolution may be accounted for by a change in elite culture, perhaps reflecting the influence of Jansenist sermons and writings, especially among parish priests. Still, interiorization and simplification of faith never signified dechristianization, and virtually all Spaniards remained loyally Catholic.[13]

Only by dominating clerical institutions could reformers expect to transform their favorite targets: spirituality, the relationship of the church with the crown and with the faithful, and the education and cultural life which the clergy influenced. Hence the reformers emphasized subjugating the clerical hierarchy and masses. By the end of the 1770s the central government had developed the instruments by which reformist politicians dominated the clergy more thoroughly than their Habsburg predecessors had dared hope. Not surprisingly, one of the outstanding historians of the Spanish church has referred to it in the later eighteenth century as the "royal church."[14] This royal church was exceptionally diverse and inconsistent. Its organization, only marginally revised since the Middle Ages, was historical rather than rational. In it were lumped together secular and regular clergy, both men and women, many of whom today would not count as clerics at all—sacristans and lay organists, for example. The secular clergy included a large number of men in minor orders, tonsured but not yet (and perhaps never) deacons or ordained priests. Typically in an Old Regime institution discrepancies of wealth were enormous, even among parish clergy. Many, especially elderly, rural parish priests suffered real poverty, while a few lived in ample comfort. Naturally, some clerics chose their calling for the relative ease it offered, including many of those who had in effect inherited family benefices. This helps explain the very uneven distribution of secular clerics across Spain's geography: large towns and cities, with their amenities and excitements, attracted clergy far out of proportion to their size and needs. This left villages and hamlets to struggle, sometimes for decades at a time, to find a resident or itinerant priest at all. The cultural level, education, and training of priests also varied widely though it improved somewhat during the century, particularly affecting urban parishes. Generally, however, it remained too low, attracting much criticism. So did the tendency for too many priests to keep concubines or to add to low stipends by indulging in uncanonical or illegal occupations. Smuggler priests in remote coastal parishes were an enduring problem, to give just one example.

The regular clergy, substantially more numerous than the seculars, also suffered many anomalies. Most regulars were friars, members of mendicant orders like the beloved and very numerous Franciscans, who lived out in the world (mainly, again, in cities and larger towns), close to the humble whom they often served with generosity and kindness. They were joined by the more privileged cloistered nuns and monks (the Hieronymites, for example) and other regulars, such as the Jesuits. Some individuals were well-off, cultivated men who made a significant contribution to contemporary culture. The well-known Benito Feijoo of Oviedo helped bring the European enlightenment into literally thousands of homes with his enduringly popular essays. His friend, Martín Sarmiento, lived in his Madrid monastery surrounded by his magnificent private library and scientific instruments and there received intellectual friends in his regular Sunday salons, a centre of the capital's enlightenment scene.[15] But Feijoo and Sarmiento, both Benedictines, were atypical. Many regular clergy lived impoverished lives, materially and culturally, and few made any lasting contribution to Spain's intellectual growth. Yet the regulars were unfairly perceived by reformers as more ignorant and superstitious than the secular clergy, and since the friars in particular wandered about, the lay authorities tended to see them as threatening order. Thus, the regulars were criticized as useless and dangerous, parasitical and backward, and were singled out for some of the enlightened reformers' harshest attacks.

If the clergy were to be remade in the image of Jansenist and other reformers, if spirituality was to be transformed, then the church itself must be remodeled. Once that had been achieved, the enlightened reformers believed they could utilize the church and clergy to help reform culture and society. Once their skills as preachers and teachers had been sharpened, and with their access to nearly all laypeople, clerics would make ideal reformist partners. Hence, the clergy, comprising about 1.5 percent of the population—declining slightly during the century—attracted the reformers' intense concern. The reformers inevitably concentrated on the influential clerical leaders, especially the sixty diocesan bishops and archbishops. In the absence of any effective clerical consultative body, the crown dealt with the bishops directly. The government issued circulars, published books, sent individual letters, decrees, and other documents informing, scolding, warning, and encouraging the prelates. But the government's greatest influence over the episcopacy was its power of appointment. The effective authority monarchs had to nominate the bishops of Spain and her overseas empire gave the crown extensive leverage, and rarely, at least after the confusion and divisions of the War of Succession, did eighteenth-century bishops openly disobey the king.[16]

The king exercised his patronage with a kaleidoscope of individuals and councils advising him. Strong-willed royal confessors like Rávago could wield an especially powerful influence. But usually, the king's confessor, the minister of Justice and the Chamber of Castile jostled for the final say in a complicated game about which we know relatively little. During the 1760s and 1770s, however, Campomanes' influence was often decisive over clerical patronage at all levels. He imposed clearly defined policies of promotion, rewarding loyalty to reform principles and Jansenist ideals.[17] Consequently, the prelates appointed by Charles III provided many models of activist renovation—spiritual, cultural, and material. One leading light among the Caroline episcopacy was Francisco Lorenzana, archbishop of Toledo, cardinal and later Inquisitor General, an accomplished intellectual, enthusiastic supporter of various enlightened reforms, a conscientious pastor, and sponsor of important economic improvements. A few were even more exceptionally active, like archbishop Armañá, who spent his entire career devotedly implementing almost every significant Jansenist and economic reform imaginable. His life, austerely Augustinian, was a wonderful advertisement of the possibilities of sincere Jansenist piety combined with a dynamic determination to better his society.[18] Thus, although disreputable bishops were not entirely unknown—like the absurdly ignorant and frivolous courtier cardinal Carlos Borja, patriarch of the Indies early in the century, the episcopacy, especially after about mid-century, enjoyed a deservedly attractive reputation.[19]

Despite the generally high quality of its leadership, inconsistencies and conflicts continued to bedevil the church. For example, many confrontations occurred between Jansenist clerics and their opponents, including Jesuits. Another rift, among Jansenists, opened up between aggressive regalists and the few Jansenists, like bishop Climent, who openly condemned regalist enthusiasm and was consequently forced to resign his Barcelona see. Oddly enough, the Jesuits, too, were divided over regalist claims. Conflicting beliefs about education, charity and mendicity, papal authority, the nature of preaching, the distribution of church wealth, the role of the religious orders, and many other issues continued to divide the clergy throughout the period. Seldom was the division simply one between reformers and traditionalists. The adherents of the two tendencies could be found on both sides of most lines of argument.[20] Since the clergy possessed no forum for debate, and no accepted chief who could have smoothed the way to compromise, every newly arisen issue almost inevitably produced another fissure. It was easy in these circumstances for the crown to appear to dominate the clergy, particularly as the ministers were nearly always supported by one clerical band or another. The regalist movement provided one of the banners around which the government's collaborators rallied.

Regalist ideas and practices encompassed a variety of assumptions and inclinations, all aiming to enhance royal control of clerical institutions. Regalists strove to eliminate clerical autonomy, to subject ecclesiastics as fully to the king's power as his lay subjects, and to undo ties with Rome which interfered with royal control. They wished to limit strictly Spaniards' dependence on Roman decisions, except on carefully defined matters of faith. At the same time, paradoxically, regalists wanted a strong church in which the clergy and their material and intellectual resources could be manipulated as instruments of social control. In this scenario the church and the crown, cooperating under the latter's command, would ensure social order and together implement the government's policies. The crown would protect the faith and permit clerics to retain some, at least, of their legal and economic privileges. Complicating this picture somewhat, from mid-century, enlightened regalists, like Campomanes, also expected the clergy to help promote cultural and material change. Regalists thus expected much from the church: for it to be powerful but subordinate; resourceful but pliant; and enlightened but pious. Regalism could be compared with Jansenism, concerned with jurisdiction, authority and power on one hand, and with encouraging change, outward and interior, among both laymen and clergy, on the other.[21]

With its late medieval roots, regalism had acquired a markedly historical character, its vigor and legitimacy resting in part on the accumulated precedents of generations of legal and political enactments. Regalists sought documents—papers which would prove their claims to solid royal authority over the clergy. Thus the eighteenth-century scholars and lawyers, among them some of Spain's foremost thinkers, who reiterated regalist ideas and claims gloried in the long history of regalism and repeatedly revived sixteenth- and seventeenth-century arguments.[22] They also absorbed the thought of foreign theorists, like Bossuet, who were increasingly influential down to the days of Scipione de' Ricci and his supporters at Pistoia.[23]

Faced with sometimes implacable opposition from Rome and occasionally from inside Spain, regalists became increasingly combative as, by the last years of the century, their enemies became more determined. When in 1799 and 1800 the Jansenists and their regalist allies seemed to some to be leading Spain into schism from Rome, the inevitable anti-Jansenist and anti-regalist reaction, supported by Pius VII and his Madrid nuncio, ended the Jansenist domination of the ministers' ecclesiastical policies. Throughout the century and despite their toughness, even the most extreme regalists continued to be seemingly sincere Catholics, like Charles III himself, Rávago, Mayans, and others.[24]

Despite the variety of regalist sympathies—more or less assertive, more or less attuned to enlightened thinking—the regalists tended to remain fairly united against those who challenged them. Few anti-regalists dared oppose them tout court for doing so smacked of plain disloyalty to the king. Instead anti-regalists usually attacked particular proposals or programs, formulating, like the regalists, legal and historical arguments. Or they worked discreetly behind the scenes to scupper regalist policies or ministers. In a few key institutions they enjoyed sufficient freedom and influence to directly confront and defeat regalist proposals. Lope de Sierra, Campomanes' fellow fiscal on the Council of Castile, used his post to crush one of the regalists' favorite projects, the enactment of legislation to restrict the acquisition of property by the church (1766). Successful opposition like Sierra's was mounted behind closed doors by the well-connected. To do otherwise, to publicize disagreement with regalist policy as the bishop of Cuenca did in 1766, was to openly challenge the king's ministers with almost invariably harsh consequences for the culprit.[25]

Yet there were some especially determined opponents of regalism who questioned not merely specific policies, but the right of the king to enact them. Their opposition, though sometimes implicit, was often enough explicit and surprisingly frank. Most prominent opponents were clerics, including papal agents who fought some regalist claims from inside Spain or from Rome. They launched their assaults mainly from privileged bodies like the Council of Castile where debate was comparatively unrestrained and the forces for and against individual regalist proposals frequently finely balanced. The Inquisition was another important forum. The latter, however, was more domesticated from the 1760s, and less openly opposed to the regalists. The Society too, in some cases, was a refuge for anti-regalist manipulations, although some prominent Jesuits, like Rávago, had impeccable regalist credentials. The Jesuits consequently gained a reputation as an anti-regalist stronghold, a perception reinforced after Rávago's fall. The *colegios mayores,* the six rich and extraordinarily well-connected university colleges, were also highly suspect to the regalists. The *colegios,* whose domination of the university system was widely and bitterly criticized by reformers, were closely related by ties of patronage and self-interest to prominent Jesuits. Some powerful regalists who truly hated the *colegios* concluded they and the Jesuits must be destroyed together. Thus it was said of Roda that he saw only graduates of the *colegios* through one lens of his eyeglasses and Jesuits through the other. It is difficult to know if this suspicion of the *colegios* was entirely justified.[26]

The first centers of resistance the regalists attacked and disarmed were papal: the Nunciature in Madrid and the Apostolic Datary in Rome. The regalists' struggle with these institutions and with the papal Curia which directed them dominated relations between Spain and the papacy, the crown and the Spanish church, in the first half of the century. At every stage were influential clerics who could be found on both sides of the church-crown dividing line, so even in these circumstances it would be misleading to see events as a struggle between church and state. Papal nuncios in Madrid were unique, enjoying fuller spiritual and jurisdictional authority over local people than in any other major state. Regalists, resenting this papal intrusion, made one of their principal aims the reduction of Nunciatural power to ensure Spaniards would be responsible to Rome only indirectly, through their bishops and ecclesiastical courts, both subject to royal scrutiny. The regalists did not achieve this goal until 1773. Meanwhile, important concessions were wrung from the Papacy which gradually whittled away what many considered a demeaning subjection of Spaniards to grasping and insensitive outsiders (usually Italian).

The regalists had another closely related goal, even more eagerly sought: to end the extensive papal patronage of thousands of Spanish benefices of almost all kinds below the rank of bishop. Patronage of church livings, with or without the cure of souls was shared by the monarch and hundreds of laypeople (usually noble), lay corporations, and the full range of clerics from bishops downward. Since the end of the Middle Ages, popes had "reserved" many thousands of benefices to be filled in Rome by the Datary. This for many Spaniards was almost intolerable. Regalists believed papal patronage provided the Curia with many opportunities to influence the Spanish church and clergy. For them, papal patronage was insulting, corrupt, and hindered church reform. How could a new kind of Spanish church be built if the pope's "rapacious henchmen" held the reins of patronage? The regalists and other reformers and successive ministers of finance also disliked seeing considerable sums of money flow from Spanish pockets into Roman coffers. Most judgments and documents—many kinds of dispensations and letters of nomination to a benefice, for example—issued by the Nunciature or Datary cost applicants sizeable sums. One recent historian has estimated that the drain of gold to the papacy amounted to the approximate annual equivalent of $25 million in today's money.[27] The regalists' repeated attacks on this double papal stranglehold led to a series of clashes which at times bordered on open war. Philip V several times severed direct relations between Spain and the papacy. When this happened the Spanish ambassador in Rome was recalled, the Madrid Nunciature was shut, and ordinary Spaniards' direct contact with papal authority ended. The breaks of 1718–20 and 1736–37 were brief. The break which began in 1709, however, lasted until 1717 when an agreement was patched together reestablishing an uneasy peace. But brief or extended these episodes were bitter affairs. In 1736–37 the Spanish even sent an army, in Italy at the time fighting the Austrians, into the Papal States to intimidate Clement XII. On these occasions clashing Spanish and papal foreign policies were one cause for ill feeling; but behind diplomacy was the politics of regalism, prepared to take relations with Rome to the brink of schism.

Not even the Concordat of 1737, a stop-gap measure in which Clement XII offered a few concessions to regalist demands, resolved the principal problems. So the war of the regalists against the Curia continued. Finally, with the accession of Benedict XIV (1740–58) began a long process of constructing a more stable and productive relationship between the crown and the papacy. The ministers and confessors of Philip V and Ferdinand VI continued to mobilize aggressive regalist propaganda, canon law, and historical research to chip away at papal claims, particularly regarding reserves. The crown employed some of the nation's most brilliant lawyers and scholars in its attack, heroes of the enlightenment like Francisco Pérez Bayer, future tutor to Charles III's younger sons. Fortunately for the regalists, Benedict XIV was a flexible and benevolent churchman, bent on securing a settlement. Still, Ventura Figueroa, the chief Spanish negotiator in Rome, needed thirteen years to finalize the agreement signed as the Concordat of 1753.[28]

The Concordat seemed to bring the Spanish Bourbons the great prize. The pope surrendered to the king his patronage of some 50,000 benefices, almost half of which were simple benefices with small incomes. The rest were a mixed bag, including several thousand attractive and lucrative canonries and prebends. Ended were certain levies the Curia had imposed on many benefices and on vacant bishoprics. These, reassigned to the crown, were used by Campomanes and other ministers to subsidize needy clergy and reformist and enlightened church projects, many of them typical Jansenist favorites. The Nunciature lost some, but not all, of its jurisdiction, and the crown compensated the Curia and various papal protegés with huge sums—a measure of the tremendous profits Rome had accrued from its judicial and patronage powers. Most regalists were jubilant, praising the Concordat to the skies. In reality, the regalists had won only half the prize. Not only did the nuncio retain for the time being a considerable jurisdictional power, but the Datary and other Curialists continued for years to hamper the fullest implementation of the Concordat. Moreover, the councilors of the Chamber of Castile, unable to cope with the vast amount of added work they had, were haphazard and even obstructive in proposing candidates for benefices. Some ministers, like Roda, frustrated and suspicious, eventually concluded that ultimate victory had been snatched from them. They sought and found the supposed culprits among the Jesuits and their friends. Thus, the disappointing triumph of 1753 ironically helped launch the decisive anti-Jesuit attack.[29]

The expulsion of 1767, once described as "the hardest and most violent manifestation of eighteenth-century regalism," was achieved by a motley army of men who both detested and feared the Society.[30]

Enlisted were ministers, influential courtiers like the very well-connected twelfth duke of Alba, enlightened intellectuals like Mayans, secular clerics like bishop Climent and respected leaders among regulars, like the Augustinian Francisco Vázquez. Each soldier in this army seemed to have slightly different reasons for joining up. Perhaps their most pervasive argument was that the Society was too powerful and ruthless; that Jesuits had acquired privileges which they used to dominate institutions as diverse as the Inquisition and the *colegios mayores;* that their determination to monopolize power made them dangerous to all except their supporters; that they promoted loyal but undeserving adherents. As Bernardo Tanucci, Charles III's Neapolitan chief minister, put it, "Once they have infiltrated a government, they wish to be the only ones to command, and to succeed in this they promote inept and even vicious men who eternally need the Society's protection." To authoritarians who cherished a united society, the Jesuits seemed to undermine order. As Charles III wrote to his cousin Louis XV in 1772, the Jesuits encouraged "that spirit of party and division which troubles and disquiets" the state.[31]

But there were other motives as well. Along with other factors, Campomanes condemned the Jesuits' wealth. The stern bishop Climent disliked them, as Jansenists generally did, for their ruthlessness and their championship of what he believed was moral and spiritual laxity. More unexpectedly, the Society was repeatedly accused of subverting learning and literature. The Anglo-Italian Hispanist, Joseph Baretti, explained how the Jesuits "have endeavoured to root out all literature . . . [to put] an end amongst us of historians, politicians, philosophers, and poets." Perceiving the close ties between the *colegios mayores* and the Jesuits, many accused the Society of building an obscurantist partnership to undermine enlightenment and university reform. Many thinkers concluded that the Jesuits were a major obstruction to their favorite intellectual reforms.[32] Finally, there is plenty of evidence to suggest that personal rancour was sometimes a factor. Some leading anti-Jesuits had seen, like Climent or Mayans, their early careers or favorite projects hamstrung by Jesuit opponents. Others, like Campomanes and Floridablanca, had long resented their exclusion from the *colegios mayores* during their student years and intended to break their and the Jesuits' arrogance and power.

Whether the expulsion was just or not is not for a historian to say. But given the very deep and obviously genuine hostility the order aroused, it is understandable that their resourceful and determined enemies should act as they did. The Society's opponents began to mobilize in a coherent way during the late 1750s, a process which intensified once Charles III arrived in Madrid. Charles's appointment to high office of Campomanes, Roda, Floridablanca, and Aranda between 1762 and 1766 marked the order's fate. From 1763 or 1764 the king began to ensure that bishoprics and other crucial church posts were filled with reliable clerics. The Augustinians and other orders, noted for their coolness toward the Jesuits—Dominicans, Discalced Carmelites and others—were mobilized. Each had its own reasons for joining the attack and helping formulate and circulate the case against the Society. By 1765 the reasons for expelling the Society were reasonably clear, but no occasion for doing so had yet arisen. Events of Easter 1766 were to furnish the justification the anti-Jesuits needed. For several weeks beginning in late March uprisings broke out in Madrid and scores of cities and towns across the country. The first, the Esquilache uprising (*motín de Esquilache*), occurred in the capital. There many factors coincided to bring crowds into the streets, taking control of the city and forcing the king to flee after dismissing the marquess of Esquilache, his tough, reformist finance minister. The marquess was disliked by rich and poor, clerics and laypeople who had many reasons to resent his policies. Aristocratic machinations combined with a subsistence crisis and other misfortunes to produce the most important urban revolt of the century. Soon the fever of rebellion spread elsewhere. Charles and his ministers were profoundly shocked; but once order was restored by late summer, Charles returned to Madrid while his ministers sought explanations or scapegoats for these events.[33]

The king established two committees of carefully chosen clerics and laymen to set the blame and ensure similar disorders would not recur. The committees, chaired in one case by Campomanes and in the other by the duke of Alba, were easily guided to their target.

Meanwhile, months of sustained pressure from other anti-Jesuit governments, the French, Neapolitans, and Portuguese, helped decide the issue. By late 1766 the committees had decided, though without anything historians have considered convincing proof, the Jesuits had instigated the riots and should be expelled from the monarchy. Charles naturally accepted this advice and set in motion the secret organization of the expulsion.[34]

The consequences of the humiliation of the Jesuits and their expulsion were enormous. Bishop Climent was correct to consider the expulsion "one of the events of the greatest political and religious import of the second half of the century," and a crucial turning point. The king and his ministers convincingly demonstrated their authority and power, reinforcing regalist claims with the full cooperation of many of the nation's most respected churchmen; they had consolidated an alliance of clerical and lay reformers which, though not always amenable to the regalists' control, was often a welcome support for them. They had ended decades of occasional Jesuit challenges to particular royal policies and to the Society's protection of institutions, above all the *colegios,* which they shielded from renovation. Added to the achievement, limited though it was, of the Concordat of 1753, the expulsion helped turn debates about religion, the clergy, the church and monarchical authority around an important corner. Henceforth, the royal church well and truly flourished.[35] Until about 1800, and despite a few notable disappointments, the combination of regalist, Jansenist, and enlightened reformist forces imposed a series of further changes on the church and clergy. It was an era during which the royal church and monarchical authority suffered few open and direct challenges by clerics. Dissatisfied clergy kept their unhappiness mainly to themselves and were content with, at worst, passive resistance.

Once accounts with the Jesuits were settled, reformers quickly refocused their energies onto other business, and the years from the mid-1760s to about 1780, coinciding with the most aggressive and successful years in office of Campomanes, Roda, and Aranda, were especially productive. Other enlightened thinkers, like the cleric Pérez Bayer and bishop Bertrán, lent invaluable support.

One of their tasks was to reduce the remaining jurisdictional role of the nuncio, a reduction sought on principle by regalists and by bishops, especially Jansenists, who believed the nunciature undermined their own judicial authority. The nuncio's authority as an ecclesiastical judge, acting for the pope, was greatly reduced in 1773, though never entirely eliminated. Two Spanish agencies were established to take over much nunciatural jurisdiction and evade most Curial excesses. The papal administration in Rome still insisted, however, on supervising a substantial number of cases and issuing some dispensations.[36] The regalists also managed to establish permanently the right of the crown to impose the so-called *exequatur,* a royal license required before bulls, briefs, and other papal documents could be delivered and implemented in Spain. Pushed by Roda and Campomanes, among others, the *exequatur,* imposed temporarily in 1761–63 was reimposed and made perpetual in 1768, despite some clerical objections. In regalist hands, the *exequatur* became an invaluable instrument helping divide the papacy from the Spanish hierarchy and to protect episcopal and royal authority.

Those few clerics who defied episcopal and royal authority to question policy and law openly were dealt with sternly. This was so even when their challenge was unintentional. Such was the case of bishop Isidro de Carvajal of Cuenca and of popular missionary preachers, who were harshly reprimanded. In most cases, their offenses represented little more than their expression of distaste for particular regalist or reform policies, and it is unlikely they intended any serious challenge to royal authority. Bishop Carvajal, aged, devout, and reform-minded, was humiliated by the Council of Castile for having questioned in writing certain regalist policies in the aftermath of the riots of 1766. More serious, because more public, were the defiances by the preachers. Their vast popularity with the Spanish masses and their ability to collect and sway large crowds with their dramatic sermonizing made them potentially dangerous. Thus, when they erred by publicly criticizing ministers and regalist and other reforms, Campomanes and the Council of Castile chastised and humiliated them. Pedro de Calatayud, a Jesuit (before their expulsion), Antonio Garcés, a Dominican, and Diego José de Cádiz, a Capuchin and the most famous missionary preacher of the century, were all at various times silenced, at least temporarily, for such offenses. The Council was effectively establishing the limits beyond which careless speech and criticism of policy would not be tolerated, making it clear that open challenges even by the most respected clerics were never acceptable.[37]

Other reforms were imposed or encouraged, often inspired by Jansenists. The tenacious hold in which the *colegios mayores* held most of the university system was, after prolonged struggles, finally loosened. This change helped a reformed and to a degree enlightened university culture take hold by the last decade or so of the century, at least in the best institutions and among younger professors and students.[38] In the church itself, bishops were encouraged to implement a wide range of improvements: to convene synods; to raise the income and educational standards of parish priests; to reorganize the distribution of benefices to make the system fairer; and to raise the spiritual character of the priesthood through regular practice of spiritual exercises. These and similar reforms were widely applauded and eagerly adopted by many prelates. Their impact, however, was sometimes superficial.

Some other reforms were more problematical. This was especially so with the financial changes Esquilache, Campomanes, and others planned to impose on the clergy. There were two fundamental issues: the extent to which the wealth and income of the church and clergy would be taxed by the crown; and the right of the monarch to regulate the church's acquisition of entailed estates (primarily as land and buildings and financial instruments of various kinds). Against changes in both of these, particularly the second, clerics offered some determined resistance. The clergy, however, were easily forced to give in over taxation. With the full cooperation of Benedict XIV, the right of the king to impose and levy a wide range of taxes on clerical income was reinforced. Taxes, most dating from the sixteenth century, which had for generations been collected on a temporary basis with papal permission, were in 1757 made permanent. The crown rationalized their administration and substantially increased their yield. Clerics, now often paying much higher sums, inevitably resented the change.[39] They generally even more decidedly opposed ministers' attempts to restrict the church's right to acquire property in entail. Entailments were the cornerstone of ecclesiastical wealth and yielded increasingly larger income as the economy expanded in the second half of the century. As by definition entailed estates could not be alienated, they expanded generation after generation as pious Spaniards donated or bequeathed property to the church. And because they were, once entailed to the church, no longer taxed directly, the tax base of the monarchy grew ever smaller. By mid-century the church owned as much as 20 or even 27 percent of the land in several provinces and received as much as one-third of all agricultural income. It owned huge amounts of urban property, too: in the city of Segovia, 53 percent of its houses. Though in some other regions and cities it owned far less, the church was overall an enormously rich institution. It has been estimated that in Castile it received nearly 28 percent of the gross income of all economic sectors.[40]

Economists, finance ministers, regalists, and others had for generations complained against this excessive wealth. And, although in the early eighteenth century a few brave reformers planned to end the continued expansion of entailments, nothing was achieved. In 1766 Campomanes proposed a law in the Council of Castile which would have effectively restricted further acquisitions by the church. He and his regalist supporters were defeated in the Council by a coalition of lay and clerical opponents led by Lope de Sierra. This defeat, coming shortly after the Esquilache riot, was probably the greatest disappointment of Campomanes' career. It undoubtedly fed his and the regalists' appetite for Jesuit blood and their determination to undo the network of obstructionists the Society seemed to lead.[41]

Once the Jesuits had been removed there was probably only one clerical institution which posed a comparably serious threat to enlightened reformers and Jansenists. The Inquisition was, if anything, even more ubiquitous than the Society, menacing both the persons and the policies of many reformers and others who disapproved of it. The latter included a wide range besides enlightened thinkers: bishops, sometimes Jansenists, who resented the inroads the Inquisition had made into their own judicial authority; patriots embarrassed by the reputation the institution had given Spain; some members of religious orders who had learned to dislike the Inquisition during the years it was under the Jesuits' shadow; magistrates who, like bishops, resented the Inquisition's intrusion into their cases, an intrusion which produced constant jurisdictional disputes; booksellers and printers whose business was sometimes threatened; and numerous ordinary Spaniards who resented the inquisitors' "prying and spying."[42]

Nevertheless, even in the last years of the century, the Inquisition had its adherents—men who wanted the Holy Office (as it was customarily called) strengthened to withstand the threatening forces of enlightenment, Jansenism, and from the 1780s, political radicalism. Its advocates helped protect the Inquisition from those who cautiously championed some degree of reform or in a few cases, outright abolition.[43]

The Inquisition, particularly from the 1770s, was itself suffused with inconsistencies: hostile to change, protecting intolerance and outmoded assumptions but also breathing a new, fresh air of progress under cultivated and fair-minded reformist inquisitor generals like bishop Bertrán.[44] Indeed, recent historians have established a strongly revisionist picture of its tribunals, highlighting its contradictions and innumerable variations.[45] The score of different tribunals, reflecting their diverse social and cultural contexts, tended to prosecute different offenses, to concentrate their efforts in varied ways, though there was a sharp and generalized decline in activity during the eighteenth century. Its methods were rational, legally cautious, and painstaking, and even its use of torture was probably more measured, possibly more humane, than in contemporary secular courts. Nor was the Holy Office indiscriminate in its censorship of books and other writings. It granted licenses to almost all more or less serious readers to consult prohibited works, particularly in the later eighteenth century. Moreover, Spaniards easily and very widely ignored the censors to read a wide range of forbidden books. Evasion was increasingly painless because the inspection process became slipshod and, at least until the 1790s, fairly half-hearted. Thus, after about 1770, Gallican, Jansenist, and radical regalist writings, both domestic and foreign, circulated readily.

Spaniards paid a price, however, for religious orthodoxy. The Inquisition's mere presence, dampening adventurous and imaginative debate, may have been its most negative aspect. Intellectuals learned to go cautiously. Hence, although through most of the century the Holy Office enjoyed a languid, largely harmless existence, with some tribunals mounting no more than a handful of investigations every year or two, it remained an intensely and fairly widely resented institution, always menacingly secretive and too often arbitrary, bothersome, and ill-informed.[46]

The sleeping dog of the Inquisition often woke and growled and occasionally bit. After mid-century its best-known victims were enlightened reformers like Jovellanos and Pablo de Olavide (the latter tried and convicted, 1776–78) whose primary offense was being too radically critical of clerical institutions or too insistent in their plans for drastic clerical reform.[47] Olavide's trial—an infamous spectacle which ended the career of this brilliant and energetic cultural and administrative reformer—was a unique but alarming expression of Inquisitorial power, as much the evidence of Olavide's political vulnerability as of clerical determination. Other potential targets, like Campomanes, escaped because they were better connected, too highly placed to be attacked. Jovellanos, the nation's foremost intellectual by the 1790s, and, like Olavide, a courageous royal servant, was attacked and destroyed (1798–1801) by a coalition including political rivals, clerical enemies in the Holy Office, and a king who had learned to distrust him.[48] Few of the prominent eighteenth-century victims of the Inquisition were destroyed by it alone. Normally the monarch and political rivals directly or passively implicated themselves in these attacks. Bourbon kings tolerated this state of affairs partly because they were genuinely anxious to protect Catholic orthodoxy, and partly because they valued the social and political control the Inquisition offered. No monarch, not even Charles III, committed himself to abolish or seriously weaken it. Consequently, the inquisitors retained sufficient freedom and authority to act occasionally even against the crown's own agents. They wisely used this power, but very rarely, to secure the most vital interests of the Holy Office and its clerical allies and, in Olavide's case, to set an example.

Yet even the Inquisition was forced to accept some reforms. During the 1760s and 1770s, ministers subjected it to a series of improvements, not always very effective, requiring it to be fairer and more open with writers and publishers. More significantly, reformist ministers ensured that the king appointed more open-minded and tolerant Inquisitor Generals. It would not be misleading to suggest that by the 1790s some Inquisitors were themselves cautious champions of the enlightenment.

In December 1788 the inexperienced and indolent Charles IV succeeded his father. The new king was utterly unprepared to confront the political and economic crises which assailed Spain for the twenty years of his reign. Moreover, neither his queen, María Luisa, nor their beloved favorite, Godoy, was able to help him surmount these challenges. Godoy, a friend of reform—though often only a lukewarm one—brought into office leading Jansenists and endorsed many of their most rigorous policies. From about 1795 to 1800 radical Jansenists and their enlightened allies enjoyed much influence. Leading Jansenist intellectuals like the Benedictine Inquisitor General, Manuel Abad y Lasierra; bishop Tavira, particularly well-known as a preacher and university reformer; and Ramón José de Arce, Inquisitor General after 1798 and chief of the king's religious household, formed a loose network. They were encouraged from abroad by their friends among the French constitutional clergy and protected at home by Godoy, Jovellanos, Urquijo, and others.[49] They encouraged the Jansenist optimism which so strongly affected intellectual culture at some Spanish universities, promoted the radical brand of thought of the Synod of Pistoia, and began, through their contacts there, to push Jansenist interests in the Curia itself. They even came close to undertaking the abolition of the Holy Office. In 1799 they embarked upon one of the most radical of Jansenist reforms. Taking advantage of the papal interregnum, Urquijo, for the time being chief minister, got the king to transfer to Spain's bishops the papal right to grant marriage dispensations. Although the measure was officially intended as a purely temporary expedient, it aroused widespread unltramontane resistance and most bishops opposed the move. They undoubtedly understood that dispensations reform could be the beginning of a deluge of anti-papal legislation, and they saw Spain on the edge of schism. The Jansenists' enemies mobilized, and with the cooperation of the wobbly Godoy, removed Urquijo from office in 1800, rescinded the decree on dispensations, and with the help of the new pope, Pius VII, convinced Charles IV to destroy Jansenist power. The ultramontanes virtually buried what Pius had condemned as the Jansenists' "spirit of innovation."[50]

By lying low after 1800, the Jansenists at least avoided the punishments the crown and Inquisition could have imposed. But until 1808, when the French invaded and Spain's Old Regime began its final, slow-motion collapse, the possibility of enacting fundamental Jansenist reforms on the national level was remote. What reforms were implemented, like the disentailment of certain ecclesiastical properties begun in 1798, tended to be cynical, makeshift measures designed to rescue the crown and its treasury or to protect Godoy and his allies.[51] The vigorous and forthright reforms of the age of Ensenada, Campomanes, and Jovellanos were now reminders of an unrepeatable past. Jansenist bishops like Tavira had to content themselves with quiet, modest, practical reforms in their dioceses. Meanwhile, the ultramontanists, ex-Jesuits—like the linguist and philosopher Lorenzo Hervás y Panduro—traditionalists, and their friends marshaled the arguments in favor of clerical and royalist reaction. The victors of 1800 thereby helped prepare the unsavory Bourbon restoration of 1814 and the bitter, bloody confrontations which divided Spaniards for the next six generations.[52] The divisions of the 1790s and the defeat of the Jansenists helped undermine the crown's authority over the clergy. Thus, with the aid of the increasingly unscrupulous Godoy and the bemused king, anti-regalists were able to destabilize and eventually, after 1808, bring to an end the eighteenth-century royal church.

Throughout Spain's early modern period the close cooperation of clergy and crown had been important. It had helped unite the Spanish kingdoms, build her American empire, dominate much of western Europe for over a century. It had helped most Spaniards achieve their identity: To be Spanish came to mean being orthodox in religion and, most of the time, reasonably loyal to the Catholic monarch. The cooperation was a source of stability and order, the clergy and crown protecting and strengthening each other. Inevitably there were occasions on which the alliance was troubled, but it endured as long as the Old Regime lasted, though like the political system itself, it was beginning to unravel by the time it failed in 1808. Thus, the crown, until the last hours, always had some loyal clerical allies to defend it. During most of the eighteenth century the clerical allies had been numerous and varied. Jansenists and other clerical reformers had married their talents and energies to those of a long series of outstanding ministers. Sharing many assumptions and agreeing on a wide range of policies, Jansenists, regalists, and men of the enlightenment (some, like Roda, were all three at once) built and consolidated the royal church. They eliminated some of their common opponents, notably the Jesuits, and diluted the authority in Spain of the popes and their nuncios. They implemented reforms, mainly moderate and fairly modest ones, of intellectual, clerical, and other institutions. Only late in the century, after about 1790, did the allies aim at more radical reform. As revolutionary political ideas began to emerge from and intrude into the Spanish consciousness, so Jansenism too rounded a corner into its most vigorous phase. At last some clerics and their lay allies rebelled. No longer content to remain quietly loyal in their cathedrals and parishes, some reacted and helped destroy the easy, old alliance which had culminated in the royal church. But until 1808 most clerics accepted the royal church because the crown, under the aegis of pious monarchs and religiously orthodox ministers, never came close to threatening the clergy's most vital interest—the Catholic monopolization of Spaniards' spiritual life.

Notes

1. Teófanes Egido briefly but effectively describes the expulsion in "La expulsión de los Jesuítas de España," in Ricardo García-Villoslada, ed., *Historia de la Iglesia en España,* 5 vols. (Madrid: La Editorial Católica, 1979, 1999),

4:750–59. See also the Consulta de la Junta de 1767, 20 Feb.1767, Archivo Histórico Nacional, Madrid (A.H.N.), Est. leg. 3517.

2. John Lynch, *Bourbon Spain 1700–1808* (Oxford: Blackwell, 1989), 182–86; Carlos Lacomb Gendry, *Vida política del P. Francisco de Rávago,Confesor del Rey D. Fernando VI* (Valladolid, 1907), 37–43; and Rafael Olaechea, "Política eclesiástica del Gobierno de Fernando VI," in *La Epoca de Fernando VI. Ponencias Leídas en el coloquio conmemorativo de los 25 años de la fundación de la Cátedra Feijoo* (Oviedo: Universidad de Oviedo, 1981), 139–225.

3. The four do not include Luis I, eldest son of Philip V. Philip abdicated in favor of his son who died after a few months (1724). Philip returned to the throne.

4. Virgilio Pinto Crespo presents a thoughtful analysis of the reformers' aims in "Una reforma desde arriba: iglesia y religiosidad," in Equipo Madrid de Estudios Históricos, *Carlos III, Madrid y la Ilustración. Contradicciones de un proyecto reformista* (Madrid: Siglo Veintiuno Editores, 1988), esp. 155–58.

5. Campomanes to Miguel de Muzquiz, 31 Aug., 1772. Fundación Universitaria Española. Archivo de Campomanes (FUE), MS27/15; J. Izquierdo Martín, J. M. López García, et al., "La reforma de regulares durante el reinado de Carlos III. Una valoración a través del ejemplo Madrileño," in Equipo Madrid, *Carlos III*, 214, 219.

6. See especially J. L. Bouza Alvarez, *Religiosidad contrarreformista y cultura simbólica del barroco* (Madrid: C. S. I. C., 1990), both the excellent prologue by A. Domínguez Ortíz and main text, 32–33, 40–45; and J. L. Sánchez Lora, "La histeria religiosa del barroco en la norma de la historia de las mentalidades: reflexiones para una apertura," in L. C. Alvarez Santaló and C. M. Cremades Griñón, eds., *Mentalidad e ideología en el antiguo régimen,* (Murcia: Universidad de Murcia, 1993), 2:119–34.

7. Domínguez Ortíz, in *Religiosidad contrarreformista,* 14.

8. Quoting Bouza Alvarez, in *Religiosidad contrarreformista,* 32.

9. Ibid.; D. L. González Lopo, "El papel de las reliquias en las prácticas religiosas de los siglos XVII y XVIII," in Alvarez Santaló and Cremades Griñón, *Mentalidad e ideología,* 247–60; A. Peñafiel Ramón, *Mentalidad y religiosidad popular murciana en la primera mitad del siglo XVIII* (Murcia: Universidad de Murcia, 1988), esp. 51–53 and 80–94, an important study of the religion of urban masses; and A. Saint-Saens, *Art and Faith in Tridentine Spain (1545–1690)* (New York: Peter Lang, 1995), 1–4, 57–90.

10. See the invaluable J. Pereira Pereira, "La religiosidad y la sociabilidad popular como aspectos del conflicto social en el Madrid de la segunda mitad del siglo XVIII," in Equipo Madrid, *Carlos III,* 223–54, (p. 224 for the quoted words); and the survey by W. J. Callahan, *Church, Politics and Society in Spain,*

1750–1874, (Cambridge, Mass.: Harvard University Press, 1984), 52–68; R. J. López, *Oviedo: muerte y religiosidad en el siglo XVIII (un estudio de mentalidades colectivas)* (Oviedo: Universidad de Oviedo, 1985), 154–63.

11. See the numerous and important works on Spanish Jansenism by Joel Saugnieux, in this case, *Le jansénisme espagnol du XVIIIe siècle: ses composants et ses sources* (Oviedo: Universidad de Oviedo. Cátedra de Feijoo, 1975), 90–102.

12. Armañá quoted in J. Saugnieux, "Foi et lumières du XVIIIe siècle," in J. Saugnieux, *Foi et lumières dans l'Espagne du XVIIIe siècle* (Lyon: Presses Universitaires de Lyon, 1985), 19; see also J. Saugnieux, *Un prélat éclairé: Don Antonio Tavira y Almazán (1737–1807). Contribution à l'étude du jansénisme espagnol* (Toulouse: Université de Toulouse, 1970). Other important studies of Jansenism include: F. Tort Mitjans, *El obispo de Barcelona Josep Climent i Avinent (1706–1781)* (Barcelona: Editorial Balmes, 1978); M. G. Tomsich, *El jansenismo en España. Estudio sobre ideas religiosas en las segunda mitad del siglo XVIII* (Madrid: Siglo Veintiuno, 1972); and R. Herr's classic work, *The Eighteenth-Century Revolution in Spain* (Princeton: Princeton University Press, 1958), chs. II and XV.

13. Saugnieux, "Foi et lumières," 9–11, and López, *Oviedo: Muerte y religiosidad*, 58–63 and 96–98.

14. Callahan, *Church, Politics and Society*, ch. 1. Chapters 1–3 of this outstanding study provide by far the best starting point for understanding the Spanish Old Regime church; a brief general analysis is found in J. Bada Elías, "Iglesia y sociedad en el Antiguo Régimen: el clero secular," in E. Martínez Ruíz and V. Suárez Griñón eds., *Iglesia y Estado en el Antiguo Régimen* (Las Palmas de Gran Canaria: Universidad de Las Palmas de Gran Canaria, 1994).

15. A. Castillo de Lucas, "El P. Feijoo y Madrid," *Anales del Instituto de Estudios Madrileños* 2 (1967): 303–21; Ivy Lilian McClelland, *Benito Jerónimo Feijoo* (New York: Twayne Publishers, 1969).

16. On royal patronage see C. Hermann, *L'église d'Espagne sous le patronage royal (1476–1834)* (Madrid: Casa de Velázquez, 1988), esp. 46–61.

17. The complexities of royal patronage are reflected in the massive documentation on its implementation in Archivo General de Simancas (AGS), Gracia y Justicia, legs 305–06, 316, 534, 600–01, and many others of the series.

18. F. Torres Amat, *Vida del illustrísimo señor don Felix Amat* (Madrid: Imp. que fue de Fuentenebro, 1835); M. R. Pazos, *El episcopado gallego a la luz de documentos romanos*, 3 vols. (Madrid: Consejo Superior de Investigaciones Científicas, Instituto Jerónimo Zurita, 1946), 3:226–42; J. Villanueva and J. L. Villanueva, *Viaje literario a las iglesias de España* (Madrid and Valencia, 1803–52), 20:64–6; Francisco Armañá, *Dos Cartas pastorales* (1783) and *Pastorales* (1794).

19. Henry Swinburne, *Travels Through Spain in the Years 1775 and 1776* (London: S. Price, R. Cross, J. Williams, 1776), 82; J. Townsend, *A Journey Through Spain in the Years 1786 and 1787*, 3 vols. (London: C. Dilly, 1791), 2:150–51; E. Appolis, *Les Jansénistes espagnols* (Bordeaux: S. O. B. O. D. I., 1966), 78; E. Armstrong, *Elizabeth Farnese. "The Termagant of Spain"* (London: Longmans, Green and Co., 1892), 146; F. Vázquez García, *El Infante don Luis Antonio de Borbón y Farnesio* (Avila: Istitución Gran Duque de Alba de la Excma. Diputación Provincial de Avila, 1990), chs. VI–VIII.

20. For Climent's fate see Tort Mitjans, *El obispo de Barcelona*, 136–60, 359–63.

21. Recent analysis of regalism may be found in A. Domínguez Ortíz, *Carlos III y la España de la ilustración* (Madrid: Alianza Editorial, 1989), 141–2; Pinto Crespo in Equipo Madrid, *Carlos III*; Izquierdo Martín et al. in Equipo de Madrid, *Carlos III*, 204–5; and F. Tomás y Valiente, "Campomanes y los preliminares de la desamortización eclesiastica," in Tomás y Valiente, *Gobierno e instituciones de la España del Antiguo Régimen* (Madrid: Alianza Editorial, 1982), 287–316.

22. J. Demerson, *Ibiza y su primer obispo: D. Manuel Abad y Lasierra* (Madrid: Fundación Universitaria Española, 1980), 16–20, 35–41; the evolution of regalist ideas may be approached in the essays by A. Domínguez Ortíz and T. Egido in García Villoslada, *Historia de la Iglesia* (Valencia: EDICEP, 1974–96), vol. 4.

23. Saugnieux, *Jansénsime espagnol*, 94–5; J. Marichal, "From Pistoia to Cádiz: A Generation's Itinerary," in A. O. Aldridge, ed.,*The Ibero-American Enlightenment* (Urbana: University of Illinois Press, 1971).

24. Charles III's piety is revealed clearly in his correspondence with his parents in 1739–40. See especially the letters of 26 February 1739 (1740?) and 12 July 1740, A.H.N., Estado, leg. 2760. Campomanes' religious sincerity is hinted at in the catalog of his library in F.U.E., MSS 39–7 and 39–9.

25. Both these incidents are discussed briefly in C. C. Noel, "Opposition to Enlightened Reform in Spain; Campomanes and the Clergy, 1765–1775," *Societas. A Review of Social History* 3 (1973): 30–32, 39–42.

26. Pedro Rodríguez Campomanes, *Dictamen fiscal de expulsión de los Jesuítas de España (1766–1767)*, ed. J. Cejudo and T. Egido (Madrid: Fundación Universitaria Española, 1977), intro., 29; R. Olaechea, "El anti-colegialismo del gobierno de Carlos III," *Cuadernos de Investigación. Geografía e Historia* 2 (1976): 53–90.

27. Hermann, *L'Eglise*, 79, and Domínguez Ortíz, *Carlos III*, 142.

28. On the career of Pérez Bayer, see J. Alvarez Barrientos and A. Mestre Sanchis, "La nueva mentalidad científica. El ensayo y la ciencia literaria," in

V. García de la Concha, ed., *Historia de la Literatura Española* (Madrid: Espasa Calpe, 1995–), 2:97–100; A. Mestre Sanchis, *El mundo intelectual de Mayans* (Valencia: Publicaciones del Ayuntameinto de Oliva, 1978).

29. On the Concordat see García Villoslada, *Historia de la Iglesia,* 4:177–89; Olaechea, "La política eclesiástica," 189–93; A. Portabales Pichel, *Don Manuel Ventura Figueroa y el Concordato de 1753* (Madrid, 1948); Ricardo Gómez Rivero, "Consultas del Inquisidor Quintano Bonifaz sobre prebendas eclesiásticas," *Revista de la Inquisición* 1 (1991): 247–67; Isidoro Pinedo Iparraguirre, "Maniobras del Gobierno de Carlos III con ocasión del Cónclave de Clemente XIV (1769)," in *Coloquio Internacional. Carlos III y su siglo. Actas,* 2 vols. (Madrid: Universidad Complutense, Departamento de Historia Moderna, 1990), 2:363–64.

30. Quoting Carlos Corona Baratech, "Sobre el conde de Aranda y sobre la expulsión de los Jesuítas," in *Homenaje al Dr. D. Juan Reglá Campistol,* 2 vols. (Valencia: Universidad de Valencia, Facultad de Filosofia y Letras, 1975), 2:80.

31. Tanucci, quoted in Domínguez Ortíz, *Carlos III,* 37; Charles III to Louis XV, 21 Sept., 1772, AHN., Est, leg, 2850–2.

32. Rodríguez Campomanes, *Dictamen fiscal,* 23–4; Antonio Alvarez Morales, *Inquisición e Ilustración (1700–1834)* (Madrid: Fundación Universitaria Española, 1982), 102; Tort Mitjans, *El obispo de Barcelona,* 71; Joseph Baretti, *A Journey from London to Genoa through England, Portugal, Spain and France,* 2 vols. (new ed., Fontwell, Sussex: Centaur Press, 1970), 2:199–200.

33. For a summary of the risings see Lynch, *Bourbon Spain,* 261–68. Of the many detailed studies, see especially Laura Rodríguez Díaz, *Reforma e ilustración en la España del siglo XVIII. Pedro Rodríguez Campomanes* (Madrid: Fundación Universitaria Española, Seminario Cisneros, 1975), chs. V–VI; Carlos Corona Baratech, "El poder real y los motines de 1766," in *Suma de estudios en homenaje al ilustrísimo Doctor Angel Canellas López* (Zaragoza: Facultad de Filosofia y Letras, Universidad de Zaragoza, 1969), 259–77; Teófanes Egido, "Madrid, 1766: Motines de Corte y oposición al Gobierno," *Cuadernos de Invesigación Histórica* 3 (1979): 125–53.

34. Corona Baratech, "Sobre el conde de Aranda," 82–106; Rodríguez Campomanes, *Dictamen fiscal,* intro.; Rafael Olaechea and J. A. Ferrer Benimeli, *El Conde de Aranda. Mito y Realidad de un político,* 2 vols. (Zaragoza: Librería General, 1978), 1:133–67.

35. Tort Mitjans, *El obispo de Barcelona,* 71.

36. On this and most of the reforms mentioned below, see C. C. Noel, "Campomanes and the Secular Clergy in Spain: Enlightenment vs. Tradition" (Ph.D. diss., Princeton University, 1970), esp. chs. III–V.

37. Charles C. Noel, "Missionary Preachers in Spain: Teaching Social Virtue in the Eighteenth Century," *American Historical Review* 90 (1985): 866–92.

38. Antonio Alvarez de Morales, *La ilustración y la reforma de la universidad en la España del siglo XVIII* (2d ed. Madrid: Ediciones Pegaso, 1979); Marichal, "From Pistoia to Cádiz."

39. For examples of the operation of these taxes, see Maximiliano Barrio Gozalo, *Estudio socio-económico de la iglesia de Segovia en el siglo XVIII* (Segovia: Caja de Ahorros y Monte de Piedad de Segovia, 1982); Callahan, *Church, Politics and Society,* 38–52.

40. Ibid., 41. Castile consisted of mainland Spain except Navarre, Aragon, Catalonia, and Valencia.

41. Noel, "Opposition to Enlightened Reform," 39–42; Tomás y Valiente, "Campomanes y los preliminares," 301–9.

42. This phrase is from Henry Kamen, *Inquisition and Society in Spain in the Sixteenth and Seventeenth Centuries* (London: Weidenfeld and Nicolson, 1985), 60. Kamen's recent updating of his research on the Inquisition scarcely deals with the eighteenth century. See Henry Kamen, *The Spanish Inquisition. A Historical Revision* (New Haven: Yale University Press, 1998).

43. Antonio Alvarez de Morales, "La crítica al tribunal de la Inquisición durante la segunda mitad del siglo XVIII," *Estudis* 6 (1977): 171–72, 179–82.

44. Marcelin Defourneaux emphasizes these contradictions. See Marcelin Defourneaux, *Inquisición y censura de libros en la España del siglo XVIII* (Madrid: Taurus, 1973), 93–103.

45. A few of the very many helpful revisionist arguments may be found in J. M. de Bujanda, "Recent Historiography of the Spanish Inquisition (1977–1988)," in M. E. Perry and A. J. Cruz eds., *Cultural Encounters. The Impact of the Inquisition in Spain and the New World* (Berkeley: University of California Press, 1991); Kamen, *Inquisition and Society in Spain;* J. Pérez Villanueva and B. Escandell Bonet, eds., *Historia de la Inquisición en España y América* (Madrid: Biblioteca de Autores Cristianos, 1984 and 1993), 2 vols; B. Bennassar, ed., *Inquisición Española: Poder político y control social* (Barcelona: Editorial Crítica, 1981); A. Alcalá, ed., *Inquisición española y mentalidad inquisitorial* (Barcelona: Ariel, 1984); J-P. Dedieu, *L'Administration de la Foi. l'Inquisition de Tolède XVIe au XVIIIe siecle* (Madrid: Casa de Velázquez, 1989); and S. Haliczer, *Inquisition and Society in the Kingdom of Valencia 1478–1834* (Berkeley: University of California Press, 1990).

46. On eighteenth-century censorship, see especially Defourneaux, *Inquisición y censura;* Saugnieux, *Le Jansenisme,* 114–33; Jean-Pierre Dedieu, "El modelo religioso: rechazo de la reforma y control del pensamiento," in Bennassar, *Inquisición Española,* esp. 253–69.

47. Olavide's career has been studied in the classic work by M. Defourneaux, *Pablo de Olavide ou l'Afrancesado (1725–1803)* (Paris: Presses Univeristaires de France, 1959), and more recently by L. Perdices Blas, *Pablo de Olavide (1725–1803) El Ilustrado* (Madrid: Editorial Complutense, 1992).

48. On Campomanes as a target of the Inquisition, see J. M. Vallejo García Hevia, "Campomanes y la Inquisición: historia del intento frustrado de empapelamiento de otro fiscal de la monarquía en el siglo XVIII," *Revista de la Inquisición* 3 (1994): 141–82.

49. For excellent analysis of these years among the Jansenists, see Saugnieux, *Un prélat éclairé,* 103ff; Herr, *The Eighteenth-Century Revolution,* chs. XIII–XV; and Callahan, *Church, Politics and Society,* ch. III.

50. Saugnieux, *Un prélat éclairé,* 153–251; Herr, *The Eighteenth-century Revolution,*chs. XIII–XV; Callahan, *Church, Politics and Society,* ch. III.; Marichal, "From Pistoia to Cádiz."

51. On the disentailment see R. Herr, *Rural Change and Royal Finances in Spain at the End of the Old Regime* (Berkeley: University of California Press, 1989).

52. On clerical reaction in Spain, see J. Herrero, *Los orígenes del pensamiento reaccionario español* (2d ed., Madrid: Alianza Editorial, 1988), 23–104; and, in contrast, M. González Montero de Espinosa, *Lorenzo Hervás y Panduro. El gran olvidado de la ilustración española* (Madrid: Iberediciones, 1994), 15–56 and 336–38.

THREE

Late Jansenism and the Habsburgs

W. R. WARD

EIGHTEENTH-CENTURY JANSENISM IS A REAL BUT ELUSIVE concept; even at the time it was both a hard reality and a very soft *Schreckenbild für Kinder* (bogeyman for children).[1] One short-cut much employed by contemporaries was simply to treat it as a cant *omnium gatherum* of opponents of the Jesuits. The famous conversation reported to Quesnel in 1688 by Louis de Vaucel, a Jansenist agent at Rome, between Cardinal Aguirre and the General of the Society of Jesus, set the pattern. The latter "spoke heatedly against the so-called Jansenists [so] the Cardinal rose and told him that it was necessary to distinguish between three sorts of Jansenists: the first, he said, are those who support the five propositions [of Jansen] and the errors which the Church has condemned in them; they are very few, since, hitherto, it has been impossible to convict anyone in a legal manner. The second are those zealous for good morality and strict discipline; and these notwithstanding the laxity of the century are a rather large number. And the third are those who, of whatever kind, are opposed to the Jesuits, and these are infinite in number."[2] Or, as the matter was put the other way round in Germany a century later, the Jesuits "Jansenise half the universe."[3]

Now the Jesuit order would not have been dissolved as it was in 1773 had not states, and especially Bourbon states, coveted its property; but there were many in the Catholic world, "Jansenised" or not, who had grievances against the way in which the Society of Jesus had set the tone in the Counter-Reformation. Augustinians and Thomists disliked the way the Council of Trent had given preference to the Jesuit formulation of the doctrine of justification, and the way the Jesuits had given preference to the late medieval scholastics over Thomas, Augustine, and the earlier Fathers. An anti-Jesuit preference for antiquity might here combine with an anti-Jesuit modernist preference for Descartes over Aristotle. And there were the perennial differences in the church over pastoral strategy between those who believed generously that they must meet people where they were, and those who believed that standards must not be compromised and that inquirers should not be misled by any shilly-shallying over what was required of them. If the Jesuits were famous for taking the first view and supporting it philosophically by Molinism and an emphasis on the role of free will in the cooperation of God and man, they also developed ethical doctrines to suit. If there was insoluble doubt whether an action was permissible or not, Jesuits would be satisfied if there was a probability that it was (Probabilism), sometimes even if there was a small probability (Laxism), and they created a science of casuistry to estimate the degrees of probability. Jansenists were very far from alone in rejecting casuistry and in playing safe morally (Rigorism or Tutiorism); and the situation was confused by the fact they attributed an unwarranted consistency of view to the Jesuits, as the Jesuits tended to abuse all their critics as Jansenists. And if there were critics of the Jesuits in theology, philosophy, and ethics, there were Piarists and Augustinians who disliked Jesuit educational methods, and many who disliked the Italianate missions with which the Jesuits had been associated, did not believe in the genuineness of many of the conversions claimed by them, and discredited both the petty devotions (*Andächtelei*) and the cult of the Sacred Heart that went with them.

If there was to be reform of the Catholic Church as the eighteenth century found it, it was therefore likely to have an anti-Jesuit slant, and by that token to gratify not only Jansenists, but many in the church who had sympathy with them on this point or that. Moreover, there was more than one style of reform from which to choose. The reform achieved in the Council of Trent had put an end to the threat of conciliarism and had issued in an enormously strengthened papacy. The papacy had called and prorogued the council at will, was commissioned to oversee the implementation of its reforms, and was empowered to complete them by preparing the Index, the new catechism, the missal, the breviary and the new edition of the Vulgate. An enormously strengthened government machine grasped the central business of the Church and held it down to the First Vatican Council and the total overhaul of canon law in 1917. Among the things which Trent did not do was to define the distribution of authority in the Church, even though its emphasis was more on the outer form than the interior life of the Church. There was inevitably a curial tradition of regarding the legacy of Trent as complete and adapting it for the future by increasingly free methods of interpretation. But it was possible to take the view that the work of Trent was incomplete, and ought to be resumed and clarified. This reform tradition was often in conflict with the first and ultimately issued in the Second Vatican Council. It is the achievement of recent work to demonstrate the breadth and diffusion of this movement. Most of this tradition (which had its roots in Italy) survived, however battered or diverted, in the Church, but some spent its course outside. Jansenism, brutally assailed by the Bull *Unigenitus* (1713), remained partly inside the Church and partly out, and became, especially in the later eighteenth century, increasingly a general movement for reform.[4] In this movement there were many who might be abused as Jansenists but were not; none at all who were willing to affirm belief in the five points of doctrine attributed to Jansen and condemned in the seventeenth century; and many who could make friendly contact on policy grounds with other reformers but might fairly be regarded as Jansenist by being Augustinian, anti-Molinist, anti-curial, and in favor of the reunion of the Little Church of Utrecht with the main Catholic body. It is indeed striking that although Jansenist reform recalls some of the points of the original Protestant program, it was a very Catholic affair. To qualify as a Jansenist it was not necessary to go as far as the celebrated Louvain canonist, Bernard Van Espen (1646–1728), who spent much of his life defending opponents of the Bull *Unigenitus,* and the friends of the church at Utrecht, and was finally exiled for his pains.[5]

At the beginning of the eighteenth century, however, the Habsburg dynasty might have been thought the last to be associated with Jansenism of any kind. They had grown great in the military struggle against the Protestants—their core territories had been Protestant territories—and had pushed back the Turks from the gates of Vienna to the southeast frontier; both these causes carried papal support. *Pietas Austriaca,* the theme of a genealogical work dedicated to the dynasty by the Franciscan Diego Tafuri, became the theme of the Habsburg family. The Habsburg eagle, represented in red, white, and red, held in its heart the sacred host. The triumphal train of "Pietas Austriaca" was preceded by a lion bearing the keys of St. Peter in its mouth. The rock on which the church was built was actually the rock of Austria. This apotheosis of the House of Austria formed the theme of the magnificent decorations of the ceremonial rooms of the rebuilt abbey of St. Florian and a hundred other baroque buildings sacred and secular. The feeling of relief with which the Turkish tide was finally turned in the later seventeenth century was marked by a great wave of baroque church-building, and the Hungarian church, which had to be reconstructed from the ground upwards after the expulsion of the Turks, was raised virtually exclusively in the baroque style. Baroque missions to the people, baroque devotions at court, Jesuit confessors to the emperors and their families, even the political record of the Habsburgs of having barred the way to the expansion of a France only too often allied with heretics and heathen, seemed to mark out the house of Habsburg as a devotee of all those Counter-Reformation traditions with which Jansenism was most uncomfortable. It was the Austrian rather than the Spanish Habsburgs who had pushed the interests of the Society of Jesus from the beginning, and it was in their domains that Jesuit influence lasted longest. The lion's share of the Protestant property confiscated for the church in Bohemia after the Battle of the White Mountain had gone to the Society of Jesus.

Realities, however, belied appearances in both Rome and Vienna. Innocent XI owed Leopold I a great deal for his long struggle with the Turks and for support in his conflict with Louis XIV. But Innocent XII was reconciled with the latter and favored the Bourbon succession in Spain. Clement XI (Pope 1700–21) did the same thing more decisively, and was regarded in Vienna as devoted to the interests of France. Open hostilities broke out between the emperor and the pope in 1708, and it has even been suggested paradoxically that the bulls issued from Rome against the Jansenists were designed to bolster up the French monarchy in moments of defeat by Austria.[6] There is no doubt that Emperor Charles VI deeply desired the Spanish inheritance and tried to make Klosterneuburg an Austrian Escorial, nor that the rabidly anti-curial Neopolitan lawyer, Alessandro Riccardi, who got into Charles's Spanish Council in these years, was in touch with the Jansenists in Flanders. The defense has been mounted for the papacy, that Clement XI was primarily interested in keeping war out of the Papal States, and that severe breaches in relations with the emperor were followed by attempts to patch things up; but the fact was that the emperor helped to see the pope contemptuously sidelined at the Utrecht peace settlement, disregarded his claims to sovereignty over Parma and Piacenza, and, in a small event which cast a long shadow before, occupied the pope's small port at Comacchio at the mouth of the Po.[7] And if by 1720 Austrian foreign policy had acquired a markedly anti-curial edge, Charles VI and his successors, faced with the complete reconstruction of the church in Hungary, were little disposed to temper the wisdom of absolutist policy by deferring to the opinions of Rome. The accession of Benedict XIV, not long before that of Maria Theresa, confronted her with a progressive pope who genuinely tried to prevent war among the chief Roman Catholic powers; but he favored the Bavarian candidate to the Empire who took office as Charles VII, together with his French and Spanish allies; and he was hostile to Maria Theresa on her accession in 1742. She replied by confiscating papal prebends on her territory and turning a deaf ear to his protests. And when the King of Naples drove the last of the Austrian troops under Lobkowitz from the Papal States, he was greeted by the pope as a liberator.[8]

If the heavy and persistent practice of baroque piety at the Vienna court did not prevent a good deal of friction with Rome, the successes of Habsburg foreign policy brought them into direct touch with Jansenism and a more open form of society than they had hitherto encountered. In 1714 in the multiple peace settlements which wound up the War of the Spanish Succession, Austria acquired not only a considerable empire in North Italy (and with it increased opportunities for friction with Rome) but also the Spanish Netherlands. The history of Jansenism here and in the United Provinces is the theme of another chapter of this book; suffice it to say that Jansen himself had been bishop of Ypres, his *Augustinus* had been published posthumously at Louvain in 1640, that Louvain remained a powerful center of Jansenist scholarship, and that the Netherlands provided a refuge for Arnauld and other Jansenists exiled from France.

Just across the border in the United Provinces the rigorist Archbishopric of Utrecht, held until 1686 by a friend of Arnauld, had passed to Peter Codde who refused to sign the anti-Jansenist formulary and was suspended by Rome in 1702. His chapter refused to accept the Pro-Vicar Apostolic and he was excluded by the States of Holland. From that moment the Church of Utrecht, the Old Catholic Church, which still exists, asserted both its independence and its desire for reunion with Rome on suitable terms; in 1724 it obtained the consecration of a new archbishop, and by its very existence created a new rallying point for the whole Jansenist world.

Thus the Jansenism of the Netherlands was now a problem of government for the Habsburgs, a problem exacerbated by the existence of a free, Jansenist, catholic church, just across the border in the United Provinces. In 1716 Prince Eugene himself became the Generalstatthalter, and speedily found himself walking a tightrope on the Jansenist question.[9] He did not enforce the observance of the Bull *Unigenitus*, but in the interests of the Quadruple Alliance and good relations with France he could not let the situation get out of hand.[10] His difficulty here was that the Jansenists set out to defend the rights of the university, while Rome and the bishops sought to put them down. He promised the Jansenists protection against unjust oppression and was several times at loggerheads with the bishops. His experience in the Netherlands gave him good grounds to distrust the pope and the Jesuits. As is well known, Eugene himself was a man of broad views and much information about the spiritual currents of the day. His celebrated library in Vienna contained Jansenist and other unorthodox works, and there were certainly Jansenists in his Vienna circle.[11] The fact that the Netherlands were fertile in intellectual skills which Vienna lacked guaranteed that others would follow.[12]

The immediate impulse to new ways came, however, from Italy, and not least from the new Habsburg empire there. For with the Habsburgs entrenched in the duchies of Milan and Mantua, and for thirty years in the Kingdom of Naples, all the Italian forces which felt in any way threatened by the policies of the curia turned to the emperor as the most obvious counterpoise. Even a minor episode such as the Austrian occupation of Comacchio (which was returned in 1725) was significant in this respect, for it was the defense of the imperial claim to that town which first brought Muratori, the great figure of the early Italian Enlightenment, to international prominence. Pietro Giannone, who wrote a famous anti-curial *Civil History of the Kingdom of Naples* and was drummed out of Naples by the church for his pains, lived in Vienna for eleven years on a pension granted by Charles VI from the revenues of that kingdom.

Paradoxically, one of the important centers of reforming and Jansenist influence, not least within the Habsburg sphere, was Rome itself. After the death of Clement XI in 1721, all the popes down to the middle of the century endeavored to reconcile the warring factions in the church. In one public respect the tide turned against the Jesuits and broke the theological uniformity they had established; Rome became increasingly hostile to their efforts to adapt Christian rites to Far Eastern understanding. Indeed, as cardinals, the nephews of Clement XII (1730–40) protected a circle of scholars with Jansenist tendencies. The leading figure in this circle was the Florentine scholar Giovanni Gaetano Bottari, who was called by the pope's great nephew Corsini in 1730 to be his librarian. He became a professor of church history. Almost all of the Italian Jansenists, including the famous Bishop Ricci, made contact with this circle when in Rome and spread its ideas throughout the peninsula. Under Benedict XIV (1740–58), who was known to say incautious things about the condemnation of Quesnel or the Bull *Unigenitus*,[13] when Jansenism was to be found even among cardinals,[14] the ideas of the early Italian Enlightenment reached their peak. Full of paradox as the story is, this Roman circle closely influenced the situation in the central lands of Habsburg influence. The Jesuits had kept a grip on the aristocratic elite which monopolized the Central European bishoprics by educating them all at the Collegium Germanicum in Rome. What now proved decisive was not the Jesuit education inside, but the Jansenist atmosphere outside, the college.[15]

Italian reform influences made themselves felt in Vienna in the first instance through Italians, mostly clergy, from the Trentino, who were brought in to manage the library of Prince Eugene. This later became the court library of Charles VI, and was greatly enlarged. At this early stage these Italians were primarily mediators of the influence of Muratori, the celebrated polymath of Modena. In fact, of Muratori's seventy-five correspondents in Austria, fifty-five were Italians or Trentiners.[16] Some of these were merely passing through, but there was a large body of permanent residents, employees of the court library, diplomatic representatives, secretaries to the upper clergy or private individuals. By the nature of their employment these Italians did not form a caste apart, but were in close contact with the influential life of the capital; they were in touch with reform circles at home; though they did not form an academy, they held informal gatherings of a similar nature, and (as we shall see) formed a refuge for the Salzburg circle. Moreover, in the period between the accession of Maria Theresa and the outbreak of the Seven Years War, when both Rome and Vienna became aware how far they had to go to catch up with the outside world, they were of real importance.

The nature of their problems only enhanced the influence of Muratori. For he was not only an archivist and librarian, not only a critical historian and editor of source materials (a crucial skill for the Jansenist appeal from the contemporary church to the early church), not only a writer on the arts and sciences, the rational ordering of law and of the devotional life, but he was adviser to the duke of Modena, whose state teetered on the brink of bankruptcy. Muratori, in short, had immediate contact with the problem confronting every ruler, and with the possibility of easing it by the use of church property.[17] Ominously for the future harmony of the Catholic world, the one cash-strapped ruler for whom this road was not open was that last-ditch defender of the Society of Jesus, the reactionary Pope Clement XIII (1758–69). Nor is there any doubt but that he gave the Habsburg family a severe push in the Jansenist direction. Not only did he decline the normal give-and-take of diplomatic relations with the curia, but he excommunicated Maria Theresa's prospective son-in-law, the duke of Parma, for seeking a way out of financial difficulties by promoting measures against the church in 1768; and to Kaunitz, Maria Theresa's chancellor, this was the last straw in enlightened times.[18]

A powerful Muratori circle established itself at Salzburg. As recently as 1731 Salzburg had witnessed one of the most dramatic episodes of the Counter-Reformation when, following Jesuit missions, a Protestant population of some 30,000 was expelled at short notice by the new archbishop, Leopold Anton Eleutherius, Baron von Firmian. In the following decade, however, a group of reformers gathered there who made contact with the Jansenists and the Italian reformers deriving from Muratori. The Salzburg group were all of importance in the church history of Austria, and exemplified a significant generational change, for four of them were relatives of the persecuting archbishop: Maria, Count Thun, his nephew and later Prince-bishop of Passau; Leopold Ernst von Firmian, dean of Salzburg (1733–39) and then bishop of Seckau; Virgil, Baron von Firmian; and Karl, Baron von Firmian, later governor of Lombardy and an ally of Kaunitz. The moving spirit in the group was a friend of Muratori, the historian Gaspari. The attraction of Salzburg for this group was that it possessed the only German Catholic university not in the hands of the Jesuits; run by South German and Austrian Benedictines, it acquired great repute for canonist and Thomist studies, and in the seventeenth century was the only Catholic *Hochschule* to accept history into its program of study. The Salzburg group, however, abused as freemasons, were defeated after a tremendous struggle in their effort to introduce the full progressive Protestant program into their university. They dispersed in 1742, but they remained in touch with the Italian group in Vienna, and those in church office began to prepare the ground for the later church reforms in Austria. When Trautson became Archbishop of Vienna he made the standard Muratorian and Jansenist attacks on the exaggerated cult of the saints and the Virgin, and began to reduce the number of saints' days; other members of the circle did the same in the sees of Gurk and Passau.[19]

These influences gained hugely in importance from covert changes in the religious psychology of the Habsburg family itself. Maria Theresa, the devout daughter of a converted Protestant mother, fully kept up the baroque observances which were part of the *Pietas Austriaca*. But from at least the time of her marriage with Francis Stephen of Lorraine in 1736, different influences were at work. The Lorraine court had been disposed to Jansenism on political grounds, and Francis Stephen brought with him a curious mixture of Stoicism, Catholicism, Quietism and Jansenism, not to mention the freemasonry into which he had been initiated by Walpole at Houghton in 1731, and which he practiced privately even in Vienna.[20] These views would not have obtained a hearing with Maria Theresa had they not involved a strictness of their own, and in both Francis Stephen and his sons this came out in a conscientious fulfilment of religious duties, daily devotion and (in the Jansenist manner) frequent confession with no corresponding obligation to frequent communion.[21] His instructions for the education of his children say nothing of the veneration of saints, the cult of Mary, processions and pilgrimages.[22]

Of course Maria Theresa had no option but to keep up a public balancing act, and, with whatever degree of conviction, maintained in public a high degree of devotion to the traditions of *Pietas Austriaca*. But the question has been quite seriously asked whether Maria Theresa was a Jansenist, and her private religious history was certainly an odd one.[23] Her mother is said to have been a rather unwilling convert who found Jansenism a more acceptable form of Catholicism than the baroque and supplied her daughter with Jansenist books. Maria Theresa also took advice from Domenico Passionei, nuncio in Vienna (1731–38), who was closely connected with Prince Eugene and later an important protector of Jansenists in

Rome. She supplied her children almost exclusively with Jansenist literature, and the flood of Jansenist translations into German in mid-century owed much to the knowledge that they would be welcome at court. The most famous of French late-Jansenist works was Mésenguy's *Exposition de la doctrine chrétienne* (1744), which after a sensational trial was put on the Index in 1761. It was, however, favored by Maria Theresa and, just after her death in 1781, it came out in four volumes in German with an imperial privilege.

The most public sign of a change came when the Habsburg family gradually got rid of their Jesuit confessors and replaced them with men of Jansenist sympathies. The process began with Isabella of Parma, the first wife of the Emperor Joseph II, who took the Jansenist Gürtler as her confessor. After her early death he took over as confessor to Joseph II's second wife, Josepha of Bavaria. In 1767 Maria Theresa took on Ignaz Müller, Provost of St. Dorothea, a moving spirit in the Vienna Jansenist circle, and a man whose theological library was predominantly French, half of it Jansenist. By this time half the court chaplains were Jansenist and half Jesuit. Before the abolition of the Jesuit order, Joseph II had got rid of his Jesuit confessor, and the only two Habsburgs who retained them were two unmarried daughters of Maria Theresa who went into convents. Not surprisingly, the Austrian Jansenists reached the peak of their influence about the time of the abolition of the Jesuit order, though Maria Theresa had firm views on the limits within which they might exercise authority on matters political. Nevertheless, the Jansenist weekly propaganda sheet, the *Nouvelles ecclésiastiques,* had frequent "occasion to applaud the zeal of the Empress-Queen," and wished only that she would be a little more tough on the ex-Jesuits.[24]

In fact after the death of Francis Stephen in 1765, Maria Theresa became steadily more melancholy, world-denying, and ascetic. The only priest she would see in her last illness was Ignaz Müller; but as one who clung to political power to the end, she could not be blind to the fact that the political forces for which the Jesuits stood had been put on the defensive but not routed; and she pursued something of a zig-zag course. The insuperable snag with the Jesuits from the empress's viewpoint was that their combination of missions and political pressure was known by the 1750s not only to have failed entirely to rid her domains of Protestants, but actually to generate revival among them; even at the end of her life she got a great mission going in Moravia, the main effect of which was to reveal a surprising number of surviving Protestants who had the boldness to petition for toleration. This was more than Maria's Jansenist soul could contemplate.[25]

While these changes had been going on at court, changes of a Jansenist and reformist kind had been taking place in the country which paved the way for the more radical church reforms of a later generation. Very early Jansenism in Austria had a lay and bureaucratic character which distinguished it completely from the later Jansenism. For at first Jansenist ideas could only be acquired by foreign travel. The Baron Franz Anton von Sporck, for example, became acquainted with Jansenism at Port Royal itself in 1680. On his return he began to translate and publish Jansenist works at his own private press, a service for which he was accused and condemned. Sporck, indeed, illustrates the vivid difference between the early and the late Jansenism. Apart from his personal contribution, only two clearly Jansenist works appeared in Austria in the first half of the eighteenth century; in the generation 1760–90 there was a comprehensive output of both original and translated material. It was a similar story with Johann Christoph von Bartenstein, a Protestant who made contact with the world of Port Royal in Paris in 1712, was converted to the Jansenist form of Catholicism, and eventually drafted the memorial for the education of the future Joseph II.

These men like the philo-Jansenist bishops did something to prepare the way for the future church reform in the Habsburg domains; but they differed notably from the late Jansenist party which was more explicitly Jansenist, almost exclusively clerical, and derived its inspiration from Italian sources. Moreover, even before Austria's experiences in the Seven Years War made the need for reform absolutely patent, Jansenism had senior clerical leadership in Vienna itself. Archbishop Trautson issued a famous pastoral letter in 1751 which tried to reduce the excesses of baroque Catholicism and take religious teaching back to essentials, a letter which Joseph II made his successor reprint thirty years later. In the current fashion he set about improving the training of the clergy and reorganized the theology faculty at Vienna. And in Jansenist style, the study of ancient languages, church councils, scripture and church history were all strengthened. Moreover, he was succeeded by the rising hope of the Jansenist party, Christoph Bartholomäus Anton, Count Migazzi.

In fact Migazzi's career, even to this point, was not unequivocal from a Jansenist viewpoint.[26] Sprung from impoverished Tirol nobility, Migazzi was trained at the Collegium Germanicum in Rome, and attached himself to the reforming circles of Count Thun and the Muratorian Dominicans. After ordination he obtained a canonry at Brixen and, continuing studies in civil and pontifical law at Innsbruck (1736–40), he became a member of the Muratorian circle there. In 1740 he accompanied Cardinal Lamberg to the conclave in Rome and came under the influence of the Austrian auditor of the Rota Romana, the reforming Count Thun. To this curial judicial post Migazzi himself succeeded (1745–51). Thun continued to assist Migazzi's career, but the job in Rome was not an easy one in those years, for the curia was on the Bourbon and Prussian side in the War of the Austrian Succession, and ran afoul of Maria Theresa and the emperor. In 1751 Maria Theresa herself rescued him from this appointment, by nominating him to Mechlin as coadjutor to the Archbishop of Alsace. The point of this appointment was that she had already sent her brother-in-law, Charles of Lorraine, as governor to the Austrian Netherlands, warning him against the advice of the archbishop, a zealous defender of the Bull *Unigenitus*. Before he set out, Migazzi was consecrated titular bishop of Carthage. A diplomatic mission to Spain on behalf of the empress followed, together with attempts by Migazzi to exchange his coadjutorship for something better. This promotion was provided by the empress in 1757 when she nominated Migazzi to succeed Trautson as Archbishop of Vienna.

It is curious to note that the empress nominated to succeed Migazzi at Mechlin the Silesian Johann Heinrich Count Franckenberg-Ludwigstorff, whom she hoped would maintain her religious and political views in the Netherlands. Franckenberg's family had lost their Silesian property to Frederick the Great and migrated to Vienna;

Franckenberg himself enjoyed the presence of Benedict XIV when he defended his thesis in canon law in Rome, and probably knew Migazzi there at the same time. As soon as Clement XIII had confirmed the appointment of Franckenberg as Archbishop of Mechlin, Migazzi consecrated him at Schönbrunn in the presence of the empress, the emperor and the future Joseph II. Maria Theresa arranged that each should be created cardinal, Migazzi in 1761, Franckenberg in 1778. Thus from an early stage were interwoven the careers of two church dignitaries, who to the dismay of Jansenists in both the Netherlands and Austria were to turn conservative together.[27]

Migazzi, however, began as so vigorous a new broom as to polarize opinion in Vienna into pro- and anti-Jesuit, pro- and anti-Jansenist with a quite new sharpness. Determined to remedy "the miserable condition of the church," he began with a visitation and an insistence upon regular catechization.[28] He followed the pattern of his mentor Thun. He was an outspoken enemy of the Society of Jesus on theological grounds. He was popular with Maria Theresa and turned her attention towards Muratori. This being opposed by one of the empress's Jesuit confessors, she replaced him on Migazzi's advice by a Jansenist. He thus came into conflict with the curia and the nuncio. Above all he aimed to give permanence to his work by creating a seminary in his diocese. The problem was to find teachers for the seminary who were not simply pale reflections of their own Jesuit tutors. So two tutors were sent off to Paris to pick up the latest wrinkles from the Sorbonne, the most famous faculty in Europe. For whatever reason, when they returned to Vienna they left the house Migazzi had created for his seminary, and were replaced by Patrizius Fast, the son of a Styrian surgeon, and three Polish Lazarist fathers. But the intention was clear. Migazzi introduced rigorist moral works, the Jansenist catechism of Montpellier, and supplied the students with the substantial Jansenist holdings from his own library. And the moving spirit in the background was Simon Ambros Stock, who had risen steadily in Vienna under the patronage of Charles VI as a preacher of Muratorian reform and reform of university studies.

Stock was born in Vienna in 1710 to a civil service family, almost all the boys of which went into the church. His special field was in the university where in 1741 he became dean of the theological faculty and in 1746, rector. In 1759 Migazzi got him made director of the Theological Faculty in place of two Jesuits. Stock had Jansenist views on church law, alarming the curia with the doctrine that the bishops, as successors of the apostles, received their authority immediately from Christ; eventually he frightened Migazzi himself by supporting the idea that secular clergy should be given opportunities to teach in the universities at the expense of the Jesuits. He boasted of having got rid of "scholastic barbarism" from the theological faculty, and was feted as the restorer of patristics, Thomism, and Augustinianism; he played a part in one of Maria Theresa's most celebrated blows against the Jesuit monopoly of higher education, the creation of chairs in Vienna for members of the Dominican and Augustinian orders so despised by the Jesuits. These were filled by two Italians, the Dominican Pietro Maria Gazzaniga and the Augustinian Guiseppe Azzoni. The great object was to treat the doctrines of grace without causing the unrest which had arisen in France and the Netherlands. Other Augustinians made their way in the other Habsburg universities—Graz, Freiburg, Prague, Olmütz, and Brünn.

The most important was Gazzaniga, who came from a teaching appointment in Bologna. A sharp anti-Jesuit and one of the few regular clergy to enjoy the respect of Kaunitz, he was regarded by the Vienna ultramontanes as an extreme adherent of Jansenism and regalianism, and was indeed at this early stage keen on the project of a reunion between Rome and Utrecht; in 1767 he became a regular correspondent of the *Nouvelles ecclésiastiques*. He kept the great organizer of the Utrecht cause, Dupac de Bellegarde, well apprised of his activities and those of his pupils. In truth he was a moderate Jansenist. He turned against Stöger's church history (see below), became alarmed at the activities of both the radical Jansenists and of Joseph II, and after the pope's forlorn visit to Vienna in 1782, he went back to Bologna and to a curial line.

Stock's role in clerical education and in the censorship made him the most important of the mid-century Jansenists, though he was not so much the leader as the spiritual father of a new generation of radical Jansenists, some of whom were pupils of the Jesuits whom he had converted to new views, and who were to be crucial to the last generation of Austrian Jansenists. His three most important disciples were Melchior Blarer, a Swiss, who did several spells in theological education abroad, including one at Amersfoort, the seminary of the church at Utrecht, Johann Baptist de Terme, and Anton Wittola. Johann Baptist de Terme, born in 1738 the son of a waggoner, became the leader of the radical Jansenists when Joseph II came to sole rule in 1788, but like the others, he had made his way under Maria Theresa. His future was secured in 1768 when he became confessor to Marie Antoinette shortly before she went off to France. Maria Theresa then gave him a canonry in the cathedral, where he became the leader of the Jansenist party in the chapter. He became the Vienna correspondent of the *Nouvelles ecclésiastiques* and railed against baroque devotions. Like Joseph II his great interest in church reform was to secure better pastoral care, and he looked to the Vienna Jansenist group to achieve it.

Wittola translated Jansenist literature from the French, pamphleteered against the fear of Jansenism, and launched his own version of the *Nouvelles ecclésiastiques*, the *Wienerische Kirchenzeitung* (1784–89).[29] This was more than a propaganda sheet; it was a link between the Austrian and Tuscan Jansenists, carrying news in common with Ricci's *Annali ecclesiastici.* Ultramontanes quipped that in the underworld evil clergy were required as a punishment to read it daily.[30] And well they might, for Wittola believed in a sort of clerical democracy on Richérist lines, and firmly championed Febronius in his crusade for the rights of the Reichskirche. He thought that the true voice of the church, the councils, was constantly being thwarted by the curialists. The center for popular devotion should be the Mass, in which there should be more popular participation. There should be vernacular hymns and psalms rather than instrumental music. He was against half-naked representations of the Virgin and Child. The doctrine of the Immaculate Conception he rejected as a Scotist school opinion, and regarded the great Austrian Marian pilgrimage places, Mariazell, Maria Taferl, and Sonntagsberg, as dens of thieves. He was among the bitterest of Austrian opponents of the devotion to the heart of Jesus. He greeted the French Revolution, the civil constitution of the clergy, and the reform laws with sympathy.

He was much too outspoken for his own good, and remained all his life a simple parish priest, writing under the pseudonym "an Austrian pastor."

A literary career like that of Wittola would not have been possible without major changes in the censorship; this therefore was another field in which the battle between, on one side, the Jesuits in possession, and, on the other, the forces of a reforming state, Catholic reform, and Jansenism was fought out. In the middle of the eighteenth century there was virtually no opposition in Austria to the censorship as such, though there was vigorous criticism of the way the Jesuits administered it—charges of ignorance, hamfistedness, prejudice, chicanery, and the desire to dominate were as common against them as they were against the state censorship at the end of the century.[31] The War of the Austrian Succession, however, had shown up the weaknesses of the Austrian system, and none of the reformers brought in from the outside, neither the Hollander Gerard van Swieten (not himself a Jansenist, though on this issue prepared to go with them), the Moravian Wenzel Anton von Kaunitz, nor the Silesian Friedrich Wilhelm von Haugwitz was disposed to shrink before the Society of Jesus. The upshot was that the censorship was absorbed into the machinery of state and bureaucratized, a result the more palatable to the church reformers when the benign rule of Benedict XIV was replaced in Rome by the pro-Jesuit reaction under Clement XIII. When Stock supplanted the rule of two Jesuits in the Theology Faculty, he and a friend replaced them on the censorship commission, and by 1759 there was a majority of Muratorians and Jansenists on the censorship commission; by 1764 the last Jesuit was gone. The result was striking. Jesuit works were banned; Jansenist works came flooding in. Not all was gain for the reformers. Migazzi as president of the Studienhof commission had to deal with the censorship decisions on the canon law works of Neller, Febronius, Kollar, and François Richer; the experience of letting in this flood finally helped to turn Migazzi away from reform into a conservative course. Not that the Jansenists were liberals; they were as prepared to turn the censorship against English deists as against Jesuits.

Migazzi's change of view was completed between 1763 and 1767. It led to his being reconciled with the Jesuits, and to some embarrassing reversals of front on his own part. In 1764 Febronius's book *De Statu ecclesiae* appeared in Vienna, and was cleared by the censorship commission, Migazzi making no objection. He then demanded of Van Swieten that, since the book was now upon the Papal Index, it be condemned out of respect to the papal court.[32] What Van Swieten could not know was that twice, in March and July 1764, Migazzi had pressed Clement XIII to take action against the book.[33] The significance of this contretemps was that Migazzi withdrew from the state censorship commission which functioned on a majority basis and took a stand upon his apostolic office. Here was being pleaded what became the standard theme of the conservatives, that the liberties of the church must be defended against aggression by the state. By contrast, Jansenists became more than ever determined to reject such right of resistance as the Jesuits had countenanced and insisted on the subject's absolute obligation of obedience to the state.[34] This breach of relations was completed when the censorship commission cleared Richer's book. Migazzi now broke with Stock. Not only did he forfeit his influence on the theological faculties and the censorship commission, he found his influence confined to the secular clergy. He had to subordinate his reform plans to papal instructions and found himself defeated by a combination of state legislation for the church and the resistance of his clergy. He was unavoidably pursued for almost the whole remaining years of his life by Jansenist propaganda of intense bitterness. If it was not that he had sold his soul for a Cardinal's hat and financial advantages, it was still darker misconduct.[35] The death of Clement XIV in 1774 (only the last, in the Jansenist belief, in a long series of Jesuit poisonings), brought Migazzi to the conclave at Rome and unmentionable foul play:[36]

> It was not rare during the reign of the former Jesuits [37] to see ambitious prelates sacrificing their lights to merit the favors of this society, and to profit by its credit. But since the downfall of the Jesuits we see the same route being taken by an Archbishop-Cardinal [Migazzi] whom one cannot treat as an imbecile since he does not pass as ignorant, who in the first years of his episcopate, declared himself zealously against lax morality, against

> probabilism, against Berruyism &c. to the point of entrusting his seminary to ecclesiastics distinguished by their piety, their knowledge, and their attachment to gospel morality. . . . It is notorious at Rome that, during the last conclave, disloyal to the instructions of the Imperial Court, he appeared willingly among the hottest partisans of the ex-Jesuits, and did not observe the ordinary decencies to those of his colleagues who were not favorable.[38]

He was now carrying off from his seminary the very books he had put in students' hands. Reduced now to tacking and dividing, he incurred the hostility of members of the royal family. As the Archduke Leopold, Grand Duke of Tuscany, noted in his journal in 1778: "The Cardinal is a great talent, very devout, but intriguing, mendacious, vindictive and ambitious, he has fallen into low intrigues, a great friend of the Jesuits whom he formerly persecuted, and on whose account he met objections in Rome, as everyone knows."[39]

Migazzi also became involved in a long-running contest, trivial as to form, but revealing as to the fluctuating fortunes of a battle over general change which had to be fought out through a backstairs conflict of religious parties. Appealing against current speculative theology to Christian antiquity, the Jansenists everywhere emphasized the importance of church history, and in company with many other German Catholics, not Jansenists, believed that the standard was now being set in the progressive Protestant University of Göttingen. It was not surprising therefore that one of the early graduates of the Vienna seminary, Ferdinand Stöger, was a church historian who in 1776 produced an *Introductio in Historiam Ecclesiasticam Novi Testamenti* (German trans., 1786). Stöger was a graduate of Migazzi's seminary, but the Cardinal broke with him for helping to clear Richer's book in the censorship commission, and, when the empress put him into a provisional chair in the Theology Faculty in 1773, and he became in effect a civil servant, Migazzi tried to put the *Alumniat* under ex-Jesuits and (as the *Nouvelles ecclésiastiques* noted) strictly to control the literature available to them. In Stöger's view, church history was to be divided by epochs as well as chronologically, it was to sharpen the moral judgment, it was to stress the relations of church and state. He received the protection of Kaunitz. In form and content the book borrowed heavily from Walch and Schrökh of Göttingen—one of Migazzi's complaints was that the book was neither Catholic nor Protestant—and there were echoes of Leibniz's propaganda for church union and of the Jansenist efforts to get up a common front against atheism, and to secure reunion with the Little Church of Utrecht.[40]

The upshot was that in 1777 Stöger left the seminary and received an appointment as *custos* of the university library. His book, however, was put on trial, and became a subject of covert politics out of all proportion to its intrinsic worth; its significance was as a public badge of the attitude of the dynasty to movements in the church. The first move was made by Giuseppe Garampi, who had been making himself expert on German affairs for some years and who became nuncio in Vienna in 1776.[41] Garampi had begun from a Muratorian standpoint with a scholarly career in view and had been pushed on by Benedict XIV. Under Clement XIII he made a decisive career change to papal diplomacy, became a German specialist, and represented the pope in the negotiations which took place to end the Seven Years War. In this period he came to believe that the German church was in a parlous state both religiously and politically, and adopted uncompromising ultramontane views. Garampi, however, remained a modernizer in the sense that he understood that the ultramontane cause would not be saved by the methods of Clement XIII, and set about creating a caucus and a spy system, rational in the Weberian sense, which would defeat the arbitrary incursions of the temporal powers in Germany upon the sphere of canon law. His frame of mind may have been somewhat less than rational, since one of his first missives to Rome was a complaint, sent in code, that he was being spied on all the time.[42] His first tactic was to build up a network to keep Maria Theresa in line, including Migazzi and Kerens, the bishop of Wiener Neustadt, to secure a retractation from Hontheim, who had campaigned for episcopalism as "Febronius," and to make an example of Stöger.

So in an audience with Maria Theresa in 1777, Garampi complained of the bad state of the theology students at the University of

Vienna, and blamed it on Stöger's book and the Protestant and Jansenist literature recommended in it. He also made the same complaints to Rome, and had his pressure on Maria Theresa reinforced by Migazzi, with material from a statement probably written by an ex-Jesuit. Migazzi also aroused support among bishops and sought official permission to send a copy of the book to Cardinal Franckenberg at Mechlin with a view to getting an opinion on it from the theology faculty at Louvain without creating a stir. Before this threat there gathered behind the empress's Jansenist confessor, Ignaz Müller, ministers and councillors of state, professors, laypeople and reforming priests and all the Jansenists, with the exception of Gazzaniga, who foreshadowed his later withdrawal from the cause by wishing to avoid scandal now. Each side circulated its propaganda. Migazzi's embarrassment was that he did not want an ecclesiastical trial of the book in Vienna, since at some stage this must involve questions of doctrine coming before a temporal judge in an absolutist state. So both he and Garampi appealed to Rome. The pressure upon the empress from opposite directions was now intense. She was inclined to believe that the whole matter arose in private resentments and party spite, and, in a game of bluff with Garampi, threatened to leave all matters of theological education to her son; this bluff Garampi was prepared to call. Rome accordingly declared that no penalty short of the dismissal of Stöger from his chair would suffice. And in November, apparently following a personal letter from the pope, Maria Theresa withdrew her *Placet* to the book and made its use in theological education impossible. Claude Fleury's *Church History* must be used instead. Migazzi's charges against Stöger were circulated in several languages; his reply never reached the public.[43]

The end of the matter was a compromise befitting Maria Theresa's trimming policies. Stöger continued to teach unharmed in the University of Vienna, and a reconstruction of theological studies proceeded there under the guidance of the Benedictine Rautenstrauch. When Joseph II entered on his mother's heritage after 1780, the duration of theological studies was several times shortened, but, in the Jansenist manner, church history was left untouched. After the Edict of Toleration of 1781, Stöger's book was openly sold, and in 1786 it appeared in German. In the same year he was sent to the Netherlands as director of the Theological Faculty at Louvain and rector of Joseph's General Seminary. Reform in the Netherlands had to come as a consequence of the abolition of the Jesuit order, but Stöger found himself faced with the same combination of enemies, and some new ones as well. A secret ultramontane combination was formed between Migazzi, Franckenberg, the nuncio, and professors at Louvain. They proved able to call on student power as well, and demagogic demands for Stöger to go. Joseph II was in no mood to buckle; he put dragoons and cannons into Louvain and even threatened to move the whole university to a barracks at Ghent. But in the end all was in vain; Stöger fled to Vienna, and lived (in a former Jesuit probation house, no less) more or less incognito. The old order at Louvain which withstood the threat of Josephinist reform had almost reached the limits of its own survival; what the emperor could not do, war and revolution did. Against them reactionary student power was of no avail.

The unimportant author of a not very significant book became the object of such intense high-level diplomacy and covert politics for two reasons. The first was that in the Habsburg sphere of influence in Italy a program of state-led church reform was unfolding which in the conservative view would be ruinous if extended further; and the second was that the balancing act among the parties performed by Maria Theresa must come to an end when she died and was succeeded (in the event in 1780) as sole ruler by Joseph II. Joseph II was not merely a very different character from his mother, but after his succession the leaders of anti-curial politics in Italy, the Habsburg lands, and Germany would be three brothers: Leopold, the Grand Duke of Tuscany, and future Emperor Leopold II; Joseph himself; and the Elector Maximilian Franz, Archbishop of Cologne, who, as a boy had been heavily exposed to Jansenist influence. The three brothers were by no means identical in their policies, but the prospect of such a combination was bound to alarm conservative sentiment in the curia.

The first area to feel the Habsburg new broom was Lombardy, which was for long a sort of satrapy to Kaunitz, ably supported by his nominee as governor, Karl Count Firmian, a relative of the reforming bishop. The Duchy of Milan preserved the administrative and political structure of a city-state, so that here Habsburg absolutism was unburdened by the feudal system which inhibited it elsewhere.[44] Early in 1767 Maria Theresa published an edict in Lombardy for the recovery of real property which had been acquired in mortmain since 1715, a policy which (the *Nouvelles ecclésiastiques* noted smugly) would cost the Jesuits more than anyone else.[45] Already church lands acquired since 1716 were subject to the same taxes as lay property, and in August 1767 a special government department (*Giunta economale*) was created to supervise church affairs; this subjected papal bulls and other ecclesiastical communications to a state imprimatur and substituted a secular censorship board for the old ecclesiastical one. It also went on to consider other reforms of a Jansenist kind, limiting the number of holy days, and converting fasting obligations into more productive channels. Kaunitz's willingness to press reform against the pope owed little to Jansenism, but it verified Habsburg credentials to men of Jansenist views.

The thing which opened the sluice gates, however, was Clement XIII's excommunication of Ferdinand, Duke of Parma, on 30 January 1768. He was Maria Theresa's prospective son-in-law, and the intention of the curia was to make an example of the weakest of the powers at that moment dealing roughly with the Society of Jesus. The effect, however, was to produce a united front of Bourbon and Habsburg, which left the papacy helpless. Kaunitz, who had been proceeding cautiously, came round to the full-blooded doctrine that "the court of Rome must be convinced once and for all, that except for matters of faith this is no longer the time for it to dictate laws to temporal princes."[46] Indeed, the pope's defense of the Society of Jesus could hardly have been better calculated to confirm the Jansenist charge that the Jesuits were a treacherous support to the lay power. This lesson was absorbed in Vienna as well as Milan; Maria Theresa transferred the policies of the *Giunta economale* to the Bohemian-Austrian Hofkanzlei, and more radical measures began to characterize the heartlands as distinct from the fringe provinces of the Habsburg enterprise.[47] And to underpin the whole enterprise, Kaunitz set about drumming up an explicit philosophical apologia.[48]

On various points Jansenists and *Aufklärers* might see eye to eye, but at bottom their premises were different. In Tuscany, however, the great opportunity for the Jansenists seemed to open. Leopold had been raised in the enlightened Catholicism of his father, Francis Stephen, to which Fénelon, Muratori, Jansenism, and even freemasonry contributed. The latter's memorandum for the education of his son relied on a mixture of Christian and Stoic doctrines. Leopold became a slave to duty, and much more of a Jansenist than his mother.[49]

Moreover, Tuscany was fertile soil for Jansenist reform. In common with other north Italian provinces, Tuscany had begun to go down the hill culturally since Europe's political and economic centers of gravity had migrated northward. But intellectual life was not dead, and Tuscany was so priest-ridden a state that it was easy for reformers and Jansenists to make common cause. Almost 3 percent of the population were in holy orders and half the land was church property. In Pistoia, a city of 9,000 inhabitants, 82,000 masses a year were said. Nor could reform wait. Leopold took over the duchy from his father in 1765, immediately after the last great famine of Italian history in 1764. The intelligentsia could approve a policy which began with free trade in corn and economy in government. In the circumstances, economy in the Church was equally appropriate. Proximity to Rome gave Tuscany the double benefit of a close view of the disorders there and the influence of the Jansenist caucus in Rome.

From the time of his arrival in Tuscany, Leopold advanced Jansenists to chairs in the theological faculties and to bishoprics, and ensured that their publications had no trouble with the censorship. Nor did he stop the Leghorn edition of the *Encyclopedia* which was on the Papal Index; but then he made Leghorn the subject of a very satisfying experiment in toleration. Leopold was not much interested in questions of doctrine, but he cared deeply about the practical cure of souls. In his "Notes on Public Education" he wrote that the business of a priest was to teach his parishioners the practice of the religion which was simple, to show them how to keep well in the country, to explain better methods of cultivation, to see that they knew some of the principles of law, a bit of medicine, and the care of bees—all of which mattered more to them than theological questions.

But as we have seen, Jansenism had long since ceased to be a theological defense of five condemned theses about the doctrines of grace and had become a general reform movement. It may be that this had become a weakness and the reason why only two of Leopold's bishops, Pannili in Chiusi and Pienza, and Ricci in Pistoia and Prato, were prepared to take the struggle against Rome to extreme limits. But to many in Tuscany as well as Rome, Leopold looked a doctrinaire Jansenist, the more dangerous, as long before the death of his mother, circumstances had enormously increased his significance in the Habsburg dynasty: the refusal of Joseph II to marry again after the death of his second wife in 1767, and the ability of Leopold to father a new child every year and produce a flock in which the great majority were boys, ensured that the future of the family was in his hands.[50]

The rest of the story in Tuscany is so well known as to require only brief reference here. Relations with the papacy deteriorated after 1780; Leopold went ahead not only with church reform on familiar lines, but in alliance with Ricci, a Jansenist in touch with the surviving leaders of the party in France. He wanted to center religious life on the parish and its liturgy, and that meant getting rid of the competition of the chapels of religious orders, private shrines, and the like. The distraction of private masses competing with the parish mass must come to an end, he felt. Financial difficulties could be met by reducing the number of clergy and pillaging the religious orders. Edifying literature was provided free for the clergy, including a signal no one could miss, Quesnel's *Moral Reflections on the New Testament.* In 1785 Leopold required all his bishops to hold a diocesan synod, and in 1786 he gave them the famous agenda of Fifty-Seven Points to get through, the slant of which was clear. They were to consider how to purge the breviary of false legends, how to encourage the reading of the Bible, how to defend the authority of the bishops from the encroachments of Rome, how to get Augustine's teaching on grace into seminaries and universities and more of the same. The principal expert present was Professor Pietro Tamburini of Pavia, very Jansenist and perhaps arriving with the draft resolutions in his pocket.

The end was not what Leopold envisaged. There was a hostile popular reaction to the revised liturgies and other changes, culminating in violent riots at Prato in response to the rumor that the bishop was about to demolish an altar dedicated to the girdle of the Virgin. Order was not restored until troops moved in. The duke continued to rule by decree for a time, but he had seen the red light. In 1789 Belgium rose against the policies, including the ecclesiastical policies of his brother Joseph, and when Leopold moved off to Vienna to succeed him in 1790, riots broke out again.[51] Leopold advised his successor that Ricci was a liability, that his resignation should be accepted and rewarded with a good pension. The alliance of prince and prelate which afforded Jansenism and Catholic reform their best chance had gone.[52]

Lombardy and Tuscany were bound to be sideshows, albeit important ones, to the main Jansenist hopes concentrated on Vienna. Once Joseph II had assumed sole rule, the tide would surely turn and the state would exercise its prerogatives in church matters for good as the Jansenists had so long hoped and prayed. The Jansenist propaganda machine hailed his advent and for a few years continued to take a laudatory view of his policies. Wisdom underpinned his government;[53] he had formed a plan of church reform before assuming sole rule, and his schemes for the wholesale creation of new parishes and a national episcopate at the expense of monastic funds were welcome;[54] he was against ransacking peasant houses for heterodox books;[55] he regulated the divine office and forbade his ecclesiastics to accept the cardinal's hat.[56] And on the party shibboleths of the late Jansenists he scored highly; he was against devotion to the Sacred Heart, in all the universities of his states he suppressed the oath to the Immaculate Conception, he prohibited the teaching of ultramontanist opinions at Louvain.[57] Moreover, Joseph's single rule commenced with a veritable flood of publications, almost a free market in books; and although this opening was exploited more effectively by enlightened than by Jansenist writers, the opportunity was there to be seized.

Yet the flood tide of the late-Jansenist movement in Austria proved to be the end of the reign of Maria Theresa, and by the death of Joseph II, the movement, though still vocal, had ceased to count. This occurred for three chief reasons. Joseph himself was not the ruler for whom the Jansenists hoped; their enemies in Rome and in the hierarchy proved too strong; and the moderate and philo-Jansenists turned out to be a broken reed. Catholic reform had given a temporary cohesion to more partners than it could unite in the longer run.

This last point applies indeed to Joseph himself, who was an unmistakable Catholic reformer. Not a *philosophe* in the Voltairian sense, he was certainly not a Jansenist, but a sort of Christian Stoic.[58] His education was a curious mixture of Jesuit logic and law taught partly from Protestant sources by Protestant converts.[59] He wanted to be shut of the Protestants in his own domains and to divide the Protestant powers abroad as much as his mother, though he was prepared to set about securing those ends in a different way; like his mother he also was prepared to tack in the direction of the Jansenists to secure support for his early church reforms; but he soon conspicuously distanced himself from them, and, like Napoleon later, he had a use for pope and clergy if he could obtain their cooperation by force or by threats.[60] Joseph possessed neither his mother's genuine devoutness, nor her capacity for manipulation. The man who put an end to *Pietas Austriaca* in court ceremonial was in fact a man of small religious conviction, as were some of his servants; but if it had been a significant public signal in the time of Maria Theresa when Jesuit confessors were replaced by Jansenists, it was equally significant when the last Jansenist royal confessor was dismissed in 1784 and replaced in the following year by an ex-Jesuit. Jansenism, moreover, was not quite what Joseph II needed. The rise of the Habsburg monarchy had been made possible against all probability by harnessing the force of the Counter-Reformation and a good deal of esoteric doctrine against the palpable targets of the Protestants and Turks, and a substantial aristocratic caucus, some of it ex-Protestant, had been built up to support it. But the unity thus achieved was a minimal unity, incapable of destroying Protestantism or insuring the regime against the strains inflicted on it by Frederick the Great. It no longer mattered that Jansenist reform carried quaint echoes of Protestantism in its anti-hierarchical aspects; it mattered a great deal that it was ill-suited to a ruler determined to use a church modernized from above as his ancestors had used the Counter-Reformation. And whereas in France, Italy, or the Netherlands, Jansenism had institutional sources of strength apart from the monarchy, in Vienna it had not. In a great measure the creation of the dynasty, its weakness was exposed when its usefulness to the dynasty ended.

It was also true that a considerable party had been built up against the Jansenists which was more than their own international conspiracy and propaganda could match. Garampi, the papal nuncio in Vienna, was a model. Garampi began as a modernizer much esteemed by Muratori, but having entered the service of the curia, he remained loyal to it. In any case, it was not difficult to recognize the threat posed to the Church by the state-church system, not only in Germany where Febronius crystallized the issue, but in Poland where a chaotic church system was threatened with further chaos by the partition of the country among three great powers, Russia, Prussia, and Austria, each with emphatic, and different, state-church traditions of its own. Even crude interest-building by promoting individuals to the cardinalate undertaken by Torrigiani, the unreconstructed Secretary of State of Clement XIII, was thought to have been sufficient to change the loyalties of Migazzi; but he was no doubt as capable as Garampi of making uncomfortable constitutional inferences from Josephism even as practiced by Maria Theresa. Nor was he alone; the great philo-Jansenist bishops of the Habsburg sphere of influence eventually went much the same way.

Moreover, Garampi exploited a split in the Jansenist party in Vienna, if he did not actually cause it, before the death of Maria Theresa. Moderate Jansenism was by this time of small consequence in Austria, and the Italians who had counted for so much in the party in Vienna remained loyal to the curia and went back to Italy. Death and these migrations left Joseph II with a radical Jansenist rump, de Terme, Wittola, and Blarer, the eloquent leaders of what was now a purely clerical party. These were in any case of limited use to the Emperor. Wittola's hopes of becoming an Austrian Ricci were effectively dashed by his launching of the *Wienerische Kirchenzeitung* in 1784, a local equivalent to the *Nouvelles ecclésiastiques*. Apart from being a prospective nuisance in taking up the cause of parish-priest democracy on Richérist lines, he was tarred with the brush of the failure of his Tuscan allies. Before the death of Joseph II he was writing in tones of resignation. As for Blarer, he had always been a wanderer and a seeker. Appointed by Maria Theresa to the new seminary at Brünn in Moravia in 1777, he enjoyed there the most successful period of his life. But he was always on the move, and foresaw very early the turn which Joseph's policy would take.

Not only were the radical Jansenists out-maneuvered by Garampi and the curia, frustrated by the old loyalties of the hierarchy, and let down by Joseph II, they were in a sense caught out by the development of the Enlightenment. The attraction of the late-Jansenist-Catholic Reform program was that it had offered a middle way between a baroque Catholicism which had failed to meet the needs of the Habsburg system or of common Catholic Christianity, and an Enlightenment not necessarily skeptical, but with apparently skeptical implications. It was indeed the Enlightenment that finished the work which Garampi (who was as irritated with Joseph II as any Jansenist) had begun. Late in life Wittola turned against the Protestant Neologists, especially Semler, whom he accused of rationalism, materialism, arianism, and socinianism. The graduates from the seminary at Brünn divided between those who turned to the Enlightenment in the full sense and those who went back to tradition. Ignaz Aurel Fessler (1756–1839), a fellow traveler with them at the time, and now immortalized in a series of vast works by Peter Barton, seemed simply to move from one thing to another.[61] Meanwhile, governments, not least those of Joseph II, were finding that ex-Jesuits were useful. As for the church in Utrecht, for so long a touchstone of orthodoxy, it had become a sideshow well before the French Revolution. The Jansenist movement, so imposing in the latter days of Maria Theresa, found that the pillars upon which it was built were few, and had crumbled successively. Almost two centuries were needed before a reform movement like it could emerge publicly in the Church again.

Notes

1. [M. A. Wittola], *Der Jansenismus ein Schrekenbild für Kinder* (Friedburg, 1776). Compare for example, the barbs of Bernard Plongeron directed against the analysis of a highly nuanced "third party" by Emile Appolis, *Le "Tiers Parti" Catholique au XVIIIe Siècle. Entre Jansénistes et Zelanti* (Paris: A. et J. Picord, 1960). Bernard Plongeron, "Was ist katholische Aufklärung?" in Elisabeth Kovács, ed., *Katholische Aufklärung und Josephinismus* (Munich: R. Oldenbourg, 1979), 51–52.

2. Lucianus Ceyssens, "Le Jansénisme. Considérations historiques préliminaires à sa Notion," *Analecta Gregoriana* 71 (1954): 7–8. Reprinted in Ceyssens, *Jansenistica Minora,* 8 vols., (Mechelen: St. Franciscus Drukkerig, 1950–64), vol. 3, for the year 1957.

3. *Neue Literatur des katholischen Deutschlands* (Nuremberg, 1785–86), 1:524, quoted in Wilhelm Deinhardt, *Der Jansenismus in deutschen Länden* (Munich: J. Kosel and F. Pustet, 1929), 94.

4. Victor Conzemius, *Katholizismus ohne Rom. Die Altkatholische Kirchengemeinschaft* (Zurich: Benziger, 1969), 15–23.

5. Michel Nuttinck, *La Vie et l'Oeuvre de Zeger-Bernard Van Espen. Un canoniste janséniste, gallican et régalien à l'Université de Louvain,* 1646–1728 (Louvain: Louvain Bureaux du Recueil, Bibliothèque de l'Université, 1969), esp. 664–69.

6. Heinrich Benedikt, "Der Josephinismus vor Joseph II" in *Österreich und Europa; Festgabe für Hugo Hantsch zum 70. Geburtstag* (Graz: Styria, 1965): 186.

7. Norbert Huber, *Österreich und der Heilige Stuhl vom Ende des Spanischen Erbfolgekrieges bis zum Tode Papst Klemens XI (1714–1721)* (Vienna: Böhlau in Kommission, 1967), 30–33, 44, 79, 82, 130, 174, 184.

8. Alfred von Arneth, *Geschichte Maria Theresias,* 10 vols., (Vienna: W. Braumüller, 1863–79), 9:1–3.

9. In 1719 he even received a solemn appeal from the rector of the University of Paris to support the calling of a council of the church to oppose the Bull *Unigenitus.* Max Braubach, "Prinz Eugen und der Jansenismus" in Hugo Hantsch et al., eds., *Historica; Studien zum geschichtlichen Denken und Forschen. Festschrift für Friedrich Engel-Jánosi zum 70. Geburtstag* (Vienna: Herder, 1965), 117–34.

10. Peter F. Barton, *Jesuiten, Jansenisten, Josephiner. Eine Fallstudie zur frühen Toleranzzeit: Der Fall Innocentius Fessler* (Vienna: Böhlau, 1978), 151.

11. Max Braubach, *Prinz Eugen von Savoyen: Eine Biographie,* 5 vols., (Vienna: Verlag für Geschichte und Politik, 1963–65), 4:164–76; 5:107.

12. For the swings in Habsburg church policy in the Netherlands after Prince Eugene's time there, see Charles de Clercq, "Documents des Archives de

l'État à Vienne concernant les archevêques de Malines, d'Alsace et de Franckenberg pour les années 1722–59" in *Sacerdos et Pastor Semper Ubique,* Festschrift for Franz Loidl (Vienna: Wiener Dom-Verlag, 1972), 225–33.

13. Emile de Heeckeren, ed., *Correspondance de Benoit XIV,* 2 vols., (Paris: Plon-Nourrit, 1912), 1:55; 2:280–82.

14. And especially Cardinal Passionei. On the whole matter see Ludwig von Pastor, *The History of the Popes, from the Close of the Middle Ages,* 40 vols., (London: J. Hodges, 1891–1953), 35:381–91.

15. Peter Hersche, *Der Spätjansenismus in Österreich* (Vienna: Österreichische Akademie der Wissenschaften, 1977), 88.

16. Elisabeth Garms-Cornides, "Zwischen Giannone, Muratori und Metastasio" in Friedrich Engel-Jánosi et al., eds., *Formen der europäischen Aufklärung,* Wiener Beiträge zur Geschichte der Neuzeit, vol. 3 (Munich: R. Oldenbourg, 1976), 224.

17. Adam Wandruszka, "Die katholische Aufklärung Italiens und ihr Einfluss auf Österreich," in Kovács, ed., *Katholische Aufklärung und Josephinismus,* 63.

18. Ferdinand Maaß, ed. *Der Josephinismus, Quellen zu seiner Geschichte in Österreich* 1760–1850, 5 vols. (Vienna: Verlag Herold, 1951–61), 1:283. For the (unconvincing) argument that Kaunitz was altogether more radical than the empress in his state-church views, see Anton Ellemunter, *Antonio Eugenio Visconti und die Anfänge des Josephinismus: eine Untersuchung über das theresianische Staatskirchentum unter besonderer Berücksichtigung der Nuntiaturberichte,* 1767–1774 (Graz: H. Böhlaus Nachf., 1963).

19. Eleonore Zlabinger, *Ludovico Antonio Muratori und Österreich* (Innsbruck: Österr. Kommissionsbuchh. in Komm., 1970), 25–40.

20. Derek Beales, "Christians and 'philosophes': the case of the Austrian Enlightenment," in Derek Beales and Geoffrey Best, eds., *History, Society and the Churches. Essays in Honour of Owen Chadwick* (Cambridge: Cambridge University Press, 1985), 174–75.

21. Adam Wandruszka, *Leopold II,* 2 vols., (Vienna: Verlag Herold, 1963–65), 1:42.

22. Hans Wagner, "Der Einfluss von Gallikanismus und Jansenismus auf der Kirchen und den Staat der Aufklärung in Österreich," in *Österreich in Geschichte und Literatur* 11 (1967): 525.

23. Peter Hersche, "War Maria Theresia eine Jansenistin?" *Österreich in Geschichte und Literatur* 17 (1971): 14–25.

24. Hersche, *Der Spätjansenismus in Österreich,* 135–36; *Nouvelles Ecclésiastiques* 1 June 1777, 89; 23 October 1779, 169.

25. Wandruszka, *Leopold II,* 2:11.

26. Even in 1770 the *Nouvelles ecclésiastiques* thought that Migazzi might bring about the regeneration of all the clergy in the Vienna diocese. *Nouvelles ecclésiastiques* 29 September 1770, 149.

27. Elisabeth Kovács, *Ultramontanismus und Staatskirchentum im theresianisch-josephinischen Staat* (Vienna: Wiener Dom-Verlag, 1975), 19–25.

28. It was thus reported to the church at Utrecht: Rijksarchief Utrecht Fonds Port Royal 2560, quoted by Kovács, *Ultramontanismus und Staatskirchentum,* 199, n. 1.

29. [M.A. Wittola], *Der Jansenismus ein Schreckenbild für Kinder.*

30. Hersche, *Der Spätjanenismus in Österreich,* 258.

31. On the whole subject see Grete Klingenstein, *Staatsverwaltung und kirchliche Autorität im 18. Jahrhundert. Das Problem der Zensur in der theresianischen Reform* (Vienna: Verlag für Geschichte und Politik, 1970).

32. Kovács, *Ultramontanismus und Staatskirchentum,* 42.

33. Pastor, *History of the Popes,* 36:287 and note 3.

34. Gustav Otruba, "Probleme von Wirtschaft und Gesellschaft in ihren Beziehungen zu Kirche und Klerus in Österreich" in Kovács, *Katholische Aufklärung,* 123.

35. Peter Hersche, "Erzbischof Migazzi und die Anfänge der jansenistischen Bewegung in Wien," *Mitteilungen des österreichischen Staatsarchivs* 24 (1971): 299 and note 85.

36. *Nouvelles ecclésiastiques* 19 December 1774, 201. It was not only Jansenists who were convinced by the rapid decomposition of the body that there had been foul play, though the Jesuits were not the sole suspects. Pastor, *History of the Popes,* 38:533.

37. The Jesuit order had been abolished by Clement XIV in 1773.

38. *Nouvelles ecclésiastiques* 11 June 1776, 95.

39. Wandruszka, *Leopold II,* 2:15.

40. Kovács, *Ultramontanismus,* 58–59.

41. For him see Dries Vanysacker, *Cardinal Giuseppe Garampi, 1725–1792: an enlightened Ultramontane* (Brussels: Institut historique belge de Rome, 1995).

42. Ibid., 150.

43. Kovács, *Ultramontanismus,* 80–90.

44. Franco Valsecchi, "Joseph II und die Verwaltungsreform in der Lombardei," in Hantsch, *Historica; Studien zum geschichtlichen Denken und Forschen,* 147–73.

45. *Nouvelles ecclésiastiques,* 5 March 1768, 40.

46. Maaß, *Der Josephinismus* 1:266–67.

47. Franz A. Szabo, *Kaunitz and enlightened absolutism, 1753–1780* (Cambridge: Cambridge University Press, 1994), 222–28; Erich Zöllner,

"Bemerkungen zum Problem der Beziehungen zwischen Aufklärung und Josefinismus," in *Österreich und Europa; Festgabe für Hugo Hantsch*, 206–7; Adam Wandruszka, "Die katholische Aufklärung Italiens und ihr Einfluss auf Österreich" in Kovács, *Katholische Aufklärung*, 67–69.

48. See for example, Eckhart Seifert, *Paul Joseph Riegger: (1705–1775) ein Beitrag zur theoretischen Grundlegung des Josephinischen Staatskirchenrechts* (Berlin: Duncker und Humblot, 1973), 345–47.

49. Leopold was, however, under his mother's instructions to make the welfare of religion his first concern in Tuscany. Adam Wandruszka, "Zur Vorgeschichte des 'Josephinismus.' Maria Theresias Instruktion für Leopold von Toskana im Jahre 1765" in Hantsch, *Historica; Studien zum geschichtlichen Denken und Forschen*, 138.

50. Wandruszka, *Leopold II*, 1:82, 182; 2:11–40.

51. On these see Hanns Schlitter, *Die regierung Josefs II in den österreichischen Niederlanden* (Vienna: A. Holzhausen, 1900), 18–29, 78; Edouard de Moreau, *Histoire de l'Église en Belgique* 5 vols., (Brussels: l'Édition universelle, 1949–52), vol. 4.

52. Wandruszka, *Leopold II*, 2:111–38; Charles A. Bolton, *Church Reform in 18th Century Italy. The Synod of Pistoia, 1786* (The Hague: Nijhoff, 1969).

53. *Nouvelles ecclésiastiques* 1782, 132.

54. Ibid., 1782, 204, 127; 1783, 65; 1784, 13.

55. Ibid., 1786, 16.

56. Ibid., 1783, 107; 1785, 164.

57. Ibid., 1781, 112; 1782, 181, 190.

58. Derek Beales, "Christians and 'philosophes': the case of the Austrian Enlightenment" in *History, Society and the Churches. Essays in honour of Owen Chadwick*, 188–89.

59. For the effectiveness of this, see Derek Beales, *Joseph II*, vol. 1 (Cambridge: Cambridge University Press, 1987), 64; Anna Hedwig Benna, "Zur Situation von Religion und Kirche in Österreich in den 50er Jahren des 18. Jahrhunderts" in *Sacerdos et Pastor Semper Ubique*, 193–224.

60. Beales, *Joseph II*, 1:120, 163, 444, 448; Gustav Otruba, "Probleme von Wirtschaft und Gesellschaft in ihren Beziehungen zu Kirche und Klerus in Österreich" in Kovács, *Katholische Aufklärung*, 108.

61. Peter F. Barton, *Ignatius Aurelius Fessler. Barockkatholizismus, Romantik, Erweckungsbewegung* (Vienna: Böhlau, 1969); Peter F. Barton, *Jesuiten, Jansenisten, Josephiner* (Vienna: Böhlau, 1978); Peter F. Barton, *Erzieher, Erzähler, Evergeten* (Vienna: Böhlau, 1980); Peter F. Barton, *Maurer, Mysten, Moralisten* (Vienna: Böhlau, 1982).

FOUR

The Religious Origins of Radical Politics in England, Scotland, and Ireland, 1662–1800

JAMES E. BRADLEY

OF THE COUNTRIES STUDIED IN THIS BOOK, THE NORTHERN German lands, and England, Scotland, and Ireland alone had established religions that were Protestant.[1] While the religious and social effects of the Reformation in these countries were profound, the political theory that grounded religious establishments remained much the same as in Catholic Europe. Protestant rulers in the British Isles, just like their Catholic counterparts on the continent, believed that religious orthodoxy expressed through an established hierarchy was essential for maintaining political order, but the English Civil War had proven that some form of accommodation for religious minorities was necessary for civic peace. From 1689 forward, dissenters in England, Scotland, and Ireland enjoyed a measure of toleration, and yet from their minority perspectives, standing as they did outside of the religious establishments, the Anglican and Presbyterian reformations had not gone nearly far enough.

The Act of Toleration of 1689 suspended the penal laws against orthodox Dissent in England, and within a year, Scottish Presbyterians once again enjoyed the status of an establishment, a status that received every possible guarantee by the Act of Union with England in 1707. Although the government of Queen Anne (1702–14) threatened to revert to an active policy of persecution, the Hanoverian accession, followed by the split in the Whig party and attempts to purchase the Dissenters' support by both parties of Whigs, finally brought relief: following the passage of the Irish Toleration Act of 1719, the toleration of Dissent seemed secure. English freedoms were widely celebrated; the breadth of religious diversity was applauded by foreigners like Voltaire almost as highly as the mixed constitution.[2] Yet Presbyterians in England and Ireland, along with English Congregationalists, Baptists, and Quakers, continued to suffer legal handicaps. The Test and Corporation acts set up serious religious barriers to their attaining public office, whether local or national; English Dissenters were denied education at Oxford and Cambridge; and a host of minor legal nuisances in such areas as marriage provided daily reminders of their second-class social status. Dissenters in Scotland soon learned that their Presbyterian brethren, when once in power, were prone to adopt the annoying habits that had characterized the Anglican establishment, and while the Presbyterian Seceders were spared the legal impositions borne by other Dissenters, they suffered the same forms of social ostracism. Irish Presbyterians who dissented from the ruling Synod of Ulster found themselves in an alienated situation very similar to the Scots Seceders and the English Nonconformists. Through a series of complex historical developments that this chapter seeks to illumine, those who dissented from the established churches in England, Scotland, and Ireland became, by degrees, leading advocates of reform and outspoken critics of civil government.

"Radicalism," of course, is the conventional term used to refer to the reformist political principles of a wide variety of disaffected groups, principles that go to the root of serious religious and civil discontent.[3] In any discussion of the origins of radicalism, however, one must concede that before the nineteenth century, radicalism was nascent and inchoate and that religion was but one of several sources of political disaffection leading eventually to organized attempts at political reform. Other ideological sources of radicalism can be traced to such well-known traditions as classical republicanism, the Commonwealthman idiom, "Country" opposition, Deism, and Freemasonry.[4] What makes the dissenting religious tradition of particular interest is that unlike these other sources, its ideology of opposition was embodied in separated ecclesiastical polities, and its religious and political expressions were thereby nurtured by separated social groups. Hence, it was not the writings of the clerical dissenting elite alone that eventually forced the majority religions to accept the principles of religious equality and pluralism, nor was it merely their theology that encouraged expressions of political discontent and calls for political reform; rather, it was the presence of hundreds of segregated, potentially seditious religious bodies scattered throughout the realms of England, Scotland, and Ireland that at length arrested the attention of the established churches and government, prompting repression in some cases, accommodation in others, and genuine efforts at reform in still others.

The theoretical grounds upon which these dissenting bodies justified their separate existence, and the specifically religious origins of their radical political disaffection, have not been sufficiently investigated. The Presbyterian tradition, in particular, provides evidence that justifies the conventional usage when referring to nascent "radicalism" and tracing its origins to religious dissent. Writing in the early 1770s, for example, the Scottish dissenting Presbyterian John Baillie argued that the principles of human equality and political representation were first instituted in dissenting ecclesiastical polity, since "the radical court in presbytery is the session," in which elders and ministers are invested in office by "the choice of the people." In a Scottish Covenanting pamphlet published at about the same time, we find that on the basis of "Scripture and right reason" the relation between rulers and those ruled in civil government was construed as both voluntary and mutual, because the "people" possess "the radical right" to choose those who rule over them, and this right is identified as the "intermediate voice of God."[5] In this statement, the paradoxical and much maligned phrase "*vox populi vox dei,*" an aspect of civil polity, is derived precisely from dissenting ecclesiastical polity. On religious grounds, dissenting theory and practice thereby radically challenged the foundations of the traditional, hierarchical view of civil, religious, and social order, an order sustained by deference to monarch, bishop, and peer. When Bristol radicals advanced the principle of universal manhood suffrage as early as 1781, it was within the ethos of a dissenting religious context.[6] And when, in 1799, the Scots dissenter Archibald Bruce defended "the radical power and inherent right of the people at large to establish, limit, or alter their government and governors," he moved but a short step from ecclesiastical to civil polity, and by this date, Bruce was already espousing what would later be known as "radicalism."[7] The origins of "radical courts," "radical rights," and "radical powers," in a word, a major source of both the terminology and the structures of radical political disaffection is thus explicitly traceable to religious dissent.

While the dissenters appealed to the spiritual nature of the church, ecclesiology for them was far more than a theological issue of proper polity, whether episcopal or congregational. Just as with an individual's conscience, chapel polity was a practical political matter with profound implications for civil government. As one opponent of church patronage in Scotland put it, studying the theory of political systems was important as a discipline of the mind, but such theory might not actually effect much change. "Some actual exercise of liberty, therefore, must be indulged to those we would wish to be its votaries. Nothing is more calculated to produce this effect with us, than our people's being allowed some interest in determining who are to be their teachers in spiritual and eternal concerns. This hath been the hinge upon which their attachment or aversion to our various princes hath turned."[8] Even during the largely placid middle decades of the eighteenth century, discussion of such matters as private judgment and ecclesiastical polity could give rise to talk of Dissenters in England making "common cause" with their dissenting brethren in Scotland, and warnings, if not threats, to both religious and civil leaders. "To impose and screw down such servitude upon societies of men" is not wise, it was said, and if the state refused to concede the justice of the Dissenters' appeals against penal legislation, then "those who have been friends will be forced to be enemies."[9]

Here the concerns of the mid-1700s are very similar to those of the mid-1600s during the Civil War. Critics of the established church in Scotland moved easily from a discussion of the unjust authority of the General Assembly in rebuking a presbytery for acting according to its collective conscience, to Parliament laying a tax of sixteen shillings on the pound upon land. In neither case, observed one author, was the issue a question of who was the proper judge of such matters, since in both cases it was assumed to be the people; rather, it was a question to be determined by the people as to whether they had judged rightly. In this instance, Scots dissenters argued, the Presbyterians in an established church who controlled the General Assembly were beginning to act just like oppressive Anglican bishops, and the former were likened to "fiery charioteers" with whips in hand who treat us like "slaves" and wish to drive the people "like beasts of burden."[10] Established churches were often associated with "princely tyranny," and hence, the Dissenters' anti-Catholicism, as we will see, characteristically veered over into a thinly veiled anticlericalism, directed as readily at Presbyterian ministers as Anglican priests.[11]

The prevailing explanation of religion in relation to English radicalism may be conveniently termed the "heresy-radicalism" thesis, a theory that focuses on individual thinkers and attempts to account for political disaffection on the grounds of their christological heterodoxy. This understanding has influenced religious explanations of radicalism for the past fifty years and more but it has recently attained great prominence: Anthony Lincoln's influential study of 1938 put the thesis categorically: "the history of significant dissenting opinion in the years 1763–1800," wrote Lincoln, "is the history of the Rational Dissenters."[12] The majority of radical publicists, whether Anglican or Nonconformist, were theologically liberal (Arian, Socinian, or Unitarian, i.e., "rational"), and research has thus centered around a relatively small, close-knit group of intellectuals in London who were mostly clergy. Past studies commonly linked the theological heterodoxy of the "rational Dissenters" and heterodox Anglicans with the social and political alienation that stemmed from the Test and Corporation acts, or the unwanted requirement of subscribing to the Thirty-Nine Articles. While virtually every study has adopted some form of the heresy-radicalism thesis, a few have recognized the importance of the social alienation of groups.[13] On the whole, however, studies of religion and radicalism have construed the subject too narrowly in terms of individuals and their ideas alone, and they have made little attempt to integrate these findings into broader, social reconstructions.

The enormous contribution of English "rational" Dissent to religious and civil liberty cannot be reasonably questioned, nor can it be doubted that anti-trinitarians, who were excluded from the benefits of the Toleration Act, suffered more than other Dissenters.[14] The importance of heterodox believers as spokesmen for political reform and sympathizers with the American and the French revolutions is beyond cavil. In the period of the American Revolution, the names of Richard Price and Joseph Priestley are eminent, but the list extends to Joseph Towers, James Burgh, Caleb Fleming, Philip Furneaux, and many others.[15] But does it follow that the Arian, Socinian, and Unitarian theology of these Dissenters was in itself the stimulus that led them to disaffection? A central problem with the heresy-radicalism thesis is that, utilizing the history of ideas, it merely reconstructs the mental world of individual Dissenters and unduly subordinates the social location and the legal conditions of Dissenting religion, lay and clerical.[16] The focus rests almost entirely on the thought and publications of the elite. The thesis also raises a major issue of the dating of religious change in relation to politics. The entire modern project of research on "rational Dissent" has concentrated on the period after 1763, and the thesis thereby neglects the earlier, more orthodox origins of political disaffection, ignoring the common heritage of all those Dissenters who worked harmoniously together on various political and social reforms, regardless of their theological differences. The thesis has served Unitarian denominational history well, and paradoxically, it also coheres with the traditional High-Anglican critique of Dissent as schismatic and thus necessarily heterodox. The ductile quality of the thesis may help account for its longevity and perennial power; it has recently been adopted and forcefully restated by J. C. D. Clark, J. G. A. Pocock, A. M. C. Waterman, and others.[17]

On the one hand, the evidence supplied in this chapter offers broad support for the growing scholarly consensus that religion in eighteenth-century Britain and Ireland was an important component of most forms of political argument. The religious resonances of the 1640s reached all the way into the new century and produced more than faint echoes in the 1770s and 1790s. Moreover, J. C. D. Clark's and David Hempton's comparative geographical perspective, underscoring the importance of denominational discourse in Ireland and Scotland, is especially valuable. Here we learn how ethnic and religious identities were intertwined and reinforced by religious rhetoric, and the relationship of this rhetoric to immigration and to a heightened sectarian identity in the colonies is shown to have important political corollaries.[18] In addition, it can now be demonstrated that the major division in local politics and in national crises like the American Revolution was not based principally in social class, although socioeconomic variations played a role, but in the religious differences between those outside the establishment and those within. Broadly speaking, Anglican ministers gave overwhelming support to the government, while Nonconformist ministers, both orthodox and heterodox, were almost unanimous in their support of the American colonists, and many were sympathetic to the French Revolution.[19] These results of recent research appear to be secure.

But what was behind the religious division and what was at the heart of the Dissenters' political disaffection? As early as 1791, trinitarian Nonconformist Robert Hall argued that the zeal of the Unitarians for freedom "cannot be imputed to any alliance between their religious and political opinions but to the conduct natural to a minority."[20] The heresy-radicalism thesis thus faces significant obstacles right at the outset. Serious anomalies in the ranks of the radical leadership should have given historians some pause; outspoken Dissenting critics of the government such as James Murray, Caleb Evans, Robert Robinson, Rees David, Samuel Palmer, and Robert Hall were orthodox trinitarians. When we find that there were actually more trinitarian Dissenting ministers who opposed the government's American policy than heterodox ones, we must search for alternative explanations in those areas of theory and practice that all Dissenters held in common.[21] An exploration of the Dissenters' common experience of a separated church polity in England, Scotland, and Ireland will locate the causes of their political disaffection principally in a commitment to individualism and self-government rather than heterodox doctrine: schism, a form of social deviance, goes further in explaining radicalism than heresy, a form of doctrinal deviance (though not without social undertones). The thesis of this chapter is that the common theology of various forms of religious dissent in Britain and Ireland was an important cause of civil disaffection, but that these theological principles, which were entirely orthodox, were effectively introduced into the civil realm through a profound experience of social alienation. Theological conviction was mediated through a religious minority's separated social identity, and both components (ideology and practice) were necessary to produce political disaffection. A comparative analysis of those who dissented from the established churches in England, Scotland, and Ireland should illumine the important bearing of private judgment and ecclesiastical polity on the origins of political radicalism.[22]

The Three Denominations in England

No detailed study of dissident English religion in relation to politics for the period 1662–1832 currently exists.[23] The salient features of denominational identity, however, can be briefly sketched in order to compare the English setting with those of Scotland and Ireland. From the ejection of some 2,000 Nonconforming ministers, lecturers, and fellows of colleges in 1662, through the penal period of Dissent to 1689, and on into the early years of Queen Anne's reign, heterodox and orthodox Dissenters alike experienced imposition and exclusion, and they were constantly under the threat of repression. The political and social implications of the sudden and irrevocable ejection of such a large body of ministers has not been sufficiently appreciated.

A vast literature on the nature of Nonconformity in relation to episcopacy (ca. 1662–1720) can be cited to illustrate the point that questions of individual conscience and ecclesiastical polity were at the heart of this Church-Dissent debate. The common practice of dating the significant religious shifts from the Act of Toleration in 1689 rather than from the ejection of Nonconformists in 1662 has allowed scholars to continue to focus on doctrine rather than the social reality of hundreds of separated, often alienated, dissident congregations. Moreover, strictly in terms of chronology, major religious debates over matters of individual conscience and ecclesiastical polity preceded in time major conflicts in Christology, and differences over polity were thereby the first matters of political debate to offer us keys into the origins of political discontent. To be sure, however, the right of private judgment and congregational polity were christologically grounded. During this period, it was the potent combination of theory and practice that mattered: the idea of the right of private judgment in the individual nurtured an egalitarian, independent disposition, and the right of congregations to appoint and dismiss their pastors betrayed an affinity for self-government that held significant promise for democracy.[24]

The Act of Toleration itself was but a small step toward liberty, in that it merely suspended the legal penalties against orthodox Dissent. Moreover, while the revolution of 1688–89 was a new beginning in some sense, for Dissenters it continued what was begun in 1662 by forcing them into a separate and politically inferior status.[25] Through the reign of Anne, this threat continued to be more than merely symbolic; these were pivotal and defining years for the Dissenters, because, as Norman Sykes observed, "within twenty years of the Revolution its religious settlement had been reversed"[26]—so decisive was the passage of the short-lived Occasional Conformity and Schism acts. The essential theoretical and practical breakthrough for English Nonconformity, therefore, came in the first two decades of the eighteenth century. On the side of theory, it was Edmund Calamy Jr., who, in his massively influential *Defense of Moderate Non-Conformity* (1703–05) showed that the essential distinction of the Nonconformists was their refusal to allow any civil or religious authority to exercise power over the individual's conscience, or for that matter, to exercise any power "derogatory to the honour of our great Master, the sole legislator in his own kingdom."[27] According to Andrew Kippis, from Calamy forward the debate between the Nonconformists and the Church of England was placed "on a new footing" of the separation of civil and spiritual authority, and the argument was always christologically grounded.[28] During the Bangorian controversy, the Low-Church Anglican Bishop of Bangor, Benjamin Hoadly, adopted Calamy's view and popularized it, bequeathing to Hoadly as much respect among Nonconformists as they later accorded John Locke. On the side of practice, the defining moment for the Nonconformists was in the events of the reign of Queen Anne. The Sacheverell affair, the Tory-inspired Occasional Conformity and Schism Bills, combined with the Bangorian controversy, helped to forge the three denominations into a cohesive religious tradition. In the first two decades of the eighteenth century, Dissenters were repeatedly put in an embattled, defensive posture; they were resented for their actions, censured for their writings, and several of them were imprisoned for what they published. This forced political exile rendered the theological differences between Dissenting denominations far less important than those principles they held in common.

On particular points of theology, of course, the English Baptists differed from the Congregationalists, and in polity, both Baptists and Congregationalists differed from the Presbyterians, but in England, all forms of Dissent adopted essentially congregational polities. The sacramental test for public office, the burdensome laws concerning marriage, and the onerous conventions regarding education put Dissenters of all varieties on the same footing.[29] Thus in relation to the established church and the state, the three denominations shared a single, coherent ideological position.[30] The ideological, or more properly, the theological, grounds of their separation from the established church were thus virtually the same in all Dissenting denominations; moreover, these grounds of opposition were the same whether a minister was orthodox or heterodox. Dissenters of all varieties appealed to the Bible as their sole source of religious authority, and they idolized the primitive church as representing a period of pristine purity in which all Christians were equal, long before the invidious introduction of church hierarchy and the imposition of canon law.[31]

Past treatments of the English Dissenters in the eighteenth century have depicted them as snugly satisfied with the Hanoverian regime and fully reconciled to the legal status they had inherited under the Revolution settlement. As long as there was a Jacobite threat, and as long as local High Anglican or Tory parties forced them to seek the favor of the government, Dissenters naturally preferred a legally handicapped survival to outright persecution. Under the benign conditions of mid-eighteenth-century England, differences with Anglicans seemed unimportant, and the dwindling number of Dissenters (among whom were many who conformed to the national church) appeared to suggest a progressively peaceful coexistence. In addition, the Dissenters' own assurances of their satisfaction with their lot was reflected in their public statements and published sermons offered on national days of thanksgiving, and these documents seemed to confirm the picture of a growing accommodation (though it should be noted that the very nature of these occasions virtually dictated the courteous tenor of their rhetoric). Finally, among Dissenters themselves was a wide range of opinion concerning the degree of their own satisfaction with Hanoverian society and politics.

What changed in the 1770s? The dominant emphasis on heterodoxy as an explanatory device has envisioned a rather sudden transformation of Dissent in this decade from dormant and benign to active and threatening, and this has drawn historians' attention away from other long-term social causes of discontent, disaffection, and local political opposition to church and government. What, then, was the long-standing theory of Dissent, and what was its practice in the chapel, the borough, at the quarter sessions, through Dissenting representatives, their lobbies, and in national, and, finally, international episodes of political agitation over the fifty-year period preceding the American crisis?

Putting the question this way, we find that there is another side of Dissent that shows a higher level of dissatisfaction, that under the best of circumstances commonly verged on disaffection, and under the worst of conditions might even turn radical. We can measure this disaffection through a variety of means, and we turn first to the formal apologies of Dissent. These treatises were written by Dissenters to help the faithful understand their tradition in relation to the national church and to catechize their youth, and they were reprinted in prodigious numbers. They portray a very different outlook and tone than the sermons Dissenters published on occasions of national gratitude. First, the apologies located their reasons for dissent in the doctrine of Christ. Here it is crucial to distinguish between the private theological conviction of individual Dissenters and the Christology which all Dissenters deployed when representing their tradition in public debate. The Dissenters' Christology in its political expression was orthodox, and the doctrine functioned identically in the mouths of Arians and trinitarians, whether the author wrote in the early, mid-, or late-eighteenth century. For example, there are no discernible differences in the three trinitarian writers, Charles Owen, Samuel Chandler, and Samuel Palmer. Following Calamy, all three authors describe Christ as the "Head" and "Sole Lawgiver" in his church, and it is this high view of the authority of Christ that establishes the two defining principles of English Nonconformity and British dissent, generally: (1) the right of private judgment (Christ as the sole Lord of conscience) and (2) the spiritual and voluntary nature of the church (Christ as sole "lawgiver" guarantees the people's right to chose their own pastors). These principles were juxtaposed to the twentieth article of the Thirty Nine Articles which declared the Anglican Church's power to decree rites and ceremonies and its authority in controversies of faith.[32]

The same verbiage and logical structure are found in the political writings of Arians such as Samuel Bourn and Micaiah Towgood.[33] By mid-century the theological base of Dissenting separatism had even begun to be worked into the title of apologetic works. The later editions of Micaiah Towgood's justly famous apology began to appear in the 1750s under the title, *A Dissent from the Church of England, Fully Justified: and Proved the Genuine and Just Consequence of the Allegiance Due to Christ, the Only Lawgiver in the Church.*[34] According to Towgood, the issue of the debate between the Anglican Church and Dissent "depends absolutely and entirely upon the single point—Is there any *other* Lawgiver or King in the *Church* of God besides *Jesus Christ;* or, is there not?"[35] Even Nathaniel Lardner, who moved all the way to a Unitarian position, adopted the language of Christ as the "Head of the Church," and "Lord and master of it."[36]

Conversely, Anglicans located the authority of Christ in the established church. Roger Altham, for example, a moderate Anglican, recognized that the dispute with Dissent was not over whether Christ is the head of the church, but the precise way in which he is head of the church, and it was exactly this question that had "brought many confusions upon the peace of the civil world." For Altham, as for Anglicans generally, the power of Christ was administered through the visible church, since Christ commissioned his apostles and their successors with his power, and the result was a civil polity in perfect harmony with the established, sacred polity of the Anglican Church.[37] Anglicans were convinced that those who insisted on the right of private judgment "first set up the idol of their own reason, and then introduce upon us an universal empire of confusion."[38] Naturally, Anglicans also attacked the right of private judgment and the spiritualized notion of the church that flowed from the Dissenters' Christology. In their view, sin in the sacred polity led inevitably to "faction in the civil polity," and therefore strict limits must be put on the exercise of private judgment: from this perspective, so-called "scruples" of Puritans and Nonconformists concerning spiritual matters were, in truth, mere pretenses and excuses that always led to the "crime of disobedience."[39]

How was such relatively abstract theology transformed into action in the civil realm, and how did it lead to radical political theory and behavior? The egalitarian and voluntaristic implications of the Dissenters' ecclesiology promoted criticism of the hierarchical and authoritarian structures of the established church.[40] The Dissenters responded to the experience of oppression in part through the development of a thoroughgoing anticlericalism.[41] It is well known that Nonconformists were inveterate opponents of Roman Catholics, but it is not often recognized that many expressions of anti-Catholicism were in fact thinly veiled attacks on the Anglican Church.[42] The anti-Catholicism of Dissent as a species of anticlericalism has not been sufficiently investigated as at the core of radical disaffection to the government. As Samuel Chandler put it, while he was willing to be known as a Presbyterian, "I am no more a believer in the divine original of the discipline of *Geneva* or *Edinburgh*, than I am in that of

Rome or *Canterbury*" because in each case, establishments used religion as "the stalking-horse to power."[43] In this way, anti-Catholicism was readily transferable into Anglican anticlericalism and a generalized anti-establishment attitude. Expressions of anticlericalism among Dissenters were thereby unavoidably tied to politics, whether the subject was their attitude toward authority in general, or bishop, magistrate, or monarch in particular.

Long before the age of the democratic revolution, certainly from the 1720s forward, in sermons, political pamphlets, and book length catechisms, Dissenters had urged that the Anglican hierarchy with the King at its head and the unjust impositions of religious tests for office holding were a kind of "popery" in politics. Dissenters construed Anglican impositions in the language of slavery and the attempt to turn their fellow human beings into beasts of burden. Charles Owen thus alluded to the clergy of the Church of England: "Are these the men that lead our gentry, as well as the common people, by the nose?"[44] The Anglican clergy promote "pulpit prostitution," revealing that they really are "wolves in sheep's clothing."[45] The Dissenters' very existence as independent congregations implied a critique of the whole social theory of the Anglican establishment. Orthodox and heterodox Dissenters worked together throughout the eighteenth century on projects of civil and religious liberty;[46] they found a common foe in a reigning Anglican establishment, and there is little evidence that the radical theory of the Nonconformists changed substantially in the 1770s. To be sure, the volume was turned up and the tone of voice became shrill, but the theoretical basis for Dissent remained the same across time and across a wide denominational and theological spectrum of writers.[47]

But the christological theory behind the anticlericalism of Dissent was no mere theory. The political disaffection of the Dissenters was sustained by their theology, by their long history of perceived oppression, and through a segregated social life organized around a separated church polity. The Dissenters' voice emerged as the voice of a minority, and the social setting of Dissent should not be isolated from its theology. The Dissenters' practice of a separated polity produced a habitual response to authority that was characterized by suspicion and vigilance. Pride at standing on principle could easily veer over into defiance of the Establishment. The privileges of worship and church government guaranteed by the Act of Toleration were claimed as natural as well as theological rights, and these privileges were frequently exercised in the local setting by reinforcing rituals that graphically, even frightfully, displayed the power of the people. First, church covenants among the Dissenters commonly bound members to Jesus Christ as their sole King and lawgiver, meaning loyalty to Christ's headship in his own church. Hence, "All human laws, which are inconsistent with the divine, ought to be disobeyed."[48] Second, there was an element of defiance at the heart of the ordination vow, and a kind of anticlericalism institutionalized in the practice; herein lay one of the sources of the power of the doctrine of Christ's sole authority in his church. At his ordination, for example, Thomas Bradbury vowed: "*I believe that in all these parts of worship*, one is our master, even Christ; *no man* having dominion over our faith, *or any right to break* the liberty wherewith he has made us free and entangle us again in a yoke of bondage."[49] Another Dissenting minister put the matter even more menacingly: "I can assure you, brother, I neither at ordination nor institution was forced to *bow my knees* before a Lord Bishop, or any other ecclesiastical superior . . . ."[50] Such an attitude was not far removed from those expressed by many defiant Dissenting ministers during the American and French revolutions.

Third, Dissenting congregations called and chose their pastors, and with intimidating frequency, actually exercised their privilege of dismissing them. Anyone who has read the church books of eighteenth-century Nonconformity will be struck by the frequency of this practice: At the Baptist chapel at Bristol in 1746, "the church made choice of the Rev'd Mr. John Needham" as assistant, but in the year 1752, "Mr. Needham was violently cast out from his office of Pastor & Minister in that place where [he] was chosen. . . ." The Congregational Church in Cambridge "could not agree on a pastor till 1734 when they chose to that office the Rev'd Joseph Dudly. Him they excluded the next year June 24, 1735." But "on July 19th 1737 the church chose for their pastor Mr. Samuel Sherie but as he proved an immoral man, they availed themselves again of that noble privilege of Protestant dissenters, & on November 7, 1738 cut him off and dismissed him."[51] The practice led naturally to the contention that "All [Dissenters] think the people the origin of power, the administrative [branch of government] responsible trustees, and the enjoyment of life, liberty and property the right of all mankind."[52] Ministers, as well, were constantly reminded of their inferior legal status as they were required to register the chapels by appearing, in what to them was a humiliating posture, before the Quarter Sessions or the Justice of the Peace. It was equally galling that Dissenting youth could not be educated at either university.

The intractableness of this ecclesiological position contributed, inevitably, to a proclivity to dissent in politics. The combination of ideology and excluded minority status was thus readily portable from the ecclesiastical to the civil realm. The Dissenters' criticism did not stop with the church; indeed, since many Justices of the Peace were also Anglican clergymen, their critique of the church inevitably included the government. The theology of Dissent was thus explicitly connected directly to political matters, and criticism of the Anglican Church regularly veered over into criticism of political structures. The connection was made at both the theoretical and the practical level. For example, Samuel Wright observed that being truly subject to Christ as the sole Lord of conscience "will regulate our submission to the *civil* power and magistrates."[53]

We can see the principles of Dissent actually at work in local borough politics where Nonconformists were anything but deferential to the Anglican structures of power. The broad generalization that Dissenters were government supporters before the American Revolution and oppositionists afterwards, while true, obscures more than it reveals. The missing element in our understanding of the Dissenters' radical politics in the eighteenth century is the borough corporation. In many of the open boroughs of England, local party behavior was characterized by endemic conflict between an Anglican-dominated corporation and an anticorporation party of Dissenters, surrounded by a group of Low-Church Anglicans. The Dissenters wielded considerable political influence in twenty-five of the thirty-five large and medium-sized freeman boroughs with electorates of more than 500 voters.[54] In every borough in England in which Dissenting ministers responded with public pro-American sermons and radical rhetoric in the 1770s, including Norwich, Bristol, Newcastle-upon-Tyne, Nottingham, York, Cambridge, and Taunton, there existed a pattern, in most cases long-standing, of rancorous party conflict between corporation and anticorporation parties defined by denomination.[55] In the Dissenters' eyes, the borough was not so far from Whitehall; a corrupt local corporation was just a step away from the most corrupt corporation of all. The Dissenters' anticorporation sentiment was deep and ingrained, and it was readily translated into antigovernment sentiment.[56]

At the national level, a variety of legal needs, grievances, and the desire for reform brought the three denominations together for cooperative political action on a regular basis after 1730. In each of the following episodes, Dissenters felt that their own interests were at stake; they produced an extensive literature in each case (with the possible exception of the Sheriffs' Cause), and the definition of an aggrieved minority with a righteous cause was reinforced proportionately. Dissenters did act in the capacity of a pressure group in the period following 1730,[57] and their history is a history of regular activity in an attempt to liberalize English law. Representatives of the Presbyterians, Congregationalists, and Baptists of London met in 1732, and while laying plans for their application to Parliament for the repeal of the Test and Corporation acts, they formed the Dissenting Deputies, a group that though based in London, was intended to represent the interests of the entire alternative nation.[58] In each of the three periods of agitation for repeal (1732–39, 1787–89, and 1790), the Deputies coordinated the Dissenters' efforts, and the organization has been rightly viewed as highly innovative in its use of lobbying techniques.[59] The repeal movement created a vigorous, in-depth literature on both sides of the debate, extensively canvassing the issues of civil and religious liberty and displaying them before the public. The controversy over the Quaker's Tithe Bill overlapped with the first agitation for repeal and carried public debate on the nature and threat of Dissent into the early 1740s (1736–42).[60] The so-called "Sheriff's Cause" claimed the attention of numerous Dissenters from the 1740s through the 1760s.[61] The publication of the fourth volume of Blackstone's *Commentaries on the Laws of England* in 1769 declaring Dissent a crime provoked some of the finest writing in defense of religious liberty ever published.[62] The agitation of 1772 for abolishing the necessity of subscribing to the Thirty-Nine Articles was a genuinely nationwide effort that collected more than 850 signatures of Dissenting ministers, most of whom were orthodox; indeed, the number of orthodox authors who wrote in support of the antisubscription cause rivaled the heterodox.[63] Each of these episodes kept the matter of the Dissenters' disaffected identity before ministers and laity alike; in each, there was a massive reiteration of the principles of Dissent by both orthodox and heterodox authors, and in each, theory was connected to a pattern of national agitation in concrete, practical attempts to redress deeply felt grievances.

The potent mix of Dissenting theology and minority status can also be seen at work in national and international politics. Dissenters may have been more actively engaged in the Middlesex election affair and issues raised by the agitation over John Wilkes in the late 1760s than heretofore thought possible. The Middlesex election affair provides us with a natural transition from the Dissenters' earlier agitations concerning their own legal status to the American conflict. Heretofore, the connections between the supporters of John Wilkes and the pro-Americans have remained obscure, but beginning with John Sainsbury's study of London, the issue has now been set on a far firmer foundation.[64] We now know, for example, that the leaders of the Middlesex petitioning movements at Bristol, Newcastle, and Coventry were the same leaders who put forth and circulated petitions protesting the use of force in the colonies in 1775, and many of these leaders were Dissenters. Moreover, Joseph Towers, a leading heterodox Dissenter, and James Murray, an orthodox Presbyterian, published pamphlets in the late 1760s that urged Dissenters to engage in such petitioning activity.[65] The Stamp Act crisis in the colonies and the excitement over an American episcopate were intimately connected, and it was the convergence of these issues that fed the heightened panic concerning bishops in 1768.[66] Micaiah Towgood wrote to his colonial correspondent, Jonathan Mayhew, on the conflation of these two issues: "Perhaps the reluctance you have shown to have episcopal bits put in your mouth, may have hastened your being saddled with that disagreeable tax. If that order of men had been established, you would probably have found not only the saddle fixed, but riders also mounted on you."[67] The government seemed to unduly favor Catholics with the Quebec Act in 1774, and the Dissenters' negative, almost violent response was entirely predictable. When Thomas Davis, pastor of the Reading Baptist chapel, expressed his sympathy for the American colonists in 1776, he was threatened with reprisals from the local Anglican priest. He replied defiantly: "The world rages, the devil roars, and the doctor of our parish said he would silence me if he went to the King in person, and the Bishop of London is his friend. I said they might tell him, if he had a mind to silence me he must take out my tongue."[68] Among Nonconformist ministers this kind of political crankiness was a constant feature in the eighteenth century, and though it often went unexpressed, it was always present and always dangerous to the Establishment in both church and state.

In short, we have the theory of Dissent—the right of private judgment, congregational polity, the evil of the alliance in church and state—reinforced by the rituals of forming churches around covenants and choosing and excluding ministers. These principles of Dissent were constantly reiterated on any and all occasions; they were reinforced by the reoccurring practice of opposition politics in Anglican-Dissenting terms in most of the open boroughs in England. We have national campaigns for repeal of odious acts concerning sacramental tests, and for relief from prosecution for non-payment of tithes. The Wilkes' affair attracted the Dissenters' attention, and in the early 1770s there was the national canvass among Dissenters for abolishing subscription to the Thirty-Nine Articles. All of this amounts to a perfectly natural preparation for a predictable Dissenting response to the events in America and later in France. What activated the disaffection of the Dissenting minister? The answer is as simple and prosaic as self- and group interest. If Georgian Anglicanism was perceived as completely benign, then some such mechanism as heterodoxy may be needed to explain the disaffection of the Dissenters. But the history of resistance to Anglican-dominated society from the 1720s to the 1770s depicts a coherent, alternative political nation, whose marginalized self-identity requires no such theory of heterodoxy as a trigger to explain radical disaffection in the age of the American and French revolutions. Are there parallels in Scotland and Ireland that can illumine the religious origins of radicalism in the late eighteenth century?

Scotland, the General Assembly, Patronage, and Secession

Following the Revolution Settlement of 1690, Presbyterians who strictly adhered to the Covenants of 1638 and 1643 refused to return to the newly reestablished Church of Scotland. These Covenanters later organized the Reformed Presbyterian Church, but they were always a tiny minority, and their theocratic ideology, while rabidly anti-erastian and always potentially disruptive, could not be reconciled with the separation of church and state or religious toleration.[69] The Covenanting tradition therefore provides limited resources for the study of late-eighteenth-century radicalism. Though broadly speaking, Covenant ideology influenced all the varieties of secession from the national church, the issue of church patronage actually served as a more potent cause of political disaffection than the national covenant. When the Scottish Church emerged from battle with the Stuarts and rejected episcopacy in 1690, the Presbyterian Parliament abolished the right of patrons to control elections of ministers to unsupplied congregations. But following the Union of 1707, lay patronage was restored. In 1712, under the Tory influence of Queen Anne's last administration, the Patronage Act was passed by Parliament, in part as an inducement to help wean the landed classes from Jacobitism.[70] By the 1720s patrons were becoming aggressive; abuses increased and the courts came by degrees to support the rights of patrons.[71] One recent study avers that the crisis over patronage was the leading political controversy of mid-eighteenth-century Scotland.[72]

The controversy reached a boiling point at Kinross in 1731–32 in a contest between the local patron and the congregation who wished to call Ebenezer Erskine, minister of Stirling. The Presbytery of Dunfirmline took the side of the congregation, and the General Assembly of 1732 debated the matter at length. Erskine emerged as the champion of the popular party, insisting on the divine right of the people to choose their pastors. The grounds of his argument and those of his three ministerial colleagues were largely christological.[73] Erskine and his colleagues like William Wilson were above all concerned that the "Crown rights of the Redeemer" were invaded by the enforcement of the law of patronage. But Christology was connected directly to polity, for the dissenters were equally concerned about the "rights, liberties, and privileges of the subjects of Christ's spiritual kingdom, against the violence done them by the present judicatories."[74] The "spiritual" nature of the kingdom of Christ was thus the basis for the voluntaristic, independent nature of the Secession Church. Erskine and the three ministers who supported him eventually formed their own presbytery and the Secession Church, which later took the name of the Associate Synod, was born.[75] Soon there were secessions from the Secession: the litigiousness of these groups caused no end of grief to the original critics of patronage. The Associate Synod itself split in 1747 over the question of taking the burgess oath: the Antiburgher (General Associate) Synod believed the oath entailed compromise with the national church and so separated from the Associate Synod. There was yet another breach in 1761, so that by that date there were three branches of the Secession.[76] Doctrine and conviction were thereby embodied in a minority social system that would soon develop an embattled, minority mentality.

The decade of the 1740s saw nearly forty disputed settlements and the growth of the Secession Church was impressive. By 1766 there were perhaps 100,000 adherents in all the varieties of secession, comprising approximately ten percent of the population. The movement had grown to embrace 190 separatist congregations by 1773, though some of these were strictly independent and not affiliated with the three secession bodies.[77] By the 1790s in some areas, like Jedburgh, dissent was in the majority, though in the era of the American and French revolutions, in the annual disputed settlements at the General Assembly, the Moderate party, who supported patronage, consistently won.[78]

We find the same constellation of ideas in all the forms of Secession—the right of private judgment; the spiritual nature of Christ's Church; anti-Catholic and anticlerical rhetoric—all related to a high Christology: the leading question for all Scottish dissenters was the question of allegiance to "the King of Zion" and the extent to which that allegiance should be taken. As defenders of Calvinistic orthodoxy, the Seceders were opposed to what they considered to be the rationalistic tendencies of the General Assembly.[79] Their high Christology was grounded primarily in Scripture, but one may detect hints of the 11th article of the Scots Confession as well, where Christ is confessed as "the only Head of his Kirk, our just Lawgiver." The National Covenant of 1638 included a personal oath of allegiance to Jesus Christ, the only Head of the church, the King of kings, and it affirmed the church's spiritual nature and independence as well.

Those who opposed patronage argued that the right of electing ministers was "the right and privilege that we believe our Lord Jesus Christ left to his church, which he purchased with his own blood."[80] The "liberty of election" honored Jesus Christ as the head of the church and advanced Christ's kingdom in the congregation. On the other hand, "the power of single persons to present and nominate pastors to vacant congregations" had always been viewed as a heavy grievance because it dishonored Christ.[81] Conversely, the defenders of the established church located the authority of Christ in the establishment. For example, John Currie, though no friend of patronage, stayed within the established church and defended it against the Secession because, he said, the judicatories of the Church of Scotland are "a court of Christ."[82] Thus defenders of the Church of Scotland, in precisely the same way as defenders of the Church of England, argued that those who left the established church were themselves "trampling upon the authority of our Lord Jesus Christ," and tearing up "his Servants' Commission, whom he has sent to dispense them [i.e., his ordinances] in his name."[83] On the other hand, dissenters like John Graham, who emphasized the right of private judgment and the spiritual nature of Christ's kingdom and detested all those "chimerical Warburtonian principles of alliance," put the case exactly: "The question with me is, where this authority is lodged. You [the established clergy] assert that it lies in the Constitutions; I say it is lodged in the members. It is *you*, therefore, who rob the church of her authority."[84] Given the prior claim of the establishment in appealing to Christ's authority, it is not surprising that those who dissented from the national church appealed to a high Christology, and located Christ's presence in the congregation.

But more was at stake than ideas. When Ebenezer Erskine broke from the General Assembly, he went outside of the accepted conventions of social control. The ideology that justified this departure was theological, but just as with the Dissenters in England, the result was an alternative social system that eventually engaged hundreds of congregations. The insistence on an independent polity, separate from the General Assembly's control, was a social as well as a theological desideratum that entailed a kind of right of self-determination. People in this alternative system resented the power of the established church, just as people in the national church resented the disaffected behavior of the dissenters. These feelings of alienation alone account for the language of disloyalty, on the one hand, and tyranny on the other. We will find that over a period of time, the dissenters developed a felt affinity for other groups challenged by similar established authority.

The controversy was thus not simply theological. The opponents of patronage called the practice "an encroachment upon the liberties of mankind, the privileges of a free-born people, and the laws of society." Congregations of Christians were understood to be "free societies, voluntarily joined together," and therefore they should enjoy "the privilege of other free societies, as republics, cities, and corporations, to choose their own officers." In addition to the issue of natural rights, this early in the century there was a class element at stake. "The exorbitant power of superiors and chieftains in *Scotland* over men's bodies and goods," had been rightly resisted, it was said, and to allow such men "to extend their superiority over the people's souls," was an evil to be equally resisted.[85] Conversely, the defenders of patronage charged the dissenters with encouraging social insubordination.[86] Erskine was reproved by the General Assembly for his opposition as a "bold, insolent man."[87] Writing in 1733, George Logan insisted that the common people should always behave in the "most dutiful and respectful manner." Logan was concerned above all by the common people's lack of respect for their "lawful superiors in the Lord." The protests against patronage led people to transgress "the line of their station," threatening "effrontery" with people having lost a proper sense of "deference and respect." Moreover, Logan argued, these people lacked the "measures of knowledge" that they claim, thus throwing doubt on their political ability.[88] Other writers put the case in similar terms: the opponents of patronage were motivated by pride and self-will, and, like children, they were not competent judges in political matters.[89] On both sides of the debate, therefore, issues of theology were inextricably mixed with questions of power and attitudes toward authority. Dissenters viewed the "intrusion" of ministers over people by patrons a "manifold" act of "violence and oppression," and such "tyrannical and arbitrary steps" justified secession.[90] Alternatively, the defenders of the national church believed the dissenters filled the people's minds "with prejudices against all ranks and orders of men, against the nobility, the gentry, the ministers, and all magistrates, supreme and subordinate."[91]

A second disaffected group of Presbyterians arose out of the Cambuslang revivals led by George Whitefield in the 1740s. These evangelicals came to be known as the "Popular party," because of their opposition to clerical patronage, but unlike the Secession party, they never severed their formal ties with the establishment.[92] The Popular party placed a premium on the liberating experience of the grace of Christ in personal conversion, and in this case, personal experience played a similar role to the Secession's right of election: Christ's authority was valued supremely, not in the congregation, but in the individual. Like the Secession, the Popular party was comprised of staunch Calvinists, and while their thought derived in part from fundamental law and the Commonwealthman tradition, it was grounded above all in radical Protestant and biblical arguments.[93]

The Popular party linked the "persecution" of patronage in the ecclesiastical realm with authoritarianism in the civil realm, and as with the Secession, the vehicle by which they linked the two was the ideology of anti-Catholicism. The need for the "assent of the people over whom the person is placed" was understood as a corrective to the corruption of "Antichrist" and the popish church. The structure of anti-Catholic thought, as it was deployed in the cause of Scottish dissent of both varieties, was rigorously logical: Popery was tyranny; clericalism and establishments, even among Protestants, were remnants of popery. Therefore both must be resisted.[94]

Secession and Evangelical ministers constantly reminded their people of past Catholic atrocities, and their appeal to current events was reinforcing: in the Forty-Five, not one Presbyterian minister had supported the Pretender, while over 1,000 Catholics had died or fled the country as a result of the attempt.[95] So while "Romanism" was still associated with Jacobitism as late as the 1770s and 1780s, the issue of patronage was used to keep the matter alive, and patronage and anti-Catholicism were mutually reinforcing. A forced settlement of a minister, said one anonymous pamphleteer, is "congenial to the hierarchy of the Romish church and breathes the spirit of despotism. Diametrically opposite to a republican constitution, it unhinges the whole frame of Presbyterian government."[96] In the terms of Archibald Bruce, "Infallibility has come/ Wrapt up with *Patronage* from *Rome*."[97] Thus, anti-Catholicism, church patronage, and civil liberty were linked. All forms of coercion in Christ's spiritual kingdom were demonized by associating the use of force with the past tyranny and the present threat of "popery." The strength of Popular party opposition to Catholic relief and the general enthusiasm for Lord George Gordon led to rioting in Glasgow (October 1778) and Edinburgh and Glasgow (January, February 1779), and following the Gordon riots in London, some fifty Scottish towns expressed sympathy for Gordon.[98] The loss of trade with America and the West Indies, especially in the west of Scotland, and the government's evident sympathy for Catholicism, expressed in the Quebec Act, undoubtedly served to cement anti-Catholicism and pro-Americanism.[99] The historian of anti-Catholicism in Scotland recognizes that the movement of the

Popular party gave rise to modern methods of political agitation, constitutionalism, and the awakening of widespread political awareness among the Scots.[100]

The Moderate party was born in the early 1750s when a small body of influential intellectuals determined to use the system of patronage to refashion the National Church. In facing the schism of Secession, the issue at hand was clearly one of power and control, for, as Alexander Carlyle said, "It was necessary to use every means in our power to restore the authority of the Church, otherwise her government would be degraded, and everything depending on her authority would fall into confusion."[101] The Moderate party linked subordination in the church with order in civil society; conversely, "licentiousness" in the church would inevitably mean "rebellion and disorder in civil government."[102] Under the leadership of William Robertson, Alexander Carlyle, Adam Ferguson, Francis Hutcheson, and others, these Moderates emphasized a rational base for religion, and their party became a leading force for the influence of enlightened thought in the Church of Scotland.

The Moderates opposed the Popular party, denigrating all forms of enthusiasm in religion, and they opposed the Secession movement as the leading expression of disorder: the control of patronage was the means for managing both. The manipulation of ministerial appointments was their main strategy for shaping the Scottish Church according to a rational vision of true religion expressed in a unified, state establishment in harmony with, and subordinated to, the English crown. The crucial connections with the English government are made obvious by the fact that crown patronage comprised about one-third of the whole, with a slight edge even over the number of livings in the gift of the Scottish nobility.[103] The Moderates became so adept at manipulating patronage that though they experienced some insecurity from the 1780s forward, they did not lose control of the General Assembly until well into the nineteenth century.[104] Moderates also generally supported relief for Catholics, a move that seemed to their opponents to be a natural confirmation of their power tactics.[105] In addition, their outlook was characterized by a distinct class consciousness, for they believed that people of property would be more inclined to support ministers who were drawn from the middling strata or higher; such ministers, they expected, would be well educated, free from enthusiasm, sympathetic to the established church, and supportive of the Whig hegemony. With their aristocratic leanings, they supported, in the felicitous phrase of Martin Fitzpatrick, a career open to the most talented.[106]

Both the political and social implications of the conflict are apparent in the connections that were drawn between the English monarchy, the Scottish upper classes, and the use and abuse of patronage. Opponents connected the crown patronage of church livings in Scotland specifically to the "woeful use that is made of that branch of the royal prerogative," and hence matters of ecclesiastical polity had a direct bearing on attitudes toward representative government and even republicanism: in one author's words, "the choice of the people" brings more worthy characters to the ministry than "those who have obtained their settlements by the gift of the Crown and ministerial favour"—indeed, it was claimed that the best ministers came "from among the very lowest of the people." In this view, the specific duty of "the representatives of the people" in Parliament was "to confine the power and prerogative of the Crown within the narrowest limits." Conversely, what was at stake in the matter of "popular election" to church livings was precisely "the rights of the people," juxtaposed to the selfish interests of the "rich and the great." In short, patronage was a "yoke" of slavery which neither "we [n]or our fathers were able to bear."[107]

The long-standing struggle of Scottish dissent against church patronage, the Moderate party, and the Catholic Church contributed directly to the dissenters' disaffection for the English government. The political overtones of the Seceders' convictions are plain, and the connections between their theology, ecclesiology, and radical thought can be illustrated during both the American and the French revolutions by the publications of three Secession ministers, John Baillie, William Graham, and Archibald Bruce. The writings of these three ministers are especially valuable because they were orthodox trinitarians, and their thought can be traced through the period of the American and French Revolutions. Baillie and Graham were ministers at Newcastle-upon-Tyne, and the contemporary episodes of Newcastle radicalism and the religious views of the two ministers were undoubtedly mutually reinforcing. All three ministers grounded their political views in a high Christology. By means of the presbyterian form of government, Christ the "Blessed Head" of the church had checked the wrong desire among men for gaining superiority one over another.[108] The principle of equality was instituted in dissenting polity, in which the method of selecting ministers was "popular election," a practice guaranteed by divine right. In such a "voluntary society" or "a free community" each member is allowed to vote in what concerns the whole.[109] Christ's authority was connected to the spiritual nature of his kingdom and the right of private judgment, so all forms of coercion in matters religious were rejected.[110]

Both Baillie and Graham blasted patronage as a crime, for it "overthrows the essential and peculiar qualities of Christ's Kingdom; and subverts his kingly authority in, and over it."[111] The anti-Catholic theme was broadened to anticlericalism in that patronage was traced to the "covetousness, ambition, and desire of domination among clergymen," and since the "*established* clergy never had the honour of beginning a reformation, since Christianity commenced in the world," it was left to common Christian people to attend "to their own sacred concerns and unalienable rights."[112] "Popery," in short, is the use of force in the affairs of the church. The patron of a village kirk is "a Protestant pope," "infallible, absolute, incontrollable."[113] Graham, like Baillie, threw doubt on the validity of establishments in both Scotland and England: it makes no difference whether the decrees of Antichrist "are dated from *Constance,* or *Canterbury;* from *Trent,* or from *Edinburgh.*"[114] As Bruce put it, we find oppression, "When *old true blue* with *surplice* meets,/ And *Kirk* the high *Cathedral* greets."[115] Anti-Catholicism thus functioned as a device for expressing anticlerical and anti-establishment views. It also opened the political vision of the dissenters to a broader, international scope. Anti-Catholicism helped people see across national boundaries and thereby transcend their characteristic penchant for provincial politics. In this generalized form, anti-Catholicism allowed the Presbyterian dissenters to charge their Presbyterian brethren in the General Assembly with behaving like episcopal prelates.

Secession ministers then broadened their thought from the oppression of church establishments to the civil realm. In William Graham, for example, the language of defiance was crafted to a fine art. He had recently made a tour through Scotland and found that "ecclesiastical oppressors have been dragging their plough with bold defiance" over the "furrowed backs" of the "best Christians" in the kingdom. He admonished the people to stir themselves up and throw off the yoke. "Shocking thought!" said Graham, "to imagine that our Lord, who redeemed his church with his blood, should leave her, at the mercy of either the precarious humours of princes, or the selfish wisdom of churchmen!" The parallels between the uncertain "humours" of princes and the touted "wisdom" of churchmen make the political implications of Graham's thought unmistakable: "The authority of Christ removes all civil distinctions, and all superiority founded upon such distinctions, in his kingdom. All are upon a level equally, as they shall soon be before the awful tribunal of the great Judge." In matters of religion and conscience, "none has dominion over another," and in civil matters, Christianity teaches superiors to treat their dependents as they would wish to be treated by their great master in heaven.[116]

But the same religious ideas were transferable to the social realm as well. The tone of the works of the Scottish dissenters was anti-authoritarian, and the social disaffection, in addition to the theological rationale, especially in the setting of revolution, becomes palpable. Writing in 1774, Archibald Bruce, a pastor of the Associate Synod, adopted the satiric style of Alexander Pope's *The Dunciad* in *The Kirkiad; or Golden Age of the Church of Scotland*. He located the causes of class distinctions and disparities in wealth in the national church, for despite the Reformation:

> . . . The wish'd for day doth dawn
> When Kirkmen, yet arra'y in lawn,
> Shall pompous reign in lordly state,
> On velvit sit, and eat on plate. (2).[117]

Bruce moved readily from criticism of the established church to criticism of patronage and the social structure, grounding his thought in the right of private judgment.

> Shall men in Bonnets, and coarse tatters
> Pretend to wisdom, like their betters?
> Can e're a man arrive at sense,
> Who does not rent a hundred pence?
> Who can his Bible understand?
> Who ne'er posses'd one foot of land?
> Can one in conscience give a rate,
> Who is himself not worth a groat?
> Who can such impudence allow
> That beggars must be choosers too? (35)

Wealthy churchmen, wealthy patrons, and wealthy nobility are in league together in their oppression of "dumb tenants," and "plebian souls," and they exercise oppression through the abuse of powerful political instruments, like Parliament.

> Tho' *Scape-grace* cannot preach or pray,
> What have plebian souls to say?
> Why should they their instructors scorn,
> Whether their food be chaff or corn?
> Whether the well be clear or stink,
> Let them no questions ask, but drink.
> For *good and all* themselves commit,
> To others' hands more wise and fit:
> About salvation take no care,
> Nor of damnation have a fear,
> While pow'rful *Patrons* stand between,
> And *Acts of Parliament,* for screen. (36)

The criticism of the higher classes is patent: "What precious privileges wait/ On him who wears a coronet!/ How wond'rous does the man appear,/ who has some thousand pounds a-year!" (36).[118]

Privileged religious status, aristocracy, and the abuse of power were thus clearly connected. But there is a possible escape for the righteous poor: "This side the globe you need not stay/ *New-Englander,* or those of *Pen',*/ Perhaps may welcome you, good men!" (2). Bruce notes that he hears rumblings already of

> —How *Democracy*, it was said,
> Deep schemes and dang'rous plots had laid,
> And muster'd forces with intent,
> *Aristocracy* to supplant (43).

In Britain's dispute with the colonies, the Seceders thus clearly favored the Americans: John Baillie and William Graham signed the document circulated by Newcastle radicals in 1775 in favor of peace with the American colonists.[119] Conversely, the Moderates who controlled the General Assembly and defended the Church of Scotland were staunch and consistent supporters of the British government during the American crisis. The unqualified defense of the government of George III in the political sermons of the leading Moderates, Alexander Carlyle, George Campbell, and Alexander Gerard, is indistinguishable from the thought of loyalist Anglican ministers in England.[120] Just as the defenders of patronage asserted the authority of the higher courts, emphasized the need for social subordination, and scorned the abilities of the common people, in a revolutionary setting the Moderates consistently exalted the authority of Parliament and the Crown, castigated the Americans, and admonished the people to be appropriately deferential and submissive. It comes as no surprise that in the 1780s the Moderates opposed the Yorkshire Association movement and parliamentary reform. Conversely, among dissenters there was a direct correlation between the desire for reform of church patronage and a plea for radical reform in the House of Commons to effect it.[121]

The Popular party mirrors exactly the political interests of the Secession during the American Revolution. Criticism of the English government for its evident sympathy for Catholicism was closely associated with, or veered over into, criticism of the government for its

American measures. The fear of an American episcopate; the Quebec Act, when combined with the denial of relief to Protestant Dissenters in England; the granting of relief to Catholics in England; and the threat of granting relief in Scotland all seemed to show against freedom.[122] In addition, there was a strong connection between the Popular party in Scotland and the New Light ministers in America, in particular through the connection of John Witherspoon, who went to the colonies as president of the College of New Jersey in 1768.[123] But beneath the anti-Catholic ideology and personal ties of friendship, there was the underlying religious conviction of the right of private judgment and a congregational polity that adumbrated all branches of the dissenters' understanding of civil authority.

Writing in the 1770s, ministers of the Popular party used the language of slavery to describe the two-thirds majority of Scots clergy who supported patronage, clergy who were given to promoting every scheme "which is laid to enslave us."[124] The "dearest and most valuable privilege" of Christians, said John Snodgrass, is "the right of choosing a minister to take care of their souls." In the words of another leading Evangelical, William Thom, patronage tended to subvert "the democratical power" of the people in the church, and it enhanced the monarchical power in church *and* state.[125] The rhetoric of a "wretched thraldom of patronage," the "arbitrary measures" of a prevailing faction, and spiritual "oppression and tyranny" was thus readily ported to the civil realm.[126] Thom juxtaposed the language of "despotism" and "arbitrary power" when describing the government to "the rights and liberties of the common people."[127] Snodgrass specifically drew the comparison between church patronage and the corruption of parliamentary elections where agreements between voters and candidates were used to keep the powerful in power.[128] Moreover, the social class element is evident in his admonishing people to resist admitting "persons of quality, or high rank" into the eldership, and the same applied to lawyers, who are the church's "inveterate and most dangerous foes."[129] In the midst of the American Revolution, Snodgrass exhorted his congregation to stir up that "love of liberty, that true patriotism, that fortitude and magnanimity in the defense of our civil and religious privileges, for which our fathers were so remarkably distinguished."[130] Thom, like Snodgrass, blamed the British government entirely for the breach.[131] Another opponent of the Scottish establishment, John Graham, writing in 1771, hoped that "the republican clergymen of Scotland, who have not [had] to cut their way through the blood and entrails of *Bishops,* will assert their rights," for then, he continued, they will set the example of religious liberty for England.[132]

Altogether, we can identify thirteen Scots ministers of the Popular party who supported the Americans through writing or preaching.[133] Many others, like John Gillies, kept close contacts with their American friends. On one occasion Charles Nisbet preached so strongly on conciliation with the colonies that the magistrates and town council of Montrose walked out of his church. Evangelicals David Grant and Ralph Bowie were both favorably disposed to Gordon's idea of a Scots' congress, or a "political Presbytery"; both were arrested in 1780 on suspicion of antigovernment activities.[134] Conversely, the Moderates attacked the Popular party in 1778 for sounding like "correspondents from Massachusetts Bay" in its synods.[135] Hugo Arnot, writing from a Moderate perspective, referred to the Popular party as "violent enemies to patronage"; men who are "bigoted in their religious principles"; and "ever inclined to advance the republican part of the constitution, and who are always endeavoring, by arts suitable to the end, to insinuate themselves with the rabble."[136] The Popular party, in turn, attacked the Moderates by associating them with the Catholics in their optimistic view of human nature and in their support for arbitrary, authoritarian government: patronage itself was viewed as a kind of medieval, Catholic survival. These associations are confirmed by areal analysis. Links between the leaders of the Popular party and the geographic centers of anti-Catholicism and sympathy for the American Revolution have been made, and these connections extend into the period of agitation over parliamentary reform in 1784 and 1785.[137]

When the impact of the French Revolution was felt in Scotland, the Moderate party had already experienced considerable challenges from the Popular party, and its dominance of the General Assembly was shaken.[138] It is not surprising, therefore, that after a brief initial ambivalence, the Moderates opposed the revolutionaries in France and the radicals in England. They were afraid precisely for the safety of religious establishments. Alexander Carlyle, Hugh Blair, and other Moderates were as vigorous as ever on the side of the established church, monarchy, and good government.[139] In the 1790s, we thus find the same themes among the Moderates as we found in the 1770s. Carlyle was proud that he could still "preach like a son of thunder . . . against the vile leveling Jacobins, whom I abhor."[140] Leading Evangelicals such as John Erskine joined with the Moderates in urging respect for government, but the Popular party did not urge social subordination as rigorously as the Moderates, and they acknowledged the need for moderate political reform.[141]

Meanwhile, the Seceders had, if anything, grown more radical. William Graham produced one of the first comprehensive comparative critiques of religious establishments in Europe. Graham embraced the "revolutions" in the "political systems of all nations" with the inflammatory words "Hail, thou auspicious age," and encouraged people to throw off the fetters of established churches, hoping thereby to produce the "total annihilation" of religious monopolies.[142] Another Scottish dissenter, James Smith, betrayed the scriptural roots of his argument in his title, *The Golden Calves of Dan and Bethel: or, the Alliance of Church and State, An Ancient Political Engine* (1795), a work which he dedicated to "the friends of civil and religious liberty" with the taunting phrase: "The Church by law established! What a pompous title!"[143] Writing at about the same time, John Baillie applauded the Americans, praised France, drew upon Thomas Paine's *Rights of Man* and Junius with the comment that they are "two of the most enlightened and informing writers of the age," and continued to write within the strict bounds of orthodox trinitarianism.[144]

In Archibald Bruce the right of private judgment was broadened to include "the right of every man to judge of the lawfulness or unlawfulness of every command of human authority." Bruce argued that a "free discussion of public affairs in church and state," including the right to censure some things in the constitution, the law, or the conduct of administration, is "undoubtedly" the prerogative of the people of God. Why? Because "the laws of God and our Redeemer have authority over all classes of men and in all sorts of acts, be they natural, civil or religious." In the midst of a pamphlet of 1799 that declares his loyalty to the House of Hanover, Bruce trenched on the borders of sedition by the way he alluded to the king's counselors, the king himself, and Parliament: "Why do the wicked Amaziahs, that haunt the court of princes, infuse jealousies into their mind, and procure orders to banish liberty of prophesying, from the vicinity of the king's courts and chapels? Why should the Herods of the earth wax wroth, and imprison and behead faithful reprovers? Why should corrupt Sanhedrins so abuse their power, and forget their interest, as to sit in council together, 'plotting against the Lord and his anointed.'"[145] Bruce despised the Hickes, the Leslies, and "the men of their stamp," and returned to his critique of higher social classes in the name of the "inferior and poorer sort of people."[146] Connections with anti-Catholicism and enthusiasm for the French Revolution can also be traced in his writings. The destruction of the French Catholic Church—an idolatrous establishment that had so long been "a yoke of iron to the oppressed church of Christ"—was, in his words, a "signal work of God."[147]

John Brims studied the contribution of the Secession church to the radicalism of the 1790s in England and Scotland. The contributions of ten leading Secession ministers show the extent to which Scottish dissent was implicated in radical politics. Three ministers of the Antiburgher church served as delegates in the Scottish radical reformers' national conventions of 1792–93, and a fourth was nominated for the proposed British convention. One of these men, John Wilson, was a leader of the Perth Association of the Friends of the People. In fact, William Skirving, who was trained at the Burgher Theological College, was the de facto secretary of the Scottish Friends of the People. Within the Burgher Church, Brims located four more ministers involved in radical reform in the 1790s, one of whom, Ebenezer Hislop, was known as the "Reverend Democrat" and was delegated to the first national convention.[148] In Stirling it was reported that the "deamon" of political jealousy originated in "dissenting principles in religion."[149] But as we have seen, these principles were not effective in isolation from social conflict and other changes in society. For example, the means of disseminating information contributed to the popular enthusiasm for revolution; from 1782 to 1790 the number of newspapers in Scotland grew from eight to twenty-seven.[150] But it took courage and conviction to defend freedom of speech, especially in the later 1790s, when such a stance was calculated to provoke the government. It is no coincidence that the defenders of a free press were dissenters. George Lawson and Archibald Bruce, both of whom were professors of divinity in Secession seminaries, forthrightly supported freedom of speech, and they did so on what are by now the familiar grounds of the authority of "the great Judge" who alone "searcheth the hearts and trieth the reins of the children of men."[151] The Unitarians in Scotland made a contribution to Scottish radicalism in the person of Thomas Fysshe Palmer, but clearly the Evangelical devotees of the Popular party and orthodox Seceders were the major players in Scottish radical politics.

Ireland, the Presbytery of Antrim, and the United Irishmen

Until the mid-1960s, Irish nationalist historiography generally dismissed the contribution of Ulster Presbyterians to politics.[152] Writing in 1959, William McMillan was the first to link convincingly the radicalism of the United Irishmen of the 1790s to the Presbyterian ministry.[153] This link has subsequently been reaffirmed by A. T. Q. Stewart and Marianne Elliott, whose works, among other things, traced the Presbyterian support for the United Irishmen and the Rebellion of 1798, and to a lesser extent, Irish Pro-Americanism, back to the antisubscriptionists of the 1720s. But Stewart and Elliott confused some Presbyterian ministers' repudiation of the Westminster Confession of Faith with theological heterodoxy and argued that it was the heretical tradition that supposedly contributed to radicalism, thereby providing an Irish counterpart to the English heresy-radicalism thesis.[154] Following the lead of McMillan, D. W. Miller challenged the connection of "rational" or heterodox dissent with radical politics and discerned instead a politically prophetic strain of divinity in orthodox Calvinism.[155] Recently, the heresy-radicalism thesis has been subjected to even more rigorous critique: Jim Smyth has shown that since both orthodox and heterodox Presbyterians were involved in revolutionary politics, their contribution must lie in what they held in common, and he locates it in providing "participatory structures" for radicalism.[156] Similarly, in a fine, carefully nuanced study of the Irish Presbyterians and radicalism, Ian McBride has argued that radical ministers of the late eighteenth century did not feel compelled to choose between the republic of virtue and the Kingdom of God.[157] The relative importance of these sources of radical thought, particularly Christology and anti-Catholicism, require further investigation; we need to know more about how questions of private judgment were connected to matters of polity and church authority, and transferred, in turn, from the theological and ecclesiastical to the civil realm. All of these issues first arose in the controversy over subscription.

When the Westminster Confession of Faith was adopted as the standard creed of the Church of Scotland in 1647, subscription to it was not required. In the 1690s, when relations between Episcopalians and Presbyterians in Scotland remained uncertain, various efforts at subscription were attempted, but in Ireland no church law required subscription in the seventeenth century.[158] In 1705, however, in the wake of the controversy over Thomas Emlyn, who was charged with Arianism, the Synod of Ulster, the governing body for Presbyterians in Northern Ireland, enacted a law of compulsory subscription for licentiates to the ministry.[159] In addition to the threat of heresy, Irish Presbyterians debated the terms on which they would accept toleration, since the Toleration Act of 1689 did not extend to Ireland. Many ministers argued in favor of subscription to the Westminster Confession of Faith, but when the Irish Toleration Act was drawn up in 1719, no doctrinal subscription was required. Since toleration was not connected to subscription to the Thirty-Nine Articles as it was in England, the subscription issue in Ireland was initially debated *within* Presbyterianism and did not, as in England, have the state or the established church as the focal point of conflict.[160]

The Belfast Society was formed in 1705 by a group of Presbyterian ministers who were opposed in principle to subscription. The society was conceived to encourage the diffusion of useful knowledge, and the ministers pledged to bring all the subjects of their discussion to the test of reason and Scripture, "without a servile regard to any human authority," as one contemporary put it.[161] Eminent among the members of the society was John Abernethy, who preached a sermon in 1719 entitled "Religious Obedience Founded on Personal Persuasion," and this sermon provoked a seven-year controversy that ultimately resulted in the exclusion of the Presbytery of Antrim from the Synod of Ulster.[162] Various attempts at compromise were suggested, but the conflict came to a head in 1726 when the synod effectively isolated all of the non-subscribing ministers in the Presbytery of Antrim in an attempt to restrict their influence.[163] The ministers who favored subscription controlled the synod and many of them believed that the nonsubscribers were harboring heretical views, despite the orthodox protests of the nonsubscribers.

The subscribing clergy focused the issue on the unity and authority of the church being grounded upon doctrinal conformity to the Westminster standards. Some ministers in the Synod were clearly worried about christological heresy, specifically Arianism. The antisubscriptionists, insisting on the right of private judgment, wished to limit the authority of church judicatories and at the same time advance the cause of toleration. They argued that the controversy was not about orthodoxy, but about the synod's new claims to church power.[164] On the question of the orthodoxy of the nonsubscribers, modern scholarship has come down decisively on the side of the nonsubscribers.[165] Further analysis of the most eminent leaders of the antisubscription party confirms this view: John Abernethy, James Kirkpatrick, Samuel Haliday, and Thomas Nevin all defended the full deity of Christ.[166] Even in the case of Abernethy, the most advanced non-subscribing thinker, there is no positive evidence that he actually embraced Arianism, though the tendency of his thought toward Arminianism and nomism is unmistakable.[167]

The arguments of the nonsubscribers were based squarely on the authority of Christ. The phrase, Christ as "the sole King and

Lawgiver" in his church, or its equivalent, runs like a refrain through all of their writings.[168] The authority of Christ as King and Lawgiver in his church is placed over against "the arbitrary will of man," "imposing terms of communion," all "human exclusive tests of orthodoxy," and any other "usurpations" of the authority of Christ.[169] Samuel Haliday and Thomas Nevin even connected their belief in the full deity of Christ directly with the appeal to Christ's authority in this controversy. Haliday confessed: "That from a sacred regard for the deity of Christ, I refuse obedience to those religious laws, which have been superadded to the laws of the Gospel, and reject all those terms of Christian or ministerial communion, which men have devised without his authority:"[170] In addition to Scripture itself, the nonsubscribers relied on the seventeenth-century Puritan divines, Richard Baxter and John Owen, as the principal sources for this emphasis.[171]

This high, christological orthodoxy served as the touchstone by which to judge all human aspects of religion. For the nonsubscribers, the very definition of Nonconformity was at stake, and for them, it was grounded on a single principle arising from a single source: the right of private judgment based directly upon Christ's authority, and the two were invariably connected.[172] If a creed or a doctrinal formula was required as a test of communion, then the nonsubscribers viewed it as inevitably usurping the place that belonged to Christ alone. Laws made by human authority and required for communion were "encroachments upon the royal authority of King Jesus." Christology thus served as the basis for the liberty of individual conscience, the corresponding right of private judgment, and it ultimately grounded the spiritual nature of Christ's kingdom. Flowing from Christ's authority were rights "which Jesus Christ has expressly granted to his subjects."[173] While the congregation's right to choose its own pastor was defended by the non-subscriptionists, it was not a major part of this debate.[174]

Perhaps the clearest statement on the right of private judgment among the nonsubscribers was made by John Abernethy. According to Abernethy, everyone is naturally endowed with reason, the faculty that allows us to form an understanding of God. Neither faith nor obedience is possible without a person being persuaded in his or her own mind freely, because, according to Abernethy, Christ called people "individually" and he "addressed his instructions to men individually." Christianity is thus based on the principle of liberty: "a right in every man to conduct himself in matters of conscience by the *persuasion of his own mind.*" Faith is essential for our salvation, and by its very nature it must be deliberate, arising from the "freest exercise of our understanding."[175] Other nonsubscriptionists endorsed exactly the same understanding of private judgment.[176] Any person's private judgment, thus, can defeat the decisions of church judicatories.[177] By insisting that there was no other way to determine the truth but by the exercise of free and impartial reason, and no other way to advance the truth than by argument, the Dissenters' understanding of private judgment supplied one of the leading vectors of enlightened thought.[178]

Considerations of church authority bore directly on civil authority. If the main principle of Nonconformity was the right of private judgment, the great prejudice against the doctrine, Abernethy observed, was that it "seems to sap the foundations of human authority," and hence both secular and established ecclesiastical powers vehemently opposed it. The implications were plain for civil jurisdiction: matters of conscience are not under any human jurisdiction. In other words, "no man can be safe in a blind submission to the decisions of others, whatever authority they have, or in whatever stations they are placed." Neither can magistrates tell us what is a matter for conscience; what is and is not a matter of conscience is to be judged only by the individual conscience. The magistrates' just power is exercised in "outward human actions" that bear upon public peace and order. "But magistrates have no more authority than any of the rest of mankind (that is, they have no proper authority at all) in matters of conscience *as such.*"[179] In other words, if church judicatories should not impose subscriptions of faith, neither should the state obtrude in matters of conscience.

Thomas Nevin, like Abernethy, moved the argument a very slight but crucial step from the authority of synods to the authority of the state. He blasted the Synod of Ulster's failure to address the proper limits of the magistrate's power: this was a topic, as he put it, "too hot for their handling."[180] Nevin based his arguments not only upon the right of private judgment, but upon the spiritual nature of the church. "Our Lord declares himself, his *Kingdom is not of this world,* and consequently, not to be supported or enlarged by the terrors of it. . . ."[181] On these grounds, Nevin championed the toleration of the Jews as boldly and vigorously as his New Light descendants would champion the toleration of Catholics, so the idiom could easily be applied universally.[182] Benjamin Hoadly's sermon of 1717 on the spiritual nature of Christ's Kingdom was read in Ireland, it was said, "with great attention, and much pleasure, by the friends of liberty."[183] Writing the year after the sermon was preached and published, Francis Hutcheson described a "perfect Hoadly mania among our younger ministers in the North. . . . Their pulpits are ringing with them [Bishop Hoadly's principles]."[184] But while Hoadly was well known and celebrated at the time, he was not the source of the Dissenters' thought.[185] Dissenters in Ireland, like those in England, merely appealed to Hoadly as the best Anglican apologist they had against the principles of established Anglican religion.

The Presbyterian Synod of Ulster opposed these arguments because for them, much like their Anglican counterparts, the authority of Christ was located, not in the individual, but "in the judicatories of the church."[186] The issues raised by the nonsubscribers, however, could not be confined to the church. In eighteenth-century Britain and Ireland, if one questioned the authority of religious establishments, one invariably questioned the authority of civil establishments. Anglican theory and practice espoused a unified notion of authority in the civil and religious spheres. In Ireland, as in England, Anglican clergymen were Justices of the Peace, and blasphemy was a punishable crime, because according to Anglican theory, its threat could not be confined to the spiritual realm alone. Hence, Nevin was charged by his opponents as "a rebel to their [i.e., magistrates'] mild and just authority." For his writings against the authority of magistrates in matters of conscience, Nevin was accused of "railing and indecent expressions to his Majesty's Justice of the Peace."[187] Naturally, both the subscribers of the Synod of Ulster and Anglicans thought the principles of the nonsubscribers dangerous.[188] Some Anglicans, like William Tisdall, the Vicar of Belfast, worried a great deal about the political implications of Presbyterianism. Tisdall argued that the Christology of the Dissenters, when applied to ecclesiastical polity, was a dangerous political principle subversive of episcopacy and monarchy.[189] A watchful eye must be kept on them, "because it is to be presum'd whenever these Directors [the factious Presbyterian leaders] shall think it seasonable shall declare for this or any other of what they call *the prerogatives of Christ's Kingdom*, they have power to spirit up their people. . . ." This "arbitrary power" of Dissenting teachers is not to be wondered at "when we consider that it is the natural result of their scheme of ecclesiastical policy, by which the *independent* government of the *kirk* is compos'd of a mixture of *lay and spiritual members*, vested with equal authority in all points. . . ." The ruling elders thus have authority delegated directly from Christ himself and exercised in the cause of Christ's kingdom. From an Anglican viewpoint, vigilance with respect to the Presbyterians was required, and the political expedience of maintaining the Test Act was obvious. Tisdall charged the Presbyterians with setting up an "*Imperium in Imperio*,"[190] a nation within a nation, that challenged the very existence of the Anglo-Irish Ascendancy, and in a sense, this is exactly what the nonsubscribers had done in relation to the Synod of Ulster.

The theory of the Dissenters was further radicalized and made concrete by their appeal to an anti-Catholic understanding of history. The Irish Presbyterians were always intensely in touch with their history, a history which at bottom was "a history of frontier insecurity, their mentality essentially a siege mentality, their symbolic dates 1641, 1689, and 1690."[191] All of the rhetoric of anti-Catholic prejudice was present in the writings of the nonsubscribers, but the sheer size of the Catholic community in Ireland may have muted the polemic. For example, anti-Catholic imagery was present in John Abernethy's writings, but it is well known that he was kindly disposed toward his Catholic neighbors.[192] In Ireland, anti-Catholicism among the nonsubscribers was used principally as a point of comparison, and "popery" was generalized into a kind of archetypical spiritual oppression. Perceptions of Rome, for example, provide ready-made comparisons with the Synod of Ulster. Nevin thought that the worst of the popish inquisitors seemed to be in the past, but now, he averred, we find Protestants adopting the same tactics. Similarly, Haliday equated spoiling the pope in the past with rejecting the power of present-day Protestant synods.[193] Alternatively, the "mock omnipotence" of the Synod was compared to the tyranny found in "popish" countries.[194] Abernethy suggested that all forms of "imposition" were "popery" and even described "a narrow spirit" in Protestantism as "popery." Similarly, for Kirkpatrick, "popery" was found in imposing rules of any kind.[195] Just as in England and Scotland, the use of force in matters of religion or conscience was understood as a species of "popery" since "servile" notions of church power would inevitably destroy a "rational choice."[196]

The concept of "popery" was also broadened to embrace the Anglican establishment. The nonsubscribers argued uniformly that to allow tests of orthodoxy was to place oneself on the same ground as the Anglican establishment. To require "tests" among Presbyterians was tantamount to admitting truth in the Anglican "pretense" with respect to the Prayer Book.[197] The imposition of the liturgy and ceremonies of the established church thus found an exact parallel in the attempt to force assent to the Westminster Confession of Faith. In the case of the established church, however, the situation was worse, in that the civil magistrate armed the imposer with a coercive power.[198] At points, the opposition to church power was broadened to a general anticlericalism: for example, it is said that the impositions of the Roman Catholic and Greek Orthodox Churches generally supported "the power, the grandeur, or the wealth of the clergy."[199] This softer form of anti-Catholicism, applied to Protestant synods and the Anglican establishment, seemed to foreshadow the future alliance of Irish dissenters and Catholics.

In a sense, as Smyth observes, the history, size, and cohesion of the Presbyterian Church in Ulster meant that the quarrel with Anglicans would be politicized.[200] But theology and political ideology cannot be sustained in a vacuum. Irish Presbyterians remained under the pressure of civil disabilities through 1780, and the legal disallowance of Dissenting marriages was particularly galling. Thus the principles of the nonsubscribers were maintained through the middle years of the century by their support of the English Dissenters' attempts at repeal of the Test and Corporation acts, and by their ongoing publications in favor of toleration.[201] Several studies have traced the spread of the nonsubscribers' ideology in the eighteenth century and its broadening influence on the Synod of Ulster. While the Presbytery of Antrim was excluded from the synod and its lower judicatories, it was not excluded from communion with the larger body, and so some fellowship continued. There was a gradual decline of the requirement to subscribe, and increasingly, the question was left to the determination of individual presbyteries. By 1751 the excluded Presbyter of Antrim was invited to sit again with the Synod of Ulster, and there are clear signs by this date that the idea of enforcing strict Calvinism was becoming less popular in the synod. As subscription became less of an issue, the nomenclature also shifted.[202] From the 1720s forward, and increasingly from the 1740s and 1750s, the non-subscribing party became known as New Lights.[203]

Presbyterian ministers gave strong support to the American colonists during the Revolution. By 1775 the majority of Presbyterians in Ulster had family members in the colonies, massive emigration continued apace, and hence it is not surprising that the Presbyterians were sympathetic to the colonists. During the Revolution, Old Light and New Light Presbyterians in northern Ireland were largely united in their support of the Americans.[204] The prominence of New Light ministers in the Volunteer movement and Presbyterian activity at the grass roots have been carefully studied by Ian McBride, and while in the last analysis the movement was largely ineffectual, the Volunteers did take the first steps toward reforming the Irish House of Commons. They also helped prompt the repeal of the Irish Test Act in 1780, and they were unquestionably behind the liberalizing of Irish law concerning Presbyterian marriages.[205] How were these activities justified? In William Steel Dickson's sermon on "Scripture Politics" in 1781, all of the foundational notions of New Light politics were still firmly in place: the supreme authority of Christ is asserted, and any attempt to enforce doctrinal conformity is viewed as usurping Christ's place as the sole head and legislator over the church. His Kingdom is not of this world, and it cannot be supported or extended by any form of coercion; the church is an independent society, sovereign in its own sphere.[206] After the American Revolutionary War, the New Light ministers of Ulster were particularly active on behalf of parliamentary reform.[207]

The contribution of Ulster Presbyterianism to the United Irishmen is perhaps more impressive. The Society of United Irishmen, founded in Belfast in October of 1791, eventually brought Protestants and Catholics together for united action against the English: at first, however, all of the founding members were Presbyterians.[208] Already in the 1780s, numerous Presbyterians, especially those in the New Light tradition, began to turn from their traditional anti-Catholicism,[209] and under the internationally disrupted political conditions of the 1790s, the political rapprochement between Old Lights and New Lights was momentarily sustained. Ian McBride has identified forty-nine Presbyterian ministers and probationers suspected of involvement in the 1798 rebellion; of these, New Light and Old Light ministers were almost equally involved, and McBride judges the majority to have been orthodox.[210] In fact, of all the New Light ministers, it has been possible to identify only six with Arian and two with Unitarian affiliations; in other words, approximately one-third of the New Light Presbyterian leaders who supported this radical cause can be considered theologically heterodox.[211] The principles held in common by all the ministers, combined with the congregational practices of the laity, were what mattered. Considered as a group, the ministers suffered substantially for their radical activities and sympathies; three were executed, eighteen were imprisoned, and twenty fled or were transported.[212]

We can discern some lines of continuity between the early and late-eighteenth-century theology and political ideology of the New Light ministers. David Bailie Warden, licensed to preach by the Presbytery of Bangor as a probationer in 1797, became a colonel with the United Irishmen, and following the Rebellion, he was arrested for his radical activities and confined in the same prison as Daniel Steel Dickson.[213] He published a pamphlet in 1798 in which he reminded his readers in the Presbytery of Bangor how they had been "the most strenuous advocates of reform" and how each of them had "both publicly and privately circulated republican morality."

Warden explained the meaning of "republican morality" in the following terms: "that religion is a personal thing—that Christ is head of the church—that his kingdom is not of this world—that the will of the people should be the supreme law."[214] New Light ministers continued to appeal to the text in the Gospel of John, chapter 18: Christ's kingdom is not of this world.[215] Evidently, the theology of Dissent was here being used directly for radical political ends.

What exactly, then, was the connection between Dissenting practice, Dissenting theology, and radical politics? McBride locates the connection in two major points: the representative nature of the church as a contractual association—Presbyterian polity fostered participatory forms of political association—and the separation between temporal and spiritual power, with the Dissenters placing the priority on Christ's spiritual headship. "The potentially explosive element in the Presbyterian idea of polity, for heterodox and orthodox alike," writes McBride, "was the insistence on Christ's headship of the church."[216] This Christology directly challenged ecclesiastical as well as civil "tyranny," but it is worth emphasizing that in Ireland, as in England and Scotland, it was doctrine embodied in, and reinforced by, separated ecclesiastical practice that contributed to radical disaffection with civil government. The political salience of these structures and ideas seems to be borne out by the strength of the Presbyterian support for the United Irishmen.

Strikingly, in light of what we know about Scotland, only two Seceding ministers were connected to the movement.[217] The behavior of the Covenanters is even more notable, in that, despite their staunch anti-Catholicism and their impeccable orthodoxy, they were deeply involved in Irish radicalism—"much greater, proportionately, than . . . any other Presbyterian denomination," writes McBride. Of the six ministers who formed the Irish Reformed Presbytery in 1792, three were implicated in the Rebellion, and later a fourth was added.[218]

The behavior of the Covenanters raises the issue of the role of anti-Catholicism in an acute form. I have argued that anti-Catholicism in England, Scotland, and Ireland was a main component of radical disaffection in the Dissenting idiom, but then, with the demise of anti-Catholicism in late-eighteenth-century Irish Dissent, we find an even greater radical engagement. In the case of the Covenanting ministers, we may simply have a case of inconsistent or contradictory behavior, for as McBride observes, Covenant political theology was an unstable mixture that could produce unpredictable results.[219] In the case of the New Light ministers, at least three considerations must be kept in mind.[220] The sheer numbers of Catholics in Ireland marked the country off from England and Scotland. The fact that a large Catholic population in Ireland was equally marginalized by the Anglican ascendancy would mean, in the short run, that the Irish-Presbyterian attitude toward Catholics could play out differently than in England and Scotland.[221] Second, the issue of private judgment was, for the Irish New Light Dissenters, the key ideological component in their battle with oppressive synods, and this doctrine was likely to work as a solvent on anti-Catholic prejudices. It would likely have more bearing on moderating denominational prejudice than that other pole of dissenting identity, namely, the right of Christians to elect their minister. There were crucial historical variations as well. For example, unlike the Catholics in Scotland, the Irish Catholics did not support the Jacobite cause in 1715 or 1745. Third, the Presbyterian-Catholic alliance was, at bottom, a short-lived marriage of convenience designed to oppose Anglican hegemony, and the alliance does not imply that Presbyterians uniformly threw off their anti-Catholic prejudices, a fact that the later history of the Orangemen makes evident.[222] As Stewart has shown, the extent of anti-Catholicism can be measured in part on the basis of geographic variations; those counties in which Presbyterians had suffered most in the seventeenth century remained the most resistant to cooperation with Catholics in the late eighteenth century. Finally, it seems likely that in Ireland, unlike Scotland, but parallel to England, there was a nexus between the growth of theological heterodoxy and the greater acceptance of Catholics.

Conclusion: The Religious and Social Origins of Radicalism

The religious seeds of late-eighteenth-century political discontent were sown in England by the ejection of ministers in 1662, in Ireland in 1705 by the Synod of Ulster's imposition of the Westminster

Confession, and in Scotland in 1712 when the General Assembly agreed to the law on patronage. In England, the Test and Corporation acts were to the Nonconformists what subscription to the Westminster Confession of Faith was to Presbyterians in Ireland and what patronage was to the Seceders in Scotland. Each of these structures of the established churches was viewed as contributing to a species of slavery, and each served as a stimulus for the Dissenters to sympathize with the claims of oppressed people and radical causes. In England there was never a centralized judicatory among the Presbyterians, and Congregationalists and Baptists had always insisted on a congregational polity. English Dissenters therefore never faced such internecine conflict as did the Presbyterians in Ireland and the Secession in Scotland. The English Dissenters' struggle was more directly related to the Anglican establishment and the need to legitimize their separate existence over against Anglicans. In Ireland the authority of the Synod of Ulster over the decision of local congregations was seldom invoked. But the synod did exert its authority in doctrinal matters, and the issue of private judgment and its proper extent became the central point of contention. In Scotland the structures of patronage shaped the struggle of the Presbyterian dissenters in a different direction. Here the doctrinal orthodoxy of the dissenters was not in question, and accordingly, matters of private judgment never come to the fore. But the Seceders did press the other pole of dissenting principle, namely, the voluntary nature of the congregation, and their insistence on popular elections functioned in much the same way as the right of private judgment functioned in Ireland. One is tempted to conclude that either aspect of the dissenting heritage, private judgment or a congregation's right to choose its pastor, was sufficient to provoke an anti-establishment stance, when the establishment seemed to threaten, a stance that in turn served to nurture theory about civil liberty, or, given the right circumstances, even promote resistance to civil authority.

If political radicalism had turned principally on heresy, or if it was a product of growing secularism, one would expect to find the emergence of heterodoxy much earlier and on a more consistent basis. In fact, heterodox and orthodox dissenters worked comfortably together in England, heterodoxy was virtually absent in the early subscription controversy in Ireland, and it was entirely absent among the Scottish Secession and the Popular party of Evangelicals. If heterodoxy was conceptually basic to most expressions of political disaffection, one might also expect to find traces of political dissidence in the Moderate party in the Church of Scotland. Instead we find the Moderate party enjoying its established status and behaving as if it were attached to power, while a strong element of political opposition emerged among the Scottish dissenters amidst a range of groups that were all unimpeachably orthodox. The ideological origins of radical disaffection cannot be located in a "low" heterodox Christology that was placed over against the institutional orthodoxy of the Anglican and Presbyterian establishments, but rather in a "high," christological orthodoxy, understood and applied in a radically different way. If we ask in each case of England, Scotland, and Ireland, what were those religious elements that were common to the emergence of political dissidence, we find, first, a minority group with a minority group consciousness that, second, was positively informed by a common ideology shaped by anti-Catholicism and anticlericalism. Third, it perceived the source of oppression in the majority, established religion that exercised political power, and fourth, was prompted to more overt, open opposition to civil authority by a revolutionary cause.

Dissenters combined a backward looking, primitive Christology with an egalitarian ecclesiology activated through the vehicle of the age-old polemic against Rome, and these doctrines were put into practice in the "unsteepled" places of worship, where, in the words of E. P. Thompson, "there was room for a free intellectual life and for democratic experiments with 'members unlimited.'"[223] In each of the countries examined here, we now need research that integrates the theology and practice of the Dissenters with the social discontent of the rank and file, many of whom were indifferent to religion.[224] Only then can we convincingly connect religious disaffection with other forms of alienation that arose from differences in status and wealth, and only then will we have a full picture of the origins of late-eighteenth-century radicalism in the British Isles.

Notes

1. The Reformed churches in Holland held a privileged status, but were not technically established. See the essays in this volume by Wayne te Brake and James Van Horn Melton and the general introduction by W. R. Ward, *Christianity under the Ancien Régime 1648–1789* (Cambridge: Cambridge University Press, 1999), 1–33.

2. Voltaire, *Letters Concerning the English Nation* (1733; Oxford: Oxford University Press, 1994), Letters I–VIII. For the legal status of English Dissent, see James E. Bradley, *Religion, Revolution, and English Radicalism: Nonconformity in Eighteenth-Century Politics and Society* (Cambridge: Cambridge University Press, 1990), 49–61; for Irish Dissent, see Toby C. Barnard, "The Government and Irish Dissent, 1704–1780," in Kevin Herlihy, *The Politics of Irish Dissent, 1650–1800* (Dublin: Four Courts Press, 1997), 7–29. English and Irish "Dissenters" when equated with Nonconformists (Presbysterians, Congregationalists, Baptists, and Quakers) are conventionally distinguished from religious "dissent" in a broad sense, but the term is characteristically not capitalized when referring to Presbyterians in Scotland or to dissenters construed as a group in the British Isles.

3. Compare Michael Walzer, *The Revolution of the Saints: A Study in the Origins of Radical Politics* (Cambridge, Mass.: Harvard University Press, 1965), 12, 13–16, 317–19; and Richard L. Greaves, *Deliver Us from Evil: The Radical Underground in Britain, 1660–1663* (Oxford: Oxford University Press, 1986), 4–8; and Bradley, *Religion, Revolution, and English Radicalism*, 417–22 with J. C. D. Clark, *English Society 1660–1832: Religion, Ideology, and Politics During the Ancien Regime* (Cambridge: Cambridge University Press, 2000); chap. 4, "Before Radicalism: The Religious Origins of Disaffection, 1688–1800," 318–400, and his "Religion and the Origins of Radicalism in Nineteenth-Century Britain," in Glenn Burgess and Matthew Festenstein, eds., *English Radicalism, 1550–1850*, forthcoming from Cambridge.

4. The ideological origins of political radicalism in late-eighteenth-century Britain and Ireland have been the subject of considerable scholarly interest: for classical humanist and republican thought (J. G. A. Pocock); Commonwealthman ideas (Caroline Robbins, Bernard Bailyn); the Country idiom of opposition (Linda Colley, H. T. Dickinson); and for Deism and Freemasonry (Justin Champion, Margaret Jacob). Alternatively, a few influential studies have attempted to locate political discontent and the impetus for reform primarily in economic and social sources (Simon Maccoby, George Rudé, John Brewer, E. P. Thompson, John Sainsbury). Until recently, however, a more or less secular interpretation of these ideas and sources prevailed; even though religious institutions

and theology were occasionally investigated, they were readily parsed into sociological categories and thereby rendered impotent. The same is true of comparative studies; cf. E. W. McFarland, *Ireland and Scotland in the Age of Revolution* (Edinburgh: Edinburgh University Press, 1994).

5. John Baillie, *The Influence of a Crucified Saviour* (Newcastle, 1772), 4. The Covenanting "Act of 1761," 109, is cited in Matthew Hutchison, *The Reformed Presbyterian Church in Scotland* (Edinburgh, 1893), 209. John Snodgrass adopts identical usage with "this radical part" of the constitution of the church, *An Effectual Method of Recovering our Religious Liberties* (Glasgow, 1770), 13.

6. Peter Marshall, "Bristol and the American War of Independence," The Historical Association Local History Pamphlets (Bristol, 1977), 24–25.

7. Archibald Bruce, *A Brief Statement and Declaration of the Genuine Principles of Seceders, Respecting Civil Government* . . . (Edinburgh, 1799), 19, 58.

8. *Tracts Concerning Patronage, by some Eminent Hands* (Edinburgh, 1770), 183.

9. *The Case of the Dissenters of England, and of the Presbyterians of Scotland, Consider'd in a True and Fair Light, with Relation to the King and Parliament* (London, 1738), 19, 23, 27.

10. Thomas Walker, *The Terms of Ministerial and Christian Communion imposed on the Church of Scotland by a Prevailing Party in the General Assembly*. . . . (Glasgow, 1753), 133, 125.

11. Caleb Fleming, *The Palladium of Great Britain and Ireland. Or Historical Strictures of Liberty* (London, 1762), x, vi, 2–3.

12. Anthony Lincoln, *Some Political and Social Ideas of English Dissent* (Cambridge: Cambridge University Press, 1938), 30; Russell E. Richey, "The Origins of British Radicalism; The Changing Rationale for Dissent," *Eighteenth-Century Studies*, 7 (Winter 1973–74): 179; Colin Bonwick, *English Radicals and the American Revolution* (Chapel Hill: University of North Carolina Press, 1977), 11, 46; H. T. Dickinson, *Liberty and Property: Political Ideology in Eighteenth-Century England* (New York: Holmes and Meier Publishers, 1977), 197–205; John Gascoigne, "Anglican Latitudinarianism and Political Radicalism in the Late Eighteenth Century," *History* 71 (1986): 30; Martin Fitzpatrick, "Heretical Religion and Radical Political Ideas in Late Eighteenth-Century England," in Eckhart Hellmuth, ed., *The Transformation of Political Culture: England and Germany in the Late Eighteenth Century* (Oxford: Oxford University Press, 1990), 338–72. The view has only recently been questioned. See Knud Haakonssen, "Enlightened Dissent: An Introduction," in Knud Haakonssen, ed., *Enlightenment and Religion: Rational Dissent in Eighteenth-Century Britain* (Cambridge: Cambridge University Press, 1996), 5, 10.

13. Ronald Stromberg, *Religious Liberalism in Eighteenth-Century England* (Oxford: Oxford University Press, 1954), 156; Isaac Kramnick, "Religion and Radicalism; English Political Theory in the Age of Revolution," *Political Theory* 5 (1977): 508; John Seed, "Gentlemen Dissenters: The Social and Political Meanings of Rational Dissent in the 1770s and 1780s," *Historical Journal* 28 (1985): 316–17; John Seed, "'A Set of Men Powerful Enough in Many Things': Rational Dissent and Political Opposition in England, 1770–1790," 143, in Haakonssen, *Enlightenment and Religion;* and Mark Philp, "Rational Religion and Political Radicalism in the 1790s," *Enlightenment and Dissent,* 4 (1985): 41. A few studies have even postulated a "natural affinity" between Calvinism and loyalism. See Seed, "Gentlemen Dissenters," 321; Gascoigne, "Anglican Latitudinarianism," 32; John Stephens, "The London Ministers and Subscription, 1772–1779," *Enlightenment and Dissent,* 1 (1982): 50. No one, however, has sought to explain how seventeenth-century Calvinist radicals were transformed into eighteenth-century Calvinist loyalists.

14. Under the Blasphemy Act of 1698 anti-trinitarians could be imprisoned for up to three years for propagating their views.

15. Some of the others include Andrew Kippis, Abraham Rees, Richard Baron, Thomas Brand Hollis, Samuel Heywood, Capel Lofft, and some of the less well-known Dissenters in the provinces, like George Walker, Joshua Toulmin, Newcome Cappe, and William Turner.

16. There are exceptions to this rule, notably, the articles by John Seed and John Gascoigne noted above.

17. The periodization as well as the substantive thesis of Anthony Lincoln has thus proven pivotal, as has the prerequisite taxonomy of chapters on Price and Priestley. J. C. D. Clark argued that "it was *heterodox* Dissent which lay at the root of the emerging radicalism of the 1770s and 1780s." J. C. D. Clark, *English Society 1688–1832* (Cambridge: Cambridge University Press, 1985), 252; see also 217, 293, n. 63, 423. Essentially the same argument is found in J. C. D. Clark's more recent work, *English Society 1660–1832,* 319, 368, sans the word "radicalism." In his 1994 book, heterodoxy is only one of several causes of political disaffection, including practical grievances and ecclesiastical polity. J. C. D. Clark, *The Language of Liberty 1660–1832: Political Discourse and Social Dynamics in the Anglo-American World* (Cambridge, 1994), 224; see also J. G. A. Pocock, "The Definitions of Orthodoxy," 36, 37, 50, in Roger D. Lund, ed., *The Margins of Orthodoxy: Heterodox Writing and Cultural Response, 1660–1750* (Cambridge: Cambridge University Press, 1995); A. M. C. Waterman, "The Nexus between Theology and Political Doctrine," 193–218, in Haakonssen, *Enlightenment and Religion;* John Gascoigne, "Anglican Latitudinarianism, Rational Dissent, and Political Radicalism in the Late

Eighteenth-Century," 219–40 in Haakonssen, *Enlightenment and Religion.* The High Anglican equating of schism (Dissent) with heterodoxy is pervasive; see Gordon Schochet, "Samuel Parker, Religious Diversity, and the Ideology of Persecution," in Lund, *Margins of Orthodoxy,* 121, 124.

18. Clark, *Language of Liberty,* 8, 16, 41, 43, 122; David Hempton, *Religion and Political Culture in Britain and Ireland* (Cambridge: Cambridge University Press, 1996).

19. James E. Bradley, *Popular Politics and the American Revolution in England* (Macon, Ga.: Mercer University Press, 1985), Tables 3.1–3.3; and Bradley, *Religion, Revolution, and English Radicalism,* Table 10.2.

20. Robert Hall, *Christianity Consistent with the Love of Freedom* (London, 1791), 16–17.

21. My study of the religious and social origins of eighteenth-century radicalism (in process) will show that in ten English boroughs, of the thirty-eight Dissenting ministers who signed petitions favoring the American colonists, the theological orientation of thirty-two can be clearly established; of these thirty-two ministers, eighteen (56%) were trinitarian, and fourteen (46%) were Arian or Socinian. Conversely, eighty-two of the eighty-six Anglican clergymen (95%) signed addresses favoring the Government's policy of coercion.

22. Ideas account for only one part of the complex causal chain of political discontent, and for this reason, the use of the term "sources" might be preferred over the more exclusive-sounding word "origins." In the study noted above (note 22), a chapter on radicalism in Bristol using quantitative data will show the importance of differences in wealth and status in accounting for political behavior, in conjunction with religious ideas.

23. We do have Douglas R. Lacey, *Dissent and Parliamentary Politics in England 1661–1698* (New Brunswick: Rutgers University Press, 1969); and Michael R. Watts, *The Dissenters* (Oxford: Clarendon Press, 1978).

24. On the congregational covenant, polity, and radicalism see Quentin Skinner, *The Foundations of Modern Political Thought,* 2 vols. (Cambridge: Cambridge University Press, 1978), 2:236–38; Christopher Hill, *A Turbulent, Seditious and Factious People: John Bunyan and his Church* (Oxford: Oxford University Press, 1988), 125; Patricia Bonomi, *Under the Cope of Heaven* (Oxford: Oxford University Press, 1986), 153–54.

25. Gordon J. Schochet, "The Act of Toleration and the Failure of Comprehension: Persecution, Nonconformity, and Religious Indifference," in Dale Hoak and Mordechai Feingold, eds., *The World of William and Mary: Anglo-Dutch Perspectives on the Revolution of 1688–89* (Stanford: Stanford University Press, 1995), 165–87; and Schochet's "Samuel Parker, Religious Diversity, and the Ideology of Persecution," in Lund, *Margins of Orthodoxy,* 127.

26. Norman Sykes, "Benjamin Hoadly, Bishop of Bangor," in F. J. C. Hearnshaw, ed., *The Social and Political Ideas of Some English Thinkers of the Augustan Age A.D. 1650–1750* (London: Barnes & Noble, 1928), 122.

27. Edmund Calamy, *A Defense of Moderate Non-Conformity,* 3 vols. (London, 1703–05). Calamy is dependent on Richard Baxter for this emphasis. The English Baptists had long affirmed such a view: "We believe . . . that the magistrate is not by virtue of his office to meddle with religion, or matters of the conscience, to force or compel men to this or that form of religion or doctrine . . . for Christ only is the king, and lawgiver of the church and consciences (James iv.12)." General Baptist Confession, 1614. From "Propositions and Conclusions Concerning True Christian Religion, 1612–1614," in William L. Lumpkin, *Baptist Confessions of Faith,* 2d ed. (Valley Forge, Pa.: Judson Press, 1969), 140.

28. Andrew Kippis, *A Vindication of the Protestant Dissenting Ministers with Regard to their Late Application to Parliament,* 2d ed. (London, 1773), 41–43. Dating the change to the first decade of the eighteenth century contradicts Richey's thesis in "The Origins of British Radicalism" (note 13 above).

29. The same is true for Ireland. *Some Considerations Humbly offer'd Touching the Administration and Receiving the Sacrament . . . as Directed by the Test Act* (London, 1726), 14, 17, 18.

30. Edmund Calamy, "A True Account of the Protestant Dissenters in England," reprinted in Charles Owen, *Plain Reasons for Dissenting from the Communion of the Church of England* (London, 1736), 6–7.

31. William Graham, *An Ecclesiastical History from the Birth of John the Baptist to the Present Times* (Newcastle upon Tyne, 1777), 77; Fleming, *Palladium of Great Britain and Ireland,* x.

32. Charles Owen's *Plain Reasons for Dissenting* first appeared in 1715 and went to 23 editions by 1736; it was republished as late as 1771; see 5, 7, 19, 20, 24; Samuel Chandler, *The Old Whig: or Consistent Protestant* (London, 1735–38), no. 4, 3 April 1735; also no. 42, 25 Dec. 1735; Samuel Palmer, *The Protestant-Dissenter's Catechism,* 3d ed. (London, 1774), 23, 27, 30–31. Similarly, "A Layman," *The Foundations of Religious Liberty Explained, or Plain Reasons for Being a Protestant Dissenter* (London, 1755), 30.

33. Precisely here, the error of past accounts' undue focus on the private beliefs of individual ministers becomes patent. According to Bourn, Dissenters suffer because of their faithfulness and loyalty to Jesus "the King of his Church." Samuel Bourn, *A Vindication of the Principles and Practice of Protestant Dissenters: . . . Designed and Fitted . . . for the Use of Dissenting Parents . . .* (London, 1748), ii, iii, 2, 3.

34. Towgood's work was published in London in 1753, but it was earlier known as "The Dissenting Gentleman's Three Letters." Christ, the King of the

Church, said Towgood, "hath expressly commanded that NO POWER of this kind [as exercised by the Anglican Church] shall ever be *claimed*, or ever be *yielded* by any of his followers." The claim is based on the practice of the early church and upon Matt. 23: 8, 10; John 18: 36. See Micaiah Towgood, *A Dissent from the Church of England, Fully Justified: and Proved the Genuine and Just Consequence of the Allegiance Due to Christ, the Only Lawgiver in the Church* (London, 1753), 2, 12.

35. Towgood, *Dissent from the Church of England*, 137.

36. Nathaniel Lardner, *Two Schemes of a Trinity Considered, and the Divine Unity Asserted* (London, 1784), 88.

37. Roger Altham, *The Harmony of the Sacred and Civil Polity* (London, 1719), 8, 27.

38. Roger Altham, *Church Authority Not an Universal Supremacy* (London, 1720), 4–5.

39. Ibid., 11, 8–9.

40. "In the province of religion, verily, every man is upon a level; the prince has no superiority to the peasant, nor the most learned cleric to the unlettered laic"; see Fleming, *Palladium of Great Britain and Ireland*, 4. "*ONE* and one only is our master and law-giver, even CHRIST; and all Christians are brethren; i.e. stand upon an equal foot; have no dominion over one another"; see Towgood, *Dissent from the Church*, 12. In the Kingdom of Christ "there is no distinction between the greater and lesser number of his subjects; . . . all are equally obliged by those [laws] of the sovereign, and by no other"; see Bourn, *Vindication of Principles*, 137, 179.

41. I have identified four English Dissenters whose anticlerical pamphlets were republished in the colonies in the 1760s to help combat the institution of bishops in America: Thomas Bradbury, James Murray, John Macgowan, and Micaiah Towgood. The first three were orthodox trinitarians.

42. For anti-Catholicism as veiled Anglican anticlericalism and the origins of radicalism, see Bradley, *Religion, Revolution, and English Radicalism*, 2, 170, 180; and James E. Bradley, "Anti-Catholicism as Anglican Anticlericalism: Nonconformity and the Ideological Origins of Radical Disaffection," in Nigel Aston and Matthew Cragoe, eds., *Anticlericalism in Britain c. 1500–1914* (Stroud, Gloucestershire: Alan Sutton, 2000), 67–92.

43. Chandler, *The Old Whig*, no. 13, 5 June 1735; no. 4, 3 April 1753.

44. Owen, *Plain Reasons for Dissenting*, 8.

45. *A Vindication of Liberty of Conscience; of the Toleration of Protestant Dissenters and of the Present Happy Establishment: In Remarks on Dr. Middleton's Sermon . . .* (London, 1734), 4.

46. For example, they worked on such important cooperative endeavors as the *Occasional Papers*, 3 vols. (London, 1716–1718); *The Old Whig, or*

Consistent Protestant (London, 1734–1738); and *The Protestant System*, 2 vols. (London, 1758).

47. Thus when the strict Calvinistic writers David Bogue and James Bennett wrote their history of Nonconformity in 1810, they deplored the doctrine of the Arians and the Socinians alike; see David Bogue and James Bennett, *History of Dissenters, from the Revolution in 1688 to the year 1808*, 4 vols. (London, 1810) 4:401. Nevertheless, they included many heterodox writers in their history, offering high praise for their contribution to the Dissenting movement. The controlling concern for Bogue and Bennett was the civil and religious liberty that these authors espoused. Hence, see their warm words of endorsement of George Benson, Philip Furneaux, Richard Price, and James Foster (401, 415, 423, 486–89).

48. Palmer, *Protestant Dissenter's Catechism*, v, vi–vii, 24. See also questions 6, 10, 11, 23, and 25 in Samuel Palmer, *A Supplement to the Assembly's Catechism; Relating to Church Fellowship, and the Principles of the Protestant Dissenters, with Scripture Proofs at Large* (London, 1780).

49. Thomas Bradbury, *A Confession of Faith. With an Exhortation by the Rev. Mr. John Shower*, 5th ed. (London, 1729), 23.

50. "A Dissenting Minister," *An Apology, and a Shield for Protestant Dissenters, in these Times of Instability and Misrepresentation. Four Letters to the Rev Mr. Newton* (London, 1784), 195.

51. Josiah Thompson, "History of Protestant Dissenting Congregations," Ms. 38.7–11, Dr. Williams's Library, London, 2:138; 1:155–56.

52. Robert Robinson, *Lectures on the Principles of Nonconformity* (1778), Lecture XI, in *Miscellaneous Works of Robert Robinson*, ed. Benjamin Flower (Cambridge, 1807), 2:248.

53. Samuel Wright, *The Lordship of Christ Considered* (London, 1724), 46.

54. James E. Bradley, "Nonconformity and the Electorate in Eighteenth-Century England," *Parliamentary History* 6 (1987): 253, 260, n. 96.

55. Bradley, *Religion, Revolution, and English Radicalism*, 257–59; a possible exception to this generalization is London.

56. Ibid., 174, 364–66.

57. Clark, *Language of Liberty*, 142.

58. N. C. Hunt, *Two Early Political Associations: The Quakers and the Dissenting Deputies in the Age of Sir Robert Walpole* (Westport, Conn.: Greenwood Press, 1979), 118.

59. Hunt, *Two Early Political Associations*, 83, 87, 157–58. In the late eighteenth century, M.P.'s who were willing to support the Dissenters in their campaigns for repeal numbered 150. See G. M. Ditchfield, "The Parliamentary Struggle over the Repeal of the Test and Corporation Acts," *English Historical Review* 89 (1974): 553–54, 558.

60. Hunt, *Two Early Political Associations,* 62–112.

61. Bernard Manning, *The Protestant Dissenting Deputies* (Cambridge: Cambridge University Press, 1952), 119–29.

62. Lincoln, *Some Political and Social Ideas of English Dissent,* 198.

63. The evidence for this assertion is derived from an exhaustive search of the "Eighteenth-Century Short Title Catalog" on CD-ROM published by the British Library and ESTC North America, 1992, and will appear in a subsequent study.

64. John Sainsbury, *Disaffected Patriots: London Supporters of Revolutionary America 1769–1782* (Kingston and Montreal: McGill-Queen's University Press, 1987), 15–18, 24–25; Bradley, *Religion, Revolution, and English Radicalism,* 421.

65. James Murray, *Sermons to Asses* (London, 1768), 63–65, 86, 100, 104–7; Joseph Towers, *Observations on Public Liberty, Patriotism, Ministerial Despotism, and National Grievances. With Some Remarks on Riots, Petitions, Legal Addresses, and Military Executions* (London, 1769), 15–16, 19.

66. Carl Bridenbaugh calls the period 1766–70 "The Great Fear"; see Carl Bridenbaugh, *Mitre and Sceptre: Transatlantic Faiths, Ideas, Personalities, and Politics 1689–1776* (Oxford: Oxford University Press, 1962), 260–87.

67. Cited in Bridenbaugh, *Mitre and Sceptre,* 243.

68. Cited in William Legg, *Historical Memorials of Broadstreet Chapel, Reading* (London, 1851), 50.

69. John Brims conflates the Covenanting tradition with the various forms of secession; see John Brims, "The Covenanting Tradition and Scottish Radicalism in the 1790s," in Terry Brotherstone, ed., *Covenant, Charter, and Party: Traditions of Revolt in Modern Scottish History* (Aberdeen: Aberdeen University Press, 1989), 51. But Seceders vigorously distinguished themselves from the Covenanters; see Archibald Bruce, *Brief Statement,* 18, 21–22, 26–27, 35; "A Society of Seceders in and about Glasgow," *A Testimony to the Original Principles of the Secession* [Glasgow, 1799], 4, 14). At the same time, the Covenanters likewise distanced their views from the Secession, precisely on political grounds; see *The Enchantments of Jannes and Jambres discovered: or the Errors and Blasphemies of the Secession, in their Principles on Magistracy Exposed* [Edinburgh, 1765], 4, 8–9.

70. Callum G. Brown, *The Social History of Religion in Scotland Since 1730* (London: Methuen, 1987), 29.

71. John H. S. Burleigh, *A Church History of Scotland* (London and New York: Oxford University Press, 1960), 279–85.

72. Richard B. Sher, *Church and University in the Scottish Enlightenment: The Moderate Literati of Edinburgh* (Princeton: Princeton University Press, 1985), 47.

73. The three colleagues were William Wilson, Alexander Mancrieff, and James Fisher. The christological thrust comes through all of the writings. See, for example, William Wilson, *A Letter from a Member of the Associate Presbytery* (Edinburgh, 1738), 9, 10.

74. Wilson, *Letter from a Member,* 8, 9.

75. The General Assembly actually deposed the Secession in 1740.

76. Associate Synod (Burgher), General Associate Synod (Antiburgher), and the Relief Church formed in 1761. The Reformed Presbyterian Church formally constituted the Covenanters in 1743.

77. Sher, *Church and University,* 50; Brown, *Social History of Religion,* 31; Martin Fitzpatrick, "The Enlightenment, Politics and Providence: Some Scottish and English Comparisons," in Knud Haakonssen, ed., *Enlightenment and Religion,* 76.

78. Brown, *Social History of Religion,* 31; Robert Kent Donovan, *No Popery and Radicalism: Opposition to Roman Catholic Relief in Scotland, 1778–1782* (New York: Garland, 1987), 285.

79. William Wilson characteristically worried about the errors of Arminianism and Arianism in the national church. See *Letter from a Member,* 17.

80. *A Plea for the Church of Scotland Against Patronages* (London and Edinburgh, 1735), 31, 33. So popular election is according to "the appointment of our Lord Jesus Christ."

81. Ibid., 34–40, 5.

82. John Currie, *An Essay on Separation: or a Vindication of the Church of Scotland* (Edinburgh, 1738), iii, xvi, 85.

83. *Proceedings, 1740, Answers to the Session of Dunfermline, to the Reasons of Secession Given in by Nine Elders* (Edinburgh, 1740), 14, 24. Since Christ is in the established church, it is a "great sin" or a most "heinous sin" to separate from it, and dissenters risk losing their salvation. See also Currie, *An Essay on Separation,* iii; and the anonymous *Friendly Admonition to such Well-meaning and Conscientious Persons* (Edinburgh, 1753), 9, 12, 14, 18–19.

84. John Graham, *The Religious Establishment in Scotland Examined upon Protestant Principles* (London, 1771), 275; see also, 61, 70, 166–67.

85. *Plea for the Church,* 9–11.

86. See *Pilulae Spleneticae: or, A Lagh from a True-Blue Presbyterian* (Edinburgh, 1736), 16–17; John Currie, *A True Narrative of the Settlement of the Parish of Portmoak* (Edinburgh, 1736), 25.

87. See *Pilulae Spleneticae,* 18, where Erskine is compared to Henry Sacheverell.

88. George Logan, *The Publick Testimony of Above 1600 Christian People . . . Being a Full Confutation of their Arguments for the Divine Right of*

Popular Elections (Edinburgh, 1733), 3, 4, 7, 11. Logan doubts the intellectual ability of the common person, and has a sophisticated awareness of the problems of a majority infringing the "sacred rights" of a minority, 24.

89. See *Friendly Admonition,* 3, 11–12, 29. This author used the same arguments as Anglicans used against Dissenters in England. Seceders, the author said, have raised a "horrid combustion" in both church and civil society.

90. Wilson, *Letter from a Member,* 18–19.

91. *Friendly Admonition,* 24.

92. Donovan, *No Popery and Radicalism,* 283, 294. On the nomenclature of parties, see Sher, *Church and University,* 17.

93. This is a point that Donovan largely misses in *No Popery and Radicalism,* 133;, but see also 41, 93.

94. *Plea for the Church,* 3–4, 12.

95. Donovan, *No Popery and Radicalism,* 163; *Plea for the Church,* 12.

96. *An Address to the People of Scotland on Ecclesiastical and Civil Liberty* (Edinburgh, 1782), 16–17.

97. Archibald Bruce, *The Kirkiad; or Golden Age of the Church of Scotland* (Edinburgh, 1774), 37.

98. Donovan, *No Popery and Radicalism,* 14, 25, 45, 49, 59; Colin Haydon, *Anti-Catholicism in Eighteenth-Century England* (Manchester: Manchester University Press, 1993), 212–13.

99. Donovan, *No Popery and Radicalism,* 187, 195.

100. Ibid., 7, 218, 222, 227.

101. Sher, *Church and University,* 50; for the origins of the Moderate party, see 52–55.

102. Ibid., 53.

103. Donovan, *No Popery and Radicalism,* 266, n. 91.

104. See Sher, *Church and University,* 45–64, 120–30; and Ian D. L. Clark, "From Protest to Reaction: The Moderate Regime in the Church of Scotland, 1752–1805," 213–14, in N. T. Phillipson and Rosalind Mitchison, eds., *Scotland in the Age of Improvement: Essays in Scottish History in the Eighteenth Century* (Edinburgh: Edinburgh University Press, 1970).

105. Donovan, *No Popery and Radicalism,* 102, 104, 107.

106. Fitzpatrick, "Enlightenment," 75; Burleigh, *Church History of Scotland,* 302; Donovan, *No Popery and Radicalism,* 231.

107. *Patronage Demolished, and the Rights of the Christian People Restored* (Edinburgh, 1769), 8, 24, 6–7, 13.

108. John Baillie, *The Influence of a Crucified Saviour* (Newcastle, 1772), 2, 9, 17; William Graham, *Candid Vindication of the Secession Church* (Newcastle, 1790), 35; see also William Graham, *An Attempt to Prove that Every Species of*

Patronage is Foreign to the Nature of the Church . . . By a Friend to the Natural and Religious Rights of Mankind (Edinburgh, 1768), 35.

109. Baillie, *Influence of a Crucified Saviour,* 4. Graham, *An Attempt to Prove,* 31, 58, 6, 43, iii.

110. Graham, *An Attempt to Prove,* 38, 69–70; Graham, *Candid Vindication,* 7. On the right of private judgment, see *Candid Vindication,* 12, 16, and *An Attempt to Prove,* 81, and for the spiritual nature of the church, see *An Attempt to Prove,* 38, 39, 69, 70. Archibald Bruce, like Graham, is well aware of such sources as the republican writings of George Buchanan, Samuel Rutherford, and others, but he relies principally on Scripture; see Bruce, *Brief Statement,* 35.

111. Graham, *An Attempt to Prove,* iii–iv, 31; Baillie, *Influence of a Crucified Savior,* 7.

112. Graham, *An Attempt to Prove,* 14, 33, 72.

113. Archibald Bruce, *The Patron's A,B,C: or, the Shorter Catechism Attempted after a New Plan* (Glasgow, 1771), 6. See also John Graham, *Religious Establishment in Scotland,* 98–99, 275.

114. See Graham, *An Attempt to Prove,* 48, 111; and Baillie on "Babylon" and Oxford, the former, a "bloody race" of cruel tyrants, the latter, "long a nursery of arbitrary power;" John Baillie, *A Funeral Discourse Upon the Death of the Papacy* (Newcastle, 1798), 3, 28.

115. Bruce, *Kirkiad,* 22, also 16.

116. Graham, *An Attempt to Prove,* 9, 5–6, 7, 66, 83, 10; Graham felt obliged to add that he did not intend to induce "violence and rebellion" but urged "all methods" consistent with peace.

117. This is a vigorous attack on the Moderate party: "O how does *Moderation* shine/ With fair and ever placid mien!" See Bruce, *Kirkiad,* 28; see also 10, 14–15, 18, 20, 28. He also attacks the practice of patronage, 17, 20, 23.

118. "He must be good, who e'er is great;/ A Christian without debate" (37). But there are preachers, "Who are so rude, and so uncivil,/as send a Ge'man to the dxxxl" (41).

119. James E. Bradley, "'Religion as a Cloak for Worldly Designs': Reconciling Heresy, Polity, and Social Inequality as Preconditions to Rebellion," unpublished paper presented at the annual meeting of the American Historical Association, Chicago, January 1995, p. 10, n. 35.

120. See the references to Carlyle's *Justice and Necessity of the War* (1777); George Campbell's *Duty of Allegiance* (1777); and Alexander Gerard's *Liberty the Cloak of Maliciousness* (1778) in James E. Bradley, "The Anglican Pulpit, the Social Order, and the Resurgence of Toryism during the American Revolution," notes, 39, 88, in *Albion* 21 (1989): 361–88. On the Moderate James Wodrow's condemnation of Wilkes and the Americans (a "rational" dissenter, who should,

according to the heresy-radicalism thesis, have supported them), see Fitzpatrick, "Enlightenment," 70. See Sher, *Church and University,* 263, on the Moderates.

121. Kenneth Logue studied numerous instances of violent intrusion of ministers on congregations in the period 1780–1815; Kenneth J. Logue, *Popular Disturbances in Scotland, 1780–1815* (Edinburgh: John Donald, 1979), 168, 176.

122. Donovan, *No Popery and Radicalism,* 277.

123. Sher, *Church and University,* 267.

124. Snodgrass, *Effectual Method,* 6–7. Robert Kent Donovan, "Evangelical Civic Humanism in Glasgow: The American War Sermons of William Thom," in Andrew Hook and Richard B. Sher, eds., *The Glasgow Enlightenment* (East Linton: Tuckwell Press, 1995), 229.

125. Snodgrass, *Effectual Method,* 13; Donovan, "Evangelical Civic Humanism," 238.

126. Snodgrass, *Effectual Method,* 5–7.

127. Quoted in Donovan, "Evangelical Civic Humanism," 235.

128. Snodgrass, *Effectual Method,* 37–38.

129. Ibid., 14. Conversely, those who defend patronage construe the judgment of the people in "the most ridiculous and contemptible light," and as a result, they were able to maintain a "yoke of bondage" around "our necks" (43). Thom had similar social concerns and criticism of lawyers; Donovan, "Evangelical Civic Humanism," 233, 239.

130. John Snodgrass, *The Means of Preserving the Life and Power of Religion in a Time of General Corruption* (Dundee, 1781), 37.

131. Donovan, "Evangelical Civic Humanism," 231, 234.

132. John Graham, *Religious Establishment in Scotland,* 62.

133. The thirteen were: John Erskine, William Porteous, Charles Nisbet, William Peterkin, Colin Campbell, John Warden, Ralph Bowie, David Grant, James Blinshall, Thomas Walker, James Morrison, John Snodgrass, and William Thom. Donovan, *No Popery and Radicalism,* 42, 268, 275–76; 280–81; John Graham cannot be positively identified as an Evangelical.

134. Donovan, *No Popery and Radicalism,* 281.

135. Ibid., 271, 275, 276.

136. Cited in Donovan, *No Popery and Radicalism,* 284–85, from Hugo Arnot, *The History of Edinburgh, from the Earliest Accounts to the Present Time* (London, 1788), 262.

137. Donovan, *No Popery and Radicalism,* 284, 287, 307–8. In Scotland only rarely did one find opposition to patronage or sympathy for the colonists from a layperson: Andrew Crosbie, a skeptic in religion, was the clear exception.

138. Emma Vincent, "The Responses of Scottish Churchmen to the French Revolution, 1789–1802," *Scottish Historical Review* 73 (1994): 193.

139. Ibid.," 194–96.

140. Sher, *Church and University,* 275, 208.

141. Vincent, "Response of Scottish Churchmen," 199–200, 204–205.

142. William Graham, *A Review of the Ecclesiastical Establishments in Europe* (Glasgow, 1792; 2d. 1796), vi, 73–86, 175. The text on the title page is John 18: 36: "My kingdom is not of this world," and he expounds it at length.

143. See page 19 and 24 of this work published in Glasgow in 1795. We find in Smith all the familiar Seceding themes; for example, in controling religion, ministers supplant the authority of Christ.

144. John Baillie, *A Sermon on the Time of the Restoration of the Jews* (London, 1792), 29. See also John Baillie, *A Vindication of the Divinity of Jesus Christ, with Impartial Observation on the Unitarian Scheme* (Newcastle, 1789), 15–26; on Graham's orthodoxy, see William Graham, *The Whole Earth Filled with the Redeemer's Glory* (Newcastle, 1796).

145. Bruce, *Brief Statement,* 19, 31, 34.

146. Archibald Bruce, *Reflections on Freedom of Writing* (Edinburgh, 1794), 88, cited in John Brims, "Covenanting Tradition and Scottish Radicalism," 55.

147. Bruce, *Brief Statement,* 59.

148. Brims, "Covenanting Tradition and Scottish Radicalism," 52–53.

149. *The Statistical Account of Scotland. Drawn up from the Communications of the Ministers of Different Parishes,* VIII (Edinburgh, 1793), 295, cited in Brims, "Covenanting Tradition and Scottish Radicalism," 53.

150. Vincent, "Response of Scottish Churchmen," 191.

151. Brims, "Covenanting Tradition and Scottish Radicalism," 53.

152. I. R. McBride, *Scripture Politics: Ulster Presbyterians and Irish Radicalism in the Late Eighteenth Century* (Oxford: Clarendon Press, 1998), 3. As late as 1981, John M. Barkley could write that the Presbyterian contribution to the United Irish movement "remains unsung." John M. Barkley, "The Presbyterian Minister in Eighteenth-Century Ireland," in J. L. M. Haire, ed., *Challenge and Conflict: Essays in Irish Presbyterian History and Doctrine* (Antrim: W. & G. Baird, 1981), 68.

153. William McMillan, "The Subscription Controversy in Irish Presbyterianism from the Plantation of Ulster to the Present Day; With Reference to Political Implications in the Late Eighteenth Century," M. A. Thesis, University of Manchester, 1959, 2 vols.

154. A. T. Q. Stewart, *The Narrow Ground: Aspects of Ulster, 1609–1969* (Belfast: The Blackstaff Press, 1977), 83, 90, 96–110, especially, 98–99. Marianne Elliott, *Watchmen in Sion: The Protestant Idea of Liberty* (Derry: Field Day Theatre Co., 1985), 11–12. While emphasizing the Presbyterian "contractual" tradition, "advanced" theology is still associated by Elliott with radical reform.

155. D. W. Miller, "Presbyterianism and 'Modernisation' in Ulster," *Past & Present* 80 (1978): 76–77. But by contrasting the "orthodox" party to the "new lights" he indirectly gave added life to the heresy-radicalism thesis.

156. Jim Smyth, *The Men of No Property: Irish Radicals and Popular Politics in the Late Eighteenth Century* (London: Macmillan, 1992), 89–91. The "democratic government" of the church is often listed as a cause of the Presbyterian propensity for radicalism; see Stewart, *Narrow Ground*, 83.

157. McBride, *Scripture Politics*, p. 6.

158. John M. Barkley, *The Westminster Formularies in Irish Presbyterianism* (Belfast: Graham & Heslip, 1956), 6–7, 9.

159. The General Synod is the annual meeting of all Presbyterian ministers in Ulster with a ruling elder and minister representing each congregation; it is the highest church judicatory in Ireland. John Abernethy, *Sermons on Various Subjects*, 4 vols. (London 1748–51), I:vi.

160. Robert Allen, "The Principle of Nonsubscription to Creeds and Confessions of Faith as Exemplified in Irish Presbyterian History," Ph.D. dissertation, Queen's University, Belfast, 1944, pp. 104–105.

161. James Duchal, in the preface to Abernethy, *Sermons*, I:xlvi.

162. John Abernethy, *Religious Obedience Founded on Personal Persuasion* (Belfast, 1719).

163. Antrim County Presbytery, *A Narrative of the Proceedings of Seven General Synods of the Northern Presbyterians in Ireland . . . 1720–1726 . . .* (Belfast, 1727), iv. With fifteen ministers, the Presbytery of Antrim comprised one-eighth of the Synod. See McMillan, "Subscription Controversy," 247–48.

164. Antrim County Presbytery, *Narrative of the Proceedings*, vii–viii. On the "exorbitant power" claimed by the church, see James Kirkpatrick, *A Scripture Plea Against a Fatal Rupture, and Breach of Christian Communion . . .* (Belfast, 1724), 13; on the "unalienable right of men's judging for themselves," see Thomas Nevin, *The Trial of Thomas Nevin. M. A. Pastor of a Church, of the Presbyterian Denomination . . .* (Belfast, 1725), 1; and Thomas Nevin, *A Review of Mr. Nevin's Trial before the Synod, 1724, Occasioned by Mr. McBride's Few Thoughts . . .* (Belfast, 1728), 52. See also Samuel Haliday, *Reasons Against the Impositions of Subscription to the Westminster-confession of Faith; or, any Such Human Tests of Orthodoxy . . .* (Belfast, 1724), xiv.

165. Robert Allen studied the theology of each nonsubscriber in detail, and pronounced them orthodox; he also noted that the Dublin ministers, all of whom were orthodox, gave unqualified support to the nonsubscribers. See "Principle of Nonsubscription," 330–57; he argued that one cannot find a stream of liberal theology in Antrim until 1794 (364). Andrew Brown agrees; see Andrew G. W. Brown "Irish Presbyterian Theology in the Early Eighteenth Century," Ph.D. diss., Queen's University, Belfast, 1977, 3, 563–64, 567–68; see also Barkley,

Westminster Formularies, 12, 28; McMillan, "Subscription Controversy," 271–72; and McBride, *Scripture Politics,* 45. "Calvin, not Athanasius," says McBride, "was to be the main victim of the New Light." Even an essay by M. A. Stewart turns out to be a study of orthodox thinkers; see M. A. Stewart, "Rational Dissent in early Eighteenth-Century Ireland," in Haakonssen, ed., *Enlightenment and Religion,* 42–63,

166. The "essential doctrines" of our faith, wrote Abernethy, are "the Deity of our SAVIOR" and "the redemption of the *elect* by his death." John Abernethy, *A Sermon Recommending the Study of Scripture-Prophecie, as an Important Duty, and a Great Means of Reviving Decay'd Piety and Charity* (Belfast, 1716), 11; also John Abernethy, *Seasonable Advice to the Protestant Dissenters in the North of Ireland; being a Defense of the Late General Synod's Charitable Declaration* (Dublin, 1722), 28, 29, 39; and John Abernethy, *A Defense of the Seasonable Advice, in Answer to the Reverend Mr. Charles Mastertown's Apology for the Northern Presbyterians in Ireland* (Belfast, 1724), 138, 139. Kirkpatrick, *Scripture Plea,* 6, 9, 13, 63, 64; Nevin, *Trial,* 8, 9, 25–26, 52, 170–73. For Haliday, see Samuel Haliday, *A Letter to the Reverend Mr. Gilbert Kennedy* (Belfast, 1725), 45–47; and Samuel Haliday, *A Letter to the Reverend Mr. Francis Iredel; Occasion'd by his Remarks on a Letter to the Reverend Mr. Gilbert Kennedy* (Belfast, 1726), 5–6, 9; and Haliday, *Reasons Against Impositions,* iii. I could not locate any references to Robert Higinbotham's christological belief, other than the vague "our great Sovereign"; Robert Higinbotham, *Reasons Against the Overtures, which were Referred to the Consideration of the Several Presbyterys . . .* (Belfast, 1726), 19.

167. Richard B. Barlow, "The Career of John Abernethy (1680–1740), Father of Nonsubscription in Ireland and Defender of Religious Liberty," *Harvard Theological Review,* 78 (1985): 418.

168. Haliday said that he sought to stand by his "avowed principle" concerning the "sole legislative authority of Christ as King of his Church"; Haliday, *Reasons Against Impositions,* vi, 15; see also 21, 27, 41, 68, 103. For equivalent phrases, see Abernethy, *Sermons,* I:lxxiv; *Seasonable Advice,* 41; Kirkpatrick, *Scripture Plea,* 8, 11–12, 52; Higinbotham, *Reasons Against Overtures,* 19; Nevin, *Trial,* 230; and Nevin, *Review of Mr. Nevin's Trial,* 66.

169. Abernethy, *Seasonable Advice,* 41; Kirkpatrick, *Scripture Plea,* 20, 52; Higinbotham, *Reasons Against Overtures,* 36.

170. Haliday, *Reasons Against Impositions,* 127–28. Nevin makes the same argument: He calls his confidence in the Savior's deity "the main foundation" of his peace and comfort. Nevin, *Trial,* 51, 69, 251.

171. Abernethy, *Defense of Seasonable Advice,* 67, 76, 82–90; Haliday, *Reasons Against Impositions,* 3; Higinbotham, *Reasons Against Overtures,* 44, 47–48, 149; Kirkpatrick, *Scripture Plea,* 18, 31, 56–61.

172. The right of private judgment is "the stable principle" of Nonconformity, with which Protestantism must stand or fall. Kirkpatrick, *Scripture Plea,* 20. The same idea of the "stable" or "main" or "essential" principle of Protestantism or dissent is found repeatedly: Haliday, *Reasons Against Impositions,* 40, also, 94; Abernethy, *Seasonable Advice,* 46; *Obedience,* 27; *Sermons* I:lxii; Nevin, *Trial,* 143, 148, 228; Antrim County Presbytery, *Narrative of the Proceedings,* vi.

173. Haliday, *Reasons Against Impositions,* 38, 68, 15–16.

174. Abernethy, *Defense of Seasonable Advice,* 107; *Sermons,* I:xliv.

175. Abernethy, *Religious Obedience,* 16, 9.

176. Haliday, *Reasons Against Impositions,* 39.

177. Higinbotham, *Reasons Against Overtures,* 20, 28–29; Haliday, *Reasons Against Impositions,* 25–26.

178. The "general advance of knowledge" is hindered when one has to fear concerning the consequences of his investigation, said Haliday. Haliday, *Reasons Against Impositions,* 84, 71, 120–21; see also, Abernethy, *Religious Obedience,* 17; Nevin, *Trial,* 140, 252; Kirkpatrick, *Scripture Plea,* 40.

179. Abernethy, *Religious Obedience,* 18, 19–20, 23.

180. Nevin, *Trial,* 36.

181. Ibid., 140; see also 21, 22; and Nevin, *Review of Mr. Nevin's Trial,* 66. Haliday, *Reasons Against Impositions,* 132.

182. Nevin, *Trial,* 8, 65.

183. James Duchal, in the preface to Abernethy, *Sermons,* I:xlv.

184. T. M'Crie, ed., *The Correspondence of Robert Wodrow* (Edinburgh, 1842–43), II:389 cited in M. A. Stewart, "Rational Dissent in early Eighteenth-Century Ireland," in Haakonssen, ed., *Enlightenment and Religion,* 52.

185. Nevin, for example, bases his thought first on Scripture—the "genius of the Gospel" is found in the fact that force should never be used in matters of conscience—then on Protestant principles, and finally on Locke's "Letter of Toleration." Nevin, *Trial,* 127–32, 140.

186. Higinbotham, *Reasons Against Overtures,* 18.

187. Nevin, *Trial,* 234, 30.

188. According to the Presbytery of Antrim County, the Anglican Church in Ireland sided with the subscribers, *A Narrative of the Proceedings,* vi. See also Presbyterian John Malcome, *Dangerous Principles of the Sectaries of the Last Age Revived Again by our Modern New Lights* (Belfast, 1726).

189. William Tisdall, *A Seasonable Enquiry into that Most Dangerous Political Principal of the Kirk in Power . . .* (Dublin, 1713), 13. Tisdall generalized from the Covenanters to the entire Presbyterian Church, 7, 14–15.

190. Tisdall, *Seasonable Enquiry,* 23–24, 28.

191. F. S. L. Lyons, "The Burden of our History," in Ciaran Brady, ed., *Interpreting Irish History: The Debate on Historical Revisionism* (Dublin: Blackrock, 1994), 98.

192. For references to Catholic tyranny, see Abernethy, *Sermon Recommending the Study,* 3–4, 9, 14, 17 ; but on Abernethy's affection for Catholics, see Duchal in preface to Abernethy, *Sermons,* I:xxxv; Kirkpatrick, *Scripture Plea,* 43; Nevin *Trial,* 229, 251. Allusions to the pope as "anti-Christ" are relatively rare. Haliday, *Reasons Against Impositions,* 55.

193. Nevin, *Trial,*174; Haliday, *Reasons Against Impositions,* 152.

194. Nevin, *Review of Mr. Nevin's Trial,* 55; and Nevin, *Trial,* 121.

195. Abernethy, *Sermon Recommending the Study,* 17; Kirkpatrick *Scripture Plea,* 18; similarly, Haliday, *Reasons Against Impositions,* 108.

196. Abernethy, *Sermons* I:xliii; Rome binds consciences; Nevin makes the same point, *Trial,* 229.

197. Abernethy, *Seasonable Advice,* 22. See also Nevin, *Trial,* 251, vi; *Review of the Trial,* 38; and Haliday, *Reasons Against Impositions,* 48, 94, 109.

198. Haliday, *Reasons Against Impositions,* 4, 66. The requirement of submission to the Thirty Nine Articles was, according to Haliday, "bad and unjustifiable."

199. Haliday, *Reasons Against Impositions,* 112.

200. Smyth, *Men of No Property,* 203, n. 48.

201. See, for example, *The Patriot Miscellany,* 2 vols. (Dublin, 1756).

202. McMillan, "Subscription Controversy," 280, 302–3. By 1820 only five of fourteen presbyteries required subscription, 285.

203. Ibid., 114: This was from the phrase first used by Malcome. John Malcome, *Dangerous Principles of the Sectaries of the Last Age, Revived Again by our Modern New Lights.*

204. Stewart, *Narrow Ground,* 104–5; McBride, *Scripture Politics,* 115–16. McBride provides a detailed study of links between Ulster Presbyterians and the colonists, 118–20.

205. McBride, *Scripture Politics,* 124–31, 146–48.

206. *Three Sermons on the Subject of Scripture Politics* (Belfast, 1793), quoted in McBride, *Scripture Politics,* 99.

207. McMillan, "Subscription Controversy," 311; Barkley, "Presbyterian Minister," 62.

208. Barclay, "Presbyterian Minister," 64.

209. This was particularly evident among the New Lights as early as 1782 and in the Presbytery of Killyleagh, one of the most heterodox of all the presbyteries. McMillan, "Subscription Controversy," 310.

210. McBride, *Scripture Politics,* 203–4, and appendix, 232–36. D. W. Miller located forty-eight ministers and probationers implicated in the Rebellion.

Miller, "Presbyterianism and 'Modernisation,'" 77–78. He then classified these in terms of "orthodox" ministers (including Seceders and Covenanters) and "new light" ministers, and he identified 46.5 percent in the first category and 53.5 percent in the second (79). This scheme does not do justice to the fact that two-thirds of the New Lights were theologically orthodox, and by the 1790s many who held to subscription had evidently adopted the radical political implications of their Presbyterian polity. Moreover, Miller plays up the millenarian themes and nearly passes over matters of private judgment and polity (82–83).

211. McMillan, "Subscription Controversy," 330–84. McBride concurs: "Arianism did not possess a distinct identity in eighteenth-century Ireland." McBride, *Scripture Politics,* 110.

212. Ibid., 207.

213. McMillan, "Subscription Controversy," 373–734.

214. David B. Warden, "A Farewell Address to the Junto of the Presbytery of Bangor" (Glasgow, 1798), printed in *Ulster Journal of Archeology,* 2nd ser., 13 (1907): 35.

215. McBride, *Scripture Politics,* 91, 99.

216. Ibid., 92.

217. Ibid., 107. McBride traces the lack of Seceder support to their having received a part of the *Regium Donum.* McBride, *Scripture Politics,* 106. On the "Royal Bounty" and its political power generally, see Stewart, *Narrow Ground,* 92–93.

218. McBride, *Scripture Politics,* 102.

219. Ibid., 104.

220. For a fine discussion of the ambivalences here, see Elliott, *Watchmen in Zion,* 20–23.

221. Stewart ultimately explains the alliance on the basis of the legally proscribed position of both Dissenter and Catholic in Ireland as persecuted minorities. Stewart, *Narrow Ground,* 103–4.

222. Ibid., 108; Elliott, *Watchmen in Zion,* 20; McBride, *Scripture Politics,* 194, 202.

223. E. P. Thompson, *Making of the English Working Class* (Harmondsworth, Penguin, 1968), 56.

224. The integration of religious and socioeconomic sources has been attempted for England, and significant research has brought scholars to the verge of fruitful comparison for Ireland (compare the studies by McBride and Jim Smyth), but research on Scotland, which has the richest sources, is still, with few exceptions (e.g., Callum Brown), at the level of denominational history.

FIVE

Religious Identities and the Boundaries of Citizenship in the Dutch Republic

WAYNE TE BRAKE

IN THE SUMMER OF 1786, A SPECIAL MUNICIPAL COMMISSION published its draft proposal for a new constitution of government for the city of Deventer.[1] Like so many other eighteenth-century constitutional documents, the new Deventer constitution began with a series of articles that defined the "Rights and Obligations" of the citizens of Deventer.[2] "All men are born equally free and independent," the first article began, "and all government or authority in Civil Society originates in the will of the People." The second asserted equally boldly that "all government should serve to promote the general welfare of the People" while the third declared that "the *Burgerij* [Citizenry] of this City has the right to govern itself and to regulate its internal affairs without the assistance or approval of anybody outside it." Thus the constitutional commissioners, all well-educated lawyers and experienced politicians, moved quickly from the principles of equality and popular sovereignty to the right of self-government.[3] Continuing, these introductory articles postulated in quick succession the right of revolution against arbitrary authority, the right of majority rule, the "inalienable" right to petition for redress of grievances, the right of free and open debate and deliberation in government, the right of the *Burgerij* to remove unworthy regents, and so on. Not incidentally, the fifteenth article also stipulated that henceforth Roman Catholics would be granted citizenship rights [*burgerrechten*] on an equal footing with Mennonites.

With the last of these articles, we move very abruptly from the general to the specific—from a strikingly bold litany of apparently universal eighteenth-century political ideals to the specific details of Dutch political reality. As it happened, in the public debates concerning Deventer's draft constitution, which were intended to lead quickly into a general referendum to adopt it, the general ideals were not particularly divisive or controversial. But the article granting citizenship rights to Catholics awakened a storm of protest. Very quickly, a group of "representatives of the *Burgerij*" petitioned the Magistracy to put an immediate stop to the constitution-writing process. Within weeks a major portion of the broadly based popular coalition that had pressed hard for constitutional reform in the previous two years defected from the self-styled Patriot reform movement and organized their own movement in opposition to the draft constitution, in general, and to the article granting citizenship rights to Catholics, in particular.

As this conflict escalated, the Patriots became ever more revolutionary in the sense that they were willing to resort to extreme, even violent, measures to suppress their opponents and to seize power in the name of "the People." Meanwhile, the new opponents of constitutional reform in Deventer deliberately allied themselves with the most obvious alternative to the Patriots on a national scale, the so-called Orangists. In the fall of 1787, the Orangists were swept into power by a Prussian military invasion to restore William V, Prince of Orange and Nassau, as *stadhouder* and captain-general of the United Provinces.[4] In Deventer, this meant that most of the ruling magistrates (*burgemeesters*) and town councillors, and even several Reformed pastors, were removed from office. Many Patriot leaders fled, and the house of the head of the Citizens Committee that had promoted constitutional reform was demonstratively "plundered."[5] Not surprisingly, under this counterrevolutionary regime, the Patriots' attempt to extend citizenship rights to Catholics was undone. But in 1795 the Patriots received a new opportunity to turn the political tide. In advance of the northward march of French revolutionary armies, the Prince of Orange fled for England, the Patriots seized power and declared the creation of the Batavian Republic, and

Catholics in Deventer, as throughout the United Provinces, were soon granted full citizenship rights under a democratically representative regime.

Rather than simply dismiss these developments in Deventer as an object lesson in the lingering significance of popular religious bigotry in the age of philosophical Enlightenment—not unlike, say, the Gordon riots in London a few years before—I should like to use them as a vehicle for exploring more generally the relationship between religious identities and citizenship in the Dutch Republic. Indeed, it is striking that in the Dutch Republic, known for the previous two centuries as a safe haven for religious dissenters, religious identities should intrude so divisively into the political process of revolution. But in the United Provinces of the Northern Netherlands, as was the case more generally in early modern Europe, religious identities or affiliations were significant markers of political and social difference—of inclusion and exclusion. As a consequence religion was necessarily entangled with politics and citizenship.

This essay underscores the peculiar institutional and cultural legacies of the Dutch Revolt against the "religious tyranny" of Spain by highlighting both the distinctive (though by no means unique) trajectory of state and political-cultural formation and the peculiar (though by no means unparalleled) pattern of religious and cultural pluralism that characterized the history of the United Provinces of the Northern Netherlands. Having thus set Deventer's Patriot revolution in an appropriately republican and pluralist context, I will show how the political dynamics of this failed revolution reveal not only the legacy of the republican past but also the origins of a broader pattern of contentious politics that has distinguished Dutch politics throughout the nineteenth and twentieth centuries—the mobilization for and institutionalization of mass national politics along confessional lines.[6]

Contentious Politics in a Confederated Republic

In the revolutionary situation that obtained in Deventer in the 1780s, we can see in bold relief two important dimensions of the political distinctiveness of the Dutch Republic. According to the first article of the Union of Utrecht, which served as the constitutional framework for the Republic, the rebellious provinces of the northern Netherlands agreed in 1579 to "ally, confederate and unite . . . to hold together eternally in all ways and forms as if they were one province" but added that "this is agreed without prejudice to the special and particular privileges, freedoms, exemptions, laws, statutes, laudable and traditional customs, usages and all other rights of each province and of each town, member and inhabitant of those provinces."[7] Though it left plenty of room for controversy and conflict, this article effectively ensured that the United Provinces of the Northern Netherlands would remain a fundamentally decentralized republic; it also gave credence to the powerful conceit that the *Burgerij* of Deventer could and should shape its collective political future without outside interference.

At the same time, the thirteenth article of the Union of Utrecht provided, "Concerning the matter of religion" that the provinces "may introduce . . . such regulations as they consider proper for the peace and welfare of the provinces, towns and their particular members and for the preservation of all people, either secular or clerical, their properties and rights, provided that . . . each individual enjoys freedom of religion and no one be persecuted or questioned about his religion."[8] As it happened, this article left ample room for official caprice in the name of "peace and welfare"; it nevertheless ensured that the Dutch Republic as a whole would remain a relatively safe haven for religious "dissenters" of an impressively broad variety. It also meant that even in a community like Deventer, where three-quarters of the population was affiliated with the Reformed (Calvinist) Church, there was a cultural space within which Catholics, Lutherans, Mennonites, and even Jews could publicly embrace their religious identities without fear of judicial prosecution.[9]

Declarations of political intent such as this, articulated in the heat of escalating military conflict, are notoriously unreliable guides to subsequent historical developments. In fact, the Union of Utrecht was forged of bitter necessity following the failure of the equally impressive Pacification of Ghent (1576) which bound all of the Low

Countries provinces into a common front in the face of Habsburg "tyranny."[10] Likewise, not all of the provisions of the Union of Utrecht were actually implemented, as was the case, for instance, with the eighth article providing for a universal militia muster to provide for the provinces' common defense.[11] For our purposes, what is particularly important is the survival and implementation of the first and thirteenth articles in a political setting hardly conducive to either one. The Union, like the Pacification on which it was modeled, was clearly a defensive alliance vis-à-vis an aggressive dynast, but after the formal Act of Abjuration by which the United Provinces renounced Philip II in 1581, the rebels were unable to find a substitute prince willing to accept their offers of very limited sovereignty. Thus by the late 1580s the Union became the de facto constitutional framework for a confederated republic.

On the face of it, then, the Dutch Republic was deeply conservative in origin. Certainly the first article of the Union underscores the essential continuity of late-medieval political institutions in its preservation of the privileges, freedoms, exemptions, laws "of each province and of each town, member and inhabitant of those provinces." Indeed, from rural communes and chartered cities to provincial estates assemblies and the Estates General, the principal institutions of the United Provinces of the Northern Netherlands all antedated the Revolt.[12] Likewise, the political thought that motivated and legitimated the resistance to Philip II was inspired by the historical legacy of medieval constitutionalism;[13] even the most innovative features of the Republic's fiscal administration, which were so critical to the success of the war effort, predated the beginning of the Revolt.[14] None of this should disguise the fact, however, that the Dutch rebels were revolutionaries—that like the Swiss before them, they expelled their sovereign prince. As the Edict of the Estates General put it in 1581, "Therefore, despairing of all means of reconciliation and left without any other remedies and help, we have been forced . . . to abandon the king of Spain and to pursue such means as we think likely to secure our rights, privileges and liberties."[15] In so declaring Philip's sovereign claims forfeit, they took up the familiar political baggage of the late-medieval corporations and set out on a new and entirely different trajectory of state and political-cultural formation.

The core, commercial provinces of Holland and Zeeland may have been among the best governed of the microstates of northwestern Europe even before their incorporation successively into the Burgundian and Habsburg domains, and thus they were eminently capable not only of bankrolling the war effort but leading the political adaptation process. By contrast, the other six provinces had been incorporated into the Habsburg domain more recently under Charles V; they were all quite different from one another, and as a group shared little in common with mighty Holland. Still, under the leadership of Johan van Oldenbarnevelt, the province of Holland led the process by which an unlikely collection of provinces was gradually shaped into a workable confederation that was committed not only to the principle of institutional continuity but of local self-governance, which required significant institutional adjustments in provinces like Overijssel and Friesland, for example.[16] This trajectory of state formation was distinctive, to be sure, but not unique in the way it consolidated an unprecedented degree of local sovereignty at the expense of all claimants to central or national power, whether royal, princely, appointive or delegated.[17] In effect, the Dutch had replaced the princely sovereign, who had originally called them into collective political being, with more than 2,000 local and provincial sovereigns embedded in a variety of corporative medieval institutions.[18] This thoroughly segmented political system not only allowed the Republic to survive but to thrive in a militarily and economically competitive world.

Two features of the political culture of the Dutch Republic deserve particular attention here: the importance of political brokers and the vitality of local politics. The existence of thousands of "sovereigns" in a segmented political system opened up remarkable opportunities for a new kind of political entrepreneur who was capable of brokering workable agreements across a fragmented institutional environment in which consensus was the decision-making norm. The importance of consensus among constitutional equals is evident not only at the level of the Estates General, where the weightiest decisions regarding war, peace, and taxation required unanimity among the seven voting provinces, but also at the provincial level, where in a province like Overijssel, as late as the 1780s, it had not been decided whether, and if so, for what issues, decisions by mere majorities could be regarded as legitimate.[19] Two early leaders of the Dutch Revolt—Johan van Oldenbarnevelt and William of Orange—modeled the principal alternative, and eventually competitive, modes of political brokerage. Oldenbarnevelt, like the famous chancellors of Italian city-states before him, was a political appointee—the *lands-advocaat* or *pensionaris* of Holland—who was an official spokesman but in no sense a sovereign.[20] His considerable influence within the confederation during its formative years derived from his ability to persuade others to undertake action for the common good, as when he led the provincial estates of Overijssel to adopt the very same kind of uniform taxation that they had always resisted under Habsburg rule—this so that the province might be able to meet its financial obligations to the Generality.[21] It is also important to emphasize that the heroic warleader of the Revolt, William the Silent, was a political appointee as well. William was Prince of Orange, not of Holland, and neither of his principal offices, as captain-general of the Union as a whole and as *stadhouder* of the provinces severally, allowed him to lay claim to the independent and final decision-making authority of a sovereign. Though his military leadership entailed both indirect influence through the patronage of the officer corps and potentially direct coercive power through conquest, William was especially scrupulous in not abusing either one.[22] What is striking, then, about the beginning of the Dutch Republic is that neither of its heroic founding fathers was, in fact, a sovereign.

Like any other fundamental political relationship, the specific dimensions of this kind of appointive leadership, as distinct from a more direct or coercive rulership, was subject to ongoing bargaining or renegotiation as part of the republican political process.[23] Without rehearsing the whole history of parties and factions in the Republic—of *prinsgezinden* vs. *staatsgezinden*—it is clear that Dutch history in the Golden Age and beyond was to a significant degree dominated at the national level by these two alternative models or modes of republican leadership. Ironically, it was the sovereign provinces led by Holland's pensionary who initially preserved and adapted the essentially anachronistic office of *stadhouder*—originally a provincial governor, with little more than symbolic authority, appointed by the princely sovereign—to the purposes of the Republic, but it was Maurice of Nassau, William's successor, who first came close to arrogating some form of direct decision-making authority to the office of *stadhouder* during his escalating competition with Oldenbarnevelt during the Twelve Years' Truce with Spain (1609–21). Using the expedient of the so-called *wetsverzetting* (a temporary suspension of the law), Maurice managed to purge enough of the municipal councils in the provinces of Holland and Utrecht to tip the political balance in favor of the political alliance he had formed with orthodox Calvinist opponents of a final peace with Spain. Though this tragic conflict resulted in the condemnation and execution of Oldenbarnevelt for treason, Maurice did not permanently transform the limited political potential of the office of *stadhouder*, although he clearly demonstrated how explosive the leadership of a *stadhouder* could be when combined with the office of captain-general.

In 1650, however, in the midst of yet another escalating conflict over military policy, William II tried to recreate the alliance with orthodox Calvinists that had served Maurice so well, but in the end he failed miserably to mobilize significant support for his military coup d'etat, and thus he failed to compromise the political independence of the city of Amsterdam, in particular, and the provinces more generally.[24] Thus his untimely death a few months later opened up the opportunity in 1652 for an ad-hoc Grand Assembly to reaffirm the principle of provincial and local sovereignty, and another *pensionaris* of Holland, Jan de Witt, emerged as the Republic's principal spokesman and diplomat.[25] Though the office of *stadhouder* was left vacant in five of the seven voting provinces, William's most zealous opponents failed to block permanently the combination of the offices of captain-general and *stadhouder* in a single person.

On the contrary, foreign invasions in 1672 precipitated another domestic crisis that resulted in the appointment of William III as captain-general of the Union and *stadhouder* in those provinces where the office had been vacant. But when his military success by 1675 had ridded the Republic of foreign troops that had occupied three of the land provinces, William did not demand direct decision-making as his political reward; he sought instead a significant expansion of the political patronage attached to the office of *stadhouder*, acquiring a gatekeeper function in the appointment of local and provincial officials.[26] Yet another military crisis in 1747, following another period without a *stadhouder* in most of the provinces (1702–47), gave William IV the opportunity to expand on these patronage prerogatives and even to have the office of *stadhouder* declared hereditary in both the male and female lines.[27] Still, the political power of the *stadhouder* remained vested in the indirect influence of a patron without being translated into the direct decision-making authority of a sovereign.[28] In short, the Dutch Republic remained a republic in the fundamental sense that it had no sovereign prince, only an influential *stadhouder*.

Replacing one territorial or princely sovereign with more than 2,000 local or provincial sovereigns not only opened up new opportunities for political entrepreneurs and brokers at the national level, but it also meant that the *real* rulers of the Dutch Republic lived in close proximity to their subjects. This is where, what Jan de Vries has called the Republic's "deviant medieval heritage" of weak seigneurialism, precocious urbanization, and strong popular associations is especially significant,[29] for the "special and particular privileges, freedoms, exemptions [and] laws" that the first article of the Union of Utrecht sought to protect belonged not only to the constituent provinces, but also to "each town, member and inhabitant of these provinces." In other words, the formal segmentation of power in the Dutch Republic presented everyone—not just rulers, but also subjects; not just burghers, but also rustics—with a distinctive set of political opportunities and challenges in which local variations are often profoundly confusing but the theme is always the same: rulers and subjects who live in close proximity to one another develop predictably different patterns of interaction than those who are separated by vast geographical and social distances.

In the Low Countries, as elsewhere in Europe, chartered cities (invariably medieval in origin) were islands of political difference where self-regulation was clearly at a premium. In the urbanized Low Countries, however, these islands were hardly exceptional; on the contrary, they constituted a remarkably dense archipelago in which the land was as prominent as the sea.[30] This was most obvious in the commercial provinces of Holland and Zeeland where cities held the overwhelming preponderance of votes in the provincial assemblies.[31] Friesland, on the other hand, where the political weight of the countryside was preponderant, also had its eleven cities.[32] Even in the land provinces like Overijssel, where the three major cities shared power equally with the nobility in the provincial estates, there were a large number of smaller chartered municipalities that, while not enfranchised in the provincial assembly and not even large enough to count as urban centers, were nevertheless self-regulating in that they made, judged, and enforced laws, assessed taxation, and administered public affairs on a routine basis.[33] Now within these islands of self-regulation, we should not expect to see some idealized form of direct popular participation in government; in fact, through the process of oligarchization a relatively small and self-selecting regent elite came to dominate municipal institutions ranging from town councils to public charities.[34] What's more, Rudolf Dekker's pioneering research on riots in Holland suggests that these urban communities were frequently dysfunctional and torn by violent conflict.[35] It is important, however, to see urban riots and demonstrations as part of a larger political conversation in which exceptional acts of deliberate violence, like the "plundering" of a public official's house, are part of a varied repertoire of contentious politics that includes less sensational, but often effective, actions like petitioning, lobbying, and boycotting.[36] It was through this larger political conversation that ordinary Dutchmen learned how to resolve differences, accommodate changing circumstances, and hold their rulers accountable.

Though there were analogous forms of self-regulation, political interaction, and conflict resolution in the Dutch countryside, what I want to underscore here is the urban and Old Regime origins of the Dutch concept of citizenship.[37] Indeed, the Dutch word for citizen is "*burger,*" which designates formal membership in the urban community. *Burgerschap,* or citizenship, in this urban context cut two ways: it emphasized the differences between citizens and mere "inhabitants" (those we might today term legal aliens) at the same time as it underscored the interdependence of citizens and magistrates. Now the specific nature of these political relationships within the urban community varied considerably, but some patterns are generally observable. In the first place, citizenship could be acquired either by inheritance—that is, by virtue of being born in a particular city or, more restrictively, by virtue of being born to a citizen of that city—or purchased, at a variable cost, provided one satisfied specific personal requirements, such as a minimum age or period of residence. Though originally *burgers* may have been directly involved in urban politics, through elections and representation, the most visible aspect of citizenship in Dutch cities in the early modern period was the right of guild membership, which is to say, participation in the self-regulation of specified sectors of the urban economy; indeed, in most places of any size, at least, one could not be active in any of the "burgher trades"—typically, retail shopkeeping and artisanal manufactures—without being a *burger.*[38] Thus, also, the most obvious difference between a citizen and an inhabitant, besides access to civic charities, was guild membership. In short, urban citizenship in the Dutch Republic was bounded in three dimensions: politically (vis-à-vis magistrates), socially (vis-à-vis inhabitants), and geographically (vis-à-vis outsiders). What the Patriot Revolution in Deventer underscores is the sense in which democratic revolution promised dramatically to alter the boundaries of republican citizenship.

Cultural Pluralism and the Politics of Religious Identity

If the general historical background of the Union of Utrecht was Habsburg dynasticism and state formation, the specific background to the thirteenth article, which asserts an inviolable right of individual freedom of conscience, was the criminalization of religious dissent in the first half of the sixteenth century. Whereas Charles V, as emperor of the Holy Roman Empire, seemed to be powerless to stem the tide of the Lutheran Reformation in Germany, he was much more successful in repressing religious dissent in the Low Countries, where he was more directly sovereign over his assorted provinces. Indeed, under the combined rulership of Charles V (1516–55) and his son Philip II (1555–98), there were at least 1,500 and possibly as many as 5,000 judicial executions of "heretics" in the Low Countries prior to the Revolt.[39] While this unprecedented and unparalleled pattern of judicial violence prevented a specifically Lutheran reformation in Low Countries, and it effectively deprived the diffuse movement for religious reform of its leadership, what it could not do was eliminate religious dissent as such. Instead, it drove the Protestants underground where a small minority of the Netherlandic population were organized as worshipping communities, inspired by the Genevan Reformation, nurtured by exile churches in London, Emden, and Wesel, and eventually linked through classes and synods.[40]

Now, against this background, the freedom of religious conscience, as asserted by Article XIII of the Union of Utrecht, was precious indeed; what's more, it was effective in the sense that it stopped the heresy trials and judicial executions permanently. What it did not do, however, was guarantee "dissenters"—that is, Lutherans and Mennonites as well as Catholics and Jews—the right of public, corporate worship, of teaching, or of proselytizing; clearly it stopped short of the kind of robust religious toleration that is enjoined in the Universal Declaration of Human Rights.[41] In fact, because this basic right of freedom of conscience left so much else open to question, it unleashed a voluminous, public, and learned debate on toleration in the Dutch Republic that reverberated throughout the seventeenth century, had important international dimensions, and still invites a large scholarly literature today.[42] For our purposes, what is important is not the moral and political desirability of a more complete religious toleration, but the more basic fact that freedom of individual conscience opened up an invaluable space for religious and cultural difference and made the Dutch Republic famous as a haven for all manner of "dissenters" by breaking the fundamental identification of the Christian church with the civic community.[43]

The organization and solidarity of the underground Reformed churches placed them in a unique position, at the time of the Revolt, to claim to be the "public" church wherever the Revolt was militarily successful after 1572. Indeed, whenever possible, the Reformed Calvinists very demonstratively occupied all of the public churches, even when they could not come close to filling them, and tried to forbid all other forms of public religious worship. But given the protection that freedom of conscience afforded religious dissenters, this *public* church, as opposed to an *established* or universal church, would never become more than a voluntary church whose fabled discipline could not reach beyond its voluntary membership. In any case, even becoming a majority church in the sense that a majority of the population were actually members, as opposed to so-called *liefhebbers* ("lovers" or affiliates), appears to have been out of the question in most places.[44] After the initial turmoil of the early Revolt, in fact, the pattern of confessionalization that emerged in the Dutch Republic entailed the simultaneous institutional growth of multiple denominations or confessions within most communities.[45] Thus the facts on the ground, if nothing else, required that the Dutch state, as distinct from the Reformed Church, move toward some form of official accommodation of religious differences that went well beyond the private freedom of religious conscience to allow corporate worship for dissenters. This proved to be relatively easy in most cases where Lutheran churches had been formed, and it even proved not to be difficult with regard to the Dutch branch of the dreaded "Anabaptists," because the Dutch Mennonites hardly constituted a threat to public order.[46] What proved to be far more difficult for many of the Reformed faithful, and especially the most zealous pastors, to accept was the formal accommodation of Roman Catholic worship. But after an initial period of relatively difficult harassment of Catholic priests and communicants, which fell far short of the judicial repression that had been the standard treatment of "heretics" prior to the Revolt, provincial and local authorities throughout the Republic worked out a series of compromises to accommodate what the Roman Catholic authorities organized as the "Dutch mission" (*Missio Hollandica*).[47]

While the freedom of religious conscience effectively decriminalized religious dissent, it did not by any stretch of the imagination depoliticize religious identities or confessional affiliations. In fact, the designation of a *public* Reformed Church drew a clear political boundary between Reformed Calvinists and dissenters of all sorts that was visible everywhere in Dutch society. This is because the *publicity* of the Reformed Church also entailed an effective monopoly on public office in the sense that appointment to public office was reserved for those who were *liefhebbers* (literally, "lovers" or visible associates, as opposed to full members who were subject to church discipline) of the "true" Reformed Christian religion. In this way, then, religious identities or affiliations served as significant markers of political differences that eventually became deeply embedded in Dutch society. These political boundaries between confessional groups were especially visible in those cities, principally in the provinces of Overijssel, Gelderland, and Zeeland, where religious dissenters were also excluded from urban citizenship and, by extension, guild membership.[48] But to the extent that public charities were also reserved for the affiliates of the public churches, religious identity served as the principal marker of a broad range of political and social differences throughout the Republic. Though these differences originated in the simple political distinction between Reformed Christians and dissenters, they became what Charles Tilly calls durable inequalities as they were embedded as well in differential patterns of occupation, residence, education, and social welfare.[49]

Like any other political relationship in the Dutch Republic, the formal claims of Reformed Calvinists to a privileged public status and the political exclusion of dissenters as well as the informal counterclaims of dissident religious groups to a legal corporate existence were subject to historically contingent bargaining and on-going reassessment at the local and provincial level. Though this makes generalization difficult, on the whole it is safe to say that active harassment of dissenters was less severe in the countryside than in the cities, that the political and social exclusions were applied more consistently to Catholics than to Lutherans and Mennonites, and that both harassment and exclusion diminished everywhere over time. Still, in the long run, historians speak of a process of protestantization, especially in the cities, for the simple reason that nominal affiliation with the Reformed Church was clearly the path of least resistance.[50] Meanwhile, in the long run, the substantial numbers of Dutch men and women who continued openly to assert "dissident" religious identities were more likely to live in the countryside than in the city, work as unskilled workers and peddlers rather than skilled artisans and shopkeepers, have less access to formal education and public assistance than those who presented themselves as Reformed Protestants; yet given the alternatives—active repression and expulsion, which were common enough elsewhere—they were willing to bear the obvious costs of this durable inequality marked by religious identity. Indeed, even Roman Catholic clerics, while officially denying the legitimacy of the Republic, were able to work out an informal modus vivendi with provincial and local authorities that yielded a modest Catholic revival after the 1620s.[51]

By the middle of the seventeenth century, then, the Dutch Republic had developed a remarkably stable religious peace that effectively banished the religious warfare of the previous century and clearly distinguished its durable, if unequal, pattern of cultural pluralism from the official confessional intolerance of most of its neighbors. This is not to say, of course, that there was no more politically significant religious conflict in the Dutch Republic; in fact, the history of the Dutch Golden Age is replete with political conflicts in which theological cleavages and ecclesiastical differences threatened the political stability of the confederated Republic. What is striking about these religious conflicts, however, is how little they have to do with the broad confessional differences—Reformed, Lutheran, Catholic, especially—that marked the bloody religious enmities of the sixteenth century. On the contrary, the most explosive and dangerous of these conflicts were *within* organized confessional groups rather than between them.

From the very beginning of its public triumph during the Revolt, the Dutch Reformed Church, especially, was riven by a series of well-known theological and ecclesiological disputes. Without reviewing the particulars of each, I should simply like to point out here the sequence of conflicts that: (1) separated the more latitutinarian Arminians from the orthodox Gomarists in 1590s and beyond; (2) created a permanent schism between the more inclusive Remonstrants and the more exclusive Counter-Remonstrants during the Truce with Spain and beyond; and (3) divided the more liberal Cocceians from the more theologically precise or rigid Voetians in the latter part of the seventeenth century and beyond.[52] The recurrent theme of these internal divisions is that those who espoused a more open or liberal theology for the Reformed Church also envisioned a more capacious, inclusive public Church within a spiritually diverse Dutch society; by contrast, those who espoused a more orthodox or stringently defined theology also envisioned a more exclusive or pure and disciplined Church that kept its distance from the rest of Dutch society. Repeatedly, these divisions within the Reformed Church became entangled with political conflicts between the parties and factions of the Dutch political elite as was the case in 1618 when Maurice of Nassau used his alliance with orthodox Calvinists to defeat his rival Johan van Oldenbarnevelt or in 1672 and 1747 when William III and William IV, respectively, used a spirited defense of both Calvinist orthodoxy and the Fatherland against French attack to revive the political fortunes of the House of Orange. Inasmuch as the influential regents of Holland typically favored a more latitudinarian and capacious community church, Jonathan Israel suggests, "Calvinist orthodoxy became the ideology of those—often guild-members, militiamen, and semi-literate artisans—who opposed the regents."[53] Though the political potency of these religiously defined coalitions was demonstrated as late as 1747, with the triumph of William IV, historians generally agree that in the course of the eighteenth century the most virulent theological disputes within the Reformed Church subsided with the gradual ascendancy of a liberal Cocceian theology among the Reformed pastorate.

But the largest groups of dissenters in the Dutch Republic were no less susceptible to internal conflict even though their fraternal differences were less immediately salient in Dutch republican politics. The Dutch Anabaptists, for example, early on were divided between "Flemish" and "Frisian" factions which, in turn, were subdivided into no less than six factions by the 1590s.[54] But undoubtedly the most serious religious conflict within a dissenting religious group involved the growing international struggle between Jesuits and

Jansenists within the Roman Catholic Church. With the regents of Holland initially supporting the significant Jansenist faction in the *Missio Hollandica,* this rift resulted in the first decades of the eighteenth century in a permanent schism between the so-called Old Catholic Church, which had opposed Jesuit involvement in the Dutch mission, and the official *Missio Hollandica,* which gradually purged Jansenists from their resident priesthood. Though the Old Catholic Church did not enjoy a proportionate share of a more general Catholic revival in the eighteenth century, it did enjoy a considerable allure in the international Jansenist movement in that it was the first "national" church to expel the Jesuits in the eighteenth century.[55]

Through all of this drama, however, the essential outlines of the Dutch religious peace among the various confessions, and the pattern of cultural pluralism that it entailed, remained intact. How and how well this peace functioned is evident in a curious "panic" that spread throughout Zeeland, Holland, and Friesland in 1734. The extremely rare coincidence of St. John's Day with Sacraments Day on 24 June of that year gave rise to both Catholic prophecies and Reformed fears that, in the ultimate reversal of the sixteenth-century Revolt, the Catholics would seize power throughout the Republic and once again occupy *all* of the public churches. The result was a series of panicky measures on the part of local authorities to forestall this eventuality, though in the end nothing of the sort actually happened. As Willem Frijhoff has shown, there is much that is intriguing and suggestive about this phantom event, but for our purposes just a few observations will suffice.[56] In the first place, it gives eloquent testimony to a larger tradition of triumphalist Catholic prophecies and expectations, but at the same time, it reveals a complementary fear among at least a portion of the Reformed community.[57] Taken together, these would suggest a lingering estrangement or misapprehension across the Reformed/Catholic divide that by this time had been embedded in Dutch society more generally. On closer analysis, however, it is also apparent that the phenomenon of official panic, though widespread, was most significant in communities and areas where Catholics constituted a relatively small proportion of the local population; by contrast, where Catholics were most numerous and visible—that is to say, where they were an integral part of daily experience for the Reformed community—there was simply no evidence of either official or popular panic. Finally, and perhaps most significantly, there is simply no evidence of concrete Catholic mobilization or action in response to the triumphalist prophecies and fearful rumors. This suggests that, in the final analysis, even Dutch Catholics, the most marginal of all dissenting groups (with the obvious exception of the much smaller Jewish population), had come to occupy a stable and familiar place as the most visible religious minority in the culturally plural and politically segmented Republic.

Deventer, as an Island of Difference, in Revolution

Against the backdrop of the political segmentation and religious pluralism that so distinguished the Dutch Republic from its political neighbors, we are now in a position to examine more carefully the dynamics of Deventer's Patriot Revolution.[58] As the noted eighteenth-century jurist and historian, Gerhard Dumbar, described the city, Deventer readily fit the profile of the kind corporative republican community that the German historian, Mack Walker, terms a "home town." It was a largely self-regulating community in which guild members and citizens projected a *burgerlijk* standard of sober Reformed values and Magistrates governed—that is, they made, judged, and enforced laws, levied taxes, and regulated public affairs—without outside intervention.[59] At the time of the Dutch Revolt, Deventer had already had a long and distinguished history as a center for trade both along the IJssel River and on the main east-west overland routes with Germany, and it had more recently emerged as a center of late-medieval Latin spirituality, learning, and publishing. By the end of the eighteenth century, however, its glory days were long past. Deventer had suffered grievously in the Eighty Years' War (1568–1648), which may have caused a population decline of nearly 30 percent from which the city never fully recovered, and its commerce and manufacturing had also been relegated to a secondary status by the spectacular growth of Amsterdam as the entrepot of the European world economy. By definition, of course, the triumph of Reformed Protestantism in the Dutch Revolt eclipsed Deventer's leadership role in the Catholic Church, but its distinguished Athenaeum also failed to win the right to grant advanced university degrees.[60] Still, Deventer remained a proud city whose political independence set the stage for a particularly divisive revolution. Let me return to this revolution by looking more closely at the issues and actors involved.[61]

The Patriot movement first emerged in Deventer in the context of the Fourth English War (1780–84). Though the Dutch had pursued a policy of strict neutrality in European affairs for most of the eighteenth century, they were dragged willy-nilly into the war of American independence when the United Kingdom declared war on the Republic following the discovery of a draft commercial treaty between the city of Amsterdam and the rebellious American colonies. Immediately, pamphleteers calling themselves "Patriots" blamed the disastrous course of the war on the pro-English proclivities of William V, who had dynastic ties with the Hanoverian house, and the first sign of a popular movement appeared with a nationwide petition campaign in the spring of 1782 in support of official recognition of the United States. In Deventer, this petition was signed by a modest number of merchants and boatmen who envisioned a rebirth for the sagging local economy through trade with America, and this vision was readily endorsed by the local magistrates who immediately charged their delegates to the provincial estates to vote in favor of recognition of John Adams as American ambassador. The initial success of the recognition campaign was followed in October by a truly massive petition campaign that garnered the support of approximately two-thirds of the adult male population of the city and, in December, by the creation of a Citizens Committee charged with overseeing local government and organizing continued action. The first fruits of the Citizens Committee's efforts were two more massive petitions in December 1782 and February 1783. In the spring of 1783, Deventer's Patriots also created a voluntary militia (*vrijcorps*) to defend the Fatherland from both external and internal enemies.

Thus even before the official end of hostilities, the Fourth English War precipitated a major popular mobilization in Deventer. The principal thrust of this movement was clearly anti-Orange: The petitions attacked especially the political prerogatives of the Prince of Orange and the alleged abuses of his patronage "lieutenants" in Overijssel while the "free" militias clearly undermined William's role as captain-general of the armed forces of the Union. As pamphleteers and publicists hammered away at the alleged abuses of William's political patronage system and the town councillors in Deventer and elsewhere began holding "free" elections of Magistrates, however, the Patriots necessarily turned their attention more generally to the issue of constitutional reform. In the principal cities of Overijssel—Kampen and Zwolle as well as Deventer—a new round of petitions in 1785 demanded constitutional change at both the municipal and provincial levels, and the generally receptive magistrates of these cities quickly established special commissions to oversee the process of evaluating popular grievances and proposing specific remedies. It was in the middle of this process that the apparent consensus on the goals of the Patriot movement broke down in Deventer.

The grievances submitted to the Citizens Committee in 1786 as part of the constitution-writing process provide us with a sense of the issues at stake.[62] Though the Citizens Committee was interested primarily in constitutional reform, only one of the thirteen submissions it eventually published represented the kind of constitutional focus the committee's leaders apparently had in mind. Instead, the committee was asked to address a whole grab bag of issues, ranging from allegations of official corruption and fiscal mismanagement to demands for the protection of local economic interests and a more equitable distribution of pews in the local churches. As diverse as these local, often parochial, grievances were, they betrayed obvious internal division on just one point: whereas three submissions to the committee, including one petition with 250 signatures, had specifically advocated the extension of citizenship rights to Catholics, another had specifically urged the restriction of citizenship rights to those who professed the "true Reformed Christian religion." Inasmuch as this opposition to citizenship rights for Catholics was linked with demands for protection of the rights and privileges of guilds, this was a clear token of the conflict to come.

For their part, the Citizens Committee underscored the primacy of constitutional reform over "lesser" grievances by attacking especially the corporative exclusivity and insularity of the current regime at the same time as they sought to defend the corporative identity and independence of the city itself. Thus, for example, their report attacked the current practices of election by co-optation and of life tenure for the members of the town council; they also sought to limit the local jurisdiction of the provincial executive and to exclude those eligible for membership in the provincial nobility (the *Ridderschap*) from serving in municipal office. Among its lesser recommendations, the committee included the suggestion that citizenship rights might be extended to Catholics without prejudice to the rights of the guilds.

The Municipal Commission, charged with acting on the citizens' grievances, quickly incorporated the Citizens Committee's recommendations into its draft constitution for municipal government. The commission endorsed the Citizens Committee's contention that constitutional reform deserved primacy over lesser grievances; as they saw it, the draft constitution, which was intended to institute a system of "democracy by representation," would have to be approved by the whole citizenry while lesser policy issues would not. Indeed, with a heavy dose of eighteenth-century optimism, they asserted that "one can reasonably expect that, once the Form of Government is arranged to the general satisfaction of the Citizenry [*Burgerij*] and Regents, that is, absolved of all dependence except on the people, then subsequent decisions of the Government will be received with greater satisfaction."[63] To the Municipal Commission as to the Citizens Committee then, "democracy by representation" seemed to be the ultimate solution to *all* of the city's problems.

The draft constitution that was appended to the commission's report was a complex fifty-two-page document consisting of 284 articles, the first eighteen of which were "Rights and Obligations of the Citizenry."[64] Whether the remaining sections of the constitution, once in place, would have lived up to these lofty principles or actually instituted a meaningful form of representative democracy is not readily apparent, but in fact they appear to have been relatively non-controversial. On the contrary, it was the general priorities expressed by the introductory articles that proved to be the stumbling block. For by endorsing the extension of citizenship rights to Catholics in Article XV, the Municipal Commission had boldly elevated this critical matter to the level of constitutional principle while relegating all other grievances to the level of policy issues to be decided at a later date, not by a general referendum, but by newly legitimated representatives of the people.

As an organized opposition to the draft constitution emerged, it became apparent that the constitutionalist priorities of the reform movement, in general, but the issue of citizenship rights, in particular, had begun to tear the Patriot movement apart. In August 1786, a prominent national periodical published the following excerpt from a petition to the Citizens Committee: "That the undersigned declare to the Representatives of the Citizens of the City of Deventer that they have learned that there are certain Articles in the Draft Constitution which are contrary to our Civic [*Burgerlijke*] Reformed Christian Religion and the Laws, Privileges and Liberties of the Guilds; besides certain Articles that are intemperate and in which self-interest is chiefly evident; that they [the undersigned] will not accept them, but consider them null and void."[65] Inasmuch as this petition went unanswered by the Citizens Committee, it was followed by two more petitions addressed to the Magistracy in November 1786. The first of these demanded the reconstitution of the Citizens Committee, and this having been denied, the second demanded the official recognition of "26 legally appointed representatives of the guilds and Citizens" to replace the existing Citizens Committee. When all of these requests were publicly rejected by the Municipal Commission, which had been charged with examining them, the new opposition Citizens Committee finally published a lengthy petition to the Town Council, which it addressed as the immediate representatives of the citizens, that attempted to clarify and defend their "most reasonable and legitimate" requests. By this time, the straightforwardly pious defense of "true" religion had given way to far more complex legal and historical arguments about sovereignty and corporate privilege. In fact, like the Draft Constitution, the opposition petition boldly affirmed that supreme authority within the sovereign city of Deventer rested in its citizens. Yet it was clear that the fifteenth article of the Draft Constitution granting citizenship rights to Catholics was the principal point of contention. This article, the petition argued, was "nothing less than a subtle blow intended at once to extinguish the privileges of the Guilds and *Burgerij* and to intrude into the electoral process . . . persons who were not enfranchised according to time-honored municipal traditions."[66] Citing both the city's charter and specific municipal resolutions, the petitioners argued that the guilds and citizenry (*Burgerij*) had possessed for more than a century and half the right to exclude "Foreigners, Roman Catholics, and Mennonites" in order to protect the interests of those who were the champions of the "true Reformed Christian Religion."

There is much that is interesting and problematic about this fissure in Deventer's body politic. When I first wrote about these developments some time ago as part of a microhistorical reconstruction of Deventer's revolution, for example, I took pains to show how the conflict over citizenship rights for Catholics masked a more fundamental economic and social division between guild-based artisans and shopkeepers oriented to the local market—who, in a difficult economic environment, desperately sought protection from outside competition—and merchants, manufacturers, and others oriented toward broader national and international markets—who sought to break down the insularity and protectionism of Deventer's traditional economy in order to foster new growth and prosperity. What is especially striking about the revolutionary situation that developed in Deventer in 1787, from this perspective, is that the overwhelming majority of the leaders of the new Orangist opposition to the Patriots' constitutional reform were defectors from the Patriot cause. In fact, approximately two-thirds of the Patriot movement's most consistent supporters, as measured by their support for Patriot petitions through 1785, defected from the movement in 1786–87; those who showed up in the leadership of the counterrevolutionary

Orangist movement were, for the most part, guildsmen and shopkeepers whose urgent pleas for economic relief had been subordinated to the interests of constitutional reform, and whose long-term economic security was directly undermined by the specific reforms that were being proposed.[67]

In this sense, it seems obvious that the interests that the champions of the "true Reformed Christian Religion" sought to protect were more clearly economic than theological: the affiliates of the *public* Reformed Church were desperately protecting the economic and social advantages that accrued to them within a particularly transparent pattern of durable inequality in Deventer. Indeed, it is the transparency of the guildsmen's claims and of the political and social inequality marked by religious identity that makes Deventer's revolutionary conflict a particularly valuable perspective from which to examine the relationship of religion to politics at the end of the Old Regime. What I want to focus on here are two additional dimensions of this escalating conflict in Deventer: first, the Patriots' proposed transformation of Old Regime citizenship; and second, the emergence of a new Catholic political identity.

Though the Dutch Patriots are often said to have failed because they were too conservative, the proposed constitution in Deventer suggests, nevertheless, that they were prepared to transform Dutch republican politics radically by changing both the political and the social boundaries of citizenship. Indeed, as no less an authority on democratic revolution than John Adams suggested in a letter to Thomas Jefferson in 1786, to institute democracy through direct electoral representation was to politicize citizenship as never before in the history of the Republic: "We were present at Utrecht," he said, "at the August Ceremony of Swearing in of their new Magistrates. In no instance, of ancient or modern History, have the People ever asserted more unequivocally their own inherent and unalienable Sovereignty."[68]

As I noted earlier, the traditional political boundaries of urban citizenship, in Deventer as elsewhere, were limited in the sense that whatever direct popular participation may originally have been part of urban politics had been eliminated both by the oligarchization of the Town Councils (that is, self-perpetuating corporations with life tenure and electoral cooptation) and the overlay of the *stadhouder's* patronage system (that is, outside interference in the selection of public officials). This is not to say that the *burgers* of Deventer were powerless, for the privileges of guilds especially limited the authority of magistrates to regulate the urban economy and to control social welfare policy. To eliminate both cooptation and patronage by means of electoral representation, however, was to redirect the focus or meaning of citizenship away from economic and social regulation toward more direct political participation. And to suggest, additionally, that citizenship could be transformed in this way without prejudice to the rights of the guilds, as did the Patriots' Citizens Committee in 1786, may be considered more than a little disingenuous, for to expand the political boundaries of citizenship in this way was to undermine the centrality of the guilds within the urban political community.

At the same time, of course, Deventer's proposed constitution was intended to expand the social boundaries of urban citizenship by including Catholics within the urban polity. This social expansion of citizenship was not at all unprecedented inasmuch as both Lutherans and Mennonites had long ago been accepted as citizens in Deventer. Indeed, the inclusion of Mennonites at the beginning of the eighteenth century served as both a precedent and a model for the Patriots, who sought to revitalize the urban economy by attracting new talent and energy, because in the course of the eighteenth century a number of prosperous Mennonites from the eastern part of Overijssel had migrated to Deventer and brought with them their connections with the growing protoindustrial production of linen and mixed-fiber cloth. Thus by the end of the century, the Patriot movement could boast not only a number of linen weavers among its supporters but even some Mennonites among its leadership.

At first, the proposal to grant citizenship to Catholics was clearly linked to giving them access to guild membership inasmuch as the fifteenth article of the constitution granted Catholics *burgerrechten* on an equal footing with Mennonites. Later the Municipal Commission amended the article to protect the rights of guilds to determine their own membership, but by that time the damage was done. After all, the ideological leader of the Patriots' Citizens Committee, Professor F. A. van der Marck of the Deventer Athenaeum, had openly ridiculed the guilds for their continued exclusion of Catholics, who might be expected to breathe new life into the local economy.[69] But Catholics, who constituted approximately 20 percent of Deventer's population, were hardly equivalent to Mennonites, who together with Lutherans and Jews made up only 5 percent of the population. To transform such a sizable minority of Deventer's population from inhabitants to citizens, even if their citizenship did not "prejudice the rights of the guilds," was virtually to eliminate the social boundaries of urban citizenship by excluding only Jews, the quintessential outsiders in European culture, and thus to come very close to identifying the political community with all of society, regardless of religious affiliation.[70]

Thus to understand the radicalism of the Patriots' redefinition of citizenship is also to understand the sense in which the opponents of Deventer's constitution got the politics of it right: To grant citizenship to Catholics was at once to undermine the guilds and to redefine the urban polity.[71] But this also begs the question of what was actually attractive in this constitutional proposal for Deventer's Catholics.[72] Unfortunately, we know relatively little about the 20 percent of Deventer's population who were willing to pay the obvious costs of openly embracing a Catholic religious identity and thus to forgo the considerable advantages that might flow from at least making a show of being a *liefhebber* of the Reformed Church. At the very least, we can say that they probably did not depart significantly from the general social profile of Catholics in the Dutch Republic.[73] By the end of the eighteenth century, as I suggested above, Dutch Catholics were, on the whole, more likely to be rustics than cityfolk; more likely to be unskilled laborers or peddlers than skilled artisans and shopkeepers; and less likely to have access to formal education in their youth and social assistance in their old age.

In principle, if such a profile is at all accurate, we might well surmise that Deventer's Catholics were not prime candidates for recruitment in the early stages of a political reform movement that most often projected itself as thoroughly middle class or *burgerlijk*. Yet it appears as if some 250 individuals, representing approximately 60 percent of the total Catholic population, were mobilized in support of the petition requesting citizenship rights for Catholics in 1785.[74] We can well imagine that many of these signatories hoped that citizenship would bring them the traditional social and economic benefits attached to it, but it is also possible that many of them welcomed as well the formal political agency that the redefined citizenship of the Patriots' constitutional draft was offering to them for the first time. Indeed, I strongly suspect, though I cannot at this point prove, that many of the unskilled workers and day laborers who signed a Patriot petition for the first time in February 1787, following the defection of many of the movement's core supporters, were Catholics who were newly entering the republican political fray.

But regardless of whether such speculation about the extent of Catholic mobilization is correct, it is clear that entering into a broad revolutionary coalition was not without difficulty for those Catholics who signed petitions or joined the voluntary militia. In the first place, it seems clear that Deventer's Catholics were being actively recruited to join the movement as junior partners; indeed, they were expected to project themselves as an aggrieved minority seeking relief rather than as the triumphant foes of Reformed domination of religion *and* politics.[75] In the political vision that the Patriots projected of Deventer's, and more broadly the Republic's, future, Catholics would have publicly to accept their place as just another religious minority in a pluralist and tolerant world. Officially, the Catholic hierarchy would not have been able to accept such a proposition, but in addition, the resident leadership of the *Missio Hollandica* were well aware of the dangers inherent in a political coalition with revolutionary challengers. To side openly with the challengers was to risk a serious backlash if the challenge were unsuccessful. Consequently, it is not surprising that the Vicar Apostolic insisted that both priests and parishioners keep their distance from the growing Patriot movement.[76] From this perspective, then, to the extent that we can discern the emergence of a new republican political identity for Catholics in the course of Deventer's revolution, we must also be impressed by the cultural and political adjustments this required of the Catholics as well as their Reformed allies who recruited them.

In the end, then, the Patriots' attempt to democratize politics in revolutionary Deventer brought together some strange political bedfellows. On the side of revolution, a sizable segment of the Catholic minority population at the social and political margins of Old Regime Deventer was aligned with the marginal elements of the regent elite—those who stood outside the Prince's patronage network—plus a broad range of educated and professional elites, who led the movement, and a faithful remnant of the Reformed artisans, shopkeepers, and merchants who stayed with the Patriot movement following the mass defections of 1786. Ironically, this pro-Catholic revolutionary coalition also included most of the city's Reformed pastors, who were later removed from office by the Orangist counterrevolution. On the side of counterrevolution, a determined core of guild-based artisans, who considered themselves, not without reason, the *burgerlijk* heart and soul of Deventer's Reformed society, was allied with an equally determined core of the regent elite who refused to cooperate with the Patriots' project of constitutional reform.[77] Ironically, this counterrevolutionary coalition was supported at least implicitly by the Roman Catholic hierarchy who were fearful of disrupting the political balances that had not only allowed the Catholic Mission to survive but to grow during the eighteenth century. In short, although revolutionary conflict in Deventer invoked religious identities like "Reformed" and "Catholic" in the struggle over the boundaries of citizenship, it did not represent a fundamental displacement or transformation of the basic conditions of religious peace and coexistence. On the contrary, it revealed just how the durable inequality of the religious peace could continue to inform Deventer's politics even in a more democratic regime in which the most obvious political boundaries between confessional groups were reduced or eliminated.

To be sure, Deventer's revolution was exceptional in the sense that the specific conflict over citizenship rights for Catholics was uniquely divisive; still, its overall dynamic reveals the long-term significance of the Republic's peculiar path of state and political-cultural formation. The segmentation of political sovereignty under the Union of Utrecht preserved the integrity of urban politics while the growing paralysis of Dutch politics as reflected in the polarization of Patriots and Orangists during the Fourth English War opened up an extraordinary opportunity for ordinary Dutch citizens not only to imagine a new world in which "the sovereignty of the People" was a possible new foundation of political affairs but actually to set out to create such a world. At the same time, the Union of Utrecht's guarantee of individual freedom of conscience nurtured an unparalleled cultural and religious pluralism in the Republic while the specific prerogatives of the *public* Church had resulted in very durable forms of inequality in which religious affiliation served as an important marker of political and social difference. The consequence was not only the massive mobilization of the first democratic and revolutionary political movement in Europe in the 1780s but also the emergence of new political cleavages that suggested that religious identities would have continued to mark political differences even if the Patriots had succeeded in institutionalizing a new, more inclusive form of active democratic citizenship within the framework of a confederated Republic.

Epilogue: Of New Endings and Old Beginnings

The Dutch Patriot Revolution succumbed to outside intervention in 1787. This was one of the obvious disadvantages, R. R. Palmer once mused, of being a small republic in world of increasingly militarized monarchies, so we will never know whether the Patriots' vision of a democratic and culturally inclusive republic was actually feasible.[78] Instead, the Orangist counterrevolution, in Deventer as elsewhere, claimed to be restoring the status quo ante while actually bringing new people into politics and depending as deeply on popular support as the Patriots' revolution had in 1787. But before there was even much time to see the tangible results of this clearly unintended outcome of democratic mobilization and conflict, the triumph of the French Revolution in 1789 and the northward expansion of the very different French version of a democratic republic in 1795 brought a new and different ending to the republican politics of the

Dutch Old Regime. Subsequently, the Dutch again learned that, however much they were convinced that a sovereign people should be free to design its own political future, there were any number of very practical reasons that the political future was not theirs to shape exclusively on their own terms. In particular the demands of French *fraternité* as often as not conflicted with the interests of Dutch *liberté,* and as a result the French had an important hand in shaping the Batavian Republic as well as the succession of regimes that followed. Eventually the French were driven out as enemies of the people in 1813, and the Dutch set about shaping a new Kingdom of the Netherlands, which reunited the southern with the northern Netherlands, also as a consequence of outside interference by the Congress of Vienna.[79]

So why should we care about a failed revolution in a small republic that before long ceased to exist? By way of conclusion, let me suggest just two reasons. In the first place, although the French had a firm hand in replacing the politically segmented Dutch Republic with a French-style unitary state, they were hardly the inventors or patrons of the Dutch version of democracy and citizenship that reemerged under the Batavian Republic. Instead, the Batavian revolutionaries went a long way toward establishing a new culturally inclusive and democratically active citizenship, based firmly on the Patriot example, within their cities and provinces prior to the adoption of a national constitution in 1798.[80] In short, while the leaders of the French Revolution imagined that they had to destroy their far more authoritarian history in order to lay the foundations of a modern citizenship, the leaders of the Dutch Revolution could readily imagine that it would require only a series of boundary adjustments—especially in social and political terms—in order to transform the *burgerschap* of old into a radically new citizenship. Thus, the principal contribution that the French armies brought with them in the 1790s was the strong push, on the grounds of fiscal efficiency as much as democratic ideology, toward the nationalization or geographical expansion of citizenship along with the centralization of the state.

The second reason we should care about Deventer's failed revolution has to do with the inevitable disappointment of its newly active Catholic minority. To be sure, most Dutch Catholics greeted the arrival of French revolutionary troops with great anticipation. Some, who still harbored a Catholic triumphalist vision of the future, thought that the French might be the answer to their prayers, but they soon discovered that these were hardly the French who might be expected to reestablish the Catholic Church.[81] Meanwhile, those who more soberly hoped that their admission to full citizenship might lead to significant improvements in their economic circumstances were equally disappointed when the French-sponsored unitary constitution of 1798 abolished the guilds, to which they might have hoped to gain entrance, and the course of the revolutionary and Napoleonic war utterly destroyed what remained of the Republic's economic prosperity.[82] But once the French were gone and the new Kingdom of the Netherlands reunited the northern provinces with the overwhelmingly Catholic southern Netherlands, Catholics soon enough discovered that, contrary to the promises of their liberally democratic allies from the 1780s onward, equal access to a radically individual and exclusively political citizenship on a political par with Reformed Calvinists would not be a sufficient answer to their prayers, either. On the contrary, the structural inequalities that had been so embedded in the Old Regime remained to frustrate their social and economic expectations under a whole succession of new regimes.[83] It is thus not surprising that in the escalating political crisis that led to the separation of the northern and southern Netherlands in 1830, Dutch Catholics once again embraced their Old Regime political identity as an aggrieved minority and, in so doing, became the first in a long series of religiously or ideologically identified political groups to mobilize massively and to bargain strenuously with the new national state.[84]

Notes

1. Deventer was, alongside Kampen and Zwolle, one of the principal cities (*hoofdsteden*) in the small eastern Dutch province of Overijssel; as chartered

cities, all three enjoyed a considerable degree of autonomy at the same time as they shared equally with the corporate body of the nobility (the *Ridderschap*) sovereignty over the rest of the province.

2. For a fuller analysis of these events in Deventer, see Wayne Ph. te Brake, *Regents and Rebels. The Revolutionary World of an Eighteenth Century Dutch City,* Studies in Social Discontinuity (Oxford: Basil Blackwell, 1989), 97; the introductory articles are quoted on p. 97. For the full text of the draft constitution, see *Tweede Rapport . . . over de Verbetering van de Stedelyke Regeeringswyze in Augustus des jaars 1786* (Deventer, 1786).

3. The opening articles of the Deventer constitution are strikingly similar to the Declaration of Rights of the Pennsylvania Convention in August 1776. For a recent edition of these, see Jack N. Rakove, *Declaring Rights. A Brief History with Documents,* The Bedford Series in History and Culture (Boston: Bedford Books, 1998), 85–87.

4. For a general survey of the revolutionary era in the Dutch Republic, see Simon Schama, *Patriots and Liberators: Revolution in the Netherlands 1780–1813* (New York: Alfred A. Knopf, 1977).

5. See Te Brake, *Regents and Rebels,* plate 3, "Het plunderen te Deventer."

6. There is a considerable literature on the so-called pillarization (*verzuiling*) of Dutch politics; in English see especially Hans Daalder, "The Netherlands: Opposition in a Segmented Society," in Robert Dahl, ed., *Political Oppositions in Western Democracies,* (New Haven: Yale University Press, 1966), 188–236; Arend Lijphart, *The Politics of Accommodation: Pluralism and Democracy in the Netherlands,* 2d ed. (Berkeley: University of California Press, 1975); and Kenneth D. McRae, ed., *Consociational Democracy: Political Accommodation in Segmented Societies,* The Carleton Library (Toronto: McClelland and Stewart, 1974).

7. E. H. Kossman and A. F. Mellink, eds., *Texts Concerning the Revolt of the Netherlands* (Cambridge: Cambridge University Press, 1974), 166.

8. Kossman and Mellink, *Texts,* 169–70.

9. The first census to record the religious affiliations of Deventer's population is from 1810; at that time, 75 percent of the households identified themselves as Reformed, 20 percent as Catholic, and the remaining 5 percent as Lutheran, Mennonite, and Jewish; see Te Brake, *Regents and Rebels,* 21.

10. For an account of the Revolt, see Geoffrey Parker, *The Dutch Revolt,* rev. ed. (Harmondsworth: Penguin, 1985); for a more general suvey of the history of the republic, see Jonathan I. Israel, *The Dutch Republic: Its Rise, Greatness, and Fall, 1477–1806,* The Oxford History of Early Modern Europe (Oxford: Clarendon Press, 1995).

11. Instead, the United Provinces developed one of Europe's most impressive mercenary armies under the leadership of Maurice of Nassau.

12. Robert Fruin, *Geschiedenis der Staatsinstellingen in Nederland tot den val der Republiek*, edited by H. T. Colenbrander, with an introduction by I. Schöffer ('s-Gravenhage: Martinus Nijhoff, 1980); Marjolein 't Hart, *The Making of a Bourgeois State; War, Politics and Finance during the Dutch Revolt* (Manchester: Manchester University Press, 1993).

13. See Martin van Gelderen, *The Political Thought of the Dutch Revolt 1555–1590*, Ideas in Context, 23 (Cambridge: Cambridge University Press, 1992); and Martin van Gelderen, ed. and trans., *The Dutch Revolt*, Cambridge Texts in the History of Political Thought (Cambridge: Cambridge University Press, 1993).

14. See James D. Tracy, *A Financial Revolution in the Habsburg Netherlands: Renten en Renteniers in the County of Holland, 1515–1565* (Berkeley: University of California Press, 1985); and James D. Tracy, *Holland under Habsburg Rule, 1506–1566: The Formation of a Body Politic* (Berkeley: University of California Press, 1990).

15. Kossman and Mellink, *Texts*, 225.

16. Cf. Wayne te Brake, "Provincial Histories and National Revolution in the Dutch Republic," in Margaret C. Jacob and Wijnand Mijnhardt, eds., *The Dutch Republic in the Eighteenth Century; Decline, Enlightenment and Revolution* (Ithaca: Cornell University Press, 1992), 67–70.

17. See Wayne te Brake, *Shaping History: Ordinary People in European Politics, 1500–1700* (Berkeley and Los Angeles: University of California Press, 1998), ch. 5.

18. The "sovereigns" I refer to here are the members of municipal councils who chose ruling magistrates and sent delegates (with limited commissions) to provincial estates assemblies; the members of corporative bodies of the nobility (the *Ridderschap*) who participated in the estates assemblies of most provinces; and the delegates, elected by enfranchised landowners, who represented the rural districts of the province of Friesland. Altogether these numbered well over 2,000. Cf. D. J. Roorda, "Het onderzoek naar het stedelijk patriciaat in Nederland," in W. W. Mijnhardt, ed., *Kantelend geschiedbeeld: Nederlandse historiografie sinds 1945* (Utrecht/Antwerpen: Uitgeverij Het Spectrum, 1983), 118–42.

19. On Overijssel, see Te Brake, *Regents and Rebels;* for a survey of the literature on Dutch politics more generally, see G. de Bruin, "De geschiedschrijving over de Gouden Eeuw," in *Kantelend geschiedbeeld*, 83–117.

20. Jan den Tex, *Johan van Oldenbarnevelt* ('s-Gravenhage: Nijhoff, 1980).

21. Te Brake, "Provincial Histories and National Revolution," 68–69.

22. In this sense, William of Orange's leadership of the Revolt was a lot like George Washington's leadership in the American War of Independence two centuries later, with the remarkable difference that William did not live long enough (he was assassinated in 1584) to trade his appointive war leadership in for a piece

of sovereign authority as Washington did later as first president of the United States, long after he had resigned his military commission.

23. For a general treatment of the Princes of Orange in the political history of the Republic, see Herbert H. Rowen, *The Princes of Orange: The Stadholders in the Dutch Republic,* Cambridge Studies in Early Modern History (Cambridge: Cambridge University Press, 1988).

24. Herbert H. Rowen, "The Revolution That Wasn't: the Coup d'Etat of 1650 in Holland," *European Studies Review* 4 (1974): 99–117.

25. Herbert Rowen, *John de Witt: Statesman of the "True Freedom"* (Cambridge: Cambridge University Press, 1986).

26. D. J. Roorda, "William III and the Utrecht 'Government Regulation': Background, Events and Problems," *Low Countries History Yearbook* 12 (1979): 85–109.

27. Jan A. F. de Jongste, "The Restoration of the Orangist Regime in 1747: The Modernity of a 'Glorious Revolution,'" in Margaret C. Jacob and Wijnand W. Mijnhardt, eds., *The Dutch Republic in the Eighteenth Century: Decline, Enlightenment, and Revolution* (Ithaca: Cornell University Press, 1992), 32–59.

28. On the function of the Prince's patronage regime, see A. J. C. M. Gabriëls, *De heren als dienaren en de dienaar als heer: Het stadhouderlijk stelsel in de tweede helft van de achttiende eeuw,* Hollandse Historische Reeks 14 ('s-Gravenhage: Stichting Hollandse Historische Reeks, 1990).

29. See Jan de Vries, "On the Modernity of the Dutch Republic," *Journal of Economic History* 33 (1973): 191–202; De Vries's delightfully contentious argument that the heritage of medieval institutions did not significantly retard the first wave of modern economic growth in the Dutch Republic is more fully elaborated in Jan de Vries and Ad van der Woude, *The First Modern Economy: Success, Failure, and Perseverence of the Dutch Economy, 1500–1815* (Cambridge: Cambridge University Press, 1997).

30. See Jan de Vries, *European Urbanization 1500–1800* (Cambridge, Mass.: Harvard University Press, 1984), and Maarten Prak, "Regions in Early Modern Europe," in *Proceedings of the Eleventh International Economic History Congress* (Milano: Università Bocconi, 1994).

31. The votes were eighteen for the cities and one for the nobility in Holland and six for the cities and one for the nobility in Zeeland.

32. In Friesland the countryside was organized in three "quarters" or districts where political office was elective and the eleven small cities (today famous for the marathon ice-skating race that connects them all) constituted the fourth quarter collectively; see J. A. Faber, "De oligarchisering van Friesland in de tweede helft van de zeventiende eeuw," *AAG Bijdragen* 15 (1970): 39–64.

33. Te Brake, *Regents and Rebels.*

34. Roorda, "Onderzoek"; for exemplary local studies, see L. Kooijmans, *Onder regenten: De elite in een Hollandse stad, Hoorn 1700–1780,* Hollandse Historische Reeks 4 (Amsterdam/Dieren: De Bataafsche Leeuw, 1985); J. J. de Jong, *Met goed fatsoen: De elite in een Hollandse stad, Gouda 1700–1780,* Hollandse Historische Reeks 5 (Amsterdam/Dieren: De Bataafsche Leeuw, 1985); and Maarten Prak, *Gezeten burgers; De elite in een Hollandse stad: Leiden 1700–1780,* Hollandse Historische Reeks, 6 (Amsterdam/Dieren: De Bataafsche Leeuw, 1985).

35. Rudolf Dekker, *Holland in beroering: Oproeren in de 17e en 18e eeuw* (Baarn: Amboboeken, 1982); Rudolf Dekker, "Some Remarks about Collective Action and Collective Violence in the History of the Netherlands," *Tijdschrift voor sociale geschiedenis* 15 (1989): 158–64.

36. Henk van Nierop, "Popular Participation in Politics in the Dutch Republic," in Peter Blickle, ed., *Resistance, Representation, and Community,* The Origins of the Modern State (Oxford: Clarendon Press for the European Science Foundation, 1997), 272–90; Rudolf Dekker, "Labour Conflicts and Working-Class Culture in Early Modern Holland," *International Review of Social History* 35 (1990): 377–420.

37. For a fuller discussion of this point and the accumulating literature around it, see Maarten Prak, "Burghers into Citizens: Urban and National Citizenship in the Netherlands during the Revolutionary Era (c. 1800)," *Theory and Society* 26 (1997): 403–20.

38. Cf. Maarten Prak, "Individual, corporation and society: The rhetoric of Dutch guilds (18th C.)," in *Statuts individuels, statuts corporatifs et statuts judiciaires dans les villes européennes (moyen âge et temps modernes)* (Leuven/Apeldoorn: Garant, 1996), 255–79.

39. Alastair Duke, "Building Heaven in Hell's Despite; the Early History of the Reformation in the Towns of the Low Countries," in *Reformation and Revolt in the Low Countries* (London: Hambledon Press, 1990), 71–100.

40. For a fuller analysis of this dynamic of repression and underground mobilization, see Te Brake, *Shaping History,* ch. 3.

41. Marijke Gijswijt-Hofstra, ed., *Een schijn van verdraagzaamheid: Afwijking en tolerantie in Nederland van de zestiende eeuw tot heden* (Hilversum: Verloren, 1989).

42. Cf. C Berkvens-Stevelinck, J. Israel, and G. H. M. Posthumus Meyes, eds., *The Emergence of Tolerance in the Dutch Republic,* Studies in the History of Christian Thought, vol. 76 (Leiden: Brill, 1997).

43. This important fact clearly distinguishes the Dutch pattern of religious reformation from others, especially the German and Swiss, which were intended to reform whole communities, with the exception of the Imperial Free Cities of

Germany, which were required to accommodate Catholic worship under the Peace of Augsburg (1555); cf. Euan Cameron, *The European Reformation* (Oxford: Clarendon Press, 1991).

44. Benjamin J. Kaplan, "Dutch Particularlism and the Calvinist Quest for 'Holy Uniformity,'" *Archiv für Reformationsgeschichte* 82 (1991): 239–55; Benjamin J. Kaplan, *Calvinists and Libertines: Confession and Community in Utrecht, 1578–1620* (Oxford: Clarendon Press, 1995); Andrew Pettegree, "Coming to Terms with Victory: The Upbuilding of a Calvinist Church in Holland, 1572–1590," in Alastair Duke, Gillian Lewis, and Andrew Pettegree, eds., *Calvinism in Europe, 1540–1620* (Cambridge: Cambridge University Press, 1994), 160–80.

45. Reformation historians use the term "confessional" to denote the various strands of theological or ecclesiastical difference (often articulated by religious leaders in formal, propositional confessions of faith) in European Christianity during and after the Reformation; the major strands (each with regional and local variations) were, thus, Lutheran, Reformed (either Zwinglian or Calvinist), Anabaptist, and Catholic. For a synthesis of the general literature on confessionalization—that is, the process by which these confessions become embedded in European politics, usually just one confession in each state—see R. Po-chia Hsia, *Social Discipline in the Reformation; Central Europe, 1550–1750* (London: Routledge, 1989); for a model study of multiple confessions in a single Dutch city, see Joke Spaans, *Haarlem na de Reformatie: Stedelijke cultuur en kerelijk leven, 1577–1620,* Hollandse Historische Reeks 11 ('s-Gravenhage: Stichting Hollandse Historische Reeks, 1989); on Dutch confessionalization in general, see Israel, *Dutch Republic,* 361–98.

46. Alastair Hamilton, Sjouke Voolstra, and Piet Visser, eds., *From Martyr to Muppy; A Historical Introduction to Cultural Assimilation Processes of a Religious Minority in the Netherlands: The Mennonites* (Amsterdam: Amsterdam University Press, 1994).

47. The Church at Rome refused to recognize the legitimacy of the Dutch Republic and, in effect, stripped the resident Catholic clergy of its episcopal structure; the *Missio* was organized in direct relationship to Rome through a Vicar-General who at first resided in Brussels, but later at Utrecht; cf. Israel, *Dutch Republic,* 377–89; the standard work is L. J. Rogier, *Geschiedenis van het Katholicisme in Noord-Nederland in de zestiende en zeventiende eeuw* (Amsterdam: Urbi et Orbi, 1947).

48. Maarten Prak, "The Politics of Intolerance: Citizenship and Religion in the Dutch Republic (17th–18th C.)," Paper presented at the workshop on "Religious Toleration and the Making of the Dutch Golden Age" at New York University (1999).

49. Charles Tilly, *Durable Inequality* (Berkeley: University of California Press, 1998).

50. Cf. J. A. de Kok, *Nederland op de breuklijn Rome-Reformatie: Numerieke aspecten van protestantisering en katholieke herleving in de noordelijke Nederlanden, 1580–1880* (Assen: Van Gorcum, 1964); and Israel, *Dutch Republic.*

51. For a survey of the relevant literature in English, see Israel, *Dutch Republic,* 361–98, 637–76, 1019–37; see also Mathieu Spiertz, "Priest and layman in a minority church: The Roman Catholic Church in the Northern Netherlands, 1592–1686," in W. J. Shiels and Diana Wood, eds., *The Ministry: Lay and Clerical* (Oxford: Basil Blackwell for the Ecclesiastical History Society, 1989), 287–301.

52. Each of these conflicts has generated a sizable literature in its own right; for a general survey, including the political implications, see Israel, *Dutch Republic,* passim.

53. Israel, *Dutch Republic,* 372.

54. See I. B. Horst, ed., *The Dutch Dissenters: A Critical Companion to their History and Ideas* (Leiden: E. J. Brill, 1986); Cornelis Krahn, *Dutch Anabaptism: Origins, Spread, Life and Thought* (The Hague, 1968); and Hamilton, Voolstra, and Visser, *From Martyr to Muppy.*

55. P. Polman, *Katholiek Nederland in de achttiende eeuw,* 3 vols (Hilversum: Uigeverij Paul Brand, 1968); for statistics on the growth and decline of the two groups, see Kok, *Nederland op de breuklijn Rome-Reformatie.* On Jansenist networks, see the chapters by Dale Van Kley and W. Reginald Ward in this volume.

56. Willem Frijhoff, "De paniek van Juni 1734," *Archief voor de geschiedenis van de katholieke kerk in Nederland* 19 (1977): 170–233.

57. Willem Frijhoff, "Katholieke toekomstverwachting ten tijde van de Republiek; structuur en grondlijnen tot een interpretatie," *BMGN* 98 (1983): 430–59.

58. For more on the divergent trajectories of state formation and political-cultural development in early modern Europe, see Wayne te Brake, *Shaping History,* ch. 5.

59. G. Dumbar, *Het Kerkelijk en Wereldlijk Deventer* (Deventer, 1732); Paul Holthuis, *Frontierstad bij het scheiden van de markt: Deventer militair, demographisch, economisch, 1578–1648* (Houten: Arko Uitgeverij, 1993).

60. See Willem Frijhoff, "Deventer en zijn gemiste universiteit: Het Athemeum in de sociaal-culturele geschiedenis van Overijssel," *Overijsselse historische bijdragen* 97 (1982): 45–79.

61. The following account in based, unless otherwise noted, on Te Brake, *Regents and Rebels.*

84. L. François, "De petitiebeweging in het Verenigd Koninkrijk der Nederlanden: Balans van het onderzoek," in C. A. Tamse and E. Witte, eds., *Staats- en natievorming in Willem I's Koninkrijk (1815–1830)* (Brussel/Baarn: VUB Press/Bosch & Keuning, 1992), 122–70.

SIX

Pietism, Politics, and the Public Sphere in Germany

JAMES VAN HORN MELTON

EMERGING IN THE FINAL DECADES OF THE SEVENTEENTH century as a reform movement within German Lutheranism, Pietism developed out of a cultural and religious milieu teeming with apocalyptic visions and chiliastic hopes. It is easy to overlook these millenarian origins, especially if one focuses exclusively on the more restrained Prussian variant of the Pietist movement that evolved in partnership with the Hohenzollern court in the early eighteenth century. In the beginning at least, Pietism was no creature of absolutist order and stability; it was born of the chaos, despair, and destruction wrought by the Thirty Years' War and its aftermath.

Pietism was a symptom of the crisis of confidence that had come to afflict German Protestantism during its second century. Even before the outbreak of war in 1618, widespread complaints of sporadic church and school attendance, ignorance of the fundamental articles of faith, and rampant immorality among the laity, had all inspired doubts about the success of Luther's enterprise.[1] In Brandenburg, disenchantment with the spiritual torpor of orthodox Lutheranism led Elector Johann Sigismund to defect to the Calvinist faith in 1613.[2] Elsewhere, the spread of mystical and spiritualist currents in German Protestantism further testified to growing disillusionment with the established Lutheran churches. Calling for a more inward and less dogmatic faith, Lutheran mystics like Jacob Böhme

(1575–1624) and Johann Arndt (1555–1621) insisted that the Reformation had yet to fulfill its spiritual promise.

As war spread throughout the empire during the 1630s and 1640s, among contemporaries the conflict assumed a cosmic and eschatological significance. Some, like the devout Lutheran Duke Ernst the Pious of Saxony-Gotha, saw it as a sign of divine disfavor, while others, like the self-appointed prophet and Silesian tanner Christian Kotter, viewed it more dramatically as a prelude to the Last Judgment.[3] The conclusion of peace in 1648 did little to dispel this mood of failure and doubt. A century after the death of Luther, extensive areas of the empire lay ravaged by war and pestilence. Although the Peace of Westphalia brought an end to the intermittent confessional struggles that had afflicted the empire since the Reformation, fresh catastrophes provoked further calls for repentance and reform. Repeated invasions by the French from the 1670s through the first decade of the eighteenth century cut a destructive swath through areas of southwestern Germany, above all the Palatinate, and added fuel to millenarian prophecies and jeremiads. Louis XIV's revocation of the Edict of Nantes and the attendant flood of Huguenot exiles into the empire heightened fears that Antichrist was afoot, as did the revived Turkish threat symbolized by the siege of Vienna in 1683.[4]

Insofar as these events seemed to offer proof of divine disfavor, Lutheran critics laid the spiritual failures of their church at the doorstep of their temporal and spiritual leaders. Lutheran princes, who like other rulers of the age increasingly indulged a taste for luxury and display in the style of Louis XIV, were an easy enough target. The Saxon electors, traditionally the political leaders of the Lutheran cause in the empire, hardly conformed to the model of the patriarchal prince tending to the spiritual welfare of his flock. As for the church, critics blamed the sterility and rigidity of post-Reformation Lutheran theology for the allegedly tepid state of lay piety. This dogmatism went along with the general hardening of divisions between the three major confessions of the empire (Catholic, Lutheran, and Calvinist) that had followed the Peace of Augsburg in 1555. In the case of Lutheranism, a need to assert its doctrinal distinctiveness vis-à-vis both Calvinists on the "left" and Catholics on the "right" had led to a renewed emphasis on polemic theology (*Kontroverstheologie*) in theological faculties of the period. Here the disputation held pride of place as the primary instrument for preserving the purity of Lutheran doctrine from any taint of heterodox belief, be it crypto-Catholic or crypto-Calvinist. Scholastic and syllogistic in form, the disputation had become an integral part of academic culture in the West since the reception of Aristotelian logic in the twelfth century. Although Luther, echoing humanist critics of scholasticism, had condemned the excesses of academic disputation for encouraging theological hair-splitting, the practice underwent a revival beginning in the second half of the sixteenth century. By the early seventeenth century, the overheated atmosphere of theological debate generated by the intensification of confessional strife had made *Kontroverstheologie* the crowning subject of theological study at Protestant universities.[5]

The Pietist call for a "Reformation in the Reformation" must be understood in the context of the crisis of confidence described above. The spiritual father of Pietism was the Alsatian-born theologian Philip Jakob Spener (1503–1705). As a student at the University of Strassburg, Spener had read copiously in Arndtian mysticism and Puritan devotional literature.[6] Arndt's *Das Wahre Christentum* (*True Christianity*, 1605), probably the most widely read devotional manual in Protestant Germany during the seventeenth and eighteenth centuries, had argued that the church was itself responsible for the rampant immorality and spiritual laxity that afflicted the laity.[7] Moral and religious reform demanded genuine repentance and conversion, which occurred not through mere outward assent to an abstract set of doctrinal principles but only through an inwardly cultivated faith. This faith, he argued, had to bear practical fruits in a Christian love for others. Christianity required not adherence to a sterile and rigid system of belief but the practice of piety in one's daily life. Also important for Spener's theological development during this period was Lewis Bayly's *Practice of Piety*, one of the most popular devotional guides in seventeenth-century England. Bayly's Bible-centered theology and his emphasis on the practical value of Scripture were to be central features of Pietism. Bayly (1580–1631) enjoyed close ties with Puritanism when his handbook appeared in 1629, and although he later distanced himself from the movement when his views incurred the disfavor of the Stuart court, his *Practice of Piety* remained popular in Puritan circles.[8]

Although Spener proved receptive to Calvinist influences, including Jean de Labadie (the fiery Huguenot minister and ex-Jesuit whom Spener befriended during a visit to Geneva in 1660), like Arndt he carefully avoided straying beyond the acceptable bounds of Lutheran doctrine. Throughout Spener's career, in fact, he showed an uncanny ability to appropriate ideas from disparate theological currents while keeping his Lutheran credentials intact—a skill that must be reckoned as key to his later success in containing separatist tendencies within the Pietist movement. That Spener remained fully in the Lutheran mainstream after receiving his doctorate at Strassburg is evident from his subsequent appointment at the age of thirty-one to the prestigious post of senior pastor in Frankfurt am Main. In addition to his duties as pastor of the Frankfurt *Barfüsserkirche,* Spener was responsible for supervising the ordination of Lutheran clergy, upholding church discipline in the city's twelve parishes, and serving as chief spokesman for the local pastorate in its relations with the city government.[9]

Spener's rigorist outlook soon attracted a following among a devout group of educated laypeople critical of public morals in the city and dissatisfied with the contentious debates of orthodox Lutheran theologians. With Spener's approval they formed what came to be known as the *Collegium Pietatis,* an informal study group devoted to fostering piety and fellowship among its members. It met at Spener's home, where readings from the Scriptures and other devotional texts were accompanied by discussion and prayer. The group soon attracted widespread attention both in Germany and abroad—William Penn paid a visit in 1674—and is generally considered the first Pietist conventicle in Germany.

The importance of the conventicle in Pietist devotional practice will be examined later in this essay. Here it need only be said that Spener's study group, as a private circle with no formal ties to the church, soon aroused fears of separatism among the more orthodox clergy and magistrates of the city. Their suspicions were confirmed when a faction in the conventicle broke away and began boycotting the Eucharist. Spener's critics seized upon the scandal in an attempt to discredit him, by which time Spener's writings and activities had begun to spark controversy elsewhere in Protestant Germany. In 1686 Spener left Frankfurt to assume a position as pastor and confessor at the Saxon court in Dresden. There, too, Spener incurred the hostility of the Lutheran establishment, which accused him and his supporters of separatist leanings. Tensions also surfaced in Spener's relationship with the Elector Johann Georg II, who grew to resent Spener's open disapproval of the dissipation and prodigality he found at the Saxon court. Spener's final break with the elector in 1691 led him to the Prussian capital of Berlin, where he served as a member of the Lutheran consistory until his death in 1705.

Pietist Inwardness and Social Reform

Central to Pietist theology was the conviction that spiritual renewal from within was far more important than the purely passive, outward observance of dogmatic principles. This belief was a central theme of Spener's *Pia Desideria* (1675), a foundational text of the Pietist movement, and the distinction between the external and internal, between outward observance and inner conviction, was to be a fundamental tenet of Pietism. For the Pietists, the outward fulfillment of one's Christian duties was less important than the spirit in which they were carried out. True Christians carried out their obligations voluntarily and with conviction, not mechanically or through coercion. Although the distinction between inner conviction and external observance had been central to Luther's doctrine of justification, the Pietists were critical of their church precisely because they believed it had lost sight of the reformer's original message.[10] "It is a disgrace to the Lutheran religion," wrote Spener, "that so many of its members believe they can be saved by observing the externals of the faith alone."[11]

Pietist inwardness was accompanied by a determined social activism. This combination at first seems paradoxical, for the Pietist emphasis on spiritual renewal from within would seem to have discounted the value and efficacy of good works. Indeed, critics of Pietism, from seventeenth-century orthodox Lutherans who viewed Pietist social activism as a heretical abandonment of Lutheran solafideism, to modern historians who see in Pietist *Innerlichkeit* the roots of the "unpolitical German," have each stressed the incompatibility of the two attitudes.

Yet the relationship between the two positions was dialectical, not contradictory. For Pietists it was precisely the individual's renewed faith and purified will that made good works possible; conversely, good works were evidence of spiritual renewal. As Spener wrote, "even faith . . . must be verified through action. This in the end is the highest proof of the power of faith."[12] Here the Pietists again followed Luther, who held that although good works were not efficacious for salvation, they did proceed logically from faith. This emphasis on the indivisibility of faith and works enabled the Pietists to validate their emphasis on social action. Moreover, because Pietists shared the Lutheran belief that grace was in principle available to all and not (as in Calvinism) reserved for an elect, they held that every individual was eligible to receive divine grace through repentance and conversion. A corollary of this position was the belief that Christians had to be concerned not merely with their own salvation but also with that of others, an idea that lay at the heart of the Pietist social ethos.[13]

Pietism owed its reputation as a social reform movement largely to the work of August Hermann Francke (1663–1727), who succeeded Spener as the leader of North German Pietism. While completing his theology studies at the University of Leipzig, Francke had undergone a conversion experience and joined a circle of Spenerian students in the city.[14] In 1688 he visited Spener in Dresden and had become an ardent disciple by the time he returned to Leipzig in 1689 and began teaching in the theology faculty. Soon Francke attracted a student following as well as the hostility of orthodox faculty at the university. Leipzig was a bastion of Lutheran orthodoxy, and Francke's insistence that the devotional study of Scripture was more important than the mastery of polemic theology raised eyebrows among those trained in the Lutheran scholastic tradition. His critics blamed Francke for declining attendance at lectures on logic and metaphysics, and a 1689 investigation revealing that some of his students were selling or even burning their philosophy textbooks and lecture notes supported these charges.[15] Even worse from the standpoint of his critics, Francke's influence had begun to spill out of the university into the larger Leipzig community. They claimed that large numbers of townspeople, especially from the city's artisan population, were attending conventicles organized by Francke and staying away from worship services. One such gathering was purportedly hosted by a washerwoman, and Francke was criticized for seeking followers among the common people.[16] Attacks on Francke grew increasingly bitter, and in 1690 the Saxon government, at the urging of Johann Benedict Carpzov and other guardians of Lutheran orthodoxy at the university, prohibited all conventicles in the city. In addition Pietist candidates for the priesthood were blacklisted, and the stipends of known Pietist students were withdrawn. These measures effectively put an end to the Pietist movement in the city, and that year Francke left Leipzig to accept a deaconate in Erfurt.[17]

The campaign against Francke in Leipzig is revealing, for it shows how Pietism was almost from the very beginning identified with two groups. One was the "common people." Although Pietism would actually win adherents from every tier of society, the movement did in fact accord the poor and the uneducated considerably more status and agency than was previously the case in Lutheran devotional life. Spener and Francke were by no means social radicals, and both accepted the hierarchical social order of their day as divinely ordained.[18] But Pietist theology and devotional practices did have egalitarian implications. The conscious reaffirmation of Luther's doctrine of the priesthood of all believers, the emphasis on feeling and emotion over intellect, the conviction that the practice of piety in daily life was more important than the mastery of theological subtleties—these beliefs not only narrowed the gulf between clergy and laity, but among the laity itself, they sanctioned and indeed encouraged varieties of religious experience available to the schooled and unschooled alike. To its enemies Pietism smacked of vulgar anti-intellectualism, a charge usually paired with mockery of the movement's plebeian overtones. The Leipzig theologian Carpzov, who was initially sympathetic to Spener's ideas but later became a critic of Pietism, noted the "disreputable entourage" surrounding Spener in Dresden and criticized Pietist assemblies for allowing servants to sit at the same tables with their masters.[19]

The charge against Francke that even Leipzig washerwomen were hosting conventicles highlights the second group associated early on with the Pietist movement, namely women. The participation of women in Pietist conventicles was probably the single most controversial feature of the movement in its early years. It scandalized opponents, who viewed the presence of women in conventicles as a cloak for female preaching and hence a violation of St. Paul's injunction (1 Corinthians 14:35) that "it is shameful for a woman to speak in church." Although Spener and Francke went to great lengths to deny this charge, Pietism was early on identified with women. The 1736 comedy *Pietism in Petticoats* (*Die Pietisterey im Fischbeinrocke*), an Enlightenment satire penned ironically by Luise Adelgunde Gottsched (wife of the Leipzig critic Johann Christoph Gottsched), ridiculed Pietism as a movement whose adherents were chiefly foolish and gullible women duped by theological charlatans and religious hypocrites.[20] Much later, Ernst Troeltsch also disparaged the affinity between Pietism and women when he observed that the movement lacked the "manly power" of Luther.[21]

Why this identification of Pietism and women? Pietism fostered the participation of women in Lutheran devotional life for the same reason it had elevated the role of the common people: by downplaying the cognitive dimensions of religious experience, it accorded a greater role to groups with limited access to formal education and positions of church leadership. Moreover, the chiliastic features of early Pietism by their very nature encouraged a suspension of standard criteria for validating religious experience. The fact that early Pietists viewed the circumstances of their age as exceptional, the prelude to the Last Judgment, served to legitimate the visions and prophecies of women claiming the inspiration of the Holy Spirit. These women could and did cite the testimony of the prophet Joel as quoted in the book of Acts (2:17–18): "In the last days it will be, God declares, that I will pour out my Spirit upon all flesh, and your sons and your daughters shall prophesy . . . . Even upon my slaves, both men and women, in those days I will pour out my Spirit."

The visibility of Pietist prophetesses reached its peak in the 1690s. The most celebrated examples were Anna Maria Schuchart of Erfurt, Magdalena Elrichs of Quedlinburg, and Katharina Reinecke of Halberstadt, the trio popularly known at the time as the "three enraptured maidens." Between 1691 and 1693 these women attracted attention and controversy throughout Protestant Germany for their religious visions, prophecies, and ecstasies. Katharina Reinecke of Halberstadt was renowned for her visions, while Anna Maria Schuchart's hour-long ecstasies included songs in which her otherwise thick Thuringian dialect unaccountably gave way to High German. Driven out of Erfurt, Schuchart fled to Halle and later emigrated to Pennsylvania with a separatist group. Magdalena Elrichs grew up in a poor neighborhood of Quedlinburg and had no education, but her religious visions reportedly attracted three hundred pilgrims and curiosity seekers to the town in one day.[22] All three women had close ties to the Pietist movement and usually experienced their visions and ecstasies in conventicles. As their self-appointed mentor, Francke at various times paid visits to all three, whom he initially hailed as signs that the Kingdom of God was near.[23] As we will later see, however, Francke and Spener would ultimately distance themselves from the female visionaries in their ranks.

Pietism and the Prussian Court

Spener and Francke arrived in Prussia in 1691, the former in the wake of his controversial tenure as court chaplain in Dresden, the latter as a refugee from the orthodox opposition he had aroused during his deaconate in Erfurt. That Prussia proved such a Pietist haven was largely due to the support of the Hohenzollern elector, Frederick I, and several of his leading advisers.[24] Frederick I was not a man of Pietist temperament, and his lavish building projects and extravagant court epitomized much of what the Pietists condemned. Like the Puritans, early Pietists like Spener criticized the luxury and ostentation of court and aristocratic life. Pietists also resembled Puritans in condemning other forms of sensual display, such as dancing and the stage, as sinful distractions. But Frederick's patronage of the Pietists was dictated more by politics than spiritual or cultural affinities. Although the Hohenzollerns had converted to Calvinism in the early seventeenth century, their subjects remained predominantly Lutheran. That the Hohenzollerns professed a religion at odds with that of most of their subjects does much to explain the dynasty's celebrated policies of religious toleration. These were motivated in part by a desire to attract colonists to Prussia's underpopulated central and eastern territories, but they also reflected the Hohenzollerns' own heterodox status in the monarchy. Ever since the Hohenzollerns had converted to Calvinism in 1613, confessional differences had been a major source of tension between the dynasty and the predominantly Lutheran territorial Estates. It was therefore in the interest of the Hohenzollerns to encourage a movement like Pietism that emphasized inward faith and compassion over divisive polemics. Although Frederick I was never able to win Pietist backing for his ecumenical efforts to unify the Calvinist and Lutheran confessions in his realm, Pietist calls for a more temperate tone in theological debates did serve the interests of a dynasty understandably wary of religious controversy.

The Hohenzollerns had other reasons for sponsoring a counterweight to Lutheran orthodoxy. In Brandenburg the established Lutheran church had close ties to the territorial nobility, whose rights of church patronage had been confirmed at the diet of 1653. The nobility had customarily controlled pastoral appointments and enjoyed those other privileges, properties, and incomes traditionally linked to their rights of patronage. The nobility likewise dominated the territorial Estates, which in the early eighteenth century still remained a potential source of opposition to Hohenzollern absolutism. This partnership between the established Lutheran church and the territorial Estates helps further explain the alliance that later developed between Hohenzollern absolutism and Prussian Pietism. To the Pietists, who themselves faced orthodox Lutheran opposition, an alliance with the monarchy against the territorial Estates made tactical sense. So, for example, in the territory of Magdeburg, where the Pietist stronghold of Halle was located, Francke staunchly supported the crown in its struggle with the Magdeburg Estates and their orthodox Lutheran allies. The monarchy, faced with potential opposition from the Estates, was for its part equally disposed to support the Pietists against their orthodox opponents.

Not long after their arrival in Prussia, Spener and Francke were able to secure the support of influential government officials like Eberhard von Danckelmann, a former tutor to the elector and now his leading adviser, and Veit Ludwig von Seckendorff, chancellor of the newly established University of Halle in 1691. As a cameralist committed to state action as a means of mobilizing the resources of society, Seckendorff looked favorably on the Pietist social gospel. It was largely through his intervention that Spener was able to secure the appointment of Francke to the Halle faculty.

Francke in fact devoted his primary energies not to his teaching but rather to his pastoral work. In Glaucha, an impoverished suburb of Halle where he served as a pastor, Francke embarked on an active campaign of moral and religious reform. He revived a town ordinance prohibiting dancing and tavern keeping on Sundays, and withheld communion from those who failed to heed his calls for reform. But Francke was convinced that the only real antidote to the moral depravity he found among the poor was education. In 1695 he founded in Halle the first of a series of schools destined to establish his reputation as one of the most influential educational reformers of the eighteenth century. Although originally aimed at children of the poor, the school soon gained such a reputation for piety and orderliness that artisans and even middle-class parents began enrolling their children there. Francke subsequently established a separate elementary school for the children of more prosperous families, and in 1701 he founded the orphanage destined to be widely emulated throughout Germany. Crowning Francke's educational complex was the *Pädagogium*, an elite boarding school for the children of prosperous nobles and burghers. To train teachers for positions in his various schools, Francke had in 1696 also established the first pedagogical seminar in the Holy Roman Empire. Pupils at this institute, the *Seminarium selectum praeceptorum,* were mainly poor theology students who received free meals at the orphanage in exchange for teaching at one of the schools in Francke's complex. Francke directly supervised their training and activities, and those who successfully completed their pedagogical apprenticeship received a permanent position at one of his schools.

By 1727, the year of Francke's death, his Halle schools contained more than 2,000 pupils and 175 teachers. The *Pädagogium* had become an elite establishment training prospective officers and civil servants, the orphanage a prototype for those established elsewhere in the empire in the eighteenth century, and the *Seminarium selectum praeceptorum* the basic model for teacher-training institutes established throughout Germany and Austria. Francke owed much of his success to the patronage of the court. By berating orthodox pastors for granting communion to "unreformed" parishioners excommunicated from his own parish, Francke became embroiled in bitter controversies with the local clergy of Halle. Only the continued support of the Prussian court protected Francke and his institutions from his opponents. Following the fall in 1697 of their chief patron, Eberhard von Danckelmann, the Pietists acquired an equally influential protector in Paul von Fuchs. As a privy councillor and supervisor of ecclesiastical and school affairs, Fuchs aided the Pietists in consolidating their position within Lutheran churches and schools. In 1702, for example, theology candidates teaching at Francke's *Pädagogium* were given official preference in all pastoral and parish-school appointments.

With Fuchs's death in 1704, however, opponents of Pietism within the Lutheran and Calvinist clergy took the offensive. They pinned their hopes on the well-known hostility of the young crown prince, Frederick William, toward the Pietists. Frederick William had blamed the mental collapse of his stepmother, Sophie Luise, on her Pietist leanings. Even worse, the military-minded crown prince suspected the Pietists of pacifism. His suspicions were not unfounded, since Francke had in numerous sermons condemned the brutalities of war. But Francke, aware of Frederick William's distrust, prudently abandoned his anti-militarist rhetoric, while the appointment of Pietist chaplains helped to forge ties between the movement and the Prussian officer corps. By the time Frederick William acceded to the Prussian throne in 1713, his initial antagonism to the Pietists had dissolved. With his simple and spartan personal habits, the king shared a certain temperamental affinity with the movement. Both had a puritanical distaste for ostentation and had disapproved of the extravagance of Frederick I's court. Pietists applauded the austerity measures that Frederick William I imposed on the court at his accession, and the practical-minded king was for his part delighted with the blend of piety and discipline he found during a tour of the Halle orphanage. The king now enthusiastically embraced the Pietist movement, installing Francke as rector at Halle and requiring that every pastoral candidate study at least four semesters at Halle or Königsberg. Since Pietists were occupying virtually every theological chair at those universities by the 1720s, Frederick's requirement gave them de facto control over admission to the Lutheran pastorate. By this time, as Mary Fulbrook has written, "Pietism had become established as the new orthodoxy of Brandenburg-Prussia."[25]

Under Frederick II (1740–1786), it is true, Pietist pastors and theologians lost the monopoly on pastoral positions and theology chairs they had enjoyed under Frederick William I. Yet it is telling that Frederick, for all his apparent hostility to the Pietists, continued to entrust to them responsibility for schooling his subjects. The *General-Landschul-Reglement* of 1763, the edict issued by Frederick in an attempt to establish a uniform system of compulsory schooling for all children between the ages of five and thirteen, was largely the work of the Pietist pedagogue Johann Julius Hecker (1707–1768).[26] A graduate of Francke's *Seminarium selectum praeceptorum* and a former teacher at the Halle *Pädagogium*, Hecker was the leading pedagogical reformer of Frederick's reign. As a Berlin pastor and later an influential member of the Supreme Consistory (the body responsible for the ordination of Lutheran pastors and the supervision of Lutheran churches and parish schools), Hecker established in the 1740s and 1750s an educational complex in Berlin modeled on that of Francke's in Halle. Just before his death in 1768 Hecker was

English translation of Francke's *Nicodemus.*[28] Francke corresponded with Cotton Mather of Harvard College, who in turn donated several of Francke's works to the Harvard library and contributed financially to the Pietist orphanage in Halle. Devotional writings circulating in Württemberg conventicles of the late seventeenth century included Jansenist works imported from France, and Nikolaus Ludwig von Zinzendorf, founder of the Pietist colony in Herrnhut (Saxony), was both an admirer of French Jansenism as well as a friend of John Wesley.

Second, if Pietism was not exclusively German in its theological origins and influence, neither was it unreservedly absolutist in its politics. To be sure, by the early eighteenth century Prussian Pietism had cast its lot with the Hohenzollern dynasty. But little in the early history of Pietism suggests that an alliance with territorial absolutism was inevitable. Saxony, still the leading Protestant territory in the empire when Pietism emerged in the 1670s, is a case in point. Spener's tenure in Saxony was difficult and his relationship with the Saxon elector was far from congenial, while Francke ultimately left the territory after the Dresden court sided against him in his struggles with Leipzig's orthodox establishment. Despite the cozy relationship they later developed with the Hohenzollern court, early Pietists had been critical of their church's excessive dependence on territorial princes. They feared that this reliance on princely power had hardened the church both theologically and institutionally, closing it off from the spontaneous spiritual impulses that had fueled the Reformation in the first place.

The most compelling case for the absence of any necessary connection between Pietism and the rise of territorial absolutism was the duchy of Württemberg. Pietism began to make headway in the duchy during the 1680s, when the first conventicles appeared and disciples of Spener among the Württemberg clergy began calling for improvements in church discipline and education. As in Prussia, the rise of Pietism in Württemberg coincided with efforts by the territorial ruler to expand his political and administrative prerogatives at the expense of the Estates. But in contrast with Prussia, the relationship of Pietism to the Württemberg court was more oppositional in character.

The difference lay in the fact that the balance of political forces was very different in the two territories: while the Württemberg Estates, as in Prussia, were closely associated with the territorial church, their position vis-à-vis the territorial ruler was stronger than that of the *Stände* in Brandenburg Prussia. Because the relatively secure political position of the established church in Württemberg allowed it to be more tolerant and flexible in its relations with the Pietist movement, the relationship between Pietism and the Estates was never as antagonistic in Württemberg as it was in Prussia.[29] Pietist pastors and theologians in Württemberg were incorporated relatively smoothly into the territorial church, even if they never had the kind of institutional power that Prussian Pietists came to wield under Frederick William I.

All of this was to have important political consequences in the early eighteenth century, when efforts by Duke Eberhard Ludwig (1692–1733) to build a standing army and curb the consultative powers of the Estates heightened political tensions. Here the Pietists, who among other things were critical of the Duke's lavish court and open cohabitation with his mistress, joined forces with the Estates in opposing ducal policies. These tensions subsided somewhat following the Treaty of Utrecht (1713), which reduced military pressures on the territory and for the moment defused the issue of the standing army. Despite continued efforts at ducal absolutism under Karl Alexander (1733–1737) and his mercurial successor, Karl Eugen (1737–1793), the financial needs of the court forced it repeatedly to compromise with the Estates and thereby temper its "sporadic despotism."[30] As a consequence, the Württemberg Estates succeeded throughout the eighteenth century in preserving the duchy's dualist constitutional structure—an achievement that led Charles James Fox, the radical Whig, to declare in the late eighteenth century that Württemberg and Great Britain were the only European polities with a genuine constitution.[31] Inner-churchly Pietism, which won formal toleration in the *Reskript* of 1743, remained tied to the cause of the Estates even if most mainstream Pietists shunned an activist political role.

Beginning in the 1780s, a more radical and "popular" Pietism emerged that would quickly overshadow the traditionalist, inner churchly variant that had dominated up to then. This new brand of

Pietism was the fruit of a century-long process of diffusion whereby Pietist ideas and devotional practices penetrated from the more urban and educated classes of the territory to the rural population of peasant smallholders, weavers, and artisans. The spread of Pietist-sponsored schooling and Pietist devotional literature throughout the countryside encouraged this process (see below). So did the rapid expansion of rural commodity production (above all linen-weaving) during the last two decades of the century, which made religious literature increasingly affordable to the proto-industrial households who benefited from rising prosperity.[32] This popular, grass-roots Pietism found expression in the formation of conventicles, which were increasingly independent from, if not in outright opposition to, the local parish church. This separatist dynamic accelerated under the impact of the French Revolution, which stimulated millenarian predictions of the Last Days and paralleled the spread of political radicalism in the duchy.

Exemplifying this development was the journeyman weaver and self-styled prophet from the village of Iptingen, Johann Georg Rapp (1757–1847).[33] During his youth Rapp's religious interests had been stimulated by visits to a conventicle sponsored by his Pietist pastor, Friedrich Christian Göz. During a stay in Tübingen in 1785, the young journeyman experienced an "awakening" in the conventicle of Johann Michael Hahn, a butcher and farm laborer who by this time had developed a sizable following as a wandering preacher.[34] After Rapp returned to Iptingen he and his wife Christina separated themselves from the local church, and Rapp began to hold Sunday morning devotional assemblies in his home. In line with the duchy's well-established tradition of toleration, the ecclesiastical authorities investigated Rapp but initially responded to his provocations with relatively mild admonitions. The patience of the authorities was tested further when some of Rapp's followers, now convinced that the established church was the Whore of Babylon, withdrew their children from the local parish school and others refused to have their children baptized in the local church. These actions led to more detailed investigations in 1787, but the Stuttgart consistory continued to counsel patience and sympathy.[35] No direct action was taken against Rapp until 1791, when the Stuttgart consistory sentenced him and one of his followers to forty-eight hours in jail for having made allegedly blasphemous statements about the church and the sacraments.[36] The punishment had no visible effect, however, and Rapp's influence in the surrounding region continued to grow throughout the 1790s.

Rapp had by this time come to believe that the Second Coming of Christ was imminent, and that he and his followers had been called upon to order their lives in accordance with the state of Adam before the fall. He also espoused ideals of communally held property and forbade his followers from entering military service. By 1800 his followers were numbered in the thousands, and the authorities grew increasingly concerned as political unrest spread throughout the duchy. Rapp himself saw Napoleon as an instrument of divine justice, and it was reported that some of his followers greeted each other with the words, "Praise God and his son Bonaparte."[37] Although the evidence suggests that Rapp and his followers were fundamentally nonpolitical and loyal to the duke, the spread of political unrest in the Württemberg countryside made the movement increasingly suspect in the eyes of church and government authorities. A church report from the nearby village of Knittlingen, which in 1800 had been a center of revolutionary unrest, claimed that in 1803 Rapp had recently preached to an assembly of hundreds in a nearby brick factory, and that those unable to crowd into the building had removed its doors and windows in order to hear his sermon. With memories of Knittlingen's earlier tumult fresh in mind, the report compared Rapp and his followers with the peasants of 1525–26 and the Münster Anabaptists of 1534–35.[38] The Knittlingen report sparked yet another investigation, which resulted in a more stringent ducal decree requiring Rapp and his followers to baptize their children and send them to school.[39]

By this time, however, Rapp had fled the duchy for the United States, he and followers having come to believe that they were the incarnation of the Sunwoman of the Apocalypse—the figure described in Revelation 12:6 who "fled into the wilderness, where she hath a place prepared by God." Over the next three decades they established a series of model religious communities in western Pennsylvania and Indiana that were to play a central role in the history of nineteenth-century utopian socialism. The most famous was New Harmony, the highly successful proto-industrial community established by Rapp and his followers in Indiana on the banks of the Wabash River. New Harmony would of course later be the site of Robert Owen's famous if ill-fated utopian community. The British industrialist and social reformer first learned of Rapp and his community from an 1812 travel account and viewed them as proof that communitarian principles could be put into practice.[40] After corresponding with Rapp in 1820, Owen began negotiating with him through American agents for the purchase of the settlement. Rapp, who by this time had decided to move his community back to Pennsylvania, agreed to the sale and left with his followers in 1824 to establish the settlement of Economy some eighteen miles south of Pittsburgh. The mismanagement and internecine squabbles that led to the failure of Owen's utopian experiment are well known, but Economy proved yet another success story for Rapp and his disciples.[41] The community prospered more than a half century after its founder's death (1847) and inspired subsequent communitarian experiments, including John Humphrey Noyes's utopian-socialist Oneida community in upstate New York. In his *History of American Socialisms* (1870), Noyes went so far as to call the Rappites the "pioneers of modern Socialism."[42]

Pietism and the Public Sphere

The vicissitudes of Pietism in the Old and New Worlds point to the dangers of associating the movement with any particular political tendency. Pietism was at best ambiguous in its political implications. As the contrasting examples of inner churchly Pietism in Prussia and Württemberg illustrate, the extent to which Pietism was supportive of or antagonistic to the rise of territorial absolutism depended less on the movement's own ideas about politics and government than it did on the particular constellation of political, social, and church relations in which it arose in any given territory. In the case of the Harmonists, we saw how the millenarian strain in Pietism could produce a movement which, if not self-consciously political in its aims, could nonetheless become an inspiration for early socialist thought in Europe and America.

Another dimension of early Pietism also raises questions about the tendency to view Pietism as implicitly conservative and quietist. That is its relationship to the Enlightenment public sphere. As elaborated by Jürgen Habermas, the concept of the public sphere is by now well known to students of eighteenth-century political culture. Since Habermas's *Structural Transformation of the Public Sphere* first appeared in German in 1962, it has informed and enriched virtually every field of early modern German scholarship.[43] Translated into French and English more than twenty years after its original publication, Habermas's study has during the past decade profoundly influenced not only historical scholarship outside Germany but also fields ranging from political theory and literary studies to art history and feminist theory. Habermas's model has attracted its share of criticism, some of it compelling, some of it less so. Critics have generally focused on his lack of concern for questions of gender and his failure to treat alternative forms of "sub-bourgeois" public space.[44]

What concerns us here is another historical dimension, that of religion, which receives adequate attention neither in Habermas's study nor in the scholarship it has inspired.[45] Habermas's public sphere was a secular phenomenon, rooted economically in the triumph of capitalism, socially in the rise of the bourgeois family, and philosophically in the Enlightenment. But as I argue below, aspects of Pietist devotional ideals and practices in the late seventeenth and early eighteenth centuries suggest another genealogy as well, for they were in various ways paradigmatic of the communicative model that Habermas associates with the more secular transformations of the eighteenth century.

As Habermas argued, the public sphere of the Enlightenment rested to a considerable degree on the explosion of print culture that occurred during the eighteenth century. In Germany, Pietism fueled this phenomenon in two ways. First, the bitter debates that raged between early Pietists and their orthodox Lutheran critics significantly broadened the audience for religious debate in late seventeenth- and early eighteenth-century Germany.[46] This controversy, which began in the 1670s and did not fade in intensity until the 1720s, generated more than 2,000 books and pamphlets, some of them in print runs of two to three thousand.[47]

Pietism further contributed to the expanding world of eighteenth-century print through its vigorous promotion of a literate devotional culture. Historians have long associated Protestantism with print, both as an effect and a cause of an expanding print culture. They usually note, for example, how Luther's Biblicism sanctioned the promotion of popular literacy by emphasizing the indispensability of lay Bible reading. In fact, we now know that Luther and other Protestant reformers were deeply ambivalent about the wisdom of making the Scriptures accessible to the laity.[48] The rise of sectarianism in the 1520s had convinced many church leaders of the need to restrict and control lay Bible reading, and they preferred instead to rely on the catechism as a safer means of inculcating the articles of faith.

It was not until the late seventeenth century, when Pietist reformers began actively promoting the diffusion of Bibles and devotional manuals, that distrust and ambivalence gave way to an unequivocal endorsement of lay Bible reading.[49] Spener's *Pia Desideria* had declared that every head of a household should own a copy of the Bible and read from it aloud as part of the family's private devotionals.[50] Francke, as pastor of the *Augustinerkirche* in Erfurt, held Bible classes after the Sunday worship service, and during his brief tenure there (1690–91) distributed some nine hundred copies of the New Testament to his parishioners.[51] In 1712 the founding of a Pietist printing press in Halle by an associate of Francke, Carl Hildebrand von Canstein, later made possible the publication of thousands of inexpensive editions of the Scriptures. Fifteen years after its establishment, the Canstein press had published more than 400,000 Bibles and New Testaments and become one of the world's leading distribution centers of religious literature.[52] Württemberg Pietism had nothing to compare with the Canstein publishing house, but there too the movement was important in promoting the spread of inexpensive

Bibles and devotional manuals. In 1704, for example, a Pietist-sponsored edition of the New Testament appeared in Stuttgart that sold for just ten Kreutzer—considerably less than the daily wage (fourteen Kreutzer) of a vineyard laborer and affordable, indeed, when one considers that the cost of a Bible in Luther's day was roughly half of what a peasant paid for a cow.[53]

The Pietist sponsorship of inexpensive Bibles and other religious works fostered a devotional culture more oriented toward print and the ownership of books. Hans Medick's study of Laichingen, a linen-weaving village in southwestern Württemberg, has shown just how deeply this Pietist culture had seeped into rural culture by the middle of the eighteenth century. Taking issue with Rolf Schenda's contention that most rural households in Germany had little contact with the book prior to the nineteenth century,[54] Medick's analysis of 557 household inventories between 1748 and 1820 found that almost a hundred percent of Laichingen households owned at least one book. Even poor, day-laborer households in Laichingen owned an average of nine to ten books—one of them contained fifty-four at the owner's death in 1786. These books were overwhelmingly religious in nature and testify to the spread of Pietism among the rural population of the duchy. Sixty percent of the inventories investigated by Medick, for example, contained at least one work by Arndt, and 57 percent contained a tract written by the Frankfurt Pietist Johann Friedrich Starck. Overall, Medick describes a village devotional culture that by the late eighteenth century had been thoroughly penetrated by the book, a world in which rural parishioners carried their Bibles and hymnals with them to Sunday worship and read Pietist tracts as part of their household devotional exercises.[55]

The Pietist promotion of primary schooling, both in towns and in the countryside, doubtless helped contribute to the spread of this literate devotional culture. Francke's complex of schools in Halle was mentioned earlier, and these were to inspire subsequent school edicts in Prussia (1717, 1736, 1763–65) and Württemberg (1729). What was notable about these Pietist-inspired reforms was not their attempt to make schooling compulsory—such efforts date back to the Reformation—but rather their active promotion of literacy.

Unlike earlier school edicts, which had placed primary emphasis on the oral memorization of the catechism, these later reforms made lay Bible reading an explicit goal. It was in this spirit that Frederick William I paid for the distribution of thousands of Bibles in East Prussian schools "so that the Word of God will be known to all my subjects."[56]

Pietism, then, contributed to the expanding print culture of the eighteenth century through the polemical wars it provoked and its efforts to foster a more literate devotional culture. But the Enlightenment public sphere as described by Habermas entailed more than just the expansion of print. It rested on new modes of sociability and communication, and here, too, analogies with Pietism deserve emphasis. In particular I now want to explore some of the homologies between Pietist devotional practices and the model of sociability which, according to Habermas, informed the communicative practices of the Enlightenment public sphere.

A defining feature of early Pietism, and certainly the most controversial as far as its contemporary critics were concerned, was the conventicle. Conventicles were lay devotional gatherings that usually met in private homes, sometimes but not necessarily with the pastor present. To understand why the Pietist conventicle proved so controversial and how it foreshadowed aspects of the Enlightenment public sphere, it is useful to look more closely at Spener's description of the Frankfurt conventicle (later known as the Collegium Pietatis, with which he was associated during most of his tenure as senior pastor in the city from 1666 to 1686).

In August 1670 several laymen in the city approached Spener about the possibility of holding small, informal devotional meetings outside of the church.[57] These men, for the most part university educated and of patrician background, expressed to Spener their desire for a place and an occasion outside of church where they could converse and enjoy fellowship free of the profanity, drunkenness, and sinful behavior they found rampant in the social life of the city. Spener welcomed the suggestion, and the group began meeting on Sunday and Monday evenings in his private study (the Sunday meetings were subsequently moved to Wednesdays). Some time later two women (also of patrician backgrounds), Anna Elisabeth Kissner and the widow Maria Juliana Baur von Eyseneck, joined the group.

Meetings opened with a prayer, followed by a reading from the Scriptures or a devotional tract.[58] Members were then free to discuss the implications of the reading for their daily conduct as Christians, or to voice disagreements about its proper interpretation as long as they avoided the contentiousness and theological hair-splitting that Spener so disliked in the Lutheran scholasticism of his day. Spener also favored the practice of *Predigkritik*, which encouraged participants to discuss and even raise objections to the sermon preached on the previous Sunday. Viewing the conventicle as a vehicle for spiritual reform—both of the clergy and of the laity—Spener welcomed specific suggestions on how abuses in the church could be eliminated and sinful behavior among the laity discouraged.

Spener's Frankfurt conventicle soon expanded from a small and exclusive discussion group into a larger, more heterogeneous assembly. By the end of 1670 the conventicle had grown to between fifteen and twenty participants, and by 1675 some fifty members comprised the group.[59] Before long it had also become a target of his orthodox Lutheran critics. Conventicles were not a Pietist invention: in his preface to the *German Mass* (1526) Luther himself supported in principle the formation of private, voluntary devotional gatherings outside the church as a means of fostering lay piety and discipline. He stopped short, however, of putting the idea into practice, believing that conditions were too unstable and leadership too scarce for the conventicle to be an effective agent of reform. But the idea reemerged in Strassburg during the 1540s, where, partly though the encouragement of Martin Bucer, various lay groups established conventicles to offer instruction in the catechism and provide an occasion for lay devotion and discussion. Distrusted by more cautious Protestant leaders in the city as a potential source of separatism, the Strassburg conventicles were outlawed in 1550.[60] Although variants of the conventicle could be found elsewhere in the Friday "congregations" of Calvinist Geneva and the "prophesyings" of English Puritans, Lutheran churches on the whole continued to frown upon devotional assemblies taking place outside of formal worship.[61]

This disapproval explains why Spener's conventicle seemed such a dangerous innovation to his orthodox critics, who attacked it on three grounds. First, they claimed that the very autonomy of the conventicle undermined the authority of the clergy and was a recipe for separatism—a fear, by the way, that proved justified in 1677 when several of its founding members split to form a separate group meeting at the home of Maria Juliana Baur von Eyseneck. The separatist dynamic accelerated when members of the Eyseneck conventicle began boycotting the Eucharist.[62] Second, as mentioned earlier, orthodox critics condemned the active participation of women in the conventicle as a violation of Pauline injunctions against female preaching. Not only did men and women mix in an inappropriate way, they charged; even common maidservants were allowed to voice their opinions and some even stood on tables to preach to the gathering.[63] Moreover, to these critics Spener's conventicle subverted relationships of authority by giving women an alternative focus of loyalty outside of church and household. Spener paraphrased this criticism as follows: "There are women and serving girls who in their separate meetings preach for hours and attack the clergy [*ministerio*] in all sorts of ways. All of this is dangerously unsettling . . . to the public good [*dem gemeinen Wesen*], to the church, and to the household, because women become less inclined to obey their husbands or care for their households, and servants less inclined to obey their lords."[64]

Spener's defense of conventicles offers a glimpse into their discursive tone and structure. He describes the atmosphere of his Frankfurt conventicle as informal, spontaneous, and conversational: "We did not observe any special order among us, or find it necessary to prescribe when one or another person should speak or address the group. Instead we conversed as one would among friends, so that whoever wanted to speak could do so and when one person was finished speaking, another who had something to say picked up the conversation, either elaborating on or confirming what was said, or voicing a different opinion."[65] Spener then went on to highlight the social heterogeneity of his conventicle: "In the beginning the group was small and consisted for the most part of learned individuals.

Now, however, all sorts of people from various ranks attend: learned and unlearned, noble and non-noble, students of theology, jurists, physicians, merchants, artisans, unmarried people. No one need petition me or others for permission to attend, and as many may come as my admittedly narrow quarters can accommodate."[66]

Spener's description contains several essential elements of public-sphere ideology that Habermas associated with Enlightenment sociability. One was the voluntary and open nature of conventicle membership: individuals joined freely and regardless of rank. Another was the intimacy, spontaneity, and conversational tone that according to Spener characterized the meetings. "We spoke as one might do among friends," and in contrast with the formal, monological style of the sermon, the communicative structure of the conventicle was that of a spontaneous, unstructured dialogue between equals. Moreover, just as Habermas's public sphere represented a realm of sociability and discussion interposed between the political and disciplinary authority of the state and the private family, so did the conventicle occupy an intermediate, relatively autonomous realm of sociability interposed between the theological and disciplinary authority of the clergy and the private devotional setting of the Christian household. Although the communicative content and contexts of these two realms were quite different, both occupied structurally analogous positions relative to the disciplinary authority of the state or clergy on the one hand and the private household on the other. In this respect, both can be considered paradigmatic of the new model of civil society that Habermas associated with the Enlightenment public sphere.

Like Habermas's enlightened public sphere, furthermore, the conventicle was conceived by Spener as a vehicle for criticism and reform.[67] Convinced that Lutheran churches had failed to fulfill the spiritual promise of the Reformation, Spener and the Pietists blamed the church establishment itself—above all the aridity and sterility of Lutheran scholastic theology—for the lukewarm state of religious faith they found among the laity. Hence spiritual reform and renewal had to originate from below, among the laity, a position Spener defended by invoking Luther's doctrine of the priesthood of all believers. Spener argued that because indeed all Christians were called upon to preach the Word, and because the pastor alone could not possibly tend to all the needs of his congregation, the conventicle was an invaluable means through which the priesthood of believers (*geistliches Priestertum*) could serve one another's spiritual needs.[68] Here Spener also viewed the conventicle as a form of lay "public opinion" that could publicize abuses and propose reform. For this reason he deemed it useful for pastors to participate, not so much in a supervisory and regulatory capacity, but in order to familiarize themselves more effectively with the needs and opinions of their flock.

Moreover, as with the salons, coffeehouses, and reading clubs that Habermas associates with the enlightened public sphere, the Pietist conventicle was an important vehicle for the reception and diffusion of the printed word. Throughout Protestant Germany, conventicles were information networks through which Pietist works were read, discussed, and publicized among a broader audience. University students, traditionally a mobile stratum in Germany, were especially important as agents of diffusion. By the early eighteenth century something akin to a "grand tour" had developed for Pietist students, for whom a pilgrimage to centers of the movement like Halle or the Harz towns of Wernigerode and Quedlinburg had become obligatory. Here the visitor customarily attended a local conventicle and perhaps learned of a recently published Pietist devotional manual, or, conversely, circulated a copy of a Pietist pamphlet unfamiliar to the group. The personal contacts and friendships growing out of these meetings in turn stimulated networks of written correspondence throughout Protestant Germany. Private letters were a favored Pietist medium, and these also served as an important vehicle through which Pietist literature was discussed and advertised. These epistolary networks served a function similar to that of book reviews later in the eighteenth century, since it was often through personal letters that one learned about the latest devotional tract or polemical debate. Johann Heinrich Reitz's *Historie der Wiedergeborenen* (History of the Reborn, 1st ed. 1698–1703), a Pietist best-seller written by a former Spener student, owed its broad distribution and spectacular publishing success to such informal marketing networks.[69]

Finally, just as the issue of women's participation in the Enlightenment public sphere revealed the limits of its inclusionary claims, so did the controversy over the visibility of women in conventicles underscore Spener's own ambivalence about the role of women in the religious life of the community. Stung by the charge that his conventicle was a forum for female preaching, Spener denied that the women who attended violated St. Paul's admonitions in 1 Corinthians 14 and 1 Timothy 2. Although he acknowledged the presence of "many Christian wives and maidens" in his conventicle, he insisted that "they are separated from the others—so that while they may listen they cannot be seen. Nor are they allowed to speak or to ask questions, and in fact none of them have ever tried to do so."[70] Here one suspects he protests too much: by Spener's own account his quarters were cramped, and it stretches the imagination to think that the "many Christian wives and maidens" in attendance could have been so easily segregated from the rest of the assembly. Moreover, the subsequent history of Spener's conventicle suggests that women played a much more active role than Spener let on. As mentioned earlier, the splinter group that seceded from Spener's conventicle in 1677 held its meetings at the home of a woman, Maria Juliana Baur von Eyseneck. Its other members included Johanna Eleonore von Merlau, who would later become the wife of the radical Pietist Johann Wilhelm Petersen.[71]

Conventicles were in fact the primary vehicle for female participation in the Pietist movement. The conventicle accorded women a devotional space outside the narrowly circumscribed world of family and household on the one hand, and the Pauline proscriptions that governed the institutional church on the other. As such it gave women access to the larger, predominantly masculine world of theological discourse, much like salons of the eighteenth century gave women a point of entry into the Enlightenment Republic of Letters.[72] During the 1690s, when female chiliasts and prophetesses reached the height of their visibility in the Pietist movement, the conventicle was often the stage for their ecstatic experiences and visions. The accessibility of conventicles encouraged some women to form their own, usually with separatist consequences. The Eyseneck conventicle in Frankfurt evolved in this way, as did the notorious sect founded by Eva Margaretha von Buttlar (1670–1721) in the 1710s.

Buttlar, the daughter of a Hessian noble, had at the age of fifteen married a Huguenot refugee who served as a tutor and *Tanzmeister* at the Saxon-Eisenach court in Thuringia.[73] In 1697 she began attending a Pietist conventicle in the neighboring town of Gotha, where a dramatic conversion experience led her to withdraw from the social and devotional life of the court. Her refusal to attend worship services or take communion soon led to her banishment from the Eisenach court, and in 1699 she left her husband (from whom she would be formally divorced in 1705) and settled in the Hessian town of Eschwege. By that time Pietism had made significant inroads into Hesse, and in Eschwege Buttlar became involved with a separatist group that was soon gathering at her home in the nearby town of Allendorf an der Werra for devotional exercises. Her conventicle, whose meetings often lasted late into the night and sparked rumors of sexual impropriety, aroused the hostility of local citizens. In 1701 this antagonism forced Buttlar and some seventy followers to flee. In the ensuing years the group wandered throughout central Germany.

The sect, which called itself the "Mother Eva Society" (*Sozietät der Mutter Eva*) but was known to its enemies as the "Buttlar Gang" (*Buttlarsche Rotte*), attracted notoriety and persecution because of its alleged sexual profligacy. The group claimed to be the first manifestation of the millennium and venerated Mother Eva, her common-law husband, Justus Gottfried Winter, and their adopted son Appenfeller (whom Eva later married after Winter's death) as incarnations of the Holy Trinity. Males were initiated into the society through a ritual that involved sleeping with Mother Eva, while the female initiate submitted to an operation in which Winter inserted his hand into her vagina and crushed her uterus. Members described these practices as rituals of sexual purification; horrified contemporaries understandably had their doubts and viewed them as a cover for sexual license. Remarkably, however, despite repeated arrests, Mother Eva always managed to escape her captors. In 1705 she and the remnants of her group fled to Cologne, where they converted to

Catholicism and then settled in Lügde (an enclave of the Paderborn cathedral chapter). There the group established its own, quasi-Catholic hierarchy and rituals and once again fell afoul of the authorities. She and her remaining followers finally found a safe haven in Altona, long a harbor for Mennonites and other radical Protestant sects, where Mother Eva lived out the remainder of her life in relative peace—though not before giving birth to her first and only child at the age of forty-three. She swore under oath that it was the child of her deceased husband, who had died thirteen months earlier.

The "Buttlar Gang" was a source of considerable embarrassment to inner-churchly Pietists. Francke condemned the sect as "filth" and even radical Pietists like Johann Wilhelm Petersen expressed outrage over "this evil enterprise."[74] Enemies of Pietism were quick to brand Buttlar and her followers as nothing more than Pietist chickens coming home to roost, and these critics had a point. The Pietist conventicle was conducive to radical-separatist movements by virtue of its relative autonomy and its function as an arena of open theological discussion. By giving women a more active and public role in devotional life, furthermore, the conventicle was a kind of associational incubator out of which self-styled prophetesses and visionaries could emerge.

Worried that the visibility of female chiliasts made the Pietist movement vulnerable to the attacks of its enemies, Spener and Francke had already in 1692 begun to distance themselves from the visionary women in their midst.[75] This disassociation was part of a general retreat from the chiliastic tendencies that had earlier marked the Pietist movement. It coincided with the arrival of Spener and Francke in Berlin, where the two now hoped to secure the patronage of the Hohenzollern court, and doubtless reflected a desire to give the movement greater respectability.

Theologically, this shift was reflected in Francke's efforts during the same period to elaborate a psychology of conversion that implicitly downgraded the ecstatic dimensions of religious experience.[76] Francke increasingly came to believe that conversion did not generally occur instantaneously in a moment of sudden illumination and inspiration. It was rather a more gradual process, occurring in distinct stages and states of mind. Here Francke viewed the conversion experience (*Bekehrung*) as an intense grappling with the self, a prolonged inner conflict that accompanied the "atonement struggle" (*Busskampf*). The resolution of this struggle came less through a dramatic, revelatory moment than it did through a gradual process of spiritual self-discipline in which the believer acquired a self-denying, passive trust in providence. Francke in effect domesticated the conversion experience by situating it existentially in the trials and labors of everyday life, rather than in the extraordinary and exceptional realm of visions and prophecies.

This shift was important. In political terms, first of all, Francke's model of conversion was an expression of Prussian Pietism's successful accommodation with Hohenzollern absolutism. The emphasis on self-discipline, self-control, and the passive acceptance of divine will was much more in line with the Hohenzollern project of state-building than the millenarian visions and prophecies of cobblers and serving women. Second, by viewing conversion as more of a quotidian process than an exceptional event, Francke's model effectively divested visionary women of the spiritual status they had come to acquire in the Pietist movement by the 1690s. Francke's emphasis on passivity and self-denial idealized the obedient housewife and selfless mother. If she had a role outside the household it was not that of the prophetess who stirred conventicles with her visions and dreams, but rather that of the charitable benefactress who visited orphans and organized collections on behalf of the poor. Women continued to play a prominent role in Prussian Pietism, but their energies were increasingly channeled into work on behalf of the movement's renowned complex of charitable institutions.

This section has focused on the relationship between Pietism and the public sphere in homological rather than causal terms. That is to say, instead of arguing that Pietism was a "cause" of the public sphere, it examined structural similarities between the two. Was there in fact a causal link between the communicative model of early Pietism and that of the Enlightenment public sphere? Here Martin Gierl's dissertation on the Pietist controversy establishes such a link.[77] He argues that the Pietist critique of the disputational practices that had traditionally prevailed in Protestant theological faculties laid the basis for a new style of learned discourse and debate. As a tool of polemic theology (*Kontroverstheologie*) based on the scholastic syllogism, the disputation was an instrument of *Konfessionsbildung* whose function was preeminently disciplinary: it served to preserve the purity of doctrine by unmasking the heterodoxy of one's opponent. Much of the Pietist controversy centered around the disputation and the broader question of how theological debate should be conducted. For Spener the disputational style of Lutheran scholasticism was counterproductive, for it served to alienate one's opponents rather than to convince and convert them.[78] Later on, in 1727, the Pietist theologian Bernhard Walter Marperger echoed this view when he argued that the arena of theological debate should be a "court of persuasion" (*Überzeugungs-Amt*), not a "court of punishment" (*Straf-Amt*).[79] As with the Pietist conventicle, the communicative model was dialogical, a process of enlightenment rather than of judgment and condemnation.

The entry of Christian Thomasius into the debate reveals the point at which the Pietist critique of the theological disputation converged with early Enlightenment pleas for toleration. Thomasius, a luminary of the early *Aufklärung*, was not a theologian but a philosopher trained in the natural-rights theories of Pufendorf and Locke. But as a professor at Leipzig he defended the Pietists against their orthodox opponents, and used their critique of the scholastic disputation to develop a broader plea for toleration and for a more moderate, less acrimonious style of scholarly debate that sought consensus with, rather than condemnation of, one's opponent. Thomasius was also editor of one of the first German literary periodicals, the *Monatsgespräche* (1688–89). The very title—"Monthly Conversations"—is illustrative of the conversational and dialogical structure that also marked the Pietist conventicle, and it was to be a hallmark of Enlightenment journals and periodicals.[80]

The alliance of *Pietismus* and *Aufklärung* proved short-lived, of course, as later became evident in 1723 when the Pietist-dominated theological faculty at Halle succeeded in expelling Christian Wolff from his university chair. This incident helps account for why historians have more often than not viewed Pietism and the Enlightenment as antithetical movements. Gierl's analysis restores some of the connections between the two, and the case of the conventicle examined earlier shows further evidence of their affinity. In Habermas's case, it is indeed ironic that religion in general and the Pietists in particular are absent from his analysis. For the looming figure behind Habermas's philosophical model is none other than Immanuel Kant, himself the Prussian product of a deeply Pietist upbringing that influenced the Königsberg philosopher probably more than either he or Habermas would have cared to admit.

Notes

1. See Gerald Strauss, *Luther's House of Learning: Indoctrination of the Young in the German Reformation* (Baltimore: Johns Hopkins University Press, 1978), 268–308.

2. Bodo Nischan, *Prince, People, and Confession: The Second Reformation in Brandenburg* (Philadelphia: University of Pennsylvania Press, 1994), 81–110.

3. August Beck, *Ernst der Fromme, Herzog zu Sachsen-Gotha* (Weimar: Böhlau, 1865), 65; Hans Schneider, "Der radikale Pietismus im 18. Jahrhundert" in *Geschichte des Pietismus,* ed. Martin Brecht et al., vol. 2: *Der Pietismus im achtzehnten Jahrhundert* (Göttingen: Vandenhoeck & Ruprecht, 1995), 395.

4. See Hartmut Lehmann, *Pietismus und weltliche Ordnung in Württemberg vom 17. bis zum 20. Jahrhundert* (Stuttgart: W. Kohlhammer, 1969), 24–27.

5. On the role of the disputation in Protestant universities during the sixteenth and seventeenth centuries, see Martin Gierl, *Pietismus und Aufklärung. Theologische Polemik und die Kommunikationsreform der Wissenschaft am Ende des 17. Jahrhunderts* (Göttingen: Vandenhoeck & Ruprecht, 1997), 65–69, 125–45.

6. On Spener's early development see Johannes Wallmann, *Philipp Jakob Spener und die Anfänge des Pietismus* (Tübingen : J. C. B. Mohr, 1970), 50–81. In what follows I have also drawn on my discussion of Pietism in *Absolutism and the Eighteenth-Century Origins of Compulsory Schooling in Prussia and Austria* (Cambridge: Cambridge University Press, 1988), 24–32.

7. Between 1605 and 1740, the work went through ninety-five German editions. See Martin Brecht, "Das Aufkommen der neuen Frommigkeitsbewegung in Deutschland," in *Geschichte des Pietismus,* 1:149.

8. On Bayly see Horton Davies, *Worship and Theology in England,* 5 vols. (Princeton: Princeton University Press, 1975), 2:112–14.

9. Martin Brecht, "Philipp Jakob Spener, sein Programm and dessen Auswirkungen" in *Geschichte des Pietismus* 1:286–87.

10. See, for example, Luther's preface to Romans, in *D. Martin Luthers Werke. Kritische Gesamtausgabe. Die deutsche Bibel,* 12 vols. (Weimar: Böhlau, 1883–), 7:4–5.

11. Spener, *Die evangelischen Lebens-Pflichten,* 3d ed., 2 pts. (Frankfurt am Main, 1715), 1:71.

12. *Pia Desideria* (Frankfurt am Main: Johann David Zunner, 1680; repr. in Philipp Jakob Spener, *Schriften,* 1. Abt., Vol. 1, ed. Erich Beyreuther (Hildesheim and New York: G. Olms, 1979).

13. On this point see Carl Hinrichs, *Preussentum und Pietismus. Der Pietismus in Brandenburg-Preussen als religiös-soziale Reformbewegung* (Göttingen: Vandenhoeck & Ruprecht, 1971) , 11–12 .

14. On Francke's early career, see Ernest Stoeffler, *German Pietism during the Eighteenth Century* (Leiden: Brill, 1973), 1–7; and Hans Leube, *Orthodoxie and Pietismus* (Bielefeld: Luther-Verlag, 1975), 174–206.

15. "Gerichtliche Leipziger Protokoll" in August Hermann Francke, *Streitschriften,* ed. Erhard Peschke (*Texte zur Geschichte des Pietismus,* ed. K. Aland, et al., Abt. II: *August Hermann Francke. Schriften and Predigten,* ed. Erhard Peschke, Vol. 1 (Berlin and New York: W. de Gruyter, 1981), 36. This collection of documents was assembled by Christian Thomasius, Francke's Leipzig colleague and supporter, and published in Frankfurt am Main in 1691.

16. "Gerichtliches Leipziger Protokoll," 16–17; Martin Brecht, "August Hermann Francke and der Hallische Pietismus," in *Geschichte des Pietismus* 1:448.

17. Brecht, "Philipp Jakob Spener," 337.

18. Koppel S. Pinson, *Pietism as a Factor in the Rise of German Nationalism* (New York: Columbia University Press, 1934), 109.

19. Ibid., 110.

20. Luise Adelgunde Gottsched, *Pietism in Petticoats and Other Comedies,* translated with an introduction by Thomas Kerth and John R. Russell (Columbia, S.C.: Camden House, 1994), 1–72.

21. Ernst Troeltsch, "Leibnitz and die Anfänge des Pietismus," in *Protestantismus am Ende de 19. Jahrhunderts,* ed. C. Werckshagen (Berlin: Wartburg, n.d.), 370. On women and Pietism see Barbara Hoffmann, *Radikalpietismus um 1700. Der Streit um das Recht auf eine neue Gesellschaft* (Frankfurt and New York: Campus, 1996), and Ulrike Witt, *Bekehrung, Bildung, and Biographie: Frauen im Umkreis des halleschen Pietismus* (Halle: Max Niemeyer, 1996).

22. On the enraptured maidens see Witt, *Bekehrung,* 24–70.

23. Ibid., 37–38.

24. Much of what follows is taken from Brecht, "August Hermann Francke und der Hallische Pietismus," 497–501; Klaus Deppermann, *Der hallesche Pietismus und der preussische Staat unter Friedrich III (I)* (Göttingen: Vandenhoeck & Ruprecht, 1961), 40–74; and Melton, *Absolutism*, 32–38.

25. Mary Fulbrook, *Piety and Politics: Religion and the Rise of Absolutism in England, Württemberg, and Prussia* (Cambridge: Cambridge University Press, 1983), 169.

26. On Hecker and his schools see Melton, *Absolutism*, 50–57.

27. See for example Pinson, *Pietism As a Factor*, 33–62.

28. *The Journal of the Rev. John Wesley*, ed. Nehemiah Curnock, 8 vols. (London: R. Culley, 1909–16), 1:301. Wesley visited Francke in Halle in August 1738. Ibid., 2:58.

29. On this point see Lehmann, *Pietismus und weltliche Ordnung in Württemberg*, 61–62, and Fulbrook, *Piety and Politics*, 174–89.

30. The term is Hans Medick's—see his discussion of the peculiarities of Württemberg government in his *Weben und Überleben in Laichingen 1650–1900*. Veröffentlichungen des Max-Planck-Instituts fur Geschichte, 126 (Göttingen: Vandenhoeck & Ruprecht, 1996), 47. The most detailed political history of Württemberg during this period is James Allen Vann, *The Making of a State: Württemberg, 1593–1793* (Ithaca, N.Y.: Cornell University Press, 1984). See also Lehmann, *Pietismus und weltliche Ordnung in Württemberg*, 22–116; and Fulbrook, *Piety and Politics*, 66–75.

31. Ibid., 67.

32. On the expansion of linen-weaving in the Württemberg countryside during the 1780s and 1790s, see Medick, *Weben and Überleben*, chapters 1–2, and David Warren Sabean, *Property, Production, and Family in Neckarhausen 1700–1870* (Cambridge: Cambridge University Press, 1990), 49–50.

33. My discussion of Rapp and his movement has relied on the excellent source collection edited by Karl J. R. Arndt, *George Rapp's Separatists, 1700–1803: A Documentary History* (Worcester, Mass.: Harmony Society Press, 1980), and Arndt's separate study, *George Rapp's Harmony Society 1785–1847* (Philadelphia: University of Pennsylvania Press, 1965).

34. On Hahn see Lehmann, *Pietismus und weltliche Ordnung in Württemberg*, 139–42.

35. Report of 20 March 1787, in Arndt, *George Rapp's Separatists*, 93–94.

36. Consistory report of 8 February 1791, in Arndt, *George Rapp's Separatists*, 180–82.

37. Quoted in Arndt, *George Rapp's Harmony Society*, 44.

38. Report of Dean Krippendorf of Knittlingen to the Stuttgart consistory, 28 February 1803, in Arndt, *George Rapp's Separatists*, 329–30.

39. Decree of 27 December 1803, in Arndt, *George Rapp's Separatists*, 404–12.

40. J. F. C. Harrison, *Robert Owen and the Owenites in Britain and America: The Quest for the New Moral World* (London: Routledge and K. Paul, 1969), 53. On Owen and the Harmonists see also Anne Taylor, *Visions of Harmony: A Study in Nineteenth-Century Millenarianism* (Oxford: Clarendon Press, 1987), 1–97.

41. Harrison, *Robert Owen*, 182–92; Taylor, *Visions of Harmony*, 115–90.

42. John Humphrey Noyes, *History of American Socialisms* (Philadelphia: J. B. Lippincott & Co., 1870), 669.

43. Jürgen Habermas, *The Structural Transformation of the Public Sphere: An Inquiry into a Category of Bourgeois Society*, trans. Thomas Burger (Cambridge, Mass.: M.I.T. Press, 1989).

44. German edition (Darmstadt, 1990), 11–19. On Habermas's neglect of alternative public spheres, see Oskar Negt and Alexander Kluge, *Public Sphere and Experience: Toward an Analysis of the Bourgeois and Proletarian Public Sphere*, trans. Peter Labanyi, Jamie Owen Daniel, and Assenka Oksiloff (Minneapolis: University of Minnesota Press, 1993); and Geoff Eley, "Nations, Publics, and Political Cultures: Placing Habermas in the Nineteenth Century," in Craig Calhoun, ed., *Habermas and the Public Sphere* (Cambridge, Mass.: M.I.T. Press, 1992). His feminist critics include Nancy Fraser, "What's Critical about Critical Theory? The Case of Habermas and Gender," in *Feminism as Critique: On the Politics of Gender*, ed. Seyla Benhabib and Drucilla Cornell (Minneapolis: University of Minnesota Press, 1987); and Joan Landes, *Women and the Public Sphere in the Age of the French Revolution* (Ithaca: Cornell University Press, 1988)—but critics of Landes have responded that her work misreads both Habermas and the Enlightenment. See for example Dena Goodman, "Public Sphere and Private Life: Toward a Synthesis of Current Historiographical Approaches to the Old Regime," *History and Theory* 31 (1992); and Keith Baker, "Defining the Public Sphere in Eighteenth-Century France: Variations on a Theme by Habermas," in Calhoun, ed., *Habermas and the Public Sphere*.

45. David Zaret, "Religion, Science, and Printing in the Public Spheres in Seventeenth-Century England," in Calhoun, *Habermas and the Public Sphere*, 212–35. Zaret notes Habermas's neglect of religion in the English context.

46. On the Pietist controversy see Gierl, *Pietismus und Aufklärung*.

47. Ibid., 26. To understand just how exceptional such a print run was at this time, one can compare it to that of popular periodicals like August Ludwig Schlözer's *Briefwechsel meist historischen und politischen Inhalts*. Published much later (1776–82), Schlözer's *Briefwechsel* had a circulation of

approximately 4,400 and was the most widely circulated German periodical of its day. See Joachim Kirchner, *Das deutsche Zeitschriftenwesen. Seine Geschichte und seine Probleme,* 1 (Leipzig: K. W. Hiersemann, 1942), 200.

48. See Richard Gawthrop and Gerald Strauss, "Protestantism and Literacy in Early Modern Germany," *Past and Present,* 104 (1984).

49. Ibid., 43–44.

50. See Spener, *Pia Desideria,* 96–97.

51. Brecht, "August Hermann Francke and der Hallische Pietismus," 450.

52. Melton, *Absolutism,* 39–40.

53. Medick, *Weben und Überleben,* 491.

54. Rolf Schenda, *Volk ohne Buch: Studien zur Sozialgeschichte der populären Lesestoffe, 1770–1910* (Frankfurt am Main: V. Klostermann, 1970) .

55. See Medick, *Weben und Überleben,* 447–560.

56. Quoted in Melton, *Absolutism,* 48. On school reform in Württemberg see Medick, *Weben and Überleben,* 476–79.

57. My description of Spener's conventicle is based on his response to his orthodox Lutheran critics, *Sendschreiben an einen Christeyffrigen ausländischen Theologum, betreffende die falsche ausgesprengte Auflagen / wegen seiner Lehre / und so genanter Collegiorum pietatis, mit treulicher erzehlung dessen / was zu Franckfurth am Mayn in solcher gethan oder nicht gethan werde* (Frankfurt am Main: Johann David Zunner, 1677); repr. in Spener, *Schriften,* 1. Abt./Bd. 1: 44–82. I have supplemented my account with material provided in Werner Bellardi, *Die Vorstufen der Collegia Pietatis bei Philipp Jakob Spener* (Giessen: Brunnen, 1994), 1–17 (a reprint of the author's 1930 Breslau dissertation), and Wallmann, *Philipp Jakob Spener und die Anfänge des Pietismus,* 253–74. See also Udo Sträter, *Meditation und Kirchenreform in der lutherischen Kirche des 17. Jahrhunderts* (Tübingen : J. C. B. Mohr, 1995), 156–66. I would also like to thank Jonathan Strom, my Emory colleague in the Candler School of Theology, for helpful suggestions and insights.

58. A favorite text was a German translation of Bayly's *Practice of Piety.* See Wallmann, *Philipp Jakob Spener und die Anfänge des Pietismus,* 50–81.

59. Ibid., 275; Martin Brecht, "Philipp Jakob Spener, sein Programm and dessen Auswirkungen," in *Geschichte des Pietismus,* 1:298.

60. On the prehistory of the Pietist conventicle, see Bellardi, *Vorstufen der Collegia Pietatis,* 32–72.

61. Brecht, "Philipp Jakob Spener," 295—although Wallmann cites some isolated instances of "Pre-Pietist" Lutheran conventicles in the seventeenth century. Spener himself mentions the conventicle of a certain Pastor Fischer in Amsterdam as the precedent for his *Collegium Pietatis.* See Wallmann, *Philipp Jakob Spener und die Anfänge des Pietismus,* 274, 269–70.

62. Wallmann, *Philipp Jakob Spener und die Anfänge des Pietismus*, 274ff.; Brecht, "Philipp Jakob Spener," 298–317.

63. Spener cites this charge in his *Sendschreiben*, 82.

64. Ibid., 78.

65. Ibid., 49–50.

66. Ibid., 62–63.

67. On this aspect of the conventicle see Markus Matthias, "Collegium pietatis and ecclesiola. Philipp Jakob Speners Reformprogramm zwischen Wirklichkeit und Anspruch," *Pietismus and Neuzeit* 19 (1993), 46–59.

68. Spener, *Pia Desideria*, 100–5. See also Spener, *Klagen über das verdorbene Christentum Missbrauch und rechter Gebrauch* (Frankfurt am Main: Johann David Zunner, 1685), repr. in Spener, *Schriften*, 1/4:188–89.

69. See Hans-Jürgen Schrader, *Literaturproduktion und Büchermarkt des radikalen Pietismus. Johann Heinrich Reitz' "Historie Der Wiedergebohren" und ihr geschichtlicher Kontext.* Palaestra, Bd. 283 (Göttingen: Vandenhoeck & Ruprecht, 1989), 245–50.

70. Spener, *Sendschreiben*, 62–63.

71. Brecht, "Philipp Jakob Spener," 298. William Penn visited the Eyseneck circle during his visit to Frankfurt in 1677, and one of its members, Francis Daniel Pastorius, emigrated with Penn to Pennsylvania to found the Quaker colony of Germantown. Ibid., 317.

72. On this aspect of eighteenth-century salons, see Dena Goodman, *The Republic of Letters: A Cultural History of the French Enlightenment* (Ithaca and London: Cornell University Press, 1994).

73. Here my account is based on the detailed study by Hoffmann, *Radikalpietismus um 1700*, 20–135. See also the brief sketch in Hans Schneider, "Der radikale Pietismus im 18. Jahrhundert," in *Geschichte des Pietismus* 2:133–35, and Willi Temme, "Die Buttlarsche Rotte—ein Forschungsbericht," *Pietismus und Neuzeit* 16 (1990), 53–75.

74. Temme, "Die Buttlarsche Rotte," 56; Schneider, "Der radikale Pietismus," 134.

75. Francke's growing ambivalence is documented in his *Entdeckung der Bossheit, so mit einigen jüngst unter seinem Nahmen fälschlich publicirten Brieffen von dreyen sobenahmten begeisterten Mägden zu Halberstadt / Quedlinburg und Erffurt begangen* (Cölln an der Spree: Jeremias Schrey, 1692), republished in Francke, *Streitschriften*, 147–59.

76. See Anthony J. La Vopa, *Grace, Talent, and Merit: Poor Students, Clerical Careers, and Professional Ideology in Eighteenth Century Germany* (Cambridge: Cambridge University Press, 1988), 137–64.

77. Gierl, *Pietismus und Aufklärung*.

78. See Spener's critique of theological "Streitsucht" in his *Pia Desideria*, 121.

79. Quoted in Gierl, *Pietismus und Aufklärung*, 321.

80. See Thomas Woitkewitsch, "Thomasius' 'Monatsgespräche': Eine Charakteristik," *Archiv für Geschichte des Buchwesens* 10 (1970).

SEVEN

Secularization and Opposition in the Time of Catherine the Great

OLGA A. TSAPINA

THE REIGN OF CATHERINE THE GREAT (1762–96), OFTEN dubbed the time of "Enlightenment" or "enlightened absolutism" in Russia, proved to be of crucial importance to the evolution of Russian political and intellectual life.[1] It was no less important for the history of church-state relations and the overall religious life of imperial Russia. Although the nature of the Russian Enlightenment and enlightened absolutism is still the subject of spirited debates, historians agree that intensive, and often forceful, secularization was one of its most prominent components.[2]

Church-state relations in Russia were indeed undergoing revolutionary change, as Peter the Great, and especially Catherine the Great, attempted to redefine these relations in accordance with the *raison d'état* of enlightened absolutism. However, the study of church-state relations has been somewhat lopsided. Scholars have paid principal attention to the government policy towards the Church, whereas the study of the reaction of the Church and clergy has been limited to the response to secularization of the church lands and the trial and persecution of Archbishop Arsenii Matseevich (1764–65).

It has been commonly assumed that the Russian Orthodox clergy was a coherent social group analogous to the clerical estates of Western and Central Europe. This axiom, however, may not reflect the real social status of the Orthodox clergy. As Gregory L. Freeze has pointed out, the notion that eighteenth-century Russian society consisted of the estates analogous to those of Western and Central Europe was actually a political and historiographical convention worked out in the next century. The social composition of eighteenth-century Russian society was extremely intricate and volatile; it responded to the changing realities of early modern times in Russia.[3] The situation of the "clerical estate" proves the point. Unlike Western clerical estates, the Eastern Orthodox clergy consisted of two large groups: the married, parish ("white") clergy and the monastic ("black") clergy. The "white" clergymen were fully integrated into the lives of local communities and often shared the plight of peasants and townsfolk, whereas the monastic clergy, on the contrary, were expected to remove themselves completely from worldly society. The monks, however, held a monopoly over the Church hierarchy and governance. This arrangement automatically put the white clergy in an inferior position.

A study of the response of the clergy to the government policies of secularization may be helpful in understanding the social status of the clergy. Indeed, if the clergy was a more or less coherent social group, we could expect a somewhat uniform response to secularization. On the other hand, if we were to find diametrically different reactions, we might assume that they were based in essential social differences. This chapter attempts to evaluate both the policy of the government of Catherine the Great and the clergy's response to it, with particular attention to the situation in the Moscow diocese during the tenure of Metropolitan Platon (Levshin) (1775–1801).

The problem of the relationship between the power of secular rulers and the authority of religious leaders troubled many generations of European statesmen. The experience of the Reformation and the Wars of Religion, the Thirty Years' War, and especially the English Revolution seems to have proven that rivalry between organized religions, or between religion and royal authority, was the principal cause of social turmoil and wars. The enlightened monarchs saw their task as reducing the power and influence of the established church, often by protecting religious minorities from harassment by the church.[4]

Russians were familiar with the theory that attributed the origins of social unrest to unorthodox religious movements. Eugenious (Voulgaris) stated, as a matter of common knowledge, that "religious differences always result in civil warfare."[5] The anonymous author of a somewhat amateurish unpublished treatise "On the Enlightenment of Common People Wandering in the Darkness of Ignorance" shared this sentiment: "Reasonable persons agree that unrest, wars and murders often arise when people of the same blood and same language differ in religion."[6]

Catherine's policy of "protection of all faiths," as outlined in her celebrated *Instruction to the Legislative Commission* (1767), clearly contradicted this maxim. Her "toleration" was largely a pragmatic measure, rather than an intention to safeguard civil rights. The experience of the revocation of the Edict of Nantes and subsequent Huguenot emigration made many European intellectuals realize that religious persecution inevitably resulted in losses for the nation's economy and public morale.[7] Besides, persecution of "fanatics" only created the halo of martyrdom for them and, in the end, even increased their authority among the "ignorant multitudes."[8] Left alone, superstition and fanaticism were expected to fizzle out. In Russia, where Eastern Orthodoxy was the predominant religion, the question of toleration of religious minorities was not so pressing, and thus, at least prior to the partition of Poland, the principle of limited toleration appeared to work rather well.[9]

The perceived transformation of the Old Belief looked like a successful experiment in pragmatic policies. The Old Belief was a rather variegated religious movement that arose in the second half of the seventeenth century. Early Old Believers, referred to as "*raskol'niki*" (Schismatics) by polemicists of the established Church, wanted to defend the traditions and rites of Russian Orthodoxy against the attempt of the Patriarch Nikon (1654–66) to make Russian practices conform to the practices of Greek Orthodoxy. The authorities launched a vigorous campaign of persecution, to which the Old Believers responded with more violence and mass suicides. Despite the fact that in the next century the Old Belief split into a dozen of different denominations and more or less adapted to the social and political establishment of Imperial Russia, mass suicides were still commonly associated with the "obstinate Schismatics."[10] The law traditionally identified Old Belief, or any religious deviation, with treason.[11] Although Peter the Great carried out a more or less tolerant policy toward the Old Believers, his *Ecclesiastical Regulation* (1721) still defined the Old Believers as "fierce enemies who always conspire against the State and Sovereign."[12] The Old Believers were also regarded as hard-liners, reactionaries, and the worst enemies of the state-sponsored "Enlightenment."[13]

Catherine's regulations regarding the Old Believers definitely broke from this tradition.[14] Even Pugachev's rebellion (1773–75) did not affect the affairs of the Old Believers. The respective instructions required that local authorities detain "agitators" who were "misleading common folks"; these measures were intended to isolate troublemakers rather than to repress Old Belief in general.[15] On the whole, there was neither repression of Old Believers nor a change in policy. The liberal policy toward the Old Believers was, to a large extent, caused by the fact that the Russian government was prone not to view the Old Belief as a serious threat to national welfare. Rather, Catherine, as well as many contemporary intellectuals, regarded the Old Belief as a living anachronism, the last remnant of old, "uncivilized" Russia, and while foolish indeed, a fairly harmless stream of popular piety. The intellectuals believed that the main reason for the existence of this "ridiculous sight" was ignorance.[16] The conviction that "the sole sources of the Old Belief deviation is the lack of grammar schooling" is found in many contemporary writings on the Old Believers.[17] Education was deemed the natural remedy for "this illness of religion." Catherine was convinced that "all schisms will disappear in sixty years after the beginning of public education. There is no need for violence and persecution."[18] To some contemporary observers, the government policy of toleration seemed to have begun to pay off. Petr Bogdanovich, a prominent journalist, even hastened to record the history and customs of northern Russia's Old Believers "before they vanished." [19]

Catherine was much more worried about competition between secular and ecclesiastical powers than potential problems stemming from religious diversity. Her concern had a foundation in Russian historical experience. Since the 1400s, the relationship between the Church and throne in Muscovite Russia had been increasingly strained.[20] The tendency to put the Tsar in a position inferior to the Patriarch was especially evident during the pontificate of the Patriarch Filaret, the father of Michael Romanov and great-grandfather of Peter the Great (1613–1632). In the 1660s this tendency resulted in an open conflict between the secular and ecclesiastical authorities. Although the trial and conviction of Patriarch Nikon (1666–67) reduced the Church to the role of a junior partner of the state, the Church retained autonomous governance, and therefore it posed a threat to the power of the monarch.[21] The intention to eliminate a potential political rival underlined the ecclesiastical reform of Peter the Great. The reform replaced the office of patriarch, the head of the Church, as independent of the secular authority, with the Holy Synod—a collegial government agency subordinated directly to the Emperor. (The main seat of the Holy Synod was in St. Petersburg; later a separate Office of the Holy Synod was established in Moscow.)[22]

However, the confrontation that characterized the Church-state relationship in Russia since the late fifteenth century, did not end with the reformer's death. There were serious attempts to reverse the effect of Peter's reforms. In May 1744 the Metropolitan of Rostov, Arsenii (Matseevich), and the Archbishop of Novgorod, Amvrosii (Iushkevich), on the pretext of suppressing religious dissenters, pleaded with Elizabeth to eliminate the Holy Synod and restore the Patriarchate.[23] The Church still enjoyed considerable influence over political and social affairs. It had full jurisdiction, for example, over monks, nuns, secular clergy, and their families. Such areas of criminal law as offenses against religion and public decency, which had rather broad connotations, and issues of marriage and divorce, all fell within ecclesiastical jurisdiction.[24] The Holy Synod carried out a rather independent policy, which too often resulted in conflicts with the secular power represented by the over-procurator (*ober-prokuror*).[25]

Catherine the Great, who was obviously concerned about the problem of the legitimacy of her rule, watched the situation within the Russian Orthodox Church very closely. She was especially worried about the theory of "two powers"—the notion of the superiority of the ecclesiastical power over that of a king.[26] Prince Mikhail Shcherbatov noted that the empress, as "a follower of the new philosophy, of course, knows the limits of the ecclesiastical power, and surely is not going to let it exceed those limits. Nevertheless, I am fairly certain that the clergy (*dukhovnyi chin*) won't miss a chance to expand their power."[27] The ecclesiastical policy of Catherine the Great intended to put an end to possible political threats.

The "theory of two powers" was thought by many to be a result of Catholic influence. Catherine's hatred of the papacy was well known. She feared, not without reason, that the majority of the hierarchs of the Russian Church were influenced by Catholic teaching. Indeed, the overwhelming majority of bishops and abbots were Ukrainians trained in Catholic schools. In order to eliminate Catholic influence, Catherine followed the Empress Elizabeth in promoting native Russian and Greek hierarchs—Dmitrii (Sechenov), Gavriil (Petrov), Platon (Levshin), Eugenious Voulgaris, and Nicephorus Theotokis.[28] Catherine never missed a chance to point out the difference between "enlightened" Russian bishops and their "fanatical" and "superstitious" Catholic counterparts. In her letter to Voltaire (17 November 1767), she praised Dimitrii (Sechenov) who was "neither a persecutor, nor a fanatic" and who "abhorred the theory of two powers."[29] Gavriil (Petrov), in Catherine's own words, was "an educated and reasonable man"; she even dedicated to him her translation of Marmontel's *Belisaire*.[30] The empress created and skillfully exploited the reputation of Platon (Levshin), then a catechism teacher, to the young Paul, praising him as a "humane" and "enlightened" cleric who represented the new generation of Russian clergy. She wanted to demonstrate to all the world that the Russian Orthodox Church was a loyal ally in her struggle to transform Russia into the promised land of the Enlightenment and tolerance.[31]

However, Catherine obviously did not think that a simple change in personnel was enough to prevent a possible resurgence of the "theory of two powers." In order to gain an upper hand in ecclesiastical affairs, she attempted to establish firmer government control over the Holy Synod. This was no easy task, since the power of the over-procurator of the Holy Synod, as outlined in the regulations of Peter the Great, was rather limited. The Instruction of 13 June 1722, defined the office as "Our [watchful] eye and a state counsel (*striapchii o delakh gosudarstvennykh*)." Since the Holy Synod, as the other state agencies established by Peter the Great, was a collegial body rather than a department directed by a state official, the over-procurator was merely to monitor its activity rather than direct the institution. Specifically, he was instructed to make sure that all operations proceeded smoothly and efficiently and in strict accordance with the Ecclesiastical Regulations and Imperial Decrees. In case of violations, he was simply to inform the Emperor rather than attempt to solve the problem himself. (This nature of the power of the over-procurator remained unchanged until the advent of ministerial form of government introduced by the reforms of Alexander I.[32]) Thus the empress had to find other ways.

The solution was found rather easily. The confessor of the Empress Elizabeth, Fedor Dubianskii, played a pivotal part in the Empress's dealings with Church administration.[33] Catherine II followed suit by giving her confessor, Ioann Pamfilov, even more power. In January 1774 Platon (Levshin), a member of the Holy Synod, asked for a year's leave of absence. His wish was eagerly granted: the Empress even retained his full pay. Then she promptly replaced Platon with Pamfilov. Unlike his monastic colleagues, Pamfilov would meticulously attend all sessions of the Holy Synod and would often show up an hour early. In the 1780s, Pamfilov and Over-Procurator Akchurin virtually ran the Holy Synod, since none of the three archbishops attended meetings.[34]

Catherine did not limit her efforts to administrative measures. In an attempt to put an end to the rivalry between the ecclesiastical and secular powers, the government strove to undermine the Church's influence by striking at the very basis of the Church's independence—Church lands. The celebrated program of the secularization of the Church lands (1764) was not an isolated measure, but rather part of the consistent policy designed to limit the area of Church jurisdiction by transferring the traditional matters of Church dominion to the jurisdiction of secular administration.

This tendency was especially evident in Catherine's policy of toleration that was clearly designed to end the monopoly of Church authority over heresies and unorthodox religious movements. For example, St. Petersburg authorities and many intellectuals believed that the Church was to blame for the excesses of Old Belief. As Ivan Melissino, the procurator of the Holy Synod, put it, the "clergy, imbued with ambition and arrogance and wielding too much power, armed itself with hatred and anger, and attempted to return their lost sheep to the fold not with the pastor's staff but with threats and torments . . . instead of teaching ignorant people the true meaning of religion."[35] Thus very often the government protected Old Believers from the abuse of the local consistories and the excessive missionary zeal of the Orthodox clergy. The local clergy were instructed to deal with the Old Believers with "patience and caution."[36] In February 1763 Catherine instructed Over-Procurator Aleksei I. Glebov to "give the Novgorod and Pskov archbishops a nudge regarding the Old Believers, as I received yet another petition from these people."[37]

In 1765, when the Old Believer Bureau (*Raskol'nich'a Kontora*) was abolished, all cases pertaining to the Old Belief were thereby exempt from the jurisdiction of the Church administration and put under the authority of the secular state. The Synod was instructed "not to establish any Old Believer agencies in the future"; all existing agencies of this sort were to be disbanded and all individuals imprisoned were to be freed.[38] In 1772 all heresies were decriminalized; the affairs concerning the Old Believers and non-Orthodox confessions were transferred from the jurisdiction of the Church to that of the Senate and other government institutions.[39] The decree of toleration (June 17, 1773) banned archbishops from any interference in the affairs of non-Orthodox faiths and conferred the full judicial and executive power over such issues to the "secular authorities."[40] In 1782 Old Believers received equal rights with all other subjects of the empire. Even the traditional pejorative term, the Schismatics (*Raskol'niki*) was replaced with the neutral phrase "Old Believers" (*starovery*).[41]

The Church antiquities, which Catherine treated as items of cultural value rather than sacred objects, became another object of secularization. Some of the most valuable objects were turned over to the control of the museum of the Armory Palace.[42] The decree of August 1791 launched the program designed to retrieve valuable historical documents from church and monastery archives. The famous collector Aleksei Musin-Pushkin, who at the time held the post of the over-procurator of the Holy Synod, was appointed as a head of the unofficial committee.[43] Catherine made an attempt to secularize ecclesiastical and religious education. The course of catechism taught in the Moscow University Gymnasium was turned into a sort of civic studies course (The textbook recommended by the Commission for the Popular Schools was *The Book of Duties of Man and Citizen*).[44] In 1765, Catherine supported a project designed to create a Faculty of Theology at Moscow University. The new faculty was supposed to prepare "pious priests and benevolent clergy of different ranks, including learned bishops."[45] The proposal signed by the loyal Moscow university faculty, a faculty that consisted mostly of German professors, emphasized that the new generation of ecclesiastical authorities "having been taught philosophy, shall be duly prepared for theological studies, and thus shall wield knowledge and ample capacity necessary to promote the general welfare by teaching the faithful to adhere to the duties required by the authorities."[46]

The most important problem, however, was the policy toward the Orthodox clergy. Catherine was obviously concerned about the proper place that clergy should occupy in a secular state. In the 1760s she even attempted to approach this problem in her article "On the Difference between Clergy and Parliament."[47] The empress had to take into account the diverse composition of the Russian clergy and the policy of her predecessors. Since the time of Peter the Great, monks and nuns had been treated as parasites who "ate off somebody else's labor" and promoted "deviation, heresy, and superstition."[48] Prompted by the policies of Frederick II and Joseph II, Catherine attempted to phase out the influence of monasticism. However, being fully aware of how the monastic way of life was valued by pious Russians, she was cautious not to aggravate the matter by such abrupt measures as Joseph II's dissolution of cloisters.[49] During the secularization of the Church lands, the number of cloisters that were funded from the state treasury ("staffed" monasteries and convents) was substantially reduced; lesser monasteries, left with no funding whatsoever, were expected to rely on the generosity of the faithful. Many provincial monasteries were simply disbanded. New monasteries were opened only in the newly conquered south frontier lands—in Kherson, Ekaterinoslav, and the Caucasus dioceses.[50] The government intended to utilize monasteries as fully as possible as asylums and mental hospitals, barracks, and veteran soldiers' nursing homes. The Spaco-Evfimiev convent was turned into a prison. The ancient Simonov Monastery was to be transformed into a military hospital.[51] Catherine wrote to Diderot with a great deal of satisfaction that the number of monks was decreasing every year.[52] In June 1789 the empress's secretary, Alexander Khrapovitskii, recorded her comments on the report from Moscow Governor General Petr Dmitrievich Eropkin regarding the Simonov monastery. The empress asked her secretary if he liked monasteries. Khrapovitskii replied just as his royal boss expected him to: "No, Your Majesty. When I look at a monastery I cannot help but think it a seat of lasciviousness."[53] According to another entry in the same journal, Catherine somewhat gleefully pointed out that "the Archimandrite Pavel delivered a very poor sermon yesterday. He is a pupil of Platon's. They [the monks] don't let anybody else be greater than they are. But nowadays white clergy [*bel'tsy*] are much more accomplished than monks [*chernetsy*]."[54]

The government indeed pursued an entirely different policy toward the white clergy. The white clergy were viewed as a "useful" social group, who, besides providing spiritual solace, were obliged to fulfill other duties: taking care of citizens' moral education, charity, and upholding social harmony. In fact, when Catherine spoke about the "clerical estate," she meant white clergy only.[55] The absolutist state was prone to regard the white clergy as an integral part of lay society. This tendency became evident during the work of the Legislative Commission (1767–68). It is a well-known fact that, unlike gentry, merchants, townsfolk, or Cossacks, the clergy were not represented in the commission as a social group. The representative from the Holy Synod was the only clergy member, and he represented a state agency, rather than the clergy.[56] The white clergy, however, were represented in the Legislative Commission. While they did not come as a separate estate, they did appear as part of the townsfolk delegations, and the clergy's wishes were included in the instructions (*nakazy*). Some clerical historians acknowledged this fact, and they interpreted it as an attempt of the clergy, who had been officially banned from participating in the Commission, to get there in a roundabout way.[57] It is unlikely, however, that the provincial town clergy were able to perform such a class action. The opinion, cautiously voiced by Viktor V. Krylov that "the clergy of certain town communities considered the city deputies as their representatives," is much more probable.[58] Indeed, the arrangement of the representation in the commission deemed the clergy an integral part of local communities. For instance, all *nakazy* were to be reviewed, registered, and endorsed by parish priests. That the clergy were not to be represented as a separate estate reflected Catherine's desire to shoot two birds with one stone: to strengthen the nascent "third estate" and to weaken the ecclesiastical power by pulling the white clergy from its jurisdiction.[59]

The same intention was behind the activity of the Committee on the People of Middling Estate, headed by Mikhail Shcherbatov. According to the draft regulation worked out by the committee, the "middling estate" was to include all educated non-nobles. Accordingly, ordained clergy were regarded as "teachers of the people" and, therefore, fell into the category of the top crust of the "third estate," along with scientists, scholars, physicians, and artists.[60] The government even took up the role of the protector of the white clergy against the Church hierarchy. This maneuver was especially evident during the secularization reform. For instance, Archbishop Arsenii Matseevich was accused by the government, among other things, with harassing parish clergy.[61] The legislation of 1764–68 significantly curtailed the financial and judicial control of bishops over parish clergy. The "white" ordained clergy was relieved from the church tax (*dannye den'gi*), seminary tax, chaplain tax (a special tax intended to maintain clergy in the army and navy), special fees for the ordination certificates (*stavlennaia gramota*), "stole" and "surplice" licenses, and transfer certificates (*perekhozhaia gramota*).

The special decree (1765) forbade bishops to defrock ordained clergy without having obtained permission from the Holy Synod. The corporal punishment of priests was banned in 1767; in 1771 the same exemption was granted to deacons. The legislation of 1765–68 provided for the white clergy's representation in local consistories,[62] which hitherto consisted exclusively of monastic elite.[63] The nineteenth-century historian P. V. Znamenskii enthusiastically believed that the reforms of 1760's for the parish clergy were what the Manifesto of 19 February 1861, was to peasants.[64] However, the reforms were primarily intended to limit the power of the hierarchy rather than improve the position of the parish clergy. While priests were protected from the abuse of bishops, in the clerical conflicts with lay authorities the government almost always took the side of the latter. For instance, in 1767 several priests of Tambov gubernia were confined to a monastery for their "impudent" complaints against an "important" lay official.[65]

Of course, the program of secularization invoked opposition. The grassroots resistance to the government's policy, which was especially evident during the time of religious revival in the 1780–1790s, should probably be qualified as intellectual dissent rather than organized opposition. On the other hand, it should not come as a surprise that the Church itself became the seat of organized opposition to secularization. Most historians of Catherine's reign regard the Church simply as a passive object of the secular government's policy. The "affair" of the Archbishop of Rostov, Arsenii Matseevich, has been regarded as the last outburst of the Church's resistance; Arsenii's severe punishment is believed to have finally intimidated the Church into complete subservience to the state. This picture, however, is not as accurate as it once appeared. Indeed, the notion of the complete subjugation of the Russian Orthodox Church to the absolutist state was to a large extent a product of the nineteenth-century debates relating to the Great Reforms and Pre-Council Committee.[66] Liberal historians emphasized the negative impact of Orthodoxy as the established religion, while clerical historians were prone to treat the history of the Russian Orthodox Church with a certain halo of martyrology. As for Soviet historiography, the interpretation of the role of the Church as a loyal ally of the imperial state clearly served the purpose of atheist propaganda.

In fact, the ecclesiastical power did not yield without serious and often effective resistance. For instance, despite the encroachments of the state, the Church succeeded in defending and even strengthening her control in matters pertaining to the family, marriage, and divorce.[67] The members of the Holy Synod successfully repelled Catherine's attacks on ecclesiastical education: they insisted that the Faculty of Theology be opened in the Zaikonospasskaia Ecclesiastical Academy rather than Moscow University. The empress had to give up the whole project.[68] The hierarchs offered considerable and often effective resistance in the affairs of the Old Believers and the Orthodox clergy.

The Church displayed a rather intransigent attitude toward the official policy of toleration. Of course, some Russian hierarchs more or less concurred with the government's handling of the affairs of the Old Believers. Dmitrii (Sechenov) and Gedeon (Krinovskii) agreed that Old Believers should be left alone as long as they "are in accord with the Orthodox Church in everything besides the rituals."[69] Especially important was Platon (Levshin) who was the first hierarch to address the Old Believers with words of pity and admonition rather than threats.[70] He was behind the compromise Uniform Faith (*edinoverie*)—an experiment designed to embrace Old Believers without enforcing the "new" rituals of the official Church upon them.[71] The voice of the opposition, however, was much stronger. The pessimists did not believe in toleration in general and especially opposed it when applied to the Old Believers. Most hierarchs insisted that the Old Believer communities were still crowds of aggressive fanatics and hotbeds of potential rebellion. In his reports to the Holy Synod, the Bishop of Tobol'sk Pavel (Koniuskevich), whom Catherine branded as "fanatic," made gloomy predictions about the grave consequences of "leniency" toward the Old Believers.[72]

The opposition got a chance to express its views in 1763–64, during the discussion about the repatriation of the Russian Old Believers living in Poland. The memorandum submitted by Gavrill (Petrov) and Amvrosii (Zertis-Kamenskii) reflected their firm stance on this matter. The very first lines of the memorandum were rather straightforward. The authors stated that religious freedom for the Old Believers was unacceptable. Moreover, they questioned the very idea of religious tolerance. They believed that one nation should be based on one religion. A monarchy was especially susceptible to the dangers posed by religious diversity: "Nothing bonds subjects to their sovereign like religious belief. Thus all intelligent people agree that allowing different religions in one state is detrimental to the welfare of the nation. Religious difference is dangerous. This is why many sovereigns destroyed and still destroy heretics. . . . Wherever the authorities are lenient to them, there are either political or religious troubles." The authors of the memorandum were convinced that the policy of toleration had not paid off as "schismatics" were "neglecting all admonitions." There was a need for stricter measures; the Church "had put up with their impudent demands for too long."[73]

The issue of the political dangers of the Old Belief was brought up again in the wake of the Plague Riot in Moscow in September 1771 in which Archbishop Amvrosii (Zertis-Kamenskii) was killed by an angry mob. The witnesses of this tragedy did not incriminate the Old Believers (though they did refer to the rebels as the mob composed of "factory workers, clerks, merchants, schismatics, serfs, cabdrivers, etc.").[74] The government did not view the riot as a manifestation of religious fanaticism. At least Voltaire, who never missed a chance to lash out at the evils of religious fanaticism, in his answer to Catherine's account of the riot, described the rebels as "merely empty-headed barbarians who deserve punishment to make an appropriate impression in their stupid heads."[75] Although in her letter to A. I. Bibikov (29 October 1771) Catherine branded the rioters as "bigots," she stressed, however, that "the investigation is under way. It is clear that there is no head or tail in the whole affair. It was nothing but an accident; everything is calm now."[76]

Public sermons delivered on this occasion pictured a completely different image. In his Sermon *On the Martyrdom of the Archbishop Amvrosii,* Aleksandr Levshin, the archpriest (rector) of the Kremlin Cathedral of the Assumption, Platon's brother, and a member of the emergency medical committee, described the rebels as "mobs of contemptible, brute, and unrestrained people imbued with madness or, more appropriately, infested with superstition. . . . They sink so low in their superstition that they consider murder, which contradicts divine and civic law, a sacrifice to God." Archbishop Amvrosii (Podobedov) regarded the murder of the Moscow archbishop as a ritual murder: "As those bigots regard suicide as a deed leading to salvation, they consider a murder as the sacrifice to God." Later Andrei Ivanovich Zhuravlev, a former Old Believer turned an Orthodox polemicist, voiced the same accusations.[77]

The difference between the attitudes of the secular and those of the ecclesiastical authorities was manifested again in 1792 when Moscow Old Believers appealed for permission to open a new chapel. The Moscow Governor General easily granted the request; he based his decision on "the manifesto of 1762 which proscribed any harassment towards Old Believers" and a special instruction of 19 April 1790, "about the secret gathering of the brotherhood" (Rosicrucian Masonic lodges). The instruction required that police "do not enter or break up any religious gatherings except those of the said brotherhood." However, Gavriil (Petrov) strictly opposed this decision. He pointed out that "there are more than twenty thousand of the followers of the Schism in the city of Moscow alone. If we allow them to build the new church, these crowds of fanatics would hold councils in Moscow. . . . That means that their followers from other *gubernias* would come to the city too. . . . It is hardly possible that these people who are devoid of any loyalty to the authorities could guarantee the safety of the city. Can we rely on their loyalty if they deem the Sovereign an infidel?"[78]

The debates in the Legislative Commission (1767–68) demonstrate that the clerical opposition was rather influential. When Catherine commissioned Gavriil (Petrov), Innokentii (Nechaev), and Platon (Levshin) to review the text of the "Instruction,"[79] the "reasonable" and "enlightened" prelates made changes that revealed their intention to expand the prerogatives of the Church and strengthen its influence over lay society.[80] For instance, the original version did not count heresy and religious offenses among criminal acts: such cases could not be presented in a court of law, and the penalties should be limited to temporary or permanent excommunication. The ecclesiastical editors altered this clause by turning religious offenses into subjects of criminal justice; thereby, the state was expected to prosecute "heretics." The original version condemned any legal actions against authors of "critical" books; the "excessive zeal" in such matters was deemed detrimental to the freedom of press. After the editors' intervention, this clause prescribed "reasonable but firm" limitations to "literary freedom."[81]

In June 1767 the over-procurator of the Holy Synod, Ivan Melissino, presented "The Articles Proposed for the Instruction to the Holy Synod Representative" to the Legislative Commission (*Punkty predlozhennye dlia sochineniia instruktsii deputatu o sochinenii novogo Ulozheniia*), which was, in fact, the government program for ecclesiastical reform.[82] The members of the Holy Synod abruptly refused even to review the "Articles," let alone to accept them. They countered the over-procurator's initiative by composing their own "Instruction" that expressed the authors' preoccupation with the problem of church-state relations. Thereby the authority of the Synod was to be made equal to that of the Senate; all religious transgressions, including failure to receive the Holy Communion, were to be treated as criminal offenses. The authors of the Synodal "Instruction" specifically emphasized the Church's role in the "betterment" and "proper education" of laity. The "Instruction" contained articles forbidding laypeople to "speak jokingly about God, the Trinity, the Savior, and the Scriptures." Such talk and even passing remarks were deemed equal to blasphemy, which, in turn, was to be treated as a criminal offense. The synodal "Instruction" also demanded that laypeople charged with such offenses be tried by a bishop rather than a court of law, thus advocating the expanding of the ecclesiastical judicial power by placing laypeople under the jurisdiction of the Church.[83]

The attempt of the Committee on the People of Middling Estate to integrate the white clergy into the "third estate" provoked the sharp criticism of Metropolitan Gavriil, the representative of the Holy Synod. He fumed that the committee guaranteed the rights of the third estate only to "white, or lower clergy while the top clergy had not been given any rights at all." The members of the Holy Synod demanded that all decisions concern "the clergy altogether rather than a part of it." They emphasized the social homogeneity of the Orthodox clergy: "The clergy is essentially one and indivisible, since the duty of all men of the cloth is to administer the sacraments, perform the Divine Service and to teach." Accordingly, the Synod proposed to replace the division of the clergy into black and white with the vertical relationship between "governing" and "governed."[84] In fact, the emphasis on the unity of "all men of the cloth" was the argument used by the hierarchy to defend its jurisdiction over the "white clergy" from the encroachment of the state. Gavriil supported his arguments against the project of the committee with a reference to the practice of the "powers that are friendly to the Russian Empire." In particular, he was referring to France, where the clergy constituted a separate estate (Gavriil would come to the sessions of the Holy Synod and the Directory Committee with lengthy statistics on the French clergy).[85]

The state was not able to overcome the resistance of the Church in the question of the social status of the white clergy. The conciliatory Church-Civic commission, created in May 1768, worked out a compromise project. The project, in an attempt to "encourage" the clergy, granted it the status of a separate estate with privileges similar to those of the nobility. The estate, however, was defined only nominally: the privileges were not transferred from father to son; they were rather benefits that came with a particular appointment.[86] Thus the white clergy found themselves in a tug-of-war between the state and the Church. But what was the opinion of the white ecclesiastics themselves? Whose side were they on? The scarcity of personal narratives of eighteenth-century white priests has made any analysis of their views very difficult if not altogether impossible.[87] Consequently, studies of the eighteenth-century Russian clergy examine mostly legal and social aspects of its history and lack a personal dimension.[88] The newly found manuscript collection of Petr Alekseev (1727–1801), the archpriest (rector) of the Kremlin Cathedral of St. Michael, offers a unique opportunity to look at the problems through the eyes of one of the most illustrious members of the white clergy.

Born into a family of a Moscow sexton, Alekseev managed to reach the top of the ecclesiastical and academic career open to a white cleric. Having completed the full course of study in the Moscow Theological Academy, he succeeded in securing the position of deacon in the Kremlin Cathedral of Archangel Michael. In 1757 he was promoted to priest, and in 1771 to the archpriest of the cathedral. Besides being known as one of the most educated priests of his time, he also enjoyed a well-deserved reputation as a lexicographer, historian, poet, and teacher.[89] Beginning in 1759 he taught catechism in the Moscow University Gymnasium, a Moscow University preparatory school. In 1771 he became the only clergy member of the Free Russian Assembly, a learned society established by Moscow University for the purpose of improving the Russian literary language. The Assembly's most important accomplishment was Alekseev's *Ecclesiastical Dictionary.* In 1783 Petr Alekseev became one of the first members of the celebrated Russian Academy. Despite these academic achievements, his ecclesiastical career was marred by prolonged confrontation with the Metropolitan of Moscow Platon (Levshin). Many of Alekseev's works remained unpublished; his manuscripts are held now in various Russian depositories. The largest collections are found in the State Historical Museum and Russian State Library.[90]

Alekseev's character became the subject of short, albeit rather heated, polemics in the 1860s. Authors close to ecclesiastical circles—N. I. Subbotin, Filaret (Gumilevskii) and A. N. Korsakov—were prone to downgrade his scholarly achievements and emphasize his "excessive loyalty" to the secular authorities and his "bad attitude" toward the ecclesiastical hierarchy and monasticism.[91] In contrast, liberal historians, such as M. I. Sukhomlinov, A. N. Pypin, and P. I. Bartenev, regarded Alekseev as a "progressive" and "enlightened" scholar persecuted by the Church.[92] Accordingly, they were inclined to avoid discussing the details of Alekseev's confrontation with the Metropolitan Platon and his involvement in the "Novikov affair." For almost a hundred years Alekseev's name was practically forgotten. In 1972 Grigorii Likhotkin published his study of Alekseev's unsavory role in the Novikov affair.[93] This study, while valuable, was laden with the stereotypes characteristic of Soviet historiography.

Alekseev's papers provide us with an opportunity to examine the views of a member of the top crust of the white clergy. The opinion of the white clergy elite—rectors, priests, and deacons of cathedrals—is especially interesting. The economic position and the place in the Church hierarchy of this upper tier of the white clergy resembled the position of the privileged monks. Unlike regular parish clerics who were elected by parishioners, the clergy of the cathedrals were appointed by the Holy Synod on the recommendation of the bishop, just like *hyegumens* (priors) and archimandrites (abbots). Their income and privileges were also comparable to those of the monastic elite. The clergy of the major cathedrals of Moscow, St. Petersburg, Rostov, and Vladimir received a fixed salary from the state treasury, quite unlike their parish colleagues whose income entirely depended on payments from parishioners and fees for rites. Education and training were the main criteria for filling such choice positions; thus the cathedral rectors, priests, and deacons, as a rule, belonged to the ecclesiastical intellectual elite. According to the scheme proposed by the Holy Synod, the archpriests fell under the category of the "governing" clergy. Therefore, one could expect that these clergymen would share the same kind of antisecularization sentiment voiced by the top clergy. In addition, a member of the clergy of the Cathedral of Archangel Michael might have held a particular grudge against the government. This cathedral, the largest landowner among all Kremlin churches, was the one that suffered most from the secularization of the church lands.

An analysis of Alekseev's writings, however, defies any such expectations. His writings are filled with bitter attacks against bishops, on one hand, and pronounced apology for the secular government, on the other. Alekseev's onslaught against episcopal power was by no means unusual for a white cleric. In the eighteenth century the white clergy and bishops were becoming more and more alienated. The extent of this alienation has even led some historians to compare them to the relations between patricians and plebeians or even serfs and lords.[94] Certain contemporaries shared such analogies. The animosity is evident in an anonymous anti-bishop pamphlet written in the early 1760s. The author, apparently a country parson, described the power of bishops in the following passionate fashion: the bishops "turned presbyters into their servants. . . . They treat God's presbyters with contempt, worse than they would treat their serfs." Indeed, they "own parish clergy like their serfs imposing unbearable levies and taxes upon them. Bishops are even harsher toward the men of God than lords are towards peasants: at least lords protect their peasants and don't burden them excessively lest they become impoverished. For a wise lord is proud to have prosperous peasants." As for bishops, "they just cannot wait to get their hands on a well-to-do priest" to extort as much money as they can. An irate bishop yells at a presbyter: rip, pierce, defrock him, cast him to prison, excommunicate him. Oh, ferocity, oh, ire!"[95]

Nineteenth-century historians tended to regard this alienation as an ethnic conflict. As the majority of bishops were of Ukrainian descent, their Russian subordinates perceived them as foreigners.[96] However, in the 1760–80s Russians replaced Ukrainians at the head of dioceses. The bishops of the new generation, such as Gavriil (Petrov) and Platon (Levshin), sons of Russian parish priests, who had first-hand knowledge of the real life of rank-and-file clergy, sincerely intended to improve their economic situation and social standing. Platon's tenure in Tver' (1773–75) and especially in Moscow has been hailed as a landmark in the history of the Russian diocesan administration.[97] Having found clergy in the Moscow diocese in the most pitiful condition—devastated by the plague of 1770–71, impoverished, and sneered at by society—Platon was proud to state that his reforms "immensely improved the clergy's general well-being, and society started to treat men of the cloth with respect."[98]

The reforms, however, led to significant resistance in the ranks of potential beneficiaries. Platon acknowledged that a great number of clerics and laymen were disgruntled by his administration. He acrimoniously described this crowd as composed of "haughty noblemen and lords, . . . drunkards and vagabonds." The important faction of the opposition included the archimandrites of privileged monasteries (*stavropigial'nye*) which traditionally were exempt from the diocesan jurisdiction and subordinated directly to the Patriarch, and then to the Holy Synod. According to Platon, all his enemies found eager support in St. Petersburg, at the quarters of his nemesis, the empress's confessor Ioann Pamfilov.[99] As all indications of the resistance against Platon's diocesan reforms were based on his "Autobiography," the nature of the opposition was conjectured, based on the assumption that Platon was an "enlightened" bishop. Accordingly, his adversaries, inevitably, were presumed to be "privileged clergy" or ignorant clerics who were opposed to the reforms per se.

Historians have regarded Petr Alekseev as the main, if not the sole, adversary of Platon in Moscow. A. N. Korsakov thought that Alekseev's animosity toward the archbishop stemmed from jealousy and envy. Kazimir Papmehl treated Alekseev's activity as a form of resistance to the reforms in the Moscow diocese conducted by the "enlightened prelate" and compared it to the opposition of the privileged clergy. But Alekseev could only nominally be classified as a member of the privileged clergy; in fact his position was significantly different from that of the heads of the privileged monasteries as well as from the clergy of the former Patriarchal cathedrals and the Cathedral of Annunciation. Indeed, the legal status of the cathedral of St. Michael was somewhat ambiguous. The "Regulation" of 1764 put the cathedral, along with the Cathedrals of the Assumption and Annunciation, within the category of privileged cathedrals financially supported by the state treasury. At the same time, the Cathedral of Archangel Michael, as the main cathedral of the Moscow diocese, remained within the direct jurisdiction of the Moscow archbishop.[100] It is important that Alekseev regarded himself as a spokesman for the parish priests rather than for the privileged clergy. When in 1786 Catherine honored him with a pectoral cross, he hailed this award as recognition of all white clergy. In his acceptance speech he addressed Catherine the Great "not on my own behalf, but on behalf of the whole white clergy who, taking heed of the favors bestowed upon their peers, awaken from the slumber of misery and enslavement and embrace the spirit of encouragement and commendable competition."[101]

The contents of Alekseev's papers reveal that he was not alone in his antipathy toward the Moscow archbishop. In fact, he was at the center of a whole group of disgruntled clergy that included Kremlin white clergy, such as Vasilii Simeonov, a priest of the church of Deposition of the Virgin Shroud and a relative of Pamfilov's; Gerasim Korenev, archdeacon of the Cathedral of the Assumption; Dmitrii Il'in, a priest of Archangel Michael; as well as ordained clergy from the Moscow parishes like Aleksei Martynov and Grigorii Petrovich, a priest of the Arbat church of St. Charitonios, Alekseev's son-in-law Petr Andreev, and a certain "parson NS." The Moscow opposition enjoyed unfailing support in St. Petersburg, in the quarters of Ioann Pamfilov.

The parsons' grievances were indeed caused by Platon's drive to impose a stricter control over the diocesan white clergy, his educational policy, and his explicit support of monasticism. Bishops had always been convinced that disorderly conduct and "lasciviousness" among lower clergy stemmed solely from the lack of episcopal control. In 1744, for example, Arsenii (Matseevich) and Amvrosii (Iushkevich) pointed out that it was the absence of an "efficient" bishop that induced priests and deacons to live in "fearlessness": "What else can one expect from priests who are not ruled by real pastor [i.e., patriarch]? Of course, they live in anarchy!"[102] Thus a stronger diocesan government was viewed as a panacea for such transgressions of the common clergy.

Platon streamlined considerably the diocesan and Synodal administration in Moscow. He subordinated the cathedrals and monasteries, which had been exempt from the diocesan jurisdiction—the Cathedral of the Assumption and the some of the *stavropigial'nye* monasteries (Vysokopetrovskii, Greek Nikovaevskii and Savvino Storozhevskii Monasteries.)[103] He also succeeded in putting under his complete control the Moscow Consistory and secured his uncontested control over the Moscow Office of the Holy Synod. When he started his term in Moscow, Platon complained that he could not "make decisions by himself" but had to "comply with other members of the Moscow Office of the Holy Synod, who had different and often self-serving objectives."[104] According to the regulations of 1762, the office consisted of a bishop (the Archbishop of Moscow, the bishop of Krutitsy, or the bishop of Pereslavl' who should go through regular rotations), an archimandrite, and an archpriest.[105] For thirty years (1768–98) the archpriest's position was occupied by Aleksandr Levshin, Platon's brother and the archpriest of the Cathedral of Assumption. The bishop's seat was kept by either Platon or his confidant, Amvrosii (Podobedov). As for the archimandrite position, it remained vacant after Damaskin (Semenov-Rudnev) was appointed to the Sev diocese; it was filled only in 1795.[106] Alekseev noted that the staff of the Moscow Office of the Holy Synod was also on Platon's side: the secretary was promoted "from a seminary teacher by the grace of His Eminence, and a minute taker is his own nephew." The procurator of the Moscow Office was not to be trusted either, since "he was indebted to the Metropolitan."[107]

Platon prided himself with the firm and strict way that he dealt with his subordinates "who have no other talent but the ability to bother, bend their spines and whine." Once he found their conduct "defying the justice of law or detrimental to the general welfare of the Flock," Platon "paid no attention either to their influential patrons, or their pleas, or their tears." It was not surprising that such firmness caused much chagrin among "governed" clergy. Platon interpreted such sentiments as the natural discontent of the lazy and drunk parsons prompted by firmer discipline.[108] The priests bitterly complained that they were subjected to unjustifiably severe disciplinary actions which included high fines "for every little error," censure, and confinement in a monastery. They were not thrilled with the methods that Platon employed to bring the clergy under a stricter discipline. (The archbishop appointed a confessor for each of his subordinates, and "in case of investigation regarding a certain priest or deacon, summoned the confessor and questioned him if the defendant is prone to such and such sin.")[109]

In his attempt to consolidate his authority in the diocese, the archbishop tended to bypass or even sabotage the secularization decrees. The somewhat scandalous story of the tax levied in 1788 on the Moscow parish priests to support the students of the newly founded Spaso-Vifanskaia seminary was one of the most publicized events of this kind. The episcopal right to tax diocesan clergy was substantially curtailed by the legislation of 1764, which relieved clergy from all taxes "established by Patriarchs." Bishops then had to resort to indirect taxes, often referred to as "voluntary contributions," which were rather hurtful to the clerics' pockets. The seminary tax of 1788 was one of those "contributions."[110] The protests from the Moscow clergy moved Catherine the Great to order Platon to stop imposing such taxes and refund the money already collected.[111] Vasilii Simeonov, the priest of the Kremlin Cathedral of the Deposition of the Shroud, summed up the situation in his letter to Ioann Pamfilov: "Our brethren priests thank you very much. It was not so much the matter of the money. The important thing is that we are not serfs (*obrochnye krest'iane*). Pamfilov's correspondent bemoaned the "sad state of affairs" when the Metropolitan arbitrarily demanded "voluntary contributions" on countless occasions, particularly favoring holidays. A priest's career often depended on the sum of his "voluntary" donations: "His Eminency acts according to his predisposition. The more you give, the better grace you are in with the Metropolitan. But if you fail to contribute as you are expected, you are under His Eminence's censure."[112]

It was Platon's rather arbitrary way of dispensing justice that bothered the white clerics of the Moscow diocese the most. In September 1789 Alekseev complained to Aleksandr Khrapovitskii, a secretary of Catherine the Great that "in the absence of a third, unbiased party [in the Moscow Office of the Holy Synod], the power of the Metropolitan is almost dictatorial."[113] Because Platon was "both a prosecutor and a judge," the archbishop's "resolutions" virtually replaced the investigation, and trials in the Consistory were conducted "by the wish of the Archbishop rather than by the letter of the law."[114] In 1792 Alekseev composed a petition on behalf of Grigorii Ivanov, a Kaluga deacon who had been confined to a monastery upon a complaint from the local *hyegumens*. He pointed out that the deacon's punishment had been decided upon "merely by the wish of His Eminence, without a proper trial." Alekseev wrote: "To push people from one place to another in such a despotic fashion was more likely to be expected from secular lords, who do so to their serfs, than from a supreme pastor."[115]

Alekseev shared Platon's concern about the pitiful condition of the clergy and their rather frequent transgressions. He was much more pragmatic, however, in his interpretation of the causes of such a state of affairs. He believed that it was impossible to demand that the "governed" clergy "were as immaculate as angels," as clerics were "human beings born with the seal of Original Sin and plagued by their human vices."[116] Since all attempts to improve human nature were futile, in order to reform the clergy the authorities had to deal with the realities that caused the clergy's low social status. Alekseev blamed the clergy's "inappropriate conduct," especially their hard drinking, on their poor economic condition: "It is well known that impoverished clergymen more often sink into drunkenness and other impudence than prosperous and well-to-do parsons."[117] Thus all attempts to improve the clergy's performance, conduct, and consequently their social status should begin with improving their economic standing.

Platon acknowledged that the economic position of the white clergy left much to be desired. Idealistic as he was, however, he believed that the material aspect of the clergy's well-being was secondary. Platon's approach was somewhat mercantilist: the main way to increase clergymen's income was to decrease their number, so fewer people could receive more allowance. The Metropolitan also made a decision to regulate the distribution of income within a parish.[118] The issue of the priests' houses provides a fine illustration of the approach of the diocesan administration. The Moscow diocesan authorities, in an attempt to uphold the tradition forbidding a priest to hold worldly possessions, consistently punished priests for their attempt to bequest or even sell their houses, which officially belonged to the diocese.[119] In contrast to Platon, Alekseev clearly regarded the clergy's possessions as private property. He stressed that the white clergy's property "does not belong to the bishop's jurisdiction and is protected by divine and civic law (*zakony bozheskie i grazhdanskie*) from violation, fines and persecution."[120] He also felt that that clergymen were entitled to a share of the church income. For instance, a part of the income from the church land which was rented to laypeople should go to the clergy of the church.[121] We should be reminded that the Committee for Middling Estates of the Legislative Commission made a point to guarantee white clergy legal protection of their private property.

One of the most complicated problems that Platon had to face was the phenomenon of "superfluous" or "excessive" clergy, caused by the disproportion between the number of ordained clergy and available parishes. The number of clerics grew because sons of priests were generally supposed to become clerics and thus remain within the confines of the "clerical estate." As a result, available positions were soon becoming fewer, as the number of priests' sons coming of age grew rapidly. Since the church legislation of Peter the Great, the growing number of tax-exempt "excessive" clerics was one of the major concerns of both ecclesiastical and secular authorities.[122] The "Instruction of the Delegate of the Holy Synod" contained a clause proposing cuts in the number of the parish clergy. In the 1770–80s the Synod issued numerous decrees that "no new priests' positions be created in churches."[123] In 1769, 1784, and 1797 all the diocesan parish clergy were subject to a "selection" program (*razbory*) that was designed to weed out "superfluous" clerics, who were to be transferred to fully taxed categories (*podatnoe sostoianie*).[124] According to the 1775 census of the Moscow diocese, conducted upon Platon's orders, the disproportion between the number of ordained clergy and number of parishes was indeed outrageous.[125] Platon consistently closed down private churches and chapels as well as old and impoverished churches and parishes. The clergy of abolished churches were either assigned to other parishes, or simply fired and thus transferred to the taxpaying estate (*podatnoe soslovie*). Thus he attempted to trim the number of the "excessive clergy" and, at the same time, streamline the diocesan administration and bring all clergy under his jurisdiction.

The white clerics shared the concern over the "superfluous clergy." In 1760s the anonymous author of an anti-episcopal pamphlet pointed out that this was one of the main defects of the Church: "Growing number of clergy causes great shame to the Orthodox Church. For the more people enter the clergy, the more idiots and crooks are found there. Besides, the church that has two, or three, or four priests faces imminent rivalry, quarrels, lawsuits, and even fist fights among them. Sometimes they fight in the very holy altar itself." The author believed, however, that bishops were to blame for such disgrace. According to him, since bishops who collected the ordination and consecration fee, they were keenly interested in "frequent ordinations or creating a separate church for a parish consisting of a mere five families." It was bishops who "for their own profit and thirst for power, have ordained clerics without number, and now prod them like cattle and shear them like sheep."[126] Alekseev, who clearly shared the anti-episcopal sentiment, believed that bishops were inept in solving the problem of excessive clergy. The policy of "weeding out," employed by ecclesiastical authorities, apparently was not working.[127] He believed that the number of the clergy could be reduced only if fewer students were admitted to seminaries.

Platon took a great pride in his educational policy, and numerous new seminaries opened in the diocese. The reform of ecclesiastical education promoted by Platon was designed to form the elite of the "clerical estate," "learned monks" who later were to take the highest positions of bishops and abbots of leading monasteries. In many instances, this aspect of the ecclesiastical education contradicted the interests of the rank-and-file parish clergy.[128] Indeed, Alekseev, who was prone to treat education as an absolute value, was highly skeptical about certain educational directives of the diocesan administration. He believed that the efforts were not only futile but largely irrelevant, inefficient, and bearing no results except for the pointless waste of the clergy's money. For example, he complained to Aleksei Musin-Pushkin, the synodal over-procurator, that sons of sextons who were required to attend the newly founded seminaries of Nikolo-Perervinskii and Savvin monasteries were supported "only by their own money. It is very burdensome for their parents, especially those who live far away from the monasteries."[129] The clause in the decree of 22 March 1800, prescribing mandatory ecclesiastical education for daughters and wives of clergy, was regarded by Alekseev as particularly meaningless.[130] Alekseev believed that the number of seminary students was being unjustifiably inflated. As a result, the graduates were forced to idly "mope around" while expecting a placement in a parish.[131] In his memorandum "On Improvement of the Clergy" (1800), Alekseev proposed that seminary and academy students of the "beginning" classes (i.e., those recruited under Platon), who were "unfit for priesthood or did not possess natural inclination to it" be "required to pursue *other secular careers,* according to the Ecclesiastical Regulation."[132]

There was nothing unusual in the proposition about expelling incapable students. Ecclesiastical authorities would rather easily get rid of the "ignorant," or what they considered the untalented, the lazy, or troublemakers.[133] One nuance in Alekseev's memorandum, however, is very important. He pointed out that not simply "ignorant" students were to be expelled, but rather those who did not feel any inclination to priesthood, or ministry (*sviashchenstvo*). Alekseev clearly regarded the Christian ministry as a secular profession: he pointed out that those individuals, who felt no call to it, should seek "other secular careers." Alekseev's definition of the priesthood as a learned profession comparable to those of artisans, physicians, jurists, military, was practically verbatim borrowed from the *Treatise of the Duties and Dignities of the Ministrie* of William Perkins, a leading figure in English Puritanism.[134] Apparently, Puritan teaching that reflected the transformation of the clergy from the "medieval conception of the clergy as a separate estate" to "one of many professions, much the worst remunerated" sounded a sympathetic chord with the Russian eighteenth century parish priests.[135] According to Alekseev, the clergy who were not involved with the ministry and work in parishes, were a "useless burden" upon the Church and society. When he referred to the "burden" he was not thinking of the "excessive" unemployed white clergy, but rather of monks. All Alekseev's writings, including his lexicographical works, were filled with the most bitter attacks against monasticism. His passionate onslaught on monasticism was largely caused by Platon's explicit support of the monastic revival.

Metropolitan Platon along with Metropolitan Gavriil (Petrov), made important contributions to the revival of monasticism. Platon's part in the revival in the late 1780s was crucial.[136] One of the most spectacular episodes of his Moscow tenure was the renovation, expansion, and adornment of the famous monastery of the Holy Trinity and St. Sergius of Radonezh (Troitsko-Sergieva Lavra). The Moscow monasteries and hermitages, Berliukova Pustyn', St. Catherine's,

St. David Hermitage, the Monastery of the Epiphany at the Market (Bogoiavlenskii monastyr' za Torgom) were practically resurrected from the ruins. Another "unstaffed" monastery, Nikolo-Perervinskii was registered as an affiliate of Chudov monastery and housed a new seminary. Especially famous was the little Monastery of Our Savior and Bethany (Spaso-Vifanskii) which Platon established as his personal hermitage; this monastery housed a new Academy, founded by Platon and kept under his patronage.[137] Altogether, during his term, Platon solicited government allowance of 200,000 rubles for the purpose of restoring of monasteries and convents.[138]

The support of monasteries was an attempt to defend monasticism against the encroachment of the secular state. In this effort Platon relied on the popular tradition of veneration of monastic life. Indeed, new grass roots monastic communities would often spring up in the very place of the disbanded cloisters.[139] The government had to abandon the plan of utilizing the Simonov Monastery largely due to the protest voiced by pious Muscovites and supported by Gavriil. Platon gave his blessing to the famous Optina pustyn', and contributed substantially to the Sarovskaia pustyn', the once abandoned hermitages that in the next century were to bloom into celebrated centers of Orthodox spirituality.[140] Alekseev was convinced that support of monasticism was fraught with the gravest consequences for both the Church and the state. He followed William Perkins in asserting that monasticism was a distortion of the traditions of primitive Christianity and a violation of human nature, which resulted in the drain of resources from society, escapism, potential political danger, and resurgence of superstition and fanaticism.[141]

Alekseev went so far as to describe monasticism as heresy: he even included the article "Hermits" in his "Dictionary of All Heretics and Schismatics." In his attempt to prove that all the heretics were monks, or at least those who favored ascetic ideals, he composed a lengthy list of heretics who "came from the monks."[142] Russia was no exception: "Who was the first to trouble the calm waters of the Russian Church? A monk Adrian. During the Time of Troubles, who looted Russia? Monks. Who was the one who converted to Islam in Yaroslavl'? A monk. Who were heretics in Novgorod? Zakhar the monk." He was convinced that monasticism was the breeding ground for Old Belief: "The Russian Schism started and is still carried out, not by the white priests, but by monks." As for the Archpriest Avvakum, the founder of the Old Belief, Alekseev tried hard to prove that "since he was a widower, he was preparing to be a monk."[143]

Alekseev also described monasteries and convents as "seats of superstition." By "superstition" he meant primarily such forms of sacral behavior as adoration of miracle-working icons, exorcism, reverence of "holy fools," and, above all, respect for ascetism, rather than popular beliefs. No wonder that Alekseev interpreted the revival of monastic spirituality as a resurgence of "superstition" and "fanaticism" and blasted Platon as a "false miracle monger" who "pandered to the superstitions of the ignorant multitudes."[144] Alekseev was especially offended by the preference that the secular public showed toward the monks. Although he was indignant that "commoners" believed that a prayer offered by a monk was "holier," he found it rather logical: since monks "live like angels, and parsons, like men, commoners were more likely to feel a veneration for mysterious monks than to their peers living next door." What he found intolerable was the fact that the popularity of monks was growing, mostly thanks to the effort of the Metropolitan. A certain "monk Melchisedek," a relative of Platon's, a self-proclaimed faith healer, was recruiting followers among Moscow parishioners, especially women, and thereby "led them away from the right clergy and right way of salvation."[145]

In his invectives against monks Alekseev cited not only English Presbyterian divines. He rather thoroughly studied the works of the German Cameralist Johann Gottlieb Justi, a French philosophe historian Giullaume Alexander de Méhégan, and the Spanish anticlerical author Campomanes. He followed Justi and Campomanes in asserting that celibacy resulted in the demographic losses for the nation: "It is well known that non-Catholic countries are flourishing" largely because "celibate clergy thwart propagation and steal people from the state before they are even born." According to the calculations of "learned people, . . . Russia alone loses one million people in 50 years due to monastic celibacy." Besides, the monastic way of life encouraged escapism and undermined private property and national economy, as gifted and wealthy individuals withdrew from the society by taking monastic vows. Moreover, "a great deal of gold and silver, necessary for the needs of society, ends up in the dead hands." Alekseev described this process as a vicious circle: people with "sizable capital" who "did not want to serve their country" would build new monasteries, take monastic vows there, and give all their possessions to their "own" monasteries. These new cloisters then attracted "commoners" who would "rush to that hermitage as to some sort of holy place and sacrifice their last kopeks to feed a parasite, often harming their lawful heirs." [146]In his scathing "Verse on the Miraculous Transformation of N. N. Vysheslatvsev, an 18-Year-Old, Who Withdrew from the Army to Become a Monk During the Last War," Alekseev lampooned a young man who traded his army uniform for the "dervish outfit." Alekseev painted him as a deserter: "While all the sons of Russia suffer in the battlefield, you enjoy yourself in the monastery! You have escaped shells, bayonets, and canons. Now all you do is drink wine and beer, stroll in the park! You don't care that the society and Church are suffering, for you have given up the world, you are headed for heaven, you are angels on earth, distant from worldly cares. You are nothing but rascals, traitors, and devils!"[147]

Celibacy was also a root of political disloyalty. Since monks have no family or property, they have nothing to cling to, and therefore, "are not afraid of anything, since they don't have a family for whose life they fear . . . you can burn them for all they care." This charge had clear political implications. Having no social attachments, monastic clergy were seen as puppets in the hands of the hierarchs who were "imbued with Popish ambitions." Alekseev stressed that monasteries "undermine the state power," as monks' "superstition" created "a state within a state, that is, some sort of separate government which confronts the power of the secular ruler."[148]

Comparison between monks and the white clergy demonstrated that the latter were "true" clergy. It was their contribution to the commonwealth rather than religious feats that made clergy orthodox. The white priests, unlike monks who were supposed to be "human angels and celestial men, . . . through wife, children and household are tied to the society." Unlike monks, they were "valued citizens" as they "gave their labor for the common cause."[149] For instance, Alekseev viewed a confessor as a sort of marriage and family counselor. Thus only a white priest could be a confessor to a layman, because only he could understand the needs and concerns of a family man. As for a monk, he "could not give advice on something that he doesn't know"; and he was even "likely to advise a faithful person not to marry at all, or to donate his money to a monastery instead of spending on his sons' education or daughter's dowry."[150] Despite the fact that there were "right" clergy, white priests were virtually subjugated to monks. Alekseev described the relationship between monks and white clergy as practically a social confrontation. Condemning the practice of monastery confinement as a form of penalty, Alekseev stressed that "the white priests are abused by monks who make fun of them and assign them without any compassion to do the hardest and dirtiest jobs around the monastery."[151] Monks apparently felt the same way. During the investigation of Melchisedek's activities, both parties described each other as representatives of the camp of the enemy. While Alekseev complained that "white clergy is trampled upon by the fanatical monks," Melchisedek branded Alekseev's accusation as a plot inflicted upon monks by the white priests.[152]

It was this profound sense of monastic oppression that shaped Alekseev's opinion of Platon's administrative reforms. Platon, who indeed tended to rely on monks in his administrative and educational endeavors, considered monastic vows as the strongest bond that could keep educated individuals in the clerical estate. He made taking the vows mandatory for all teachers in seminaries and academies.[153] In an attempt to tighten his control over the Moscow Consistory, he changed its composition by increasing the number of monks. In 1775 the Consistory included one archimandrite and three archpriests; after the reforms, in 1775–86, the number of archimandrites was tripled.[154] Alekseev felt that these innovations left white clergy at the hands of the enemy, without any legal protection whatsoever. This feeling underlay Alekseev's account of the story of the investigations of his report about the "superstitious actions of the monk Melchisedek" that took place in 1789–90. Alekseev handed a "private" report to Platon instead of filing an official complaint, lest the "commoners" would be "led into a temptation," and "many an important name" would be smeared. Platon, however, insisted that Alekseev file an official report with the Consistory.[155] Alekseev suspected that this demand was a trap. Alekseev pointed out that Consistory judges were "mostly monks," with the Metropolitan presiding. Unlike the Holy Synod, the Consistory did not have a secular procurator; therefore, a parish priest was entirely at the mercy of the monks.[156]

An accused priest could appeal to the Holy Synod in St. Petersburg. The Ecclesiastical Regulations guaranteed the right to every clergyman, whether ordained or not, to appeal to the Synod. Alekseev insisted that a petition to the Holy Synod must be regarded as an appeal rather than a denunciation.[157] However, the cost of such a venture, which involved travel expenses to St. Petersburg, bribing officials, and so forth, as well as fear of a possible retaliation from the bishop, prevented many potential petitioners from such actions. Grigorii Ivanov, the accused and demoted Kaluga deacon, tried to seek justice in St. Petersburg.[158] He had to ask for a passport to St. Petersburg, which his superiors regarded as insubordination and even blasphemy. Platon, who referred to Grigorii Ivanov as "a shameless deacon, a slime with whom I am forced to engage in litigation," was indeed exceedingly annoyed by priests and deacons who appealed to the Synod for justice.[159] In his "Autobiography" he could not conceal his displeasure about the fact that "some petitioners to the Synod appeared, which was unheard of before."[160] In the end of the 1790s, quite possibly not without Platon's influence, direct appeals to the Holy Synod, as well as direct petitions to the monarch, became illegal.[161]

Alekseev was convinced that appeals to the Holy Synod were ineffective anyhow because an archbishop could not be trusted as an independent arbiter. During the investigations in August of 1785, Alekseev confided in Ioann Pamfilov: "I have reported this matter to the Archbishop of Novgorod. However, I know that it is pointless to complain to one archbishop against another. My hopes are pinned on you."[162] Pamfilov indeed actively lobbied his case. An appeal directly to the secular authorities seemed to be the only way to escape the monastic tyranny. In his letter to Pamfilov of 12 November 1789, Alekseev described his skirmish with the Metropolitan in vivid detail: "His Eminence, as usual, yelled at me and threatened to drag me through the Consistory courts for three years, and denounced me as a squealer." Alekseev, however, did not lose his confidence: "The nightmare is dreadful, but God is merciful. The power of the bishop is great, but the power of the monarch is much greater."[163] As the story of the "seminary tax" shows, sometimes appeals to the imperial authority were indeed effective. Often, however, the secular authorities preferred not to get involved with the diocesan affairs. A decree of the Holy Synod (1773) forbade direct appeals to the secular authority.[164] In the end of his memorandum "The Opinion on Improvement the Clergy" (1800), Alekseev burst out: "Oh you, poor white clergy! Who is to defend you? Only God and the Sovereign: but God is high above and the Sovereign is far away. Now the bishop can do whatever he wants to you. In the past [priests] were allowed to protest against a harassing bishop to the patriarch [crossed out], and later to the Holy Synod. But now this channel has been closed. Even a peasant has a right to appeal to the governor and protest against the cruel lord. But a priest has nowhere to turn."[165]

Alekseev was convinced that the white priests should have a greater say in the ecclesiastical courts. For instance, he proposed that consistory judges "be elected by the white priests and approved by the Holy Synod, similar to the secular courts. Thus no archbishop could fire them." That would be a fair arrangement, since all decisions would be made "based on the Holy Scriptures, rules of the Ecumenical Council, Ecclesiastical Regulation and civil laws, rather on the resolutions of His Eminence."[166] Alekseev attempted to implement such principles in the Cathedral of Archangel Michael. In his inaugural speech to the subordinates he pointed out that culprits would be sent to the authorities not by his own decision but only if "everyone agrees upon it."[167] Alekseev believed that the white ecclesiastics should be the ones to determine the punishment for their peers. Accordingly, he proposed that the confinement in a monastery be replaced with "sending the culprits to their confessors for repentance." In contrast to the physical and mental abuse that the white clergy suffered in monasteries, the repentance supervised by culprits' peers who "hold the same title of presbyter and perform the same ministerial duties" would be truly effective. Following the examples of "individuals respected by white priests," and being admonished by a "friendly" colleague, the priests were more likely to be rehabilitated in "the spirit of brotherly love."[168] Alekseev believed that white clergy should be represented in the local ecclesiastical administration. The archpriest proposed to introduce the institute of "deans" in "ten church districts." Unlike *blagochinnye* (the supervisors appointed by the archbishop), these "inspectors" were to be elected by the white clergy.[169] According to Alekseev, the white clergy should have their delegates in state institutions as well. He was convinced that the income of the Archangel Michael's clergy was so notoriously meager because there were no representatives from the white clergy during the work of the Commission on Church Possessions (1764): "The monastic members of the Commission cared only about the welfare of the bishops and monasteries. As for the state officials, they have no idea about the needs of the white clergy. It is like the old Russian saying that reads: 'Unless a child cries, the mother never knows [what the baby needs].'"[170]

According to Alekseev, the monks' dominance in the Russian Orthodox Church was a distortion of the historical tradition. The debate over the terms "*pop*" and "presbyter" was especially interesting.[171] The word *pop*, originated from the Greek *papas* (father), was a traditional Russian term denoting a priest. However, in the late 1700s the term had acquired a distinctly negative and scornful meaning. Alekseev believed that the word "*pop*" was "a barbarian and vile expression."[172] He even petitioned Platon to banish this "unintelligible" word. Platon was not sympathetic. He believed that the term was a sign of "filial love." Nevertheless, Platon bristled at Alekseev's somewhat tongue-in-cheek suggestion that the archbishop be called "*archpop*," by way of analogy.[173] Alekseev proposed to replace *pop* with the term "presbyter." It is important that Alekseev insisted on the Latin title "presbyter" rather than Greek "*ierei,*" more traditional in Russia. The anonymous author of the anti-episcopal pamphlet also consistently used this term.[174] Both Alekseev and the anonymous author insisted that "bishop" and "presbyter" were essentially synonyms. In his memorandum entitled "Can an Honorable Priest Become a Bishop Without Taking Monastic Vows?" Alekseev cited two meanings of the word "bishop": in the "tradition of the Apostles" and "in the modern usage." According to the "teaching of Apostles," as well as the writings of John Chrysostom, Ambrose of Milan, and Jerome, "bishop and presbyter is the same title." Alekseev did not interpret the other connotation since "it needed no explanation," thereby implying that the modern usage contradicted the tradition of the primitive Church.[175] Alekseev insisted on the equality of presbyters and bishops, and regarded the power of bishops as an illegal usurpation. Citing the first epistle of Paul to Timothy (4:14) and the Epistle to the Trallians of St. Ignatius, he asserted that priesthood, as a collective noun, meant an "assembly of presbyters," in which bishop was merely a "president" elected by the assembly. Thus a bishop wields only the power delegated to him by presbyters, and, therefore, "does not possess monarchical and despotic power over presbyters."[176]

This argument was evidently influenced by Presbyterianism, with its special emphasis on the equality of ministers.[177] Indeed, Alekseev borrowed the arguments from the works of the English Puritan theologians—William Perkins (1558–1602) and John Lightfoot (1602–75). For instance, he cited Lightfoot's *Hebrew and Talmudical Exercitations upon the Evangelist St. Matthew* in his attempt to prove that the word "bishop" was not "some grand rank" but meant simply "overseer," or in Latin, "superintendent."[178] Alekseev indeed obviously favored English Presbyterianism. His unpublished "Dictionary of All Heretics and Schismatics" which listed all non-Orthodox denominations, does not contain any articles on Presbyterians, while there are two lengthy and rather passionate articles on the Independents who are criticized as the adversaries of Presbyterians.[179] Alekseev also lent a sympathetic ear to the arguments of the Erastians.[180] He felt that in the absence of the "right" church government, the jurisdiction over the secular clergy ought to belong to the secular state rather than to monastic bishops. It is not surprising, therefore, that his views on church government were very much in accord with the government's secularization policy.

A comparison between Alekseev's writings and the government program of church reform laid out in the Melissino's *Articles for the Instruction for the Synodal Deputy* (1767) reveals a striking resemblance.[181] Although the "Articles" have not yet been a subject of study, historians seem to have formed rather arbitrary opinions of their content. The "Articles" are usually described as a "liberal escapade" filled with the "anticlericalism" and "French philosophy," and thus "having nothing to do with the social interests of the Russian clergy."[182] The "Articles," however, clearly related to some needs of the white clergy, although quite possibly only the white clergy elite. Article 9 that proposed to elect "bishops and other prominent pastors from learned priests and preachers" and thereby allow bishops to marry "in accordance with the practice of the primitive Church," is the most obvious case.[183] The same intention was voiced by Alekseev as well as by the anonymous author of the anti-episcopal pamphlet.[184] The same goes for the articles regarding marriage and divorce, which repeated the proposals found in Alekseev's papers almost verbatim.[185] Alekseev vigorously advocated lifting marriage restrictions and giving the prerogative of divorce to the state. He also suggested that a fourth marriage be legalized. Questions about marriage and divorce were indeed rather painful for clerics. Intricate marriage traditions, an especially complicated system of degrees of kin, and the ban on marriages between in-laws and godparents, could put a priest in a rather difficult position. Not only the "dubious" marriage was likely to be dissolved by the bishop, the priest who had performed the sacrament could be severely punished. Alekseev also emphasized that such perplexing and antiquated marriage customs, in fact, prevented the growth of the population. Marriage laws became the subject of similar debates in the 1860–80s.[186]

Alekseev described the power of monastic hierarchs in the Russian Orthodox Church as "Popery," meaning the power of monastic clergy over laymen. He was convinced that monastic bishops had nothing in common with secular priests and, therefore, had no right to govern them. The protests against episcopal power were shared by other Russian white clerics. For instance, Kirill Vasiliev, the sacristan from Astrakhan, blamed bishops for the poor state of the Orthodox Church.[187] Therefore, the alienation between bishops and the white clergy obviously exceeded the confines of ethnic and cultural differences. As Gregory L. Freeze pointed out, after the reforms of Peter the Great, the parish clergy received the status of subordinates in the bureaucratic Holy Synod. They were not salaried, however; their income still depended on the parishes.[188] Therefore, the authority of bishops was of a purely bureaucratic nature. Contemporaries perceived it as the tyranny of "heretical" monks. It was the profound notion of the tyranny of the episcopal power that brought learned white priests to the side of a secularist government.

Catherine the Great utilized the services of white clerics. They became especially useful during the late years of her reign which was marked by the religious revival and the spread of mystical teachings. Many intellectuals, who were disillusioned with the rationalism of the Enlightenment and distrustful of the established Church, took up Roman Catholicism, mystical Freemasonry, and even the Old Belief.[189] Intellectuals also manifested keen interest in Eastern Orthodox spirituality. The "enlightened" society, including Catherine II, viewed this revival with growing alarm. The hostility towards mysticism was a complex phenomenon. Its components ranged from common fear of insanity or mental illness, to the theologians' alarm at a possible proliferation of heresy and witchcraft, to the philosophe's concern over a potential resurgence of obscurantism, superstition, religious fanaticism, and persecution. The alarm resulted in heated polemics against mysticism in which Catherine participated actively.[190]

This fear was one of the principal factors shaping "the Novikov affair." The story of the government persecution of the prominent leader of the Russian Enlightenment and a distinguished Freemason is one of the most intriguing subjects in the history of early modern Russia.[191] Certain circumstances indicate that the whole affair in fact stemmed from the fear of a Masonic conspiracy. Catherine the Great shared rather widespread public concern over the nature and goals of the Moscow-based Masonic lodges. The object of these suspicions was not Freemasonry per se, but rather a mystical strand in the Masonic movement known as "Martinism." In the 1760s the image of the "evil Mason," which resembled that of a wicked witch or a sorcerer, was found only in urban folklore and popular tales. Satirists viewed this fear of Freemasons as a typical peasant superstition. As for Masonic lodges, they were regarded as a "toy" of city fops—a ridiculous, although innocuous, diversion of bored aristocrats.[192] By the early 1780s, the fear of Freemasonry seems to have reached a more sophisticated audience.[193] The growing suspicion that the educated public showed toward Masonic lodges coincided with the spread of mystical and occult brands of Freemasonry, especially Rosicrucianism, a part of which was the Moscow Novikov circle.[194] It is worth noting that simultaneously with the "Novikov affair," the persecutor Aleksandr Prozorovskii investigated activities of the Russian mystical sect *skoptsy*.[195]

Alekseev's papers and other contemporary accounts demonstrate that the suspicion of "Martinists" was to a large extent produced by the frustration that many European observers experienced watching the resurgence of mysticism. The charges of "fanaticism" are of particular importance. Alekseev's writings, especially his lexicographical works, show that "fanaticism" was equated with "enthusiasm" and defined as "any excess in religion and piety."[196] Both church polemicists and philosophe authors regarded fanaticism as a principal cause of the religious warfare of the Reformation, the Thirty Years' War and the English Revolution.[197] This interpretation of fanaticism helps explain why the Martinists, politically the most conservative strand of the Masonic movement, were so persistently linked with the origins of the French Revolution. This notion was explicitly voiced by Alekseev as well as by many of his contemporaries. Just as the German Anabaptists were blamed for the atrocities of the Peasant War in Germany, English "fanatics" for the excesses of the English revolution, and the Russian Old Believers for the riots of the first years of Peter the Great's reign, Martinists, by way of analogy, were held responsible for the outbreak of the French Revolution. The myth of Masonic conspiracy, therefore, was a result of the crisis in the traditional way of interpretating the origins of social conflicts. That is, these disturbances were the result of the sinister activity of "enthusiasts" and "fanatics."

Alekseev was among the most ardent critics of the Moscow Martinist circle of Novikov. It was not their charitable works or educational projects which worried him; rather he fumed over the spread of mystical and occult teachings, which he regarded as "enthusiasm," and "superstition." He acknowledged that Martinist teachings found a rather eager response among an educated public fascinated with the occult and things mysterious. He also saw a connection between this trend and the revival of monastic spirituality.[198] The impassioned diatribes against "Martinists" found in the Alekseev papers correspond very well with the criticism of the teaching of Saint-Martin and his followers expressed by many Russian rationalists. Although strikingly similar, the anti-Martinist invectives had different sources. Alekseev and other clerical critics based their onslaught on "Martinists" on the sixteenth- and seventeenth-century theological refutation of enthusiasm.[199] Such celebrated secular authors as Pafnutii Baturin, Aleksandr Radishchev, Gavriil Derzhavin, and Catherine the Great founded their lines of criticism on the postulates of the European Enlightenment. The result was the same: mystical Freemasonry was viewed as a threat to everything that civilized society stood for—family, social ties, education, progress, and political stability. The political implications of the Martinist teaching especially troubled Alekseev. He feared that mystical individualism would first lead to anarchy and then to tyranny by the "illuminated" and "chosen" leaders. In fact, the Moscow Rosicrucians were regarded as a totalitarian quasi-religious cult that lured followers by promises of ultimate spiritual illumination and then exploited them.

Catherine was especially worried about a possible alliance between "enthusiasts" and the church hierarchy. The dispatches from Moscow made her conclude that Platon, who consistently resisted secularization, had formed an alliance with the Rosicrucian Masonic lodge, headed by the famous and popular publisher Nikolai Novikov. It was Alekseev, a white priest known for his secularist sympathies, who was commissioned to find out about the ties between the

Novikov circle and the Moscow clergy, especially the Metropolitan Platon.[200] Catherine was not as paranoid as she may sound today. Platon indeed supported Novikov's charities. He transferred some students from the Academies to the schools sponsored by the Rosicrucian Friendly Society. When commissioned to examine Novikov's religious beliefs, Platon replied that he "wished there were more such perfect Christians as Mr. Novikov." Assigned to examine the contents of Novikov's publications, he avoided any comments on mystical books but blasted the editions of Voltaire and Diderot as "disgusting and harmful books of insane Encyclopedists."[201] Apparently, with his profound mystical sense and ascetic aspirations, Platon found a kindred spirit in Novikov. Accordingly, Alekseev saw no difference between the self-proclaimed faith healer Melchisedek and the prominent journalist Novikov. Both were "enthusiasts" and "fanatics," and both were protected by the Metropolitan Platon. Apparently, this picture looked rather plausible to Catherine.

Conclusion

The secularization carried out by Catherine the Great between 1760 and 1790 was a complex policy with economic, political, and cultural components, designed to strip the Church of her traditional areas of jurisdiction and thereby eliminate a potential political rival. One of the most important components of this program was the attempt (possibly not without the influence of Protestant practice in Western Europe) to integrate the parish clergy in lay society, and thus turn it into part of the nascent "third estate." At the same time, the government aspired to limit the influence of monasticism, and eventually phase it out. The government policy of secularization invoked a rather influential opposition headed by the bishops. Quite logically, the support of monasticism and the strengthening of the episcopal power over the white clergy were deemed the best tactic in confronting the government policy. After the end of the Legislative Commission, the resistance to government policy continued on the diocesan level. The Metropolitan of Moscow, Platon, viewed the Moscow diocese as a testing ground for his attempt to preserve the integrity of the Church. Very soon, however the testing ground turned into a battlefield.

The writings of Petr Alekseev, many of which were inspired by the prolonged conflict with Platon, substantially correct the somewhat roseate picture of the diocesan reforms found in traditional historiography. This picture was largely based upon Platon's "Autobiography" and the documents of the Moscow Consistory—a judicial organ of the diocesan administration, which was under complete control of the Metropolitan.[202] The severity of the conflict and the fact that Alekseev enjoyed the support of clerics in the Moscow diocese and in St. Petersburg suggests that the confrontation exceeded the limits of a personal squabble. Indeed, as many similar confrontations in the intellectual history of early modern Russia, the personal antipathy was fused with theoretical disagreement. The apple of discord was the position of the married "white" ecclesiastics versus monastic clergy and the revival of Eastern Orthodox spirituality.

Alekseev's ideals of priesthood resembled more the ideals of the Protestant ministry than those of Eastern Orthodox asceticism. We cannot interpret these views, however, simply as a result of foreign influence. Since the curriculum in Russian theological schools was not consistent in preferences, and since books of both Catholic and Protestant authors were equally available, educated clergymen were able to choose from a wide variety of European theological traditions.[203] The choice of preferences was, to a large extent, stipulated by the social standing of individual clergymen. It is no accident that married, parish clergymen demonstrated such keen interest in the polemics over the "bishop question," Erastianism, Presbyterianism, and the critique of "enthusiasm."

An analysis of Alekseev's writings shows that educated white clergy were prone to identify themselves with the secular society. This tendency is especially obvious in the alternative solutions to the problems of the Church—the clergy's low social standing, the excessive number of clergy, and the reform of ecclesiastical education. Alekseev felt that the income of the clergy, and consequently their social status and morale, could only be improved by turning a priest into a proprietor and making his income dependent on his performance in the parish rather than by imposing disciplinary and administrative regulations.

Alekseev and other white priests described the episcopal power as tyranny, comparable to the foreign oppression. The bishops, perceived as monastic tyrants, were clearly regarded as centers of power, completely alienated from the "governed" clergy. Sooner or later, the outcry similar to "no taxation without representation" was bound to appear among discontented parish priests. It is not surprising that this sentiment appeared among the cathedral clergy, the most educated and outspoken layer of the clerical estate. Alekseev believed that the white priests or "presbyters," as the only "true" clergy, alone had the right to govern the Church. The views voiced by Alekseev and his associates prepared the way for similar debates in the period of the Great Reforms and the Pre-Council Committee. In the conflict between Church and State, secular priests were more likely to side with the secular state than with the church hierarchy.

The events of the last years of Catherine's reign, however, showed that the government was losing the battle for secularization. The religious awakening manifested itself in the revival of monastic spirituality, the spread of popular mystical sects, and the evolution of mystical brands of Freemasonry. Some of the trends of this revival were supported by the hierarchs of the Russian Orthodox Church, and without their support, it would be hard to account for their blossoming during the reign of Paul I and especially Alexander I.

Notes

1. L. N. Pushkarev, "Svoeobrazie russkoi kultury poslednei treti XVIII v.–vremeni Ekateriny II," *Russkaia kultura poslednei treti XVIII veka–vremeni Ekateriny Vtoroi: sbornik statei* (Moscow: Rossiiskaia akademia nauk, Institut rossiiskoi istorii, 1997), 3–12. For a general overview of the times of Catherine the Great, see Isabel de Madariaga, *Russia in the Age of Catherine the Great* (London: Weidenfeld and Nicholson, 1981); Aleksandr B. Kamenskii, *The Russian Empire in the Eighteenth Century: Searching for a Place in the World*, trans. David Griffiths (Armonk, N.Y.: M. E. Sharpe, 1997).

2. P. N. Berkov, "Osnovnye voprosy izucheniia russkogo prosvetitel'stva," *Problemy russkogo Prosveshcheniia v literature XVIII v.* (Moscow and Leningrad, 1961), 3–21; D. M. Griffiths, "In Search of Englightenment: Recent Soviet Interpretations of Eighteenth Century Russian Intellectual History," *Canadian American Slavic Studies* 6 (1982); 317–56; I. B. Torbakov, "Vek Prosveshchenia: nekotorye istoriograficheskie nabliudeniia," *Spornye problemy istorii russkoi obshchestvenno-politicheskoi mysli do nachala XIX veka: nauchnaia koferentsiia, Moskva, 12–14 maia 1992 g.: tezisy dokladov* (Moscow: Institut rossiiskoi istorii, 1992), 80–82. In this article the term "secularization" is used to denote a government policy toward the established church rather than a social and intellectual process in which religious beliefs, interests, and concerns are replaced by rational, critical evaluations and by pragmatic and utilitarian standards.

3. Gregory L. Freeze, "The Soslovie (Estate) Paradigm and Russian Social History," *American Historical Review* 91 (1989): 11–25. As Elise Kimerling Wirtschafter has demonstrated, even the nobility, the most distinctive class in imperial Russia, lacked precise social boundaries. Elise Kimerling Wirtshafter, *Social Identity in Imperial Russia* (DeKalb, Ill.: Northern Illinois University Press, 1996), 36.

4. J. G. Gadliardo, *Enlightened Despotism* (New York: Crowell, 1967), 49–51, 69–72; Leonard Krieger, *Kings and Philosophers 1689–1789* (New York: W. W. Norton. 1970), 284–85.

5. OR RNB (Manuscript Division, Russian National Library, St. Petersburg). Fond Sankt Peterburgskoi Akademii, no. 162, f.1.

6. OR RNB. Fond. 329, no. 6.

7. René Pomeau, "Une idée nouvelle au XVIIIe siècle, la tolérance," *Bulletin de la Société de l'Histoire du Protestantisme Français* 134 (1988): 195–206.

8. M. Deleyre, "Fanatisme," *Encyclopédie, ou Dictionaire raisonnée des sciences, des arts, et des métiers* (Paris: Plasson, 1756) 6:393–401.

9. O. A. Omel'chenko, "Tserkov' v pravovoi politike prosveshchennogo absolutisma," *Istoriko-pravovye voprosy vzaimootnoshenii gosudarstva i tserkvi v istorii Rossii: Sbornik nauchnykh trudov* (Moscow, 1988), 40–42. Gregory L. Bruess, "Religious Toleration in the Reign of Catherine the Great," *International Perspectives on Church and State: Proceedings of the Fourth Annual Symposium of the Philip M. and Ethel Kutznick Chair of Jewish Civilization* (Omaha, Neb., 1993), 299–313.

10. For the general discussion of the history of the Old Belief see Pavel S. Smirnov, *Istoriia russkago raskola staroobriadchestva* (St. Petersburg, 1895); Robert O. Crummney, *The Old Believers and the World of Antichrist: The Vyg*

Community and the Russian State, 1694–1855 (Madison, Wis.: University of Wisconsin Press, 1970); Roy. R. Robson, *Old Believers in Modern Russia* (DeKalb: Northern Illinois University Press, 1995).

11. V.A. Rogov, "Grekhovnoe i prestupnoe v prave Moskovskoi Rusi," *Istoriko-pravovye voprosy vzaimootnoshenii gosudarstva i tserkvi v istorii Rossii* (Moscow, 1988), 5–21.

12. Part 2, article 6.

13. D. O. Ezhov, "O tserkovno-religioznom obrazovanii v Rossii v XVIII v.," *Strannik: Dukhovnyi ucheno-literaturnyi zhurnal* 1 (1896): 73.

14. See Pia Pera, "Dispotismo illuminato e dissenso religioso: il Vecci Credenti nell'età di Caterina II," *Rivista Storica Italiana* 2 (1985): 501–617.

15. N. I. Pokrovskii, *Anti-feodal'nyi protest uralo-sibirskikh krestian-staroobriadtsev* (Novosibirsk: Nauka, 1971), 341–42.

16. *Zhivopisets* (Moscow, 1759), 33–47.

17. OR RNB. Fond St. Peterburgskoi Akademii, No. 329; RGADA (Russian State Archives of Ancient Acts, Moscow). Fond. 18, delo. 304, f. 6.

18. A. V. Khrapovitskii, *Dnevnik A. V. Khrapovitskogo c 18 Ianvaria 1782 po 17 Sentiabria 1793 goda* (Moscow: v universitetskoi tipografii, 1901), 3.

19. P. I. Bogdanovich, *Istoricheskoe izvestie of raskol'nikakh* (St. Petersburg, 1791), 5.

20. See R. G. Skrynnikov, *Gosudarstvo i tserkov' na Rusi XIV–XVI vv.* (Novosibirsk: Nauka, 1991).

21. On Patriarch Nikon, see N. F. Kapterev, *Patriarkh Nikon i tsar' Aleksei Mikhailovich* (Sergiev Posad: Tipografiia Sviato-Troitskoi Sergievoi lavry, 1909–12); Mathew Spinka, "Patriarkh Nikon and the Subjection of the Russian Church to the State," *Church History* 10 (1941): 347–66; O. F. Kozlov, "Delo Nikona," *Voprosy Istorii* 1 (1976): 102–14.

22. See James Cracraft, *The Church Reform of Peter the Great* (Stanford: Stanford University Press, 1971).

23. RGADA. Fond 199, opis' 1, portfel' 14, chast'. 3, no. 2.

24. A. S. Ikonnikov, "Arsenii Matseevich," *Russkaia Starina* 27 (1880): 177–79; Gregory L. Freeze, "Handmaiden of the State? The Church in Imperial Russia Reconsidered," *Journal of Ecclesiastical History* 36, no. 1 (1985): 82–102; Gregory L. Freeze, "Bringing Order to the Russian Family: Marriage and Divorce in Imperial Russia, 1760–1860," *Journal of Modern History* 62, no. 12 (1990): 709–26.

25. See: V. F. Blagovidov, *Ober-prokurory Sviateishago Sinoda* (Kazan': Tipo-Lit. Imp. universiteta, 1899).

26. On the secularization of the church lands see Aleksei A. Zav'ialov, *Vopros o tserkovnykh imeniakh pri imperatritse Ekaterine II* (St. Petersburg: Tip.

A. P. Lopukhina, 1900); A. I. Komissarenko, *Russkii absolutizm i dukhovenstvo v XVIII veke: Ocherki istorii sekularizatsionnoi reformy 1764 g.* (Moscow: Izd-vo Vses. zaochnogo politekhnicheskogo instituta, 1990)

27. M. M. Shcherbatov, "Statistika v razsuzhdenii Rossii," *Sochineniia kniazia M. M. Shcherbatova,* ed. I. Khrushchev (St. Petersburg: Tov. Pechatnia S.N. Iakovleva, 1896), 1:571–72.

28. On the careers of Gavriil, Platon, Voulgaris and Theotokis respectively see B.V. Titlinov, *Gavriil, mitropolit Novgorodskii i Sankt-Peterburgskii* (St. Petersburg: Tip. M. Melkusheva, 1916); Kazimir A. Papmehl, *Metropolitan Platon of Moscow (Petr Levshin, 1737–1812): The Enlightened Prelate, Scholar, and Educator* (Newtonville, Mass.: Oriental Research Partners, 1983); Stephen K. Batalden, *Catherine II's Greek Prelate: Eugenious Voulgaris in Russia, 1771–1806* (Boulder, Colo.: East European Monographs, 1982); Gregory L. Bruess, *Religion, Identity and Empire: a Greek Archbishop in the Russia of Catherine the Great* (Boulder, Colo.: East European Monographs, 1997).

29. *Sbornik Russkogo Istoricheskogo Obshchestva* (St. Petersburg, 1871), 10:160.

30. V. M. Zhivov, "Gosudarstvennyi mif v epokhu Prosveshcheniia," *Iz istorii russkoi kul'tury* (Moscow: Shkola iazyki russkoi kul'tury, 1996), 4:669–71.

31. Papmehl, *Metropolitan Platon of Moscow,* 24.

32. A. V. Kartashov, *Ocherki po istorii russkoi tserkvi* (Paris: YMCA Press, 1959), 2:370.

33. Blagovidov, *Ober-prokurory Sviateishago Sinoda,* 211.

34. Papmehl, *Metropolitan Platon of Moscow,* 40.

35. *ChOIDR* (Chtenia v obchshestve istorii i drevnostei rossiiskikh) Moscow, 4 (1889): 165–67.

36. *PSPiR* (Polnoe Sobranie postanovlenii i rasporiazhenii po vedomstvu Pravoslavnago Ispovedaniia Rossiiskoi Imperii: tsarstvovanie . . . Ekateriny Vtoroi. St. Petersburg, 1910–15), 2:365, 401, 1096.

37. *Sbornik Russkogo istoricheskogo obshestva* 7 (1868), 234–35.

38. *PSPiR,* 1:320.

39. Rogov, *Grekhovnoe i prestupnoe v prave Moskovskoi Rusi,* 22.

40. *PSZ* (Polnoe sobranie zakonov Rossiiskoi Imperii: sobranie tret'e. St. Petersburg, Gos. tip., 1885–1916), 19:13996.

41. *PSPiR,* 2:30–31.

42. Ibid., 194–97.

43. V. P. Kozlov, *Kruzhok A.I. Musina-Pushkina i "Slovo o polku Igoreve"* (Moscow: Nauka, 1981), 91–114.

44. D. P. Sokolov, "Istoricheskii ocherk prepodavaniia Zakona Bozhiia," *Rukovodstvo k prepodavaniu obshcheobrazovatel'nykh predmetov* (St. Petersburg,

1874), 1:158–59; *O dolzhnostiakh cheloveka i grazhdanina, kniga k chteniu opredelennaia v narodnykh gorodskikh uchilishchakh Rossiiskoi Imperii, izdannaia po vysochaishemu poveleniu tsarstuiushchei imperatritsy Ekateriny Vtoryia* (St. Petersburg: Tip. Akademii nauk, 1783).

45. Kh. "Proekt Bogoslovskogo fakul'teta v Moskovskom universitete," *Vestnik Evropy* (St. Petersburg, 1873), 12:317.

46. "Mnenie ob uchrezhdenii i soderzhanii imperatorskogo universtiteta i gimnazii v Moskve," *ChOIDR* (1875), 2:190, 198.

47. E. R. Dashkova, *Zapiski* (Moscow, 1990), 302.

48. I. A. Chistovich, *Feofan Prokopovich i ego vremia* (St. Petersburg: v Tip. I. Akademii nauk, 1868), 709–18; Mikhail Stepanovich Popov, *Arsenii Matseevich i ego delo* (St. Petersburg: M.I. Frolova, 1912), 170; V. Ivanovskii, *Russkoe zakonodatel'stvo XVIII i XIX vv. v svoikh postanovleniakh otnositel'no monashestvuishchikh lits i monastyrei: Opyt istoriko-kanonicheskogo issledovaniia* (Khar'kov, Tip. gubernskago pravleniia, 1905), 23–25.

49. Voltaire, then an avid admirer of the Prussian king, supported Catherine's policy toward monasteries. *Sbornik Russkogo istoricheskogo obshchestva* (1871), 10:96; M. S. Popov, Arsenii Matseevich, 170–71.

50. See N. N. Grigorovich, *Obzor uchrezhdeniia v Rossii pravoslavnykh monastyrei. So vremeni vvedeniia shtatov po dukhovnomu vedomstvu* (1764–1869) (St. Petersburg: Synodal'naia Tipografiia, 1869).

51. Brenda Meehan-Waters, "Russian Convents and the Secularization of Monastic Property," *Russia and the World of the Eighteenth Century: Proceedings of the Third International Conference . . . September 1984* (Columbus, Ohio: Slavica Publishers, 1988), 113; A. S. Prugavin, *Monastyrskie tiur'my v bor'be s sektantstom: k voprosu o veroterpimosti* (Moscow, 1905), 17–23; *PSPiR*, 2:32–33.

52. "O sostoianii Rossii pri Ekaterine Velikoi. Voprosy Diderota i otvety Ekateriny," *Russkii Arkhiv* (Moscow, 1880) 3:17–19.

53. A. V. Khrapovitskii, *Dnevnik*, 23.

54. Ibid., p. 168.

55. "O sostoianii Rossii pri Ekaterine Velikoi. Voprosy Diderota i otvety Ekateriny," 17–19.

56. V. V. Krylov, "Ekaterinskaia komissiia v eia otnoshenii k dukhovenstvy kak k sosloviiu," *Vera i razum* (Khar'kov, 1903): no. 9–11: 467–83, 553–84, 622–39, 695–723, 758–71.

57. Ibid., 469.

58. Ibid., 478.

59. On the general discussions of the attempt to create a third estate in Russia see S. M. Troitskii, "Dvorianskie proekty sozdaniia "tret' ego china,"

Rossiia v XVIII veke: Sbornik statei i publikatsii (Moscow: Nauka, 1982), 192–204; David M. Griffiths, "Eighteenth Century Perception of Backwardness: Projects for the Creation of a Third Estate in Catherinian Russia," *Canadian American Slavic Studies* 13 (1979): 452–72.

60. O. A. Omel'chenko, *Tserkov' v pravovoi politike prosveshchennogo absolutisma*, 46–47.

61. The special addenda to the Moskovskie Vedomosti published in French and German were devoted entirely to these accusations. *Pribavlenie k Moskovskim Vedomostiam* 31 (1763); Gregory L. Freeze, *The Russian Levites: Parish Clergy in the Eighteenth Century* (Cambridge, Mass.: Harvard University Press, 1977), 69.

62. Consistories, judicial and executive offices of the diocesan administrations, were established in 1744. They replaced old "*prikazy dukhovnykh del*" or "*razriady*," that had dealt with judicial and administrative affairs, and "*kasennye prikazy*," which were in charge of financial matters.

63. *PSZ*, 16:12060; 17: 12596; 18: 12471, 13163; 19: 1309. Freeze, *The Russian Levites*, 64; N. D. Zol'nikova, *Soslovnye problemy vo vzaimootnosheniiakh tserkvi i gosudarstva v Sibiri (XVIII v.)* (Novosibirsk: Nauka, 1981), 8; Papmehl, *The Metropolitan Platon of Moscow*, 75.

64. P. V. Znamenskii, *Prikhodskoe dukhovenstvo v Rossii so vremeni reformy Petra* (Kazan', 1873), 617.

65. *Russkii Arkhiv* (Moscow, 1870): 750–52.

66. See Gregory L. Freeze, *The Parish Clergy in Nineteenth Century Russia: Crisis, Reform, Counter-Reform* (Princeton, N.J.: Princeton University Press, 1983); James W. Cunningham. *A Vanquished Hope: The Movement for Church Renewal in Russia, 1905–1906* (Crestwood, N.Y.: St. Vladimir's Seminary Press, 1981.)

67. See Freeze, "Bringing Order to the Russian family."

68. Kh. *Proekt Bogoslovskogo fakul'teta v Moskovskom universitete*, 317.

69. E. V. Barsov, ed., *Novye materialy po istorii staroobriadstva* (Moscow: Tip. Moskovskovo universiteta, 1890): 15.

70. Platon (Petr Levshin), *Ot pravoslavno-kafolicheskia tserkve: Uveshchaniie byvshim svoim chadam, nyne nedugom raskola nemotstvuiushchim* (St. Petersburg: Synodal'naia tipografiia, 1765); See N. V. Lysogorskii, *Mitropolit Platon kak protivoraskol'nichii deiatel'* (Rostov-na-Donu, 1907); Pia Perra, *Dispotismo illuminato e dissenso religioso*, 550–66.

71. On Edinoverie see S. S-v, *Istoricheskii ocherk edinoveriia* (St. Petersburg, 1867); S. Shleev, *Edinoverie v svoem vnutrennem razvitii* (St. Petersburg, 1910); N. Lysogorskii, *Mitropolit Platon kak protivoraskol'nichii deiatel'*; Roy R. Robson, *Old Believers in Modern Russia*, 29–30.

72. Pokrovskii, *Antifeodal'nye protesty uralo-sibirskikh krest'an - staroobriadtsev v XVIII veke*, 297.

73. *Novye materialy po istorii staroobriadstva*, 63.

74. On the Plague Riot see I. K. Kuprianov, "Materialy dlia istorii chumy v Moskve i ubienia episkopa Amvrosia 1771 goda," *Russkoe Slovo* 11 (1867): 247–72; N.N. Bantysh-Kamenskii, "Pis'mo uvedomitel'noe o ubienii v Moskve miatezhnikami vo vremia morovoi iazvy arkhiepiskopa Amvrosia, k Iovy Bazilevichu, episkopu Pereslavskomy," *Pribavlenie k Chernigovskim eparkhial'nym izvestiam* 12 (1862): 433–39; Dmitrii Iazykov, "Chuma v Moskve u ubienie moskovskogo arkhiepeskopa Amvrosia v 1771," *Dushepoleznoe chtenie* 3 (1871): 22–41; A. A. Sablukov, "Moskva v 1771 godu," *Russkii Arkhiv* (Moscow, 1866): 330–39; D. Mordovtsev, "Chuma v Moskve 1771 goda," *Drevniaia i novaia Rossia* 2 (1875): 6–19, 104–128; P. Alefirenko, "Chumnoi bunt v Moskve v 1771 godu," *Voprosy Istorii* 4 (1947): 82–88; M. F. Prokhorov, "Moskovskoe vosstanie v sentiabre 1771 goda," *Russkii gorod: Issledovaniia i materialy* (Moscow: Izd-vo Moskovskogo universiteta, 1979), 2:114–40; John T. Alexander, *Bubonic Plague in Early Modern Russia: Public Health and Urban Disaster* (Baltimore: Johns Hopkins University Press, 1980).

75. *Perepiska rossiiskoi imperatritsy Ekateriny Vtoryia s g. Vol'terom s 1763 po 1778 god* (St. Petersburg: Pri Imperatorskoi Akademii nauk, 1802): 54.

76. *Russkii byt po vospominaniiam sovremennikov* (Moscow, 1912): 2:179.

77. Aleksandr Georgievich Levshin, *Slovo na ubienie preosviashchenneishago Amvrosiia arkhiepiskopa Moskovskogo, uchinennoe chern'iu 1771 goda, sentiabria 16 dnia* ([St. Petersburg], 1771), 2. Amvrosii (Podobedov), *Slovo skazyvannoe pri pogrebenii preosviashchennago Amvrosiia, arkhiepiskopa Moskovskogo i Kaluzhskago* ([Moscow], 1771), 3. Andrei Ivanovich Zhuravlev, *Polnoe istoricheskoe izvestie o staroobriadtsakh, ikh uchenii, delakh i raznoglasiiakh* (St. Petersburg: Tip. Sviateishago Sinoda, 1794), 78–80.

78. Sergei Mikhailovich Solov'ev, "Zametka o deiatel'nosti mitropolita Gavriila po voprosu o raskole," *Pravoslavnoe obozrenie* 11 (1875): 430–34.

79. Kazimir A. Papmehl, *Freedom of Expression in Eighteenth Century Russia* (The Hague, Nijhoff, 1971): 53 (f).

80. *Nakaz* was likewise severely criticized by the aristocratic critics whom Catherine had asked to review the first version of the document. See A. A. Kizevetter, "Pervoe piatiletie pravlenia Ekateriny II," *Sbornik, posviashchennyi P. N. Miliukovu* (Prague, 1929), 309–26.

81. I. M. Pokrovskii, *Ekaterininskaia komissia o sostavlenii proekta novogo Ulozhenia i tserkovnye voprosy v nei* (Kazan', 1910): 12–13.

82. RGADA. Fond 18, delo. 225; *ChOIDR* (1871): 3:114–21.

83. Krylov, *Ekaterininskaia komissiia v eia otnoshenii k dukhovenstvu kak sosloviiu*, 558–59.

84. *PSPiR*, 1: 467–68.

85. Krylov, *Ekateriniskaia komissiia v eia otnoshenii k dukhovenstvy kak k sosloviu*, 559.

86. O. A. Omel'chenko, *Tserkov' v pravovoi politike "prosveshchennogo absolutisma" v Rossii*, 58.

87. The fragments of the memoirs of A. Efremov, I. V. Pinegin, A. Sil'vestrov, G. A. Skopin, and A. Mikhailov, priests of Vladimir, Voronezh, Viatka, and Moscow dioceses respectively are the only materials of this kind available in print. See *Istoria dorevolutsionnoi Rossii v dnevnikakh i vospominaniiakh* (Moscow: Kniga, 1976), 1:157–59, 209; Manuscript collections are likewise rather scarce. One of them is the semi-cataloged collection of Ioann Pamfilov, the confessor of Catherine the Great (OR RNB. Fond 559). The papers of Aleksei Samborskii, priest of the Russian church in London, cover a very specific aspect of the history of the white clergy. Anthony G. Cross, *By the Banks of the Thames: Russians in Eighteenth Century Britain* (Newtonville, Mass., Oriental Research Partners 1980), 35–36.

88. See *Zol'nikova, Soslovnye problemy vo vzaimootnosheniakh tserkvi i gosudarstva v Sibiri*; Komissarenko, *Russkii absolutism i dukhovensto v XVIII v. Ocherki istorii sekularizatisonnoi reformy;* Freeze, The *Russian Levites;* Erich Bryner, *Der geistliche Ständ in Russland* (Göttingen: Vandenhoeck & Ruprecht, 1982.)

89. For the biography of P. Alekseev see Nikolai Pavlovich Rosanov, "P. A. Alekseev i ego vremia," *Dushepoleznoe chtenie* 1 (1869): 11–26; Mikhail I. Sukhomlinov, *Istoriia Rossiiskoi akademii* (St. Petersburg: Tip. Akademii nauk, 1875), 1:280–343, 424–27; A. N. Korsakov, "P. Alekseev, protoierei Arkhangel'skogo sobora," *Russkii arkhiv* 2 (1880): 153–209. The article of N. P. Rozanov is, in fact, a guide to the materials in the Archives of the Moscow Consistory relating to Alekseev.

90. OR RGB (Manuscript Division of Russian State Library, Moscow). Fond 557, No. 62 & 91; OR GIM (Manuscript Division of State Historical Museum, Moscow), Chertkov, no. 91, 99. Excerpts from Alekseev's papers were published by A. N. Korsakov in "Iz bumag protoiereia P. Alekseeva," *Russkii arkhiv* 3 (1882): 68–90; "Bumagi protoiereia P. Alekseeva," *Russkii arkhiv* 4 (1892): 449–66.

91. N. I. S[ubboti]n, "Rasskaz Petra Velikogo o Nikone Patriarkhe," *Russkii Vestnik* (St. Petersburg, 1762) 49, no. 1: 320–33; Filaret (Gumilevskii), the Archbishop of Chernigov, *Obzor russkoi dukhovnoi literatury* (St. Petersburg: Izdanie knigoprodavtsa I. L. Tuzova, 1884), 383–85; Korsakov, *Petr Alekseev, protoierei Arkhangel'skogo sobora.*

92. P. I. Bartenev, ed., "Anekdot o patriarkhe Nikone," *Russkii Arkhiv: God pervyi* (1863), 2d ed. (Moscow, 1866), 482; Sukhomlinov, *Istoriia Rossiiskoi Akademii*; A. N. Pypin, *Istoria russkoi etnografii* (St. Petersburg: Tip. M. M. Stasuilevicha, 1890): 174–78.

93. G. A. Likhotkin, *Oklevetannyi Kolovion* (Leningrad: Izd-vo Leningradskogo universiteta, 1972).

94. Znamenskii, *Prikhodskoe dukhoventsvo*, 617; Freeze, *The Parish Clergy in Nineteenth Century Russia*, 205–15.

95. V. I. Savva, *Sochinenie protiv episkopov XVIII v* (Moscow, Tip. Moskovskogo universiteta, 1910), 22–24.

96. K. V. Kharlampovich, *Malorossiiskoe vliianie na velikorusskuiu tserkovnuiu zhizn'* (Kazan, 1914), 459.

97. Platon was appointed to the post of the Archbishop of Moscow and Kaluga diocese in 1775. Although his official tenure lasted until 1799, since the early 1780s, Platon repeatedly expressed an ardent desire to retire. In 1792 the empress allowed Platon to transfer his administrative duties to the Vicar archbishop, the bishop of Krutitsy Amvrosii (Podobedov) and retreat to the monastery of Holy Trinity.

98. I. M. Snegirev, *Zhizn' moskovskogo mitropolita Platona* 2 (Moscow, 1891), 229–30. The administrative side of Platon's life and career has hardly been studied. See [V. Vinogradov], "Ob izuchenii zhizni i trudov i chestvovaniia pamiati Platona, mitropolita Moskovskogo," *Bogoslovskii vestnik* 5 (n.p., 1912): 214–15. The book by N. P. Rozanov, *The History of the Moscow Diocese Administration* (Istoriia Moskovskogo eparkhial'nogo upravleniia), was, in fact, a guide to the Archives of the Moscow Consistory. In 1882, a student of St. Petersburg Academy, P. Chistoserdov, defended a dissertation, "Platon II (Levshin) and his role in the diocesan administration"; the dissertation remains unpublished. The most thorough treatment of Platon's administrative career is found in the Papmehl's biography of Platon, *Metropolitan Platon of Moscow*, 46–55. Papmehl supplemented the information found in Platon's *Autobiography* with the materials of Synod legislation.

99. Snegirev, Zhizn' moskovskogo mitropolita Platona, 235–36.

100. In 1776, Platon sent out a special circular outlining the duties and responsibilities of the Cathedral's clergy. Rozanov, *Istoriia moskovskogo eparkhial'nogo upravleniia*, 35–36, 40 (f. 103), 220.

101. OR RGB. Fond 557, no. 90, ff. 325–25 v.

102. RGADA. Fond 199, opis' 1, portfel'. 184, chast'. 3, no 2, ff. 4 v.–5 v.

103. Rozanov, *Istoria moskovskogo eparkhial'nogo upravleniia*, 41, 14 (f. 32).

104. Snegirev, *Zhizn' moskovskogo mitropolita Platona*, 233; Rozanov, *Istoriia moskovskogo eparkhial'nogo upravleniia*, 41.

105. T. V. Barsov, *Sinodal'nye uchrezhdenia nastoiashchego vremeni: Vypusk 1: Moskovskaia Kontora Sv. Sinoda* (St. Petersburg: Tip. A. P. Lopukhina, 1899), 35–37.

106. Ibid., 42–43.

107. The procurator of the Moscow Office of the Holy Synod Gur'ev was indeed deeply in debt. In 1789 he declared bankruptcy. *PSPiR*,3:24–25.

108. Snegirev, *Zhizn' moskovskogo mitropolita Platona,* 74.

109. OR ORB. Fond. 557, no. 90, ff. 384–384v.

110. P. V. Znamenskii, "Chtenia iz istorii russkoi tserkvi epokhi Ekateriny II," *Pravoslavnyi sobesednik* (1875): 375; Freeze, *The Russian Levites,* 89.

111. *Russkii Arkhiv* 10 (1872): 302–3.

112. OR RNB. Fond 599, Pereplet 2, ff. 270–270 v.

113. OR RGB. Fond 557, no. 90, f. 313; *Russkii Arkhiv* 3 (1882): 75–76.

114. OR ORB. Fond 557, no. 90, f. 384–384 v; *Russkii Arkhiv,* (Moscow, 1871): 213–14. Alekseev was not the only person who bemoaned the partiality of the archbishop's justice. A priest named Pyliaev, and later his widow, complained about unjustifiably harsh treatment they had received in the diocesan offices and cited Platon who had been heard saying: "I hate the Pyliaevs, and I will not rest until I do away with the whole clan." Rozanov, *Istoriia Moskovskogo eparkhial'nogo upravleniia,* 185 (f. 600).

115. OR RGB. Fond 557, no. 90, ff. 384–384 v.

116. OR RGB. Fond 557, no. 62, f. 28.

117. Ibid., l. 31.

118. Rozanov, *Istoriia moskovskogo eparkhial'nogo upravleniia,* 148–50.

119. Znamenskii, *Prikhodskoe dukhovenstvo,* 153; Freeze, *The Russian Levites,* 190–91.

120. OR RGB. Fond 557, no. 62, f. 323.

121. Ibid., f. 32.

122. Cracraft, *The Church Reform of Peter the Great,* 246–48.

123. *PSPiR,* 2, 752, 818, 835, 889, 937, etc.

124. Ivan Stepanovich Znamenskii, *Polozhenie dukhovenstva v tsarstvovanii Ekateriny i Pavla* (Moscow: M. N. Lavrov, 1880), 74–79.

125. Snegirev, *Zhizn' moskovskogo mitropolita Platona,* 229.

126. Savva, Anonimnoe sochinenie protiv episkopov, 33–34.

127. For instance, no sooner had the authorities finished "cleansing" the clerical estate of unemployed clergy sons fifteen years and older than the new generation came of age, and they had to face the same task over and over again. The last "selection," which involved transferring all ordained clergy sons to the tax categories, was completed in 1797. Only three years later, in 1800, Alekseev again suggested that all "clergy children who live with their parents as well as orphans who are fifteen years or older be free to pursue a secular

career, without having to attend a seminary." OR RGB. Fond 557, no. 62, ff. 30–30 v.

128. Freeze, The Russian Levites, 78–104.

129. OR RGB. Fond 557, no. 90, f. 273.

130. The lower clergy, custodians, and bell ringers, "little lettered and often downright illiterate," who collected five rubles a year, simply could not afford to educate their children. Besides, ecclesiastical education, although elementary, made little sense for young girls and women who were "engaged in weaving, spinning, and other useful work appropriate for their gender, and were not preparing for priesthood or convent." OR RGB. Fond 557, no. 62, ff. 33–33 v.

131. OR RGB. Fond 557, no. 90, f. 353 v.

132. OR RGB. Fond 557, no. 62, f. 32 v., 32 v.

133. *PSPiR*, 1:789.

134. OR RGB. Fond 557, no. 62, ff. 372–74 v.

135. Christopher Hill, *The Century of Revolution, 1603–1714* (Edinburgh: T. Nelson 1961), 243.

136. See A. A. Beliaev, "Mitropolit peterburgskii Gavriil kak ustroitel' monasheskoi zhizni," *Dushepoleznoe chtenie*, 1 (1889): 34–63.

137. V. V. Zverinskii, *Materialy dlia istoriko-topograficheskago izsledovaniia o pravoslavnykh monastyriakh v Rossiiskoi Imperii: 1. Preobrazovania starykh i uchrezhdeniia novykh monastyrei* (St. Petersburg: Tip. V. Bezobrazova, 1890): 80–81, 98–99, 113–14, 193–194; A. Beliaev, *K istorii Spaso-Vifanskogo monastyria i Spaso-Vifanskoi seminarii* (Moscow, 1894).

138. Rozanov, *Moskovskii mitropolit Platon*, 29.

139. Meehan-Waters, *Russian Convents and the Secularization of Monastic Property*, 112–24.

140. V. P. Vinogradov, *Platon i Filaret, mitropolity moskovskie* (Sergiev Posad: Tipografiia Sviato-Troitskoi Sergievoi lavry, 1913), 22; S. Chetverikov, *Optina pustyn'* (Paris, YMCA Press, 1988), 31–39.

141. William Perkins, "An Exposition of the Symbole or Creed of the Apostles, According to the Scriptures and the consent of Orthodox Fathers of the Church," *The Workes* (London: John Legatt, 1612): 1:205.

142. OR GIM. Chertkov, no. 99, ff. 33–33 v.; no. 91, ff. 255–262 v.

143. OR RGB. Fond 557, no. 90, ff. 71–72 v., 260–262 v.

144. OR RGB. Fond 557, no. 90, ff. 73, 224–25; OR GIM, Chertkov, no. 91, ff. 283–84.

145. OR RGB. Fond 557, no. 90, ff. 90–1; no. 62, f. 207.

146. OR RGB. Fond 557, no. 90, ff. 138, 149, 156 v., 182–2 v.

147. Ibid., ff. 378–378 v.

148. OR RGB. Fond 557, no. 62, f. 206.

149. OR RGB. Fond 557, no. 90, f. 149.

150. OR RGB. Fond 557, no. 62. f. 207; OR RNB, f. 559, pereplet 2, ff. 400–2.

151. OR RGB. Fond 557, no. 90, ff. 190–190 v.

152. Ibid., f. 83; OR RNB, f. 599, pereplet 2, f. 204; *Russkii Arkhiv* (Moscow, 1871): 223–24.

153. P. V. Znamenskii, *Dukhovnyie shkoly v Rossii do reformy 1808 goda* (Kazan', 1881), 679–80.

154. Rozanov, *Istoria Moskovskogo eparkhial'nogo upravleniia*, 27–28.

155. OR RGB. Fond 557, no. 90, ff. 63–143 v.

156. Indeed, if he had lost the suit, which was very likely, Alekseev could face grave consequences, including defrocking. As a result, he had chosen to follow the advice of his crony, a Consistory secretary Ivan Vinogradskii, withdrew the report, and offered formal apologies to Platon. OR RGB. Fond 557, no. 90, ff. 190–190 v.

157. OR RGB. Fond 557, no. 90, ff. 110–111 v.

158. OR RGB. Fond 557, no. 90, ff. 323–24 v.

159. Platon, *Pis'ma moskovskogo mitropolita Platona* (Moscow, 1870), 33.

160. Snegirev, *Zhizn' moskovskogo mitropolita Platona*, 23.

161. *Polnoe sobranie postanovlenii i rasporiazhenii po vedomstvu pravoslavnago ispovedaniia. Tsarstvovanie imperatora Pavla* (Petrograd, Gos. Tip. 1915): 72–73.

162. OR RNB. Fond. 599, Pereplet 2, f. 26 v.; *Russkii Arkhiv* (Moscow, 1871): 231–32.

163. Ibid.

164. *PSZ*, 10:13996.

165. OR RGB. Fond 557, no. 62, ff. 38–38v.

166. OR RGB. Fond 557, no. 90, ff. 353–353 v; Cf. OR RNB. Fond. 599, pereplet 2, f. 127–8v.

167. OR RGB. Fond 557, no. 90, ff. 354–354 v.

168. OR RGB. Fond 557, no. 62, f. 28 v.

169. OR RGB. Fond 557, no. 90, ff. 282–282 v.; *Russkii Arkhiv* 2 (1882): 79.

170. OR RGB. Fond 557, no. 90, f. 358 v.

171. OR RGB. Fond 557, no. 90, ff. 170–71 v.

172. OR RNB. Rukopisnoe sobranie Pogodina, no 258, f. 387 v.

173. OR RNB. Fond 599, pereplet 2, f. 123; *Russkii Arkhiv* (Moscow, 1871): 229.

174. Savva, *Sochinenie protiv episkopov XVIII v.*

175. OR RGB. Fond 557, no. 62, ff. 282–2 v.; *ChOIDR* (Moscow, 1872):3: 21–22.

176. OR RGB. Fond 557, no. 90, l. 141 v.

177. Hill, *The Century of Revolution, 1603–1714,* 81–88.

178. OR RGB. Fond 557, no. 62, f. 367. Cf. John Lightfoot, *The Workes,* 2 (London, printed by William Rawlins for Richard Chiswell, 1684): 133.

179. OR GIM. Chertkov, no. 99, ff. 98 v.–101.

180. OR GIM, Chertkov, no. 99, ff. 85–5 v.

181. I. Smolitsh, *Geschichte der Russischen Kirche 1700–1917* (Leiden : E. J. Brill, 1964), 422–27; Perra, *Dispotismo illuminato e dissenso religioso,* 573–74 (f. 181).

182. Blagovidov, *Ober-prokurory Sviateishago Sinoda,* 258–60; Krylov, "Ekateriniskaia komissiia v eia otnoshenii k dukhovenstvu kak sosloviiu," 474–75; I. M. Pokrovskii, *Ekaterinskaia komissiia o sostavlenii proekta novogo ulozheniia i tserkovnye voprosy v nei;* P. G. Ryndziunskii, "Tserkov' v dvorianskoi imperii," *Russkoe pravoslavie: Vekhi istorii* (Moscow: Politizdat, 1989), 295–96; Kartashov, *Ocherki po istorii russkoi tserkvi,* 2: 484–86.

183. *ChOIDR* 3 (1871): 116.

184. Savva, *Sochinenie protiv episkopov,* 12.

185. OR GIM. Chertkov, no. 91, f. 286–318; Savva, *Sochinenie protiv episkopov,* 26; *ChOIDR* 3 (1871): 119–20.

186. Freeze, *Bringing Order to the Russian Family,* 725–27.

187. V. V. Mitrofanenko, "Kliucharevskaia letopis'—pamiatnik russkoi obshchestvennoi mysli kontsa XVIII—pervoi chetverti XIX v.," *Spornye problemy istorii russkoi obshchestvennoi mysli* (Moscow, 1992), 98–99.

188. Freeze, *The Russian Levites,* 34–56.

189. V. Lamanskii, "Evdokim Mikhailovich Kravkov, dvorianin–starover," *Pamiatniki novoi russkoi istorii,* ed. N. N. Kashpirev 1 (St. Petersburg, 1871), 36–48. For the history of Roman Catholicism in Russia see Dmitrii Tolstoy, *Le Catholicisme Romain en Russie* (Paris: Dentu, 1863–1864); On Russian monastic mysticism see: Serge Bolshakoff, *Russian Mystics,* (Kalamazoo, Mich.: Cistercian Publications, 1977).

190. Aleksei Nikolaevich Pypin, *Russkoe masonstvo* (St. Petersburg: Ogni, 1915), 262–94.

191. For the bibliography of the "Novikov affair" see W. Gareth Jones, *Nikolai Novikov, the Enlightener of Russia,* (Cambridge: Cambridge University Press, 1984); Isabel Madariaga, "Some New Publications on Nikolay Ivanovich Novikov: A Review Article," *Studies in History and Politics* (1985): 4: 173–81. See also: Douglas Smith, *Working the Rough Stone: Freemasonry and Society in Eighteenth Century Russia* (DeKalb, Ill.: Northern Illinois University Press, 1999).

192. M. D. Chulkov, *Slovar' russkikh sueverii,* (St. Petersburg, 1782), 252; OR RGB. Fond 557, no. 90, f. 114 v.; A. P.Sumarokov, "Kto khulit vsekh

frankmasonov," *Polnoe sobranie vsekh sochinenii* 8 (Moscow, N. Novikov, 1781): 8:308–9. Cf. Smith, *Working the Rough Stone*, 136–75.

193. A. Semeka, *Russkie rozenkreitsery i sochinenia imperatritsy Ekateriny II protiv masonstva* (St. Petersburg, 1902), 5–7; Pypin, *Russkoe masonstvo,* 267–69. *N. I. Novikov i ego sovremenniki,* (Moscow, izd-vo Akademii nauk, 1961), 461–62.

194. See In-Ho Ryu, "Moscow Freemasons and the Rosicrucian Order," John G. Garrard, ed., *The Eighteenth Century in Russia* (Oxford: Clarendon Press, 1973), 198–232.

195. "Podlinnye cherty i sluchai iz istorii raskola (1792–1807): Bumagi kniazia Prozorovskogo, Arkharova i grafa P.I. Saltykova," *Russkii Arkhiv* (Moscow, 1864), 7–8, 720–25.

196. OR GIM. Chertkov, no. 99, f. 84.

197. Henry Kamen, *The Rise of Toleration* (London: Weidenfeld and Nicolson, 1967), 194; H.R. Trevor-Roper, "The Religious Origins of the Enlightenment," *Religion, the Reformation and Social Change* (London: McMillan, 1984), 193; Peter Gay, *Voltaire's Politics: The Poet as Realist* (New Haven: Yale University Press, 1988), 250–51; A. Haynal, M. Molnar, G. de Puymege, *Fanaticism: A Historical and Psychoanalytical Study* (New York: Schocken Books, 1983), 23–28.

198. OR RGB. Fond 557, no. 62, f. 39–66 v.

199. See: Susie I. Tucker, *Enthusiasm: A Study in Semantic Change,* (Cambridge, Cambridge University Press, 1972); Ronald A. Knox, *Enthusiasm: A Chapter in the History of Religion* (Notre Dame, Ind.: University of Notre Dame Press, 1994); Michael Heyd, *"Be Sober and Reasonable": The Critique of Enthusiasm in the Seventeenth and Early Eighteenth Centuries* (Leiden: J. Brill, 1995); Lawrence E. Klein and Anthony J. La Vopa, eds., "Enthusiasm and Enlightenment in Europe, 1650–1850," Huntington Library Quarterly 60, no. 1, 2 (1998).

200. *N. I. Novikov i ego sovremenniki,* 452; OR RGB. Fond 557, no. 90, f. 146 v.

201. Platon, *Pis'ma mitropolita Platona,* 5; M.M. Longinov, *N. I. Novikov i moskovskie martinisty,* (Moscow, Tip. Gracheva, 1867), 034–035; Papmehl, *Metropolitan Platon of Moscow,* 89–90.

202. Znamenskii, *Prikhodskoe dukhovenstvo,* 644–50;. Rozanov, *Istoriia Moskovskogo eparkhial'nogo upravleniia,* 36–37; Papmehl, *Metropolitan Platon of Moscow,* 36–39.

203. A. S. Lappo-Danilevskii, *Istoriia russkoi obshchestvennoi mysli i kul'tury XVII–XVIII vv.* (Moscow: Nauka, 1990), 168–204.

Index